Jean Anderson's
New *Processor Cooking*

BOOKS BY JEAN ANDERSON:

The Art of American Indian Cooking
  (with Yeffe Kimball)

Food Is More Than Cooking

Henry the Navigator, Prince of Portugal

The Haunting of America

The Family Circle Cookbook
  (with the Food Editors of *Family Circle*)

*The Doubleday Cookbook (with Elaine Hanna)

Recipes from America's Restored Villages

The Green Thumb Preserving Guide

The Grass Roots Cookbook

Jean Anderson's Processor Cooking (1979)

**Half a Can of Tomato Paste & Other Culinary
  Dilemmas (with Ruth Buchan)

Jean Anderson Cooks
  Unforbidden Sweets

Jean Anderson's *New* Processor Cooking

*Winner of the R. T. French Tastemaker Award,
Best Cookbook of the Year (1975)

**Winner of the R. T. French Tastemaker Award,
Best Specialty Cookbook of the Year (1980)

JEAN ANDERSON'S *NEW* PROCESSOR COOKING

By Jean Anderson

WILLIAM MORROW AND COMPANY, INC.

NEW YORK   1983

Library of Congress Catalog Card Number: 83-61742

ISBN: 0-688-02254-5

Printed in the United States of America

Revised Edition
1 2 3 4 5 6 7 8 9 10

For John,
one of the best cooks I know

Foreword

If *Jean Anderson's Processor Cooking* had been around in the early seventies when I was struggling to master a French Magi-Mix, the forerunner of today's food processors, I would have avoided many disasters. At that time, directions and recipes were skimpy and I succeeded in producing liquid instead of chopped onions, gluey mashed potatoes, and overmixed quick breads. Even then, a food processor could perform an incredible range of cooking tasks in seconds, with minimal effort on our part, but it did not lend itself well to guesswork (and still doesn't). Then, in 1979, came this book, the first comprehensive book of processor technique to take all the guesswork out of using food processors.

Processors, in a mere four years, however, have changed dramatically, and fierce competition among manufacturers has produced many improvements at record speed. *Jean Anderson's New Processor Cooking* embodies this well-known author's systematic experimenting with many new machines, both standard and oversize, and the host of new blades and features. It is a well-organized, no-nonsense book that starts with a rundown of techniques that has distinguished it since it was first published, with extensive updating. Whether you have just bought your first processor or have owned one for a while, you will find her information invaluable.

In PART I there is an excellent section on processor accessories, descriptions of their capabilities, and clear guidelines on using a machine safely that go beyond the suggestions of some manufacturers. There follow three alphabetical charts that will be as helpful to experienced cooks as to neophytes. The first details how to operate the food processor to chop, slice thin or thick, grate, make crumbs, dice, shred, knead (the list is long), including how to time processes by numbers of seconds or on-and-offs of the motor. The second chart lists dozens of

7

ingredients, from almonds to zucchini, with precise instructions for cutting, grating, shredding—whatever is appropriate for the ingredient and its later uses in recipes. (And Jean Anderson never leaves a reader holding something like a coconut, wondering how to get the pieces of nutmeat ready to put in the processor. She tells you how to drain the milk, crack the shell, peel the skin. This kind of basic information always turns up throughout the book when you need it.) The third chart gives approximate yields for ingredients after processing: If a recipe (in this book, another book) calls for 1 cup of coarsely chopped green pepper or 1 cup of ground beef, this chart clues you in on the number of peppers or the weight of meat to start with.

Ms. Anderson definitely feels that even today the miracle processor should not be asked to do *everything*, and she advises against throwing out your blender and mixer, which still do a better job of whirling a daiquiri, whipping cream or egg whites, and mixing most cake batters. Or, chopping two sprigs of parsley or cutting three slices of lemon in the processor is impractical; a knife is easier to wash. But you can chop a big bunch of a fresh herb if it is carefully dried first—one of many small but important processor secrets you will find in this book.

In PART II, the generous recipe section, the same common sense is evident. Don't let the length of the directions scare you; on the contrary, they answer every processor question that could possibly arise. This section not only gives you a full range of dishes carefully picked so that the processor can significantly slice the time it takes to prepare them. It will also help you stock your freezer, refrigerator, and pantry with ingredients to keep on hand—broths, grated cheese, flavored butters, mayonnaise—many things you might not bother to prepare ahead without a processor. Look, especially, in this revised edition for breads and pastas that were simply not feasible with earlier machines.

Jean Anderson understands good food and her dishes are delicious. She makes no compromise on quality, whether a recipe is for *quenelles* or codfish cakes. Once you have learned to make pasta, pastry, *ratatouille*, and many other old favorites with a food processor, you will understand the techniques and can apply them to your own recipes. The uses are endless. Keep your processor working as this book directs and you'll consistently turn out terrific meals with a minimum of effort and in a fraction of the time it took before.

—JEAN HEWITT

New York, 1983

Acknowledgments

I SHOULD LIKE TO THANK the following individuals, companies and corporations, without whose valuable cooperation and assistance this book could not have been written: Geri Brin, North American Philips Corp., New York, N.Y.; Ruth Buchan, New York, N.Y.; Denise Cosimano, Sanyo Electric, Inc., Moonachie, N.J.; Kathy Cripps, Farberware, Bronx, N.Y.; Victor Golbe, Welco Manufacturing and Trading, Inc., New York, N.Y.; Barbara Kafka, Food Consultant, New York, N.Y.; Shirley Kaiser, KitchenAid Division, Hobart Corporation, Troy, Ohio; Mayburn Koss, Cuisinarts, Inc., Greenwich, Conn.; Sallie Kreda, Kreda Associates, Inc., New York, N.Y.; Barbara McGrath, Selz, Seabolt & Associates, Inc., Chicago, Ill.; Toni Mundt, Sunbeam Corporation, Oak Brook, Ill.; Rochelle Narotsky, Hamilton Beach Division, Scovill, Waterbury, Conn.; Grace D. Polk, General Electric News Bureau, New York, N.Y.; Marcia Powell, Zigman-Joseph-Skeen, New York, N.Y.; W. I. Pillow, Sears, Roebuck and Co., Chicago, Ill.; Mal Sherman, American Electric Corp., Culver City, Calif.; Wayne R. Smith, Sunbeam Corporation, Oak Brook, Ill.; and Glenn Spoerl, Sears, Roebuck and Co., Chicago, Ill.

Finally, a very special thanks to Carl G. Sontheimer, President of Cuisinarts, Inc., Greenwich, Conn., who some ten years ago introduced to America a newfangled French appliance called "the food processor," thereby launching a culinary revolution that is affecting millions of Americans; also to Narcisse Chamberlain of William Morrow and Company, Inc., for her editorial guidance, insight and judgment.

Contents

PART TWO:

270 Recipes Developed Especially for the Processor

Introduction

WHEN THE CUISINART® FOOD PROCESSOR was unveiled at the Chicago housewares show in January, 1973, it scarcely could have been called a hit. Indeed, myopic department-store and kitchen-shop buyers failed to see the machine as anything more than a souped-up blender with an exorbitant price tag. In other words, a white elephant.

Some white elephant. In just ten years it has spawned scores of imitations and turned America into a food-processor society. No one knows (or to be more accurate, *no one will say*) how many millions of food processors have been sold across the country since Cuisinart's® inauspicious debut, but what is known is that there are some thirty different brands on the market today, not to mention more models and attachments than you can shake a whisk at.

All because Carl G. Sontheimer, a retired electronics engineer and dedicated amateur chef from Connecticut, haunted the French housewares show in Paris in 1971 looking for a project to occupy his spare time. That project turned out to be a powerful, compact French machine that could grind, chop, mince, slice, purée, pulverize, mix and blend with stunning speed. Sontheimer and his wife Shirley were fascinated. They tracked down the machine's inventor, Pierre Verdun, who had also invented its precursor, Le Robot-Coupe, a heavy-duty restaurant machine dubbed "the buffalo chopper" by American chefs.

Sontheimer secured distribution rights for the machine in the United States, then shipped one dozen back to Connecticut to tinker around with in his garage. He took them apart, reassembled them, took them apart again, analyzing their strengths and shortcomings. He kitchen-tested them, his wife kitchen-tested them, and he tinkered some more. He refined the French processor's design, improved its slicing and shredding discs, incorporated safety features and rechristened it the Cuisinart®.

Undaunted by the Cuisinart's® tepid reception in Chicago among the housewares buyers, Sontheimer set out to demonstrate his machine and to convince America's best-known food gurus personally that

15

it was indeed a miracle worker. It won their unanimous blessings and was praised to the skies—in print, where the rest of us read of its wizardry.

So much for the making of a machine. The rest is history.

It was inevitable, of course, that the appearance of a new kitchen appliance as revolutionary as the food processor would produce an avalanche of food-processor cookbooks.

And so it has, this one included, which I wrote originally after long consideration of what and how much there then was to know about using a processor. This book, also unlike many of the others, dealt not with a single brand of food processor—nor with a combination of processors, blenders, mixers and other multi-function machines—but with processors *exclusively* and with all of the major models then available. It showed how to use each to best advantage and to the hilt.

My purpose was to teach new processor owners how to "drive" their machines effortlessly, expertly, safely by being as specific as possible about terms, techniques and times right down to the split half-second. Telling someone merely "to process" the onions was insufficient. How, precisely, did one mince onions without reducing them to mush? How long did it take? How did one grind beef without churning it to paste? How did one make *pâtés* and pastries by processor, to say nothing of mousses and *quenelles*?

Judging from the hundreds of comments and letters received since the original edition of JEAN ANDERSON'S PROCESSOR COOKING was published nearly five years ago, the book fulfilled its early premise and promise: to anticipate the new processor owner's questions and to answer them, to foresee problems and solve them, to devote itself not only to processor techniques but also to recipes for which the use of a processor is fundamental. Specifically, these were the kinds of recipes we hadn't tried or had seldom bothered to make because of their irritating inconvenience of preparation. And there were the time-consuming old standbys that we had been plodding through forever that had suddenly become a snap to make, thanks to the food processor.

I have now spent eight years working with more than two dozen different processors, trying and testing each new brand or model as it appeared on the market. I have put dozens of attachments—the optional extras as well as the standard equipment—through their paces. I have seen—praised be!—the arrival of big and powerful new models that can cope with five pounds of bread dough at a time (enough for two big loaves), work bowls that can accommodate more than a gallon of sliced or shredded foods all at once, even six cups of liquid as a result of redesigned central spindles that eliminate leakage.

These newest models and attachments mean that the processor is even more of a miracle worker, a speed demon of greater flexibility and control that resembles the early models about as much as an SST does a DC-3. By teaming the prowess of these new processors with a college major in food chemistry and physics, I have learned to perform tasks once thought impossible: to processor-mash potatoes, for example, to whip egg whites to moist and billowing hillocks (if not to stiff, dry peaks), a technique best demonstrated in my silken, fresh Ginger Root Mousse (see Index for recipe page number).

In the pages of this new edition of JEAN ANDERSON'S PRO-CESSOR COOKING, you will find this greater processor flexibility covered together with the techniques, tricks and tips I have learned since the first edition was published. You will also find new recipes here—among them wonderful whole-grain breads, a rainbow array of pastas (tomato, fresh basil, whole-wheat) and another of frozen puréed fruits that can be buzzed to fluff in no time flat. All have been tested once and some two and three times to refine methods or techniques.

My choice of recipes, as before, is based wholly upon the practical use of the processor: the amount of time and labor saved, the skills the processor performs best and—a crucial point—the chemical and physical properties of the food being processed. For example, because machine-mincing garlic intensifies its pungency, it may be necessary to reduce somewhat the quantity that is called for in the traditional *aïoli* and *pesto*. Also, you will still not find recipes here for yellow or silver, sponge or angel cakes because I still believe that they are better when mixed by hand or with an electric mixer. But you *will* find a variety of new quick breads, which I've streamlined for processor preparation—a fine and feathery loaf buzzed up out of fresh hazelnuts, for example, and another made of shredded butternut squash.

Because food processors are so versatile, so phenomenal, the temptation has been for recipe writers to use them like a new toy for virtually every cooking task. I disagree. Common sense must be exercised. I find it idiotic to machine-mince a couple of shallots or a few sprigs of parsley when you can do both faster by hand—certainly faster than you can set the processor up, dismantle it and wash all the component parts. A processor, moreover, should not replace the electric mixer (still the master when it comes to mixing batters, or whipping egg whites and cream) or, for that matter, the electric blender (which excels both at liquefying solid foods and at buzzing up frothy drinks). Each machine is a specialist and should be used for what it does best.

It may seem that some of my recipes run long, but I have deliberately described in detail each processor technique as it came along, specified processing times to the second, and alerted you to any unexpected (though normal) developments that may occur in the course of preparing a recipe. Processor techniques have been given short shrift in print so far, and it is my intention to be as explicit and helpful as possible.

The food processor, after all, isn't merely a new machine. It has meant a whole new way of cooking.

—JEAN ANDERSON

New York, 1983

Jean Anderson's
New Processor Cooking

Part One

THE
PROCESSOR

The Processor

LET ME SAY AT THE START that the way (and the speed with which) a specific food is chopped, minced, puréed, blended, creamed, kneaded, emulsified or whatever will vary somewhat from processor to processor because of the differences in horsepower and in revolutions per minute of blades and discs—and indeed the subtle divergencies of sharpness and contour of blades and discs. The wisest policy, obviously, is to study, thoroughly, the instruction manual that accompanies your particular food processor, then to experiment with simple jobs—slicing or shredding potatoes, chopping onions, crumbing bread—so that you get the feel of your machine and discover its strengths and weaknesses before you attempt a costly or complicated recipe.

The Standard Processor Accessories

Work Bowl and Lid: The designs vary somewhat from machine to machine, as do the work-bowl capacities, but in every case the work bowls and lids are made of clear, durable, heavy-duty plastic (most are dishwasher-safe). Each lid has a tall, chimney-like feed tube (or food chute) through which ingredients are fed into the processor. Liquids and such dry ingredients as sugar and flour can be poured directly down the feed tube from a measuring cup, but solids to be sliced, shredded or chopped must be eased down the feed tube with the accompanying plastic *pusher* (see next page). Most feed tubes, by the way, stand 4 inches high (and the GE Food Processor's is 5 inches)—longer than the longest fingers—so there is little danger of anyone's catching a finger in a cutting disc should (s)he be so careless as to hand-feed food into a processor. The most innovative recent development is Cuisinart's® expanded feed tube, which enables you to slice onions, potatoes, tomatoes, lemons and the like *whole*. Its big and powerful new DLC-X model, moreover, boasts a feed tube large enough to accommodate *small whole grapefruits* and a work bowl that can hold more than a gallon of sliced or shredded food at one time, thereby eliminating the bother of having to slice or shred foods batch by batch. Robot-Coupe™, not to be outdone, equips its 2800 model with "Le Grand Opening" in which the feed tube *is* the lid, making it possible to slice as many as four tomatoes at one time.

Because all processors are so powerful and so fast, and because their blades are razor-sharp, each manufacturer has devised fail-safe mechanisms to minimize the risk of accidents—that is, the processor motors will not operate until *after* the work bowl and lid have been securely locked into place.

On many early processors, the Lid-Lock doubled as the On-Off switch: lock the lid into place on the work bowl and the motor started, unlock it and the motor stopped. The majority of today's models feature *separate On-Off switches* (ever so much handier than swiveling the work-bowl lid back and forth) together with *Pulse buttons or switches* enabling split-second, fingertip control of the *On-Off technique* so integral to successful chopping and mincing.

Finally, newest models (of the more expensive processors, at least) offer instant (or almost instant) braking action, meaning that the cutting blades and discs come to a stop almost as soon as the motor is switched off. A most welcome new safety feature.

It goes without saying that you should study—not merely read—the instruction manual accompanying your processor before you so much as slice a carrot. Also read—memorize—the safety guidelines discussed in the section *How to Use the Processor*—SAFELY, which follows.

Pusher: Made of plastic, these fit the work-bowl feed tube snugly and should be used instead of fingers for guiding foods into the processor's cutting discs or blades—again a safeguard against accidents. Some pushers are designed to serve as measuring cups, others have a small hole at the bottom through which you can drizzle liquid ingredients into the work bowl (as when making mayonnaise), and still others are simply closed plastic cylinders. Cuisinart's® new expanded feed tube has two pushers: one that fits the expanded feed tube and a small, round central feed tube and pusher through which you can add liquids and small ingredients without pressing the entire (and somewhat cumbersome) expanded feed-tube assembly into service.

Metal Chopping Blade: You will soon discover that this—the scalpel-sharp S or double scimitar—is the most indispensable processor accessory; you will use it for everything except slicing, shredding, julienning and—if you should have the new stubby plastic blade redesigned specifically for bread-making—kneading. I use it for mixing and blending in preference to the plastic mixing blade, which most manufacturers have now either discontinued altogether or refashioned (see Plastic Blade, which follows). The metal chopping blade is also the blade that requires the greatest skill and restraint to operate. If, for example, you intend to chop or mince onions, you must develop a quick trigger finger on the control switch, pulsing the machine smartly until the onions are as coarse or fine as you want them. Otherwise you will get mush.

Using short bursts of speed is critical to the optimum performance of the chopping blade—except when you are making a purée or paste, a mayonnaise or flavored butter, etc.—because it is the only way in which you can control the texture of the chop, mince, grind or crumb.

The stop-start or pulse method of processing also helps to keep foods bouncing around the work bowl and in the path of the cutting blades, thereby eliminating the need to stop the machine frequently to scrape down the work bowl. Few chopping-blade jobs require longer than 15 or 20 seconds, and virtually none longer than 1 minute (peanut butter being the one conspicuous exception).

Plastic Blade: Its original purpose was to blend or mix foods—when you wanted to retain a modicum of texture—but so many people preferred the metal chopping blade that many manufacturers have discontinued it. Cuisinart®, however, always the innovator, has come up with a sturdy, stubby new plastic blade that does a better job of kneading big batches of bread dough (containing more than 3½ cups of flour) than the metal chopping blade because it has no pointed ends to become ensnarled in the dough and stall the motor. And KitchenAid, which introduced its first full-fledged food processor only at the end of 1982, equips it with a similarly stubby plastic "dough blade." Both dough blades actually knead the dough, churning it into a ball and rolling it around the work bowl with a washing-machine-like action.

Slicing Disc: The standard accessory for most food processors is the medium-slicing disc, averaging between 6 and 8 slices to the inch, which is a good all-around thickness for the majority of recipes. Using the slicing disc is a straightforward operation, although you *can* thicken or thin the slices simply by varying the amount of pressure with which you push the food down the feed tube—the lighter the pressure, the thinner the slice. For see-through-thin slices, I exert no pressure at all and let the action of the disc pull the food down the feed tube of its own accord—this works especially well with potatoes and cucumbers. NOTE: *Unless the slicing disc is serrated, it will not slice meats cleanly.*

Shredding Disc: A medium-shredding disc accompanies most food processors as standard equipment, and it's a good choice for most shredding tasks. There is no particular trick to using this blade—simply push food down the feed tube with gentle but steady pressure. Exerting heavy pressure will not hasten shredding, but it *will* increase the decibels to ear-shattering level (especially if the food is hard), and it may also deform or dull the shredding disc.

Additional Accessories: French-fry cutters . . . crinkle cutters . . . slicers, shredders and julienners fine and coarse . . . fruit juicers . . . pasta makers . . . and "whips" that will actually processor-whip egg whites and cream to peaks. These are just a few of the extra processor attachments now available for some—but not all—of the different brands. More and more accessories are being introduced, with Cuisinart® continuing to lead the way.

How to Use the Processor—SAFELY

DESPITE THE FACT that each food-processor manufacturer has built myriad safeguards into his machine and clearly spelled out the Do's and Don't's for its safe operation, accidents can and do happen. No machine is 100 percent safe, and must thus be used with extreme care, alertness and respect. Although the various processors differ somewhat in design and operation, the following safety guidelines apply to all:

• STUDY your processor's instruction manual thoroughly until you are completely familiar with its care and use. Pay particular attention to the discussions of the various discs and blades, the assembling and disassembling of the machine's component parts, the On-Off mechanism and, needless to add, the safe operation of the processor.

• NEVER push food down the feed tube with your hand. Always use the plastic pusher. And never stick your fingers down the feed tube when the machine is running.

• NEVER fit a blade or disc on the power base's spindle without first setting the work bowl into place. You *might* accidentally activate the motor (possible if you depress the small red dot at the center-front of the original Cuisinart® or the small white dot, center-front, on the old American Food Processor). Newer models, however, are very nearly fail-safe and both the new KitchenAid and Robot-Coupe™ food processors feature magnetic safety systems that make it impossible to turn the motor on until the bowl and lid are both securely in place.

• NEVER UNCOVER A WORK BOWL UNTIL AFTER THE BLADES OR DISCS HAVE COME TO A COMPLETE STOP. I cannot emphasize this strongly enough because people, in their haste, have been badly cut by opening the work bowl before the blades have ceased to spin. This is particularly hazardous when you're using the slicing or shredding discs, which ride at the top of the work bowl and look less formidable than the metal chopping blade. With some processors (the original Cuisinart®, Norelco, American, to name a few), the blades spin for some seconds after the motor is shut off and with momentum enough to give you a fierce cut. More accidents have been caused by opening the work bowl too soon than by anything else, with the result that several processor manufacturers (Waring, Sunbeam, Hamilton Beach, Kitchen-Aid and both Cuisinart® and Robot-Coupe™ for their newer models) have installed braking actions to halt or slow the blades of their machines almost as soon as the motor is turned off. I wish more manufacturers would follow suit, and they probably will. What they have done, meanwhile, is to print stern warnings on the lids of their work bowls (or on the machine's power base)—constant reminders not to uncover the work bowl until after the blades have come to a dead stop.

• NEVER force your processor beyond its capability: applying pressure on the pusher to speed the slicing or shredding of a coarse or hard food, trying to slice meat with a nonserrated slicing disc, overfilling the work bowl, starting the chopping blade with one or two large lumps of hard food in the work bowl, all of which may jam the blade and stall the motor. NOTE: *Every processor has an automatic overload shut-off to prevent the motor from burning out. Read your instruction booklet*

*carefully for directions on what to do should this happen to your
processor.*

• ALWAYS leave the metal chopping blade in place when lifting the
work bowl from the power base (this is to prevent leakage down the
central spindle).

• ALWAYS remove the metal chopping blade *before* emptying the
work bowl—with one exception: *liquids* that can be poured from the
work bowl. You must, however, hold the chopping blade in place while
pouring (lest it fall into the soup) by pressing down on the plastic hub.
And—common sense should tell you that you should remove the chopping blade before scraping out the bowl with the plastic spatula. For all
other foods—whether puréed, chopped, minced, emulsified (as when
making hollandaise, béarnaise or mayonnaise), I lift out the chopping
blade as soon as I have removed the work bowl from the power base,
using the plastic spatula to scrape any food clinging to it directly into
the pan, skillet or mixing bowl I'll be using to complete the recipe. I
then set the blade flat in the sink and run a thin stream of water over it
to simplify washing it later. When loading the dishwasher, I set the
chopping blade or cutting disc on the top rack—*front-center* where I
can see it the minute I open the dishwasher. NOTE: *Slicing and shredding discs can be removed from the processor work bowl before it is
lifted off the power base unless the food sliced or shredded is watery
and apt to ooze down the central spindle. Sometimes the discs are difficult to lift off—grasping them by the sides and rocking them slightly
back and forth usually loosens them quickly. The brand-new Kitchen-
Aid and also the newest Cuisinarts® and Robot-Coupes™ have detach-
able leakproof spindles onto which a variety of different cutting discs
fit. These slip on and off easily and simplify storage no end.*

• ALWAYS stop the machine when arranging a new batch of foods to
be sliced or shredded in the feed tube. Doing so not only reduces the
risk of accident but also assures you of precisely cut slices or shreds.
There are times, however, when foods should be added with the motor
running, but only when the metal chopping blade or plastic mixing or
dough blades are being used. Some examples: dropping ice cubes
down the feed tube to be crushed (or chunks of Parmesan cheese to be
grated), adding liquids or dry ingredients to batters or doughs, adding
oil to mayonnaise, etc.

• ALWAYS unplug the processor when changing discs or blades or
when disassembling the machine. And store the machine unplugged.

• ALWAYS disassemble and store your processor as the manufacturer recommends. No machine should ever be stored with the work-bowl lid locked in place or with the On or Pulse buttons depressed because the delicate, spring-operated motor switch can be damaged or broken altogether.

• ALWAYS handle all processor blades and discs as gingerly as you would your sharpest carving knife. Store them immediately after washing them—well out of reach of small children, well away from counter or shelf edges where they may tumble off and hurt someone.

A Dictionary
of Processes &
Techniques

PROCESS	DEFINITION	ACCESSORY TO USE
Beat	To whir or churn one or more ingredients until completely smooth or homogeneous, as when beating egg yolks (solo or with sugar) until thick. The processor does a stellar job of beating egg yolks and sugar to "ribbon" consistency in seconds—until stiff enough that a bit of the mixture, when dropped from a spoon, forms a flat, thick ribbon that folds back on itself and does not flatten or disappear immediately.	*Metal Chopping Blade*
Blend	To combine two or more ingredients until absolutely uniform, as when preparing a dip, spread or creamy-smooth *pâté*.	*Metal Chopping Blade or Plastic Mixing Blade*
Chop	To cut food into small pieces. For a coarse chop, the pieces, though	*Metal Chopping Blade*

PROCESS	DEFINITION	ACCESSORY TO USE
	irregular, should average about ¼ inch; for a fine chop, about ⅛ inch.	
Chunk	To cut food into chunks of about 1 inch. Unlike cubes, chunks need not be square or even uniform in shape.	*This you do by hand to prepare food for the processor.*
Cream	To beat a fat (butter, margarine, cream cheese, etc.) solo or together with one or more other ingredients (sugar, for example) until light and creamy.	*Metal Chopping Blade*
Crumb	To reduce pieces of bread, crackers or cookies to coarse or fine crumbs.	*Metal Chopping Blade*
Crush	To pulverize ice to a fine pebbly or snowy texture.	*Metal Chopping Blade*
Cube	To cut food into cubes of uniform size, usually between ½ and 1 inch in size.	*This you do by hand to prepare food for the processor.*
Cut In	To incorporate shortening (butter, lard or vegetable shortening) into flour when making pastry.	*Metal Chopping Blade*

PROCESS	DEFINITION	ACCESSORY TO USE
Dice	To cut food into small, uniform cubes, usually from ⅛ to ¼ inch in size.	*Thick-Slicer. If appearance is important, I prefer to do the job by hand. It's likely to be quicker than restacking and recutting slices to form the tiny cubes.*
Emulsify	To combine an oil or egg yolks or eggs with a non-oily liquid such as vinegar or lemon juice and churn until smooth and billowing. This is the process for making mayonnaise, hollandaise and béarnaise.	*Metal Chopping Blade*
Flake	To break up chunks of tuna, salmon or cooked meat into fairly uniform flakes (the texture is flatter and coarser than that of a chop).	*Metal Chopping Blade*
French	To slice green beans moderately thin lengthwise.	*Medium Slicing Disc*
Grate	Grated food, technically, is finer in texture than shredded food. In this book I use the term *grate* primarily for processing Parmesan	*Metal Chopping Blade*

cheese, cabbage, chocolate and coconut.

PROCESS	DEFINITION	ACCESSORY TO USE
Grind	To reduce to uniformly fine texture with sharp cutting blades. In this book, I use the term *grind* principally to refer to meats, either cooked or raw. The processor actually chops the meat, but the end result is almost the same as when meat is put through a meat grinder.	*Metal Chopping Blade*
Juice	To extract juice from a food. You can use the processor's chopping blade to juice grapefruit chunks, also fully ripe tomatoes. **NOTE:** *The KitchenAid and certain models of the Cuisinart® and Robot-Coupe™ have citrus-juicing attachments; other brands may follow suit.*	*Metal Chopping Blade or Citrus Juicer Attachment*
Julienne	To cut food into matchstick-slim slivers. It's a snap with the fine, medium or coarse julienne disc (optionals available with later Cuisinart® and Robot-Coupe™ models). But you can approximate a julienne with a coarse-shredding disc, or if you have the patience to slice, restack and slice again, you can do a more meticulous job using the thick- or medium-slicing	*Coarse, Medium or Fine Julienne Disc, Coarse-Shredding Disc, Medium- or Thick-Slicing Disc*

disc. (See **Carrots,** in *A Dictionary of Foods & How to Process Them,* for detailed directions.)

Knead	To manipulate dough or pastry in order to develop the strands of gluten (protein) present in flour so that it will have the elasticity to form the framework of bread or pastry. **NOTE:** *The newest processor attachment, now available as standard equipment with the KitchenAid and also with late-model Cuisinarts® looks like the old plastic mixing blade with the ends sawed off. It is actually a new blade made of sturdy plastic whose short, stubby ends can knead the heaviest doughs without complaint or complication. KitchenAid recommends that its Kneading Blade be used only for doughs containing more than 3 cups of flour and Cuisinart® its Dough Blade for doughs containing more than 3½ cups flour.*	*The stubby plastic Dough or Kneading Blade or Metal Chopping Blade*
Mash	To reduce chunks of food to a paste-like consistency. What's the difference between *mashing* and *puréeing?* I like to think of it as a degree of texture—*mashed* avocados will be lumpy, *puréed*	*Metal Chopping Blade*

ones silky-smooth. NOTE: *When I first wrote this book, I said that you couldn't processor-mash potatoes, that they would have all the appeal of library paste. Well, in the intervening years, I have learned how to produce fluffy mashed potatoes in the processor (see Index for recipe page number).*

PROCESS	DEFINITION	ACCESSORY TO USE
Mince	To cut food into very fine particles—smaller than a chop, meaning less than ⅛ inch.	*Metal Chopping Blade*
Mix	To combine two or more ingredients until well blended.	*Metal Chopping Blade or Plastic Mixing Blade*
Pulse	To use repeated short churnings of the processor motor by depressing, then releasing the *Pulse button or switch,* a refinement now available on the majority of processors. *Pulsing* provides split-second control of slicing and shredding discs as well as of the metal chopping blade.	
Purée	To reduce food to a smooth paste.	*Metal Chopping Blade*

Shred	To cut into fine, medium or coarse strips or shreds.	*Fine-, Medium- or Coarse-Shredding Disc*
Slice	To cut into thin, medium or thick slices.	*Thin-, Medium- or Thick-Slicing Disc*
Whip	To beat air into a food (especially egg whites or heavy cream) so that it increases dramatically in volume. **NOTE:** The processor *will* whip cream to soft mounds, but *not* to the peaks expected of a dessert topping. It will also whip egg whites to exceptionally fine, foamy hillocks provided you add both a little sugar (about 1½ to 2 teaspoons per large egg white) and a little acid (about 1 teaspoon lemon juice or vinegar or a hefty pinch of cream of tartar for 4 to 6 large whites) to help stabilize the beaten whites. Drizzling a little boiling-hot sugar syrup (preferably one with a little lemon juice, vinegar or cream of tartar added) into the egg whites as you beat them will also increase their stability as proved by my recipe for Ginger Root Mousse (see Index for recipe page number). But you cannot obtain the stratospheric heights you need for soufflés or the stiff, dry mixture	*Plastic Mixing Blade or Metal Chopping Blade*

needed for meringues because the
processor's powerful cutting action
knocks the air out of the whites
almost as fast as it is beaten in.
Waring and Robot-Coupe™ have
developed "whips" for their
processors that will whip both egg
whites and cream to peaks, but
other brands have yet to follow
suit.

What the Processor
WON'T *Do*

Grind spices to powder
Grind coffee beans
Grind whole grains to flour
Whip cream to great heights ⎫ Unless you have Waring's or
   or stiff peaks   ⎬ Robot-Coupe's™ "whip" attachments
Whip egg whites to great   ⎭
   heights or stiff peaks
Mash Maine, Eastern, All-Purpose or other waxy potatoes (it turns
   them to glue)*
Slice or shred most cooked potatoes (again, it makes them gluey)
Churn butter
Chop dried currants or raisins (unless they have first been softened
   in liquid or chilled well [about 15 minutes in the freezer], then
   dredged with flour [use about ¾ cup of the flour called for in the
   recipe you are preparing for each 1 to 1½ cups fruit]). NOTE: *This*

chill-and-dredge technique also works well for sticky, difficult-to-chop items such as dates, prunes, dried apricots and peaches and the entire repertoire of candied or glacéed fruits.

NOTE: When processors first began revolutionizing our way of cooking some ten years ago, everyone expected these miracle machines to mash potatoes to uncommon fluffiness. They failed miserably. In fact, try as I would to processor-mash potatoes, I invariably churned them to glue. I have subsequently learned a few tricks that make it possible to mash baking potatoes (Russets or Burbanks) in the processor. They may not be as creamy-light as those my mother used to mash by hand, but they are wholly acceptable and infinitely easier to prepare. Try my new recipe for Fluffy Mashed Potatoes (see Index for recipe page number). I think you'll find them to your liking.

A Dictionary of Foods & How to Process Them

Almonds:

To Blanch: Plunge almonds into boiling water, let stand 30 seconds, drain, then slip off the skins.

To Chop: Equip the processor with the metal chopping blade, then add blanched or unblanched nuts (whichever the recipe specifies) to the work bowl. For coarsely chopped nuts, let the motor run nonstop for 10 seconds; for moderately finely chopped nuts, 15 seconds; and for fine, powdery nuts, 20 seconds. **NOTE:** *For best results, do no more than 1 cup of nuts at a time.*

Almond Paste: See Index for recipe page number.

Apples:

To Chop: Peel the apples, core and cut into 1-inch chunks. Equip the processor with the metal chopping blade. Add apple chunks to work bowl (no more than 2 cups of them at a time). For a moderately coarse chop, pulse or snap the motor on and off quickly 3 times; for a finer chop, use 5 or 6 pulses or on-offs of the motor. **NOTE:** *Try Fresh Chopped-Apple Pie with Butter-Crumb Topping (see Index for recipe page number), for which the apples are not peeled.*

Apples,
cont.

To Slice: Peel, quarter and core the apples. Slip the medium-slicing disc into place, then put the work-bowl lid on, but do not turn the motor on. Lay enough apple quarters on their sides in the feed tube for a fairly snug fit (about 4 quarters), hold in place by exerting gentle pressure on the pusher, then snap the motor on or depress the Pulse button. Repeat until all apples are sliced. DO NOT ARRANGE APPLES IN THE FEED TUBE WITH THE MOTOR ON.

TIP: To keep chopped or sliced apples from darkening, sprinkle immediately with lemon juice.

Apricots:

See **Peaches.**

Artichokes,
Jerusalem:

To Prepare for the Processor: These knobby tubers, also called sunchokes, are pesky to peel. Leave the skins on, if you like, but *do* scrub each choke well with a vegetable brush under cool running water; also remove all blemishes. If you choose to peel the artichokes, you'll find the going easier if you scrape them with a sharp paring knife instead of trying to cut the thin skin off.

To Chop: Cut the prepared artichokes into 1-inch chunks, and place no more than 2 cups of them in the work bowl of a processor fitted with the metal chopping blade. For a coarse chop, pulse or snap the motor on and off quickly 2 or 3 times; for a finer chop, 4 or 5 times. The best use I know for chopped artichokes is Jerusalem Artichoke Pickle Relish (see Index for recipe page number).

To Slice: Equip the processor with the medium-slicing disc. Most Jerusalem artichokes are small enough to be fed whole into the processor feed tube, and if you stand them in the feed tube vertically, you will be able to accommodate two of them,

Artichokes, cont.

perhaps three. The point is to wedge them in—with the processor motor *off*—so that they neither wobble nor slither around as they are sliced. To slice them lengthwise, simply lay the artichokes on their sides in the feed tube, again fitting in as many as needed for a snug fit. Snap the processor on or depress the Pulse button and push the chokes down the feed tube with steady but light pressure.

To Shred: I don't recommend shredding Jerusalem artichokes unless they are to be used raw in salad; shredded chokes, when cooked, are limp, watery and unappetizing. Equip the processor with the medium-shredding disc, then stand in the feed tube as many prepared chokes as needed for a firm fit; turn the motor on or depress the Pulse button and push them down the feed tube with moderate pressure.

Avocados:

To Chop: Do not expect avocado to chop neatly; if it is ripe enough to eat, it is too soft to chop and will be reduced to lumpy mush (perfect for Guacamole; see Index for recipe page number). If you must chop raw avocado—for a salad or casserole, for example—pick fruits that are a shade underripe, halve them, remove the pits, peel and cut into 1-inch chunks. Equip the processor with the metal chopping blade, add no more than 2 cups of avocado chunks to the work bowl, then, using 1 or 2 pulses or on-offs of the motor, coarsely chop. There is no point in aiming for a fine chop—the avocado will be mashed.

To Slice: Halve firm-ripe avocados, pit and peel them, then cut each half in half (or in thirds if avocados are very large). Equip the processor with a medium- or thick-slicing disc, then arrange two avocado wedges in the food-processor feed tube back to back (that is, with the two convex or peeled sides abutting one another), with one wedge broad-side

**Avocados,
cont.**

down and the other broad-side up—this for a tighter fit, which will keep the avocado from slithering about the feed tube, thereby ensuring neater slices. Snap the motor on or depress the Pulse button and, using gentle pressure, push the avocado down the feed tube. Repeat until all are sliced, making certain that you turn the motor off each time you reload the feed tube.

To Mash or Purée: Choose soft, ready-to-eat avocados showing no signs of blackening on the skin. Halve them, remove pits, peel and cut into 1-inch chunks. Equip the processor work bowl with the metal chopping blade, add avocado chunks (no more than 2 cups at a time) with the juice of ½ lemon. **To mash:** Run the motor 5 seconds nonstop, scrape down the work bowl, then pulse or snap the motor on and off smartly one or twice. **To purée:** Simply run the processor an additional 5 seconds until avocado is creamy-smooth.

TIP: To prevent chopped or sliced avocados from darkening, sprinkle immediately with lemon juice.

Bananas:

To Slice: First of all, choose firm bananas. Peel them, then halve crosswise. Equip the processor with either a medium- or thick-slicing disc; stand two banana halves in the feed tube, cut surfaces down, and with the outer curve of one banana half fitting spoon-fashion into the hollow of the other half. Turn the motor on or depress the Pulse button and guide the banana halves through the feed tube, exerting minimal pressure on the pusher. Dip slices at once in lemon or orange juice to prevent browning.

To Mash or Purée: Select soft-ripe bananas, peel them and cut into 1-inch chunks. Equip the

Bananas, cont.

processor with the metal chopping blade. Add 2 cups of banana chunks to the work bowl (no more) with the juice of ½ lemon. **To Mash:** Let the motor run 5 seconds, scrape down the sides of the work bowl, then pulse or snap the motor on and off once or twice. **To Purée:** Buzz about 5 seconds longer until uniformly smooth.

Beans, Green or Wax:

To French: Wash and tip the beans, then cut into uniform lengths that are the width of the food-processor feed tube—about 2 to 2½ inches, depending upon the processor. Equip the processor with the medium-slicing disc and set the lid in place. With the motor off, stack the beans neatly in the feed tube, laying them on their sides and filling the feed tube almost to the brim. Insert pusher to steady the stack of beans, turn motor on or depress the Pulse button and guide the beans down the feed tube, using gentle pressure. Repeat until all beans are frenched.

To Purée Cooked Beans: See **Purées**, discussed later in this section.

Beef, Raw:

To Grind: The best cuts to use for processing are top and bottom round, because they are relatively lean and require the least amount of trimming. (I actually prefer the flavor of chuck, but it is so shot through with gristle, sinew and fat that it is scarcely worth your while to excise them all before grinding.) Trim most of the fat and all of the sinew from the meat, then cut into ¾-inch to 1-inch cubes. Equip the processor with the metal chopping blade. Unless you have one of the big new heavy-duty processors that can grind as much as 4 cups (2 pounds) of meat at a time, place no more than 1 cup of beef cubes in the processor work bowl. (**NOTE:** *Read your*

**Beef,
cont.**

processor's instruction manual carefully; some manufacturers recommend that you drop the cubes of meat down the feed tube while the motor is on and the blade is spinning.) For a coarse grind, pulse or snap the motor on and off 3 or 4 times; for a moderate grind, use 5 or 6 pulses or on-offs of the motor; and for a fine grind, let the motor run nonstop for 8 to 10 seconds. Keep an eye on the work bowl at all times and, as soon as the meat reaches the texture you want, shut the motor off.

To Slice: Again top and bottom round are the best cuts, or, if you're making one of the Oriental stir-fried dishes, tenderloin (not as much of an extravagance as you may think, because there is very little waste with tenderloin). Trim the meat of fat and sinew, then cut into chunks about the width of your processor feed tube and about ½ inch shorter than the tube. Wrap each piece of meat individually in foil or plastic food wrap and set in the freezer for 1½ to 2 hours, or until beginning to freeze. This is to firm the meat up so that it will offer some resistance to the slicing disc and will cut neatly. Equip the processor with the *serrated* medium-slicing disc (note the word *serrated*—if your slicing disc is not serrated, it will not be able to slice raw meat). Stand a piece of the semifrozen beef in the processor feed tube, turn the motor on and push the beef through the slicing disc with moderate pressure (the machine will make a ferocious racket and some of the lighter models will dance about your counter). **NOTE:** *Before attempting to slice raw beef, consult your processor's instruction manual; some manufacturers caution against trying to slice raw meat with their processors; others recommend that the meat merely be well chilled, not partially frozen.*

To Shred: For certain Chinese stir-fried dishes, you will need shredded meat, which I've found a way to prepare in the processor—at least in the top models

**Beef,
cont.**

that have the razor-sharp stainless steel French-fry cutter. Use tenderloin, trim it well of fat and connective tissue, cut into chunks about the size of the processor feed tube, wrap in foil or plastic food wrap and set in the freezer for 1½ to 2 hours until partially frozen. Equip the processor with the French-fry cutter, stand the meat in the feed tube, turn the motor on and push the meat down the feed tube, using moderate but steady pressure. There will be a terrific racket as the meat is shredded, and some tag ends may catch in the cutter. Stop the machine after each chunk of meat is sliced, remove the French-fry cutter and clean out any bits of stuck meat. Reassemble and continue until all meat is shredded. WARNING: *This process is not recommended for any but the sturdiest machines, and in truth, you will not find any manufacturer recommending that you attempt to shred meat with the French-fry cutter at all. I tried it because I wanted to determine just how versatile the processor was (the French-fry cutter, too). It worked well for me several times, but if you are hurried or haphazard (as indeed a friend of mine was), you may jam your processor (as indeed she did), damaging the motor and dulling the cutting disc. If you are to succeed, you must be unusually meticulous about the cut of meat you choose to shred (tenderloin for beef, loin or tenderloin for veal, also top round for baby veal), you must trim it of every scrap of fat, sinew or connective tissue that might "gum up the works," you must freeze the meat just to the point that it is firm outside but still moderately soft inside. Finally, you must exert no more than a modicum of pressure as you guide the meat down the feed tube. If you have reservations, if you cannot be bothered with following the steps outlined above, if you're worried about straining, stalling (or possibly damaging) your processor, by all means hand-shred your meat.*

Beef, Cooked: **To Grind:** Trim the meat of fat and gristle; cut into
¾-inch to 1-inch cubes and chill them well (about 20
minutes in the freezer, two hours in the
refrigerator). Equip the processor with the metal
chopping blade, place no more than 1 cup of meat
cubes in the work bowl (unless you have one of the
big powerful machines that can cope with 4 cups—2
pounds—of meat at one time), then grind as follows:
Pulse or snap the motor on and off at 1-second
intervals 3 to 4 times for a coarse grind, 5 or 6 times
for a moderate grind, and 7 or 8 times for a
moderately fine grind. For a truly fine and feathery
grind, use two to four 5-second churnings of the
motor or one 15- to 20-second churning. Both
methods work well.

To Slice: Trim away all fat and gristle, then cut the
meat into chunks approximately the width of the
food-processor feed tube, but slightly shorter. Chill
the chunks 30 to 40 minutes in the freezer, just until
firm. Equip the processor with the medium-slicing
disc, stand a chunk of meat in the feed tube, switch
the motor on and push the meat through with
moderate pressure.

Beets: **To Prepare for the Processor:** Whether you intend
to slice or shred beets, you should cook them first—
partially, at least—with the skins, root ends and
about 1 inch of the stems left on, so that the beets
do not lose their rich ruby color. I parboil them for
20 to 25 minutes, or until firm-tender, in enough
boiling water to cover. Then peel, trim off roots and
stems, shred or slice and finish cooking with
whatever seasonings a particular recipe calls for,
adding, if necessary, a small amount of water to keep
the beets from scorching.

To Slice: So that the beets will produce nice round
slices, pick those small enough to fit into the feed

Beets,
cont.

tube whole. Prepare as directed above, then stand one or two beets in the feed tube of a processor fitted with the medium- or thin-slicing disc, turn the motor on or depress the Pulse button and push them down the feed tube, using gentle pressure.

To Shred: Use a medium-shredding disc for the best results, then push the prepared beets down the feed tube one at a time with moderate pressure. **NOTE:** *You'll have greater control over the shredding process if you depress the Pulse button instead of simply snapping the machine on.*

To Purée Cooked Beets: See **Purées**, discussed later in this section.

Brazil Nuts:

To Chop: Do not blanch. *For coarsely chopped nuts,* equip the processor with the slicing disc (the thin-slicing disc, if you have one). Place nuts in feed tube, turn motor on or depress the Pulse button, then push nuts through the slicing disc with moderate pressure. *For more finely chopped nuts,* equip the processor with the metal chopping blade. Place no more than 2 cups of nuts in the processor work bowl, then let the motor run nonstop for 10 seconds for chopped nuts of medium texture; use two or three 10-second churnings for finely or very finely chopped nuts.

Bread Crumbs: See **Crumbs.**

Broccoli:

To Chop: I do not recommend chopping raw broccoli, because it will lose flavor and absorb water during cooking. It's better to parboil it first in lightly salted water, just until crisp-tender (8 to 10 minutes). Trim away coarse stems first (with a processor to break up the tough fibers, these can be

Broccoli,
cont.

used in meat or fish loaves such as Salmon-Broccoli Loaf with Dill and Capers; see Index for recipe page number). Wash trimmed broccoli and divide into flowerets. When cooked until crisp-tender, drain broccoli well, place in a processor equipped with the metal chopping blade (no more than 2 cups of flowerets at a time for best results), then chop as follows: 2 or 3 pulses or on-offs of the motor for coarse; 4 or 5 pulses or on-offs for medium; 6 or 7 for moderately fine and about 8 for quite fine.

To Purée Cooked Broccoli: See **Purées,** discussed later in this section.

Brown Sugar:

To Pulverize Hard, Dry Chunks: Break sugar into 1-inch pieces. Equip the processor with the metal chopping blade and snap the motor on. Now quickly drop the pieces of sugar down the feed tube—no more than 2 cups of them at a time. You'll have to shield the feed tube with your hand as you add the sugar, to deflect the smoke-like white powder that billows up from the work bowl (avoid breathing these "fumes"). As soon as all pieces of sugar have been added, insert the pusher and hold it firmly in place, again to contain the sugar dust within the work bowl. Let the processor run nonstop for about 30 seconds, or until sugar is uniformly fine (you can tell by the sound of the motor—it will hum smoothly). Snap the motor off, but leave both the lid and the pusher in place for several minutes to allow the sugar dust to settle. **NOTE:** *The pulverized sugar is now closer in texture to "brownulated" or granular brown sugars than to the sugar in a freshly opened package; it lacks the softness and moistness that enable you to pack fresh brown sugar firmly into a measuring cup. So, I suggest that you do not use pulverized dried brown sugar in recipes for cakes, quick breads, cookies or confections where precise measurements are critical to the recipe's*

Brown Sugar, cont.

success. Use it instead for streusel toppings, for flavoring fruit pies, for sweetening custards and dessert sauces, for making pancake syrups.

Cabbage:

To Chop: Using the metal chopping blade produces "grated" cabbage of about the degree of coarseness you would get by using the second-coarsest side of a four-sided hand grater. Trim and discard coarse outer leaves, quarter the cabbage and slice off the core at the point of each quarter. Cut cabbage into 1-inch chunks. Equip processor with the metal chopping blade, place cabbage chunks in the work bowl (no more than 2 cups of them at a time), then chop moderately coarsely, using 5 or 6 pulses or on-offs of the motor. For finer texture, use 7 or 8 pulses or on-offs.

To Shred: In processor language, this is something of a misnomer, as the shredding is best accomplished by using the coarse- or medium-slicing disc; most shredding discs reduce the cabbage to pulp. Trim the cabbage, quarter and core (as directed above for chopping), then cut the cabbage into columns about the height and width of the food-processor feed tube. Equip the processor with the medium-slicing disc, stand a column of cabbage in the feed tube, switch the motor on or depress the Pulse button and push the cabbage down the tube with gentle pressure. The texture of this "shred" is about the same as that achieved by grating cabbage on the coarsest side of a four-sided grater.
NOTE: *Cuisinart's® redesigned, made-in-Japan, medium-shredding disc produces shredded cabbage of fine, even texture. And when teamed with the expanded-feed-tube lid, it enables you to shred a quarter or half of a small cabbage at a time. All you need do is halve the cabbage from top to stalk end, remove the cores via deep wedge-shaped cuts, then, if necessary, halve each half crosswise and stand*

Cabbage, **cont.**	*core-side down on the medium-shredding disc. Lock the lid assembly into place, depress the Pulse button and guide the cabbage down the feed tube using moderate but steady pressure.*

Carrots:	**To Chop:** How coarse or fine you chop the carrots and how long the process takes depends both upon the firmness of the carrot (those held too long in the supermarket or refrigerator may be limp) and upon how much carrot you attempt to chop at one time (the larger the amount, the longer the processing time). But the timings given here are a fairly reliable guide. First, trim the carrots, peel and cut into 1-inch lengths. Equip the processor with the metal chopping blade. Place the carrot chunks (no more than 2 cups of them at a time) in the work bowl and chop as follows: 2 or 3 pulses or on-offs of the motor for a coarse chop; 4 or 5 for a moderate one; 6 or 7 for a moderately fine one. For a fairly fine chop, I use 10 seconds nonstop for a small amount—say 1 or 2 medium-size carrots. For more carrots, I may let the motor run nonstop for 20 or 30 seconds, and for maximum quantity, as long as 60 seconds nonstop.

To Slice: With the processor, you can slice carrots into either *rounds* or *oblongs. For rounds,* cut the peeled and trimmed carrots into 4-inch lengths and stand them on end in a food processor fitted with the slicing disc of your choice (thin, medium, thick). For completely uniform slices, wedge as many lengths of carrots into the feed tube as possible, so that they will not wobble once the machine is turned on. Switch the motor on or depress the Pulse button, then guide the carrots down the feed tube, using moderate but steady pressure. For somewhat thicker slices, increase the pressure; for thinner ones, lessen the pressure or simply allow the carrots to self-feed down the feed tube. *For oblong slices,* cut the carrots into lengths that will fit inside the

Carrots, cont.

feed tube when laid on their sides. Fill the feed tube almost to the brim, snap the motor on or depress the Pulse button and push the carrots through the slicing disc with steady, moderate pressure.

To Shred: As with slicing, you again have a choice—short shreds or long. If you stand the prepared carrots on end in the feed tube, you will obtain short shreds; but, if you lay lengths of carrot horizontally in the feed tube, you will get long shreds. And if you use a coarse-shredding disc, you can approximate julienne strips.

To Julienne: Unless appearance is critical, I recommend the coarse-shredding method described above. But if presentation is essential to a recipe's success, you must be more meticulous. Cuisinart's® 2mm and 3mm square julienne discs whiz out the most precise julienne faster than you would have dreamed possible, and Robot-Coupe's™ julienner does a creditable job, too. But if you have neither of these machines or optional attachments, you may find it quicker and easier to hand-cut a julienne of vegetables than to use the two-step, slicing-disc method. Basically, it is the same for carrots and other foods: Be persnickety, first of all, about the foods you choose to julienne. If they are cylindrical—carrots, cucumbers, summer squash, etc.—pick out the chunkiest ones you can find. If, on the other hand, they are spherical—potatoes, beets, turnips, etc.—select the most elongated specimens. Cut elongated foods into lengths that will fit sideways into the feed tube; for spherical foods, simply trim and peel. Equip the food processor with the thick- or medium-slicing disc. Lay the food horizontally in the feed tube, enough pieces for a snug fit, secure with the pusher, switch the motor on or depress the Pulse button and push through the feed tube with moderate pressure. Remove the slices from the feed tube and restack as uniformly as

Carrots,	possible. Now stand on edge in the feed tube as
cont.	many restacked slices as needed for a snug fit, their
	cut surfaces parallel to the front of the feed tube.

Carrots, cont. possible. Now stand on edge in the feed tube as many restacked slices as needed for a snug fit, their cut surfaces parallel to the front of the feed tube. Turn the motor on or depress the Pulse button and slice as before.

To Purée Cooked Carrots: See **Purées,** discussed later in this section.

Cauliflower:

To Chop: See **Broccoli.**

To Slice: You can slice raw flowerets, but there will be considerable waste—crumbly bits that splinter off the floweret at impact with the slicing disc (save these to add to a soup or stew). Trim flowerets so that they will lie sideways in the processor feed tube. Equip the processor with the medium-slicing disc. Now lay the flowerets in the feed tube, one facing one way, the next facing the opposite direction, until the feed tube is almost full. Steady the flowerets with the pusher, snap the motor on or depress the Pulse button and push the cauliflower firmly through the slicing disc.

To Purée Cooked Cauliflower: See **Purées,** discussed later in this section.

Celery:

To Chop: Wash celery, trim off coarse leaves and cut into 1-inch lengths. Equip the processor with the metal chopping blade. Place celery chunks, no more than 2 cups of them at a time, in the work bowl and chop as follows: 2 or 3 pulses or on-offs for a coarse chop; 4 or 5 for a moderate one; and 6 or 7 for a fine one.

To Slice: Cut washed and trimmed celery ribs into 4-inch lengths; equip the processor with the slicing disc of your choice, then stand in the feed tube as

Celery, cont.

many pieces of celery as needed for a tight fit. Turn motor on or depress the Pulse button and push celery down the feed tube with moderate pressure.

Celery Root (Celeriac):

To Prepare for the Processor: Because celeriac is so hard and fibrous, all but the most powerful machines with the sharpest blades are likely to balk when put to the test of slicing or shredding it. The celery root will slice and shred much more easily if it is first parboiled. Wash, peel and cut into oblongs about the height and width of the processor feed tube. Parboil in lightly salted water in a covered saucepan 20 to 25 minutes, or until firm-tender. Drain well; cool.

To Slice: Equip the processor with the medium-slicing disc, stand a piece of parboiled celeriac in the feed tube, snap the motor on or depress the Pulse button and push the celery root down the feed tube with firm, steady pressure. NOTE: *The new heavy-duty processors do have power enough (and redesigned blades sharp enough) to slice celeriac raw. They can also shred and julienne it raw—good news to lovers of* Céleri Rémoulade.

To Shred: Equip the processor with the medium-shredding disc, then proceed just as you would when slicing the celeriac.

To Julienne: See Carrots.

To Purée Cooked Celery Root: See Purées, discussed later in this section.

Cheeses:

Hard (Parmesan, Romano, Pecorino, etc.): To Grate: Cut into 1-inch cubes. Equip the processor with the metal chopping blade. NOTE: *Carefully read the directions in the instruction manual*

**Cheeses,
cont.**

*accompanying your particular processor. Some
manufacturers recommend that you add the cubes of
cheese down the feed tube while the blade is
spinning. Others recommend that you place the
cubes—no more than 1 cup of them at a time—in
the work bowl, then snap the motor on.* Timing? It
depends upon whether you add the cubes down the
feed tube or place them in the work bowl, also upon
how coarse or fine a texture you want. It's best to
begin by pulsing or snapping the motor on and off 4
to 5 times once all cheese cubes are in the work
bowl; this will give you coarsely grated cheese. For
finer texture, run the processor nonstop 10 to 15
seconds and for a fine and feathery consistency, buzz
nonstop for another 10 to 15 seconds—20 to 30
seconds, total.

**Medium Hard (Cheddar, Gruyère, etc.): To slice or
shred:** First cut well-chilled cheese into blocks about
the size of the food-processor feed tube. Equip the
machine with either the medium-shredding disc or
the medium-slicing disc. Stand a block of cheese in
the feed tube, then turn the motor on or depress the
Pulse button and push through with light but steady
pressure.

Soft Cheeses (Mozzarella): If you are to have any
luck slicing soft cheeses, they must be semi-frozen
(yet not so hard you cannot stick the point of a knife
into them), otherwise the processor will mash rather
than slice them. Cut into blocks about the width and
height of the feed tube; chill ¾ to 1 hour in the
freezer; equip the processor with the medium- or
thick-slicing disc. Stand a block of cheese in the feed
tube, snap the motor on or depress the Pulse
button, and push the cheese down the feed tube.
NOTE: *You will have more luck chopping Mozzarella
than shredding it. Cut into 1-inch cubes, then set in
the freezer about 30 minutes until quite firm. Equip
the processor with the metal chopping blade, place*

Cheeses, cont.	*up to 2 cups cheese cubes in work bowl, then pulse or snap the motor on and off 5 to 6 times; this will give you coarsely chopped cheese. For finer texture, pulse or snap the motor on and off another 5 to 6 times, checking the texture after each pulsing.*

Chestnuts:

To Prepare for the Processor: If you are dealing with fresh chestnuts, you are in for a tiresome chore, because the nuts must be shelled, then skinned. Here's how: Cut an X into the flat side of each chestnut shell; place nuts in a saucepan, cover with cold water, bring to a boil, then boil for 2 minutes. Remove from the heat, but do not drain. Working with several nuts at a time, lift them from the pan with a slotted spoon, peel away the hard outer shell, then scrape away the inner brown skin with a sharp paring knife, paying special attention to the crevices. NOTE: *I much prefer to work with the shelled and skinned, dried or frozen Italian chestnuts, which are available the year around in specialty groceries across the country.*

To Soak Dried Chestnuts: For each 1 cup of chestnuts, allow 2 cups cold water. Place in a heavy saucepan, bring to a boil, then remove from heat, cover and allow to stand at room temperature for 4 hours. Drain well, then pick over the chestnuts, removing any stubborn bits of brown skin with a paring knife.

To Chop: Equip processor with the metal chopping blade. Place chestnuts (no more than 1 cup of them at a time for best results) in the work bowl, then pulse or snap the motor on and off 3 or 4 times for coarsely chopped nuts, 5 or 6 for medium, and 8 or 10 for fine.

To Purée Cooked Chestnuts: See the recipe for **Chestnut Purée** (consult Index for recipe page number).

Chicken, Game Hen, Turkey and Other Poultry:

Raw Meat: To prepare for the processor, remove skin, bones, fat and all connective tissue.

To Grind: Cut meat into 1-inch cubes and chill well. Equip the processor with the metal chopping blade. Place meat (no more than 1 cup of cubes at a time unless you own one of the big heavy-duty machines that can cope with 1 quart—2 pounds—of meat at one time) in the processor and pulse or snap the motor on and off quickly 2 or 3 times for a coarse grind; use 4 or 5 pulses or on-offs for a medium grind; use two or three 5-second churnings of the motor for a fine grind.

To Slice: You will not have much success slicing poultry unless you are dealing with large pieces— turkey or chicken breast, for example. Prepare as directed above, then cut into columns about the size of the processor feed tube (although slightly shorter); wrap pieces individually and set in the freezer for about 1½ hours, or until firm but not frozen. Equip the processor with the medium-slicing disc; stand a piece of meat in the feed tube, switch the motor on and push the meat down the feed tube with steady, firm pressure.

Cooked Meat: To prepare for the processor, skin and bone the meat; also remove fat and sinew; chill the meat well if it is soft.

To Chop: Cut the meat into ¾-inch to 1-inch cubes. Equip the processor with the metal chopping blade. Place the meat—no more than 2 cups of it at a time unless you have a large, powerful machine that can accommodate more—in the processor work bowl. For a coarse chop, use 2 or 3 pulses or on-offs of the motor; for a moderately coarse chop, 4 or 5 pulses or on-offs; for medium texture, 6 or 7, and for fine, 8 to

Chicken, Game Hen, Turkey and Other Poultry, cont.	10 pulses or on-offs or if you prefer, two or three 5-second churnings of the motor.

To Slice: Few processors slice cooked poultry neatly, and unless you have a *serrated* slicing disc, it is pointless even to try. As with slicing raw poultry, you will need pieces of meat large enough to be cut into blocks about the size of the processor feed tube. Cut the prepared meat to size and chill well. Equip the processor with the *serrated* medium-slicing disc, stand a piece of meat in the feed tube, snap the motor on or depress the Pulse button, then push the meat down the feed tube with light but steady pressure. |
| **Chinese Cabbage:** | **To Slice:** Trim cabbage of coarse outer leaves and wash. Now pull off 3 or 4 leaves, lay one on top of the other and roll into a tight bundle that is fat enough to fit snugly in the processor feed tube when stood on end. Equip the processor with the medium-slicing disc, wedge the cabbage roll in the feed tube, click the motor on or depress the Pulse button and push the cabbage gently down the feed tube. Repeat until you have stripped away enough leaves for the remaining cabbage heart to be fed whole down the feed tube. |
| **Chocolate:** | **To Grate:** If you are making a recipe where it is important that flecks of chocolate be visible (Filbert or Almond Meringue Cookies, for example; see Index for recipe page number), you should chill the chocolate well. As a matter of fact, you should chill sweet chocolate no matter how it is to be prepared, because it is much softer than unsweetened or semisweet chocolate. Break each square of chocolate in half at the natural separation; equip the processor with the metal chopping blade. Add chocolate (no |

Chocolate, cont.

more than 6 ounces at a time) and for a coarse chop (*for unsweetened or semisweet chocolate*), use one or two 10-second bursts of speed; for a medium chop, two or three 10-second churnings of the motor; and for a very fine chop, four 10-second churnings. For sweet chocolate use the same number of churnings recommended above, only *shorter* ones—about 3 seconds each instead of 10.

Citrus Rind (Lemon, Lime, Orange, Grapefruit):

To Chop or Mince: Using a swivel-bladed vegetable peeler, take off the colored part of the rind only (the zest) in long thin strips. Equip the processor with the metal chopping blade and turn the motor on. Drop the strips of rind down the feed tube and let the motor run nonstop for 8 to 10 seconds, or until the rind is as finely chopped or minced as you like. NOTE: *If the chopped or minced rind is to be used in a sweet or a dessert, add to the work bowl along with the rind about ½ cup of the sugar the recipe calls for, and run the motor 10 to 20 seconds nonstop, or until the degree of fineness you want is reached. The sugar's abrasiveness facilitates the chopping of the rind. Recently, when I had the rinds of 4 oranges and 2 lemons to grate for a butter-cream frosting, I discovered that they can be buzzed to fine shreds with confectioner's sugar. I used a full pound of it and three to four 10-second churnings of the motor. It worked like a charm.*

Clams:

To Chop Raw: Surprisingly, raw clams (hard-shell) can be chopped without being reduced to paste— but *only* if you'll settle for a moderately coarse texture (best for most recipes, anyway). Drain the clams well and place 1 cup of them in the work bowl of a food processor fitted with the metal chopping blade. Pulse or snap the motor on and off smartly 5 times—that's all there is to it.

Clams,
cont.

To Chop Cooked: Equip processor with metal chopping blade; place clams (no more than 2 cups of well-drained, cooked clams) in the work bowl and chop as follows: 2 or 3 pulses or on-offs of the motor for a coarse chop; 4 or 5 for medium; and 6 or more for fine.

Coconut:

To Prepare for the Processor: Pierce two of the coconut's "eyes" with a nail or icepick, then drain out and reserve all liquid. Tap the coconut all over firmly with a hammer (this is to loosen the meat from the shell), then break the coconut into small pieces with the hammer. If shell does not separate easily from the meat, pry off with a screwdriver. With a swivel-bladed vegetable peeler, peel the brown skin away from the snowy meat. Rinse the coconut meat well and pat very dry on paper toweling.

To Grate: Cut the prepared coconut into 1-inch chunks; assemble the food processor, fitting the metal chopping blade into place. Turn the motor on, then drop the coconut chunks (but for best results, no more than 2 cups of them at a time) down the feed tube into the spinning blade. Churn 10 seconds nonstop for coarsely grated coconut; for moderately finely grated coconut, use two 10-second churnings and for finely grated coconut, three 10-second churnings. Inspect the coconut after each churning and stop "grating" it the minute you achieve the texture you want.

To Shred: I don't recommend this unless you have a powerful processor with an unusually sharp medium-shredding disc, because the coconut is hard and may stall the motor or dull and deform the cutting disc. Cut the prepared coconut into pieces about the height and width of the processor feed

Coconut, *cont.*	tube. Equip the processor with the medium-shredding disc, stand on edge in the feed tube as many pieces of coconut as will fit snugly, snap the motor on and push the coconut down the feed tube with firm, steady pressure. The racket will be ear-shattering. Do not increase the pressure you exert on the pusher; you won't hasten the shredding of the coconut and you may damage the blade.
Cookie Crumbs:	See **Crumbs,** opposite.
Corn:	**To Prepare Cream-Style:** Cut the kernels from the cobs whole, or, if you prefer, use thawed, frozen whole-kernel corn. Fit the processor with the metal chopping blade, add corn (no more than 2 cups of kernels at a time) and chop, using four 1-second bursts of speed.
Cracker Crumbs:	See **Crumbs,** opposite.
Cranberries:	**To Chop:** Wash and stem cranberries. Equip the processor with the metal chopping blade, add 1½ to 2 cups cranberries and chop moderately coarsely by pulsing or snapping the motor on and off 2 or 3 times. For a finer chop (and there is some risk of reducing the berries to mush), pulse or snap the machine on and off once or twice more.
Cream, Heavy:	**To Whip:** Don't expect your processor to whip cream to snowy peaks (unless you have a Waring or Robot-Coupe™ and their "whip" accessories). The processor will, however, churn cream to soft, billowing mounds—perfect for chiffon pies, ice creams, etc. Chill the cream well (and avoid using the new "super" or "ultra" pasteurized heavy

Cream, Heavy, cont. creams, which seem disinclined to whip at all). Place the well-chilled cream (for best results, about 1½ cups at a time) in a food processor fitted with the metal chopping blade. Whip the cream nonstop for 10 seconds, scrape down the work bowl, re-cover and whip 5 seconds longer. Again scrape down the work bowl and inspect the consistency of the cream carefully. It should, at this point, be stiffening. Re-cover work bowl and whip 5 to 10 seconds longer, or until cream mounds softly. Watch closely after the cream begins to thicken, so that you don't overwhip it and wind up with flecks of butter.

Crumbs: **Bread Crumbs (Soft):** Tear slices of bread into small pieces and equip the processor with the metal chopping blade. For best results, do not try to crumb more than 4 slices of bread at one time. Place the pieces of bread in the work bowl and, for moderately fine crumbs, pulse or snap the motor on and off 5 or 6 times; for finer crumbs, use two or three 5-second churnings. NOTE: *You may be interested to know that you can mince up to 1 cup of loosely packed parsley sprigs at the same time you crumb the bread—handy for meat loaves, stuffings and other recipes calling for both crumbs and minced parsley. And, to give you an idea as to quantity, 1 slice of bread will equal about ½ cup crumbs, 1 cup loosely packed parsley sprigs between ⅓ and ½ cup minced parsley. Just make sure that the parsley is thoroughly dry, otherwise the bread crumbs will not be nice and fluffy.*

Bread Crumbs (Dry): Dry out slices of bread in a slow oven (300° F.) for about 30 minutes, or until crisp and golden; break into small chunks. Equip the food processor with the metal chopping blade, place 2 cups of bread chunks in the work bowl and buzz to fine crumbs by letting the motor run nonstop for about 10 seconds.

**Crumbs,
cont.**

Cookie Crumbs: Choose crisp, dry cookies such as vanilla wafers, gingersnaps or chocolate wafers, and if the cookies are large, break them into approximately 1½-inch pieces. Place about 2 cups cookies in a food processor fitted with the metal chopping blade and buzz to fine crumbs, using four 5-second churnings of the motor.

Saltine Cracker Crumbs: The 2-inch-square saltines are the handiest size to use. Place crackers (no more than 2 dozen at a time) in a processor equipped with the metal chopping blade and whir to fine crumbs by letting the motor run nonstop 10 to 15 seconds.

Graham-Cracker Crumbs: The 2⅜-inch-square size is the best to use. Place crackers, no more than 12 at a time, in a food processor fitted with the metal chopping blade and buzz to fine crumbs by letting the motor run nonstop for 60 seconds. These are for very fine crumbs that can be used for pie crusts. For coarser crumbs, run the motor for 15-second periods and stop processing the minute the crumbs have reached the degree of coarseness or fineness you want.

Cucumbers:

To Chop: Peel the cucumbers, halve lengthwise, scoop out and discard all seeds, then cut cucumbers into 1-inch lengths. Equip the food processor with the metal chopping blade. Place cucumber in the work bowl (no more than 1½ cups at a time for best results), then pulse or snap the motor on and off about twice for a coarse chop, 3 times for medium, and 4 or 5 for fine. You must watch the chopping carefully and exercise utmost control or the cucumbers, because of their high water content, will turn to soup.

To Slice: If you want to slice whole cucumbers, choose those slim enough to fit in the feed tube.

Cucumbers, cont. Peel them (unless the skins have not been waxed) and cut into lengths slightly shorter than the height of the feed tube. Equip the processor with the slicing disc of your choice (thick, medium or thin), wedge two cucumber pieces in the feed tube, snap the motor on or depress the Pulse button and push them through the feed tube gently. If, on the other hand, you want crescent-shaped slices, halve the peeled cucumbers lengthwise and scoop out all seeds. Again cut the cucumber in lengths about the height of the feed tube, then fit two or more pieces of cucumber together spoon-fashion—however many are needed for a snug fit—and slice as directed above.

Eggplant: **To Slice:** Wash and dry the eggplant, then cut it into columns about the height and width of the processor feed tube. Equip the processor with the *serrated* medium-slicing disc, then arrange a column of eggplant in the feed tube with the skin side toward the back of the tube (this is so that the cutting edge of the blade will slice through it first, minimizing ripping and tearing); snap the motor on or depress the Pulse button and push the eggplant down the feed tube with steady, moderate pressure. **NOTE:** *If you have a Cuisinart® with the expanded feed tube, you will be able to slice small eggplants whole.*

Eggs, Hard-cooked: **To Chop:** Peel the eggs, chill well, then halve lengthwise. Slip the processor's metal chopping blade into place, add the eggs (up to but not more than 6 halves at a time), then chop as follows: 2 pulses or on-offs of the motor for a coarse chop, 3 pulses or on-offs for a moderately coarse chop, and 4 or 5 pulses or on-offs for a finer chop.

Fennel (Finocchio): **To Chop:** Wash, trim and separate into stalks; cut each into 1-inch lengths. Place fennel in a processor

Fennel (Finocchio), cont.	fitted with the metal chopping blade (no more than 2 cups at a time), then pulse or snap the motor on and off 2 or 3 times for a coarse chop; 4 or 5 times for a moderate one; and 6 or 7 times for a fine one.

To Slice: Cut washed and trimmed fennel stalks into 4-inch lengths. Equip the processor with the medium-slicing disc, then fit together, spoon-fashion, as many stalks of fennel as needed to fill the feed tube. Snap the motor on or depress the Pulse button and push the fennel down the feed tube with steady, moderate pressure. |
| **Filberts, Hazelnuts:** | **To Blanch:** Boil the nuts for 6 minutes in enough water to cover; drain well, then bundle up a cup or so of nuts in a dry Turkish towel and rub briskly to remove the skins. You'll have to peel off any recalcitrant bits of skin by hand, and this is a tedious job, alas.

To Chop: Place about 1 cup of nuts (either blanched or unblanched—many recipes call for unblanched nuts) in a processor fitted with the metal chopping blade. For coarsely chopped nuts, let the motor run nonstop for 10 seconds; for moderately finely chopped nuts, 15 seconds; and for finely chopped nuts, 20 seconds. |
| **Fish, Raw:** | **To Grind:** Remove all skin and bones, cut fish into 1-inch chunks and chill well (25 to 30 minutes in the freezer). Equip the processor with the metal chopping blade. For fairly coarsely chopped fish, pulse or snap the motor on and off at 1-second intervals about 4 times; for a finer chop, 5 or 6 times. Watch the texture closely and stop processing the minute the fish is as coarse or fine as you want. *For a fine paste,* essential when making fish puddings or *quenelles,* do not chill the fish in the |

Fish, Raw,
cont.

freezer. And instead of pulsing the motor, let it run nonstop for 60 seconds. For best results, do not attempt to process more than ½ pound of raw fish at a time unless you have one of the rugged new machines that can handle up to 2 pounds (4 cups) of raw meat or fish at one time.

Fish, Cooked
or Canned:

To Flake: Canned tuna or salmon or any firm, cooked fish can be flaked quickly and easily in the processor. Drain, remove bits of skin and bone, then cut or break into 1- to 1½-inch chunks. Equip the processor with the metal chopping blade, add fish (no more than 2 cups at a time), then pulse or snap the motor on and off briskly twice—no more.

To Grind: This simply is taking the flaking process one step further. Pulse or snap the processor on and off 4 to 6 times until the desired texture is reached.

Fruits,
Candied:

To Chop: If the fruits are to be used in a fruitcake, steamed pudding or other recipe calling for flour, they can be successfully chopped in the processor—candied cherries, citron, angelica, orange or lemon rind. Cut larger fruits into 1-inch chunks. Equip processor with the metal chopping blade. Add 2 cups of candied fruits and 1 cup of the flour called for in the recipe to the work bowl and process for 3 seconds, snapping the motor on and off, or using the Pulse button if your machine has one. Watch the fruits closely as they chop, and if they seem to be gumming up or chopping too fine, stop the motor at once.

Garlic:

To Mince: It's scarcely practical to use the processor to mince just one clove of garlic. Many recipes, however, call for several cloves or, as in the case of some Oriental stir-fried dishes, garlic plus cubes of

Garlic, *cont.*	fresh ginger root—the two can be minced together or singly. Peel the cloves of garlic (also the ginger root). Equip the processor with the metal chopping blade, turn the motor on, then drop the garlic cloves and/or ginger down the feed tube. Process until reduced to fine particles—this sometimes takes as long as 30 seconds nonstop, depending upon how fast the bouncing chunks of food catch in the teeth of the chopping blade.

Ginger Root, Fresh:	**To Mince:** The technique is precisely the same as for **Garlic,** above. But first cut the ginger into 1-inch cubes and peel.

Ham:	**To Chop:** Cut the ham into 1-inch cubes and trim off fat and sinew. Equip the processor with the metal chopping blade, add up to 2 cups of ham (or twice that if your machine is big and strong) and process as follows: 2 or 3 pulses or on-offs of the motor for coarse; 4 or 5 pulses or on-offs for medium; and 6 to 8 for fine.
	To Grind: Prepare the ham as for chopping and equip the processor with the metal chopping blade. Place ham cubes (2 to 4 cups of them depending upon the capacity and strength of your machine) in the processor and grind by using three 5-second churnings of the motor. This is a moderately fine grind, good for meat loaves and croquettes. If you prefer a coarser grind, use two 5-second churnings or, if you prefer, three 2-second churnings.
	To Slice: You will need, first of all, the *serrated* medium-slicing disc—without it, the ham will shred and tear. Trim ham of fat and connective tissue, then cut into columns about the height and width of the feed tube; chill the meat until firm (about 25 minutes in the freezer) if it is soft. Equip the

Ham,
cont.

processor with the *serrated* medium-slicing disc, stand a column of ham in the feed tube, snap the motor on or depress the Pulse button, then push the ham down the tube with steady pressure.

Herbs, Fresh: See **Parsley.**

Horseradish:

To Grate: This is best accomplished with the metal chopping blade. Wash the horseradish root, pare, then cut into ½-inch to 1-inch cubes. Place 1 cup of the horseradish cubes in the processor work bowl fitted with the metal chopping blade and grate fairly fine, using three or four 10-second churnings of the motor. Because of the pungency of horseradish, it's not likely that you'll want a coarser texture.

To Shred: I don't recommend this. Because horseradish root is so tough and fibrous, trying to force it through a shredding disc may stall the machine and dull the blade.

Ice:

To Crush: Check, first of all, your processor instruction booklet to see whether or not the manufacturer recommends using the processor to crush ice—many don't. Some, moreover (KitchenAid and Robot-Coupe™, to name two), offer (as optional discs) sturdy ice crushers or shredders, which are far less likely to dent, dull or deform than standard discs or blades. If you merely want to crush ice—not to mix a crushed-ice cocktail in the processor—do it this way: Equip the processor with the metal chopping blade, turn the motor on, then drop ice cubes (no more than 12 altogether) down the feed tube, one at a time, but in rapid succession. The minute the ice is crushed to the desired degree of fineness, stop the machine. When mixing such drinks as frozen daiquiris, you will have to alter the

Ice, *cont.*	ice-crushing method somewhat so that the ice doesn't go to mush the minute the alcohol is added. I dump the solidly frozen cubes in the work bowl, fitted with the metal chopping blade, grind furiously for 30 to 45 seconds, then pour the liquor and various flavorings down the feed tube with the motor running. The ice seems to hold up better with this method.
Lamb:	See **Beef**, discussed earlier in this section. **NOTE:** *The best cuts of lamb to grind or slice in the processor are boneless leg (best of all because it contains little fat or sinew) and shoulder (more succulent than leg because it is more heavily marbled with fat, but more sinewy, too, and thus more difficult to trim).*
Leeks:	**To Prepare for the Processor:** Because they are grown in sandy soil, leeks must be carefully washed. Trim off tops and roots, also peel away coarse outer layers, then wash under running tepid water, letting it run down between the leeks' layers, flushing out any bits of grit. Pat leeks dry on paper toweling. **To Chop:** Cut prepared leeks into 1-inch chunks, then chop as follows in a food processor fitted with the metal chopping blade: 2 or 3 pulses or on-offs of the motor for a coarse texture; 4 or 5 for medium; and 6 or 7 for fine. **To Slice:** Cut prepared leeks into 4-inch lengths, then stand enough of them in the feed tube of a processor fitted with the medium-slicing disc (or the thin- or thick-slicing disc, if you prefer) for a snug fit. Turn the motor on or depress the Pulse button and push the leeks down the feed tube with firm pressure.

Lemons,	**To Slice:** Choose a seedless variety of lemon, lime or
Limes,	orange, also fruits firm enough to withstand the
Oranges:	machine's powerful action without bruising or

To Slice: Choose a seedless variety of lemon, lime or orange, also fruits firm enough to withstand the machine's powerful action without bruising or mashing and slim enough to fit into the feed tube whole. NOTE: *Unless you have a work bowl with an expanded feed tube, you will have to halve the oranges (slice from stem to blossom end).* Peel the fruit or not, as you wish. Then slice off both ends so that the fruit will stand square and the pusher will not wobble as you guide the fruit through the slicing disc. Equip the processor with the *serrated* medium-slicing disc, ease the prepared fruit down the feed tube so that it rests on the slicing disc; snap the motor on or depress the Pulse button, and steady the fruit as it slices by exerting moderate pressure on the pusher.

To Juice: A number of processors (KitchenAid, Robot-Coupe™ and Cuisinart®) offer citrus juicer attachments, available at extra cost. In each case, use as the manufacturer recommends.

Mushrooms:

To Chop: Wipe mushrooms with a damp cloth and remove stems (these may be chopped, too, but trim off coarse or withered stem ends). If mushrooms are small, they may be put in the processor whole; if they are medium-size, halve them; if large, quarter. Equip the processor with the metal chopping blade, add up to 2 cups of prepared mushrooms, then chop as follows: 3 or 4 pulses or on-offs of the motor for coarse; 5 or 6 for medium; and 8 to 10 for fine.

To Mince: Prepare the mushrooms as for chopping and equip the processor with the metal chopping blade. Place up to 2 cups of prepared mushrooms in the work bowl, then begin mincing with two 5-second bursts of speed; scrape down the work bowl, re-cover and give two or three additional 5-second

Mushrooms, cont.

bursts of speed, until mushrooms are of a very fine, uniform texture. NOTE: *Also see the recipe for* Duxelles, *a seasoned mushroom paste that keeps well in refrigerator or freezer and can be dipped into as needed to flavor soups, sauces and stews (see Index for recipe page number).*

To Slice: Choose medium-size mushrooms and those that are as nearly uniform as possible; wipe clean with damp cloth, then slice off the coarse stem ends. Equip the processor with the medium-slicing disc. Lay the mushrooms on their sides in the feed tube (they will fit more securely and snugly if you alternate the direction the caps face—one to the right, one to the left, and so on). Fill the feed tube almost to the top, place the pusher on the mushrooms to steady them, snap the motor on or depress the Pulse button, then guide the mushrooms down the feed tube with gentle but steady pressure.

Okra:

To Slice: Choose pods of approximately the same length, wash, then trim off caps and pointed tips. Equip the processor with the medium-slicing disc. Stand in the feed tube as many okra pods as needed for a snug fit (also stand every other pod upside down for a tighter pack). Snap the motor on or depress the Pulse button, then push the okra down the feed tube with moderately firm pressure.

Olives:

To Chop: Place 1 cup pitted ripe or green olives (or pimiento-stuffed olives) in a food processor fitted with the metal chopping blade. Use 2 or 3 pulses or on-offs of the motor for a coarse chop; 4 or 5 for medium; and 6 to 8 for fine.

To Slice: I find it faster and more reliable to hand-slice olives, but you may disagree. For what it is

Olives,
cont.

worth, here is the technique recommended for processor-slicing olives. Assemble the machine with the medium-slicing disc. Set the work-bowl lid in place, just so you can determine the size of the area on the slicing disc just underneath the feed tube. Stand 5 or 6 olives, broad-sides down, in this area, *directly on the slicing disc.* Carefully replace the work-bowl lid, then insert the pusher in the feed tube to steady the olives. Snap the motor on or depress the Pulse button—and presto!—sliced olives.

Onions:

To Chop: Peel the onions and if they are very large (Bermudas, for example, or Spanish onions), cut into 1-inch chunks. If medium-size, cut into slim wedges (6 to 8 wedges per onion), and if small, halve or quarter the onions. Equip the processor with the metal chopping blade. You will be able to chop about 2 medium-size onions at one time (or 2 cups of onion chunks). Empty these into the processor, then, for a coarse chop, pulse or snap the motor on and off quickly once or twice; for a moderately coarse chop, 2 or 3 times; for a medium chop, about 4 times; and for finely chopped onions, about 5 times.

To Mince: This is simply carrying the chopping a bit further—6 to 8 pulses or on-offs of the motor should do it. Just don't over-mince so that you end up with mush. The pulsing or on-off technique is the key.

To Slice: If you intend to slice onions whole, you must find those slim enough to fit into the feed tube (unless you are lucky enough to have a work bowl with an expanded feed tube). Otherwise, halve or quarter the onions lengthwise, or if they are very large, simply cut into columns about the height and width of the feed tube. Insert the medium-slicing disc in the processor, stand the onion in the feed

Onions, *cont.*	tube, switch the motor on or depress the Pulse button, then push the onion down the tube with light pressure.
	To Purée Cooked Onions: See **Purées.**
Oranges:	See **Lemons.**
Oysters:	See **Clams.**
Parmesan:	See **Cheeses.**
Parsley, Fresh Leafy Herbs (Mint, Basil), Watercress:	**To Chop:** Wash well, remove coarse stems, then pat very dry on paper toweling; pile sprigs or leaves loosely in a measuring cup (for best results, do not try to processor-chop less than ½ cup or more than 2 cups). Equip the processor with the metal chopping blade and add the parsley or herb to the work bowl. For a coarse chop, pulse or snap the motor on and off 3 or 4 times; for a moderate chop, 5 or 6 times; and for a finer one, 7 or 8.
	To Mince: The preparation and technique are the same as for chopping, except that you should give the motor two or three 5-second churnings. This will produce a lovely, uniform mince.
Parsnips:	These are chopped, sliced and shredded exactly like carrots (see **Carrots**, discussed earlier in this section).

Peaches,	**To Chop:** Blanch the fruits for 20 to 30 seconds in
Apricots and	boiling water, then drain and slip off the skins.
Other Soft,	Halve, remove pits, then cut each half in half, or if
Fleshy Fruits:	fruit is large, in thirds or quarters. Equip the

To Chop: Blanch the fruits for 20 to 30 seconds in boiling water, then drain and slip off the skins. Halve, remove pits, then cut each half in half, or if fruit is large, in thirds or quarters. Equip the processor with the metal chopping blade. Place no more than 2 cups prepared fruit in the processor, add the juice of ½ lemon (to prevent darkening of fruit), then pulse or snap the motor on and off once or twice for a coarse chop (perfect for shortcakes), or 3 or 4 times for a finer chop (good for an ice-cream or cake topping).

To Slice: Your processor slices will be prettier and neater if you choose a freestone variety of peach. Blanch the fruits as described above, then halve and pit. Equip the processor with the medium-slicing disc (or the thick-slicing one). Fit two halves of fruit together so that they form a whole, pitted fruit, then lay sideways in the feed tube with the stem end of the fruit pointing to the right. Steady the halves with the pusher, snap the motor on or depress the Pulse button and guide them through the feed tube with light but steady pressure.

Peanuts:

To Prepare for the Processor: If nuts are unblanched, immerse them in boiling water for 30 seconds, drain well and slip off the skins. If nuts are unroasted, here's an easy way to do it. Spread the nuts out one layer deep in an ungreased, shallow baking pan, set, uncovered, in a slow oven (300° F.) and roast about 45 minutes, or until richly golden brown. You'll have to stir the nuts once or twice as they roast. Cool well before using.

To Chop: Place no more than 2 cups of pre-pared peanuts in a food processor fitted with the metal chopping blade. For a coarse chop, use two 5-

Peanuts, *cont.*	second churnings of the motor; for medium, three 5-second churnings; and for fine, four or five 5-second churnings.
	To Make Peanut Butter: See Index for recipe page number.
Pears:	**To Slice:** Quarter pears lengthwise, peel and core (or, if you prefer, leave the pears unpeeled). Equip the processor with the medium-slicing disc. Stand two pear quarters in the feed tube this way: with their outer, curved sides abutting (the skin sides) and with one quarter arranged broad-end down and the other broad-end up. Place the pusher in the feed tube to steady the pears, snap the motor on or depress the Pulse button and push the pears down the feed tube with steady but gentle pressure.
	TIP: Sprinkle pear slices with lemon juice to keep them nice and white.
Pecans, **Walnuts:**	**To Chop:** Place no more than 2 cups shelled nuts at a time in a processor fitted with the metal chopping blade. For a coarse chop, pulse or snap the motor on and off twice; for a medium chop, 3 or 4 times; and for a moderately fine one, 5 or 6 times. To chop, indeed, *to grind,* the nuts very fine as when making *Baklava* (see Index for recipe page number), let the motor run nonstop for 10 to 15 seconds.
Pepperoni and **Other Hard** **Sausages:**	**To Slice:** Cut the sausage into 4-inch lengths and peel off the casings. In the feed tube of a processor fitted with the *serrated* medium-slicing disc, stand as many lengths of sausage as will fit tightly. Turn the motor on or depress the Pulse button and push the sausage down the feed tube with firm, steady pressure.

Peppers,	**To Chop:** Wash, halve, core and seed the peppers,
Sweet:	then cut into 1-inch pieces. Place no more than 2
	medium-size cut-up peppers (or 2 cups) in the work

Peppers, Sweet:

To Chop: Wash, halve, core and seed the peppers, then cut into 1-inch pieces. Place no more than 2 medium-size cut-up peppers (or 2 cups) in the work bowl of a processor fitted with the metal chopping blade. For a coarse chop, pulse or snap the motor on and off once or twice; for a moderately coarse chop, about 3 times; for a medium chop, 4 times; and for a moderately fine one, 5 times. You can, if you like, chop 1 medium-size yellow onion and 1 medium-size sweet pepper together in the processor. Use the above times as a guide.

To Mince: This means simply chopping the pepper finer—6 to 8 pulses or on-offs of the motor should be sufficient.

To Slice: You will need smallish peppers, which, when halved, will fit upright in the feed tube. Wash the peppers, halve, core and seed. Equip the processor with the medium-slicing disc. Stand a pepper half in the feed tube, turn the motor on or depress the Pulse button and push the pepper gently down the feed tube.

Pineapple:

To Prepare for the Processor: Remove spiky tops; peel the pineapple and dig out the "eyes" with the point of a small knife. Quarter the pineapple, slice off the cores at the point of each quarter, then divide each quarter in half lengthwise.

To Chop: Cut the prepared wedges of pineapple into 1-inch lengths, then place no more than 2 cups of them at a time in a food processor fitted with the metal chopping blade. To chop fairly coarsely, use about two 3-second bursts of speed; for a finer chop, use three or four 3-second bursts of speed.

To Slice: Cut the prepared wedges of pineapple into 4-inch lengths, and if they are too chunky to fit into

Pineapple, cont.	the feed tube, trim or halve lengthwise. Equip the processor with the medium-slicing disc, stand 1 or 2 wedges of pineapple in the feed tube, snap the motor on or depress the Pulse button and push the pineapple through the slicing disc with firm pressure.
Pine Nuts (Pignoli, Piñon Nuts):	**To Chop:** Equip the processor with the metal chopping blade. Add up to 2 cups of shelled pine nuts and, for a coarse chop, use two 3-second churnings of the motor; for medium, three 3-second churnings; and for fine, four or five 3-second churnings.
Pistachio Nuts:	**To Blanch:** Immerse the nuts in boiling water for 30 seconds, then slip off the skins. Or, quicker, drain the nuts well, bundle them up, about 1 cup at a time, in a dry, thick Turkish towel and rub briskly in the towel to take off the skins.

To Chop: In a food processor fitted with the metal chopping blade, place up to 2 cups of blanched or unblanched pistachios (whichever your recipe specifies), then process as follows: For a coarse chop, pulse or snap the motor on and off 2 or 3 times; for a medium chop, 4 or 5 times; and for a fine chop, 6 to 8 times.

To Grind: Place prepared pistachios (again no more than 2 cups at a time) in a food processor equipped with the metal chopping blade, snap the motor on and allow to run nonstop for 15 seconds. |
| **Pork:** | See **Beef**, discussed earlier in this section. The best cuts of pork to grind or slice (both raw and cooked) are boneless loin and fresh ham, because they contain less sinew and interlarding of fat than |

**Pork,
cont.**

shoulder or butt. NOTE: *Be especially meticulous about the way you wash all parts of the processor after you have dealt with raw pork (indeed, all utensils used with the raw pork). There exists in much of the raw pork sold in this country a microscopic parasite called* trichina, *which, when ingested live, can cause an often fatal illness known as* trichinosis. *It is for this reason that in many states butchers are forbidden by law to grind fresh pork unless they have a grinder used exclusively for pork. Few do. Fortunately, the* trichinae *are easily killed by heat (temperatures above 140° F.). As a precaution, I scald all processor parts in simmering water (about 160° to 180° F.) before I load them into the dishwasher, and I would recommend that you do the same. Do not soak the processor parts in the simmering water, merely pour it carefully over them. It goes without saying that you should also wash your hands thoroughly in as hot water as you can stand after working with raw pork (make sure that you clean underneath your nails, too). And, of course, never taste any recipe containing raw pork until after it has been thoroughly cooked. I cannot stress this strongly enough, so be particularly cautious about the way you prepare the terrines, sausages, and* pâtés *in this book, all of which contain raw pork.*

**Potatoes, Irish
and Sweet;
Yams:**

To Chop: Peel the potatoes and cut into 1-inch cubes. Place no more than 2 cups of cubes at a time in a processor fitted with the metal chopping blade, then pulse or snap the motor on and off 4 times. This will yield a coarse chop, perfect for hashes. Longer chopping will reduce the potatoes to mush.

To Mash: It *is* now possible to processor-mash certain potatoes as my recipe for Fluffy Mashed Potatoes readily proves (see Index for recipe page number).

Potatoes, Irish and Sweet; Yams, cont.

To Slice: Choose potatoes slim enough to fit whole in the feed tube (new potatoes, for example, or California Long Whites, although if you have a work bowl with an expanded feed tube, you can slice all but truly whopping potatoes whole). Peel the potatoes (if not, scrub well with a vegetable brush). Stand a potato in the feed tube of a processor fitted with a slicing disc—medium for scalloped potatoes, thin for chips—turn the motor on or depress the Pulse button and push the potato firmly down the feed tube.

To Shred: The technique is precisely the same as for slicing potatoes; only the disc changes. For most recipe needs, the medium-shredding disc is best.

To Cut French Fries: See recipe for French Fried Potatoes (consult Index for page number).

Purées:

The technique is similar whether you are puréeing cooked vegetables, raw berries or other fruits, or soups. The attachment to use in all instances is the metal chopping blade, and, for best results, do not attempt to purée more than 2 cups of food at a time.

Berries and Fruits: Most are juicy enough to purée without additional liquid, but should any be needed, add a little lemon or orange juice (usually ¼ cup to 2 cups fruit is sufficient). Process the fruits in 5-second increments, inspecting the texture after each churning, and stopping as soon as a velvety purée is achieved.

Cooked Vegetables: Do not attempt to purée starchy vegetables (potatoes, for example) because they will become as sticky and drab as library paste. The vegetables that purée the most successfully are those containing a fair percentage of water: carrots, beets, turnips, green beans and peas, onions, mushrooms, broccoli, cauliflower, asparagus and, of course, such leafy greens as spinach and cress. Whatever the vegetable, it should be cooked until tender and drained. Cut, if large, into 1-inch cubes, then place in the processor fitted with the metal chopping blade. Except for leafy greens, which need no additional liquid at all, I customarily add 2 to 6 tablespoons of reserved cooking water, chicken or beef broth, milk or cream to each 2 cups of vegetable—the drier vegetables (green peas, turnips, carrots, etc.) getting the larger amounts of liquid. Sometimes I also will add a small lump of butter. Purée the vegetables using three to four 5-second churnings, scrutinizing the texture after each churning and stopping the instant you achieve a silky texture.

Leftover Cooked Vegetables: Here's a wonderful way to utilize odds and ends. Some compatible combinations: broccoli and spinach; spinach and watercress; cauliflower, turnips or parsnips with mashed potato (purée everything but the potato in the processor); carrots and mushrooms; onions and almost anything. Warm the vegetables briefly and independently in just enough broth, milk or cream to keep them from scorching, then dump them into a processor fitted with the metal chopping blade and buzz together until fine and smooth. Season to taste and serve.

Soups: For most soups, you should strain out the solids, then purée 2 cups of them at a time in a processor fitted with the metal chopping blade with just enough of the soup liquid to facilitate puréeing (⅓ to ½ cup liquid per 2 cups of solids is a good average). Purée until smooth—I usually do this in 5- or 10-second bursts of speed (depending upon how hard the solids are), inspecting the mixture closely after each churning.

Radishes:	**To Chop:** Trim and wash the radishes and, if they are large, halve them. In a food processor fitted with the metal chopping blade, place up to 2 cups of radishes. Chop coarsely by pulsing or snapping the motor on and off 2 or 3 times, or moderately coarsely by using about 4 pulses or on-offs of the motor. If you attempt to chop the radishes more finely, you risk ending up with mush.

To Slice: Trim and wash the radishes, then pile them whole, the cut ends down, in the feed tube of a processor fitted with the medium-slicing disc. Insert the pusher into the feed tube to steady the radishes, then turn the motor on or depress the Pulse button and push them firmly down the feed tube. |
| Rhubarb: | **To Prepare for the Processor:** The roots and leaves of rhubarb are poisonous, so trim the stalks carefully. Also wash them well. If the rhubarb is to be chopped, cut into 1-inch lengths; if sliced, cut into 4-inch lengths.

To Chop and Slice: See **Celery,** discussed earlier in this section. The techniques for chopping and slicing rhubarb are the same. |
| Rutabaga: | **To Prepare for the Processor:** Peel. If the rutabaga is to be chopped, cut it into 1-inch chunks; if it is to be sliced or shredded, cut it into columns about the height and width of the food-processor feed tube.

To Chop, Slice or Shred: Follow the directions given under **Turnips.** |

Scallions: **To Chop:** Trim, wash and cut scallions into 1-inch lengths. Equip the processor with the metal chopping blade. Add up to 2 cups of prepared scallions and process this way: 2 or 3 pulses or on-offs of the motor for a coarse chop; 4 for medium; and about 5 for fine.

To Mince: This is merely carrying the chopping one step further, to obtain a finer texture. Usually, 6 to 8 pulses or on-offs of the motor will mince scallions nicely.

Scallops: **To Chop Raw:** Drain the scallops very well, then wash and pick over carefully to remove any hidden bits of shell. For best results, do not attempt to chop more than 1 cup of scallops at a time. If you are using sea scallops, cut them into 1-inch cubes; bay scallops are small enough not to require cutting. Equip the processor with the metal chopping blade, add the scallops, then pulse or snap the motor on and off quickly 1 or 2 times for a coarse chop, 3 or 4 times for a finer one. If you chop much longer, you will be *grinding* the scallops to paste. For some recipes, of course—mousses, *quenelles* (see the recipe for Mousse of Bay Scallops listed in the Index)—a fine paste is precisely what you want. *To grind scallops*, let the metal chopping blade run 60 seconds nonstop.

To Chop Cooked Scallops: Drain the scallops well, and if they are large, cut them into 1-inch chunks. Place no more than 2 cups of prepared scallops at a time in the food processor fitted with the metal chopping blade. Pulse or snap the motor on and off 2 or 3 times for a coarse chop, 4 times for medium, and 5 for fine.

Scallops,	**To Mince Cooked Scallops:** Place no more than 2
cont.	cups of drained, cooked scallops (again, cut any large
	ones into 1-inch chunks) in a food processor fitted
	with the metal chopping blade and churn 5 seconds
	nonstop. If the texture is not as fine as you would
	like, buzz for 3 to 5 seconds longer.

Shallots: **To Mince:** See **Garlic**, discussed earlier. The technique is the same.

Shrimp: **To Prepare for the Processor:** Shell and devein the shrimp and halve crosswise any that are very large.

To Chop Raw or Cooked Shrimp, or to Mince: Follow the directions given above for **Scallops**.

Squash,
Summer:

To Chop: Wash and trim the squash and cut into 1-inch chunks. Place in a food processor fitted with the metal chopping blade (no more than 2 cups of squash chunks at a time), then process as follows: one or two 1-second bursts of speed for a coarse chop; three 1-second churnings for a medium texture; and four or five 1-second bursts for a fairly fine chop.

To Slice: Wash and trim the squash and cut into 4-inch lengths. Equip the processor with a slicing disc (thick, medium or thin), stand as many pieces of squash in the feed tube as will fit, turn the motor on or depress the Pulse button and push the squash firmly down the feed tube.

To Shred: The technique is exactly the same as for slicing squash, only the disc used is the coarse- or medium-shredding disc instead of a slicing disc. The fine-shredding disc is not a good choice, because it forces a great deal of water out of the squash.

Squash, *Summer,* *cont.*	**To Cut for French Frying:** See Index for the recipe for Batter-Fried Zucchini Sticks. **To Purée Cooked Summer Squash:** See **Purées,** discussed earlier in this section.

Squash, **Winter:**	**To Purée Cooked Winter Squash:** See **Purées,** discussed earlier in this section.

Strawberries:	**To Chop:** Rinse and hull the berries and halve any that are large. Place no more than 2 cups of prepared berries in a processor fitted with the metal chopping blade, and pulse or snap the motor on and off 2 or 3 times—no more or you will get mush. **To Slice:** I am not convinced that this is a worthwhile operation, especially if the berries are juicy and ripe, but many processor manuals recommend it. Wash and hull the berries, then arrange them on their sides in the feed tube of a processor fitted with the medium-slicing disc; alternate the direction in which the tips of the berries point—some right, some left. Continue until feed tube is full. Turn motor on or depress the Pulse button and push *gently* down the feed tube.

Tomatoes:	**To Chop:** Wash the tomatoes, core and cut into slim wedges. You can chop about 2 medium-size tomatoes at one time in the processor (or about 2 cups of wedges). Fit the machine with the metal chopping blade, add the tomatoes, then pulse or snap the motor on and off briskly 2 or 3 times—no more or the tomatoes will become mushy. **To Juice:** Choose dead-ripe tomatoes at their peak of flavor; wash, core and cut into slim wedges. Fit the processor with the metal chopping blade, dump in

Tomatoes, cont.

up to 2 cups of tomato wedges, then reduce to juice with two to three 20-second churnings of the motor. Strain mixture through a fine sieve to remove seeds and bits of skin.

To Slice: Some processor manuals describe how to do this, but I find nothing challenging or tedious about hand-slicing tomatoes. It goes quickly—as quickly as you can set up the processor and arrange the tomatoes in it. Because good tomatoes are ripe tomatoes, they are too soft to slice cleanly in the processor.

Turkey:

See **Chicken.**

Turnips:

To Chop: Peel the turnips, cut into 1-inch chunks, then place—about 1 cup of chunks at a time—in a food processor fitted with the metal chopping blade. For a coarse chop, use one or two 3-second churnings of the motor; for a moderate, three or four 3-second churnings; and for fine, five to eight 3-second churnings—depending upon how finely chopped you want the turnips to be.

To Slice: Choose turnips, if possible, that are slim enough to stand whole in the feed tube (easy if you have an expanded feed tube). Otherwise, halve them lengthwise. Peel the turnips, then stand, one at a time, in the feed tube of a processor fitted with the medium-slicing disc. Turn the motor on or depress the Pulse button and push the turnip firmly down the feed tube.

To Shred: Equip the processor with the medium-shredding disc, then follow all the steps described above for slicing turnips. The techniques are the same—only the cutting disc changes.

Turnips, cont.	**To Purée Cooked Turnips:** See **Purées**, discussed earlier in this section.

Veal:	See **Chicken**. Because veal is so like chicken in texture, it can be chopped and sliced the same way. NOTE: *The all-around best cut of veal to use for processor preparation is round—either top or bottom round (scaloppine is cut from the round). The veal should, of course, be well trimmed of fat and sinew before it goes into the processor.*

Walnuts:	See **Pecans**.

Watercress:	See **Parsley**.

Zucchini:	See **Squash, Summer**.

Some Useful Equivalents

THIS INFORMATION is for helping you adapt your own recipe favorites to processor preparation. Because many recipes call for ingredients by the cup rather than by the piece or pound—½ cup chopped onion, for example, 1 cup fine bread crumbs, 2 cups leftover ground ham—it is useful to know just how much onion you must processor-chop to obtain ½ cup, how many slices of bread it takes to equal 1 cup of fine crumbs, how many ounces of leftover ham will, when processor-ground, amount to 2 cups.

The following table is arranged alphabetically, food by food. The equivalents, it should be stressed, can only be approximate, because of the subtle differences that exist from processor to processor and because each cook's techniques will vary, too.

FOOD AND AMOUNT	HOW PROCESSED	EQUIVALENT YIELD
Almonds, 1 cup, whole	*Coarsely chopped*	*1 cup*
	Finely chopped	*1¼ cups*
Apples, 1 medium	*Coarsely chopped*	*½ cup*
	Finely chopped	*⅓ to ½ cup*
	Sliced medium thick	*¾ cup*

FOOD AND AMOUNT	HOW PROCESSED	EQUIVALENT YIELD
Artichokes, Jerusalem, 1 cup, whole	*Coarsely chopped*	*¾ to 1 cup*
	Moderately finely chopped	*⅔ to ¾ cup*
	Sliced medium thick	*¾ cup*
Avocados, 1 medium	*Coarsely chopped*	*1¼ cups*
	Sliced	*1½ to 2 cups*
	Puréed	*¾ to 1 cup*
Bananas, 1 medium	*Sliced*	*1 cup*
	Mashed or puréed	*⅔ cup*
Beans, green or wax, 1 cup, cooked	*Puréed*	*½ cup*
Beef or Pork (raw or cooked), ½ pound, boneless, well trimmed	*Ground coarse or fine*	*1 cup*
	Sliced medium thin	*1½ cups, loosely packed*
Beets, 1 medium	*Sliced medium thin*	*⅔ cup*
	Shredded	*½ cup*
	Puréed (cooked)	*⅓ cup*
Brazil Nuts, 1 cup, whole	*Coarsely chopped*	*1 cup*
	Finely chopped	*¾ to 1 cup*

FOOD AND AMOUNT	HOW PROCESSED	EQUIVALENT YIELD
Bread, 2 slices with crusts	*Crumbed*	*1 cup*
Broccoli, cooked, 1 cup flowerets	*Coarsely chopped*	*¾ cup*
	Puréed	*½ cup*
Cabbage, raw, 1 medium head, trimmed and cored	*Coarsely chopped for slaw*	*8 cups*
	Shredded (sliced) for slaw	*10 cups*
Carrots, 1 medium	*Chopped coarse or fine*	*½ cup*
	Sliced medium thin	*½ cup*
	Shredded	*½ cup*
	Puréed (cooked)	*¼ cup*
Cauliflower, cooked, 1 cup flowerets	*Coarsely chopped*	*¾ cup*
	Puréed	*½ cup*
Celery, 2 medium-size ribs	*Chopped coarse or fine*	*⅔ cup*
	Sliced medium thick	*¾ cup*
Celery root, 1 medium	*Sliced medium thick*	*¾ cup*
	Shredded	*¾ cup*
	Puréed (cooked)	*⅓ to ½ cup*
Cheeses:		
Parmesan, ½ pound	*Grated*	*1¾ cups*
Cheddar, ½ pound	*Shredded*	*2 cups*

FOOD AND AMOUNT	HOW PROCESSED	EQUIVALENT YIELD
Cheese, cont. Gruyère, ½ pound	*Shredded*	*2 cups*
Chicken, Turkey (raw or cooked), ½ pound, boneless, trimmed	*Ground or chopped* *Sliced*	*1 cup* *1½ cups, loosely packed*
Coconut, 1 medium	*Grated (chopped)* *Shredded*	*5 cups* *7 cups*
Corn, 1 cup, whole kernels	*Chopped cream style*	*½ cup*
Cranberries, 1 cup, whole	*Coarsely chopped*	*¾ to 1 cup*
Cucumbers, 1 medium, peeled and seeded	*Coarsely chopped* *Sliced medium thin*	*1 cup* *1¼ cups*
Crumbs (fine): Saltines, 28 (2-inch) squares	*Crumbed*	*1 cup crumbs*
Graham Crackers, 15 (2⅜-inch) squares	*Crumbed*	*1 cup crumbs*
Vanilla Wafers, 24	*Crumbed*	*1 cup crumbs*
Chocolate Wafers, 16 (2-inch diameter)	*Crumbed*	*1 cup crumbs*

FOOD AND AMOUNT	HOW PROCESSED	EQUIVALENT YIELD
Crumbs, cont.		
Gingersnaps, 24	*Crumbed*	*1 cup crumbs*
Filberts, Hazelnuts, 1 cup, whole	*Coarsely chopped* *Finely chopped*	*1 cup* *1¼ cups*
Ham, ½ pound, boneless, well trimmed	*Chopped or ground* *Sliced medium thin*	*1 to 1¼ cups* *1½ cups loosely packed*
Ice Cubes, 3 (2½ inches x 1 inch)	*Crushed*	*1 cup*
Lamb (raw or cooked), ½ pound, boneless, well trimmed	*Ground coarse or fine* *Sliced medium thin*	*1 cup* *1½ cups, loosely packed*
Leeks, 2 medium-size, trimmed	*Coarsely or finely chopped* *Sliced medium thin*	*1 cup* *1 cup*
Mushrooms, ¼ pound, trimmed	*Coarsely chopped* *Minced* *Sliced medium thin*	*1¼ cups* *¾ to 1 cup* *1½ cups*

FOOD AND AMOUNT	HOW PROCESSED	EQUIVALENT YIELD
Onions, yellow:		
1 medium-size	*Coarsely or moderately coarsely chopped*	*½ cup*
	Minced	*⅓ cup*
	Sliced thin	*½ cup*
1 large	*Coarsely or moderately coarsely chopped*	*1 cup*
	Minced	*⅔ cup*
	Sliced thin	*1 cup*
Parsley, Fresh Herbs, Watercress, 1 cup loosely packed sprigs or leaves	*Coarsely or moderately coarsely chopped*	*½ cup*
	Minced	*⅓ cup*
Peaches, 1 medium	*Coarsely chopped*	*½ to ⅔ cup*
	Sliced medium thin	*⅔ to 1 cup*
Peanuts, 1 cup whole	*Coarsely chopped*	*1 cup*
	Finely chopped	*1 cup*
2 cups, whole	*Made into peanut butter*	*1 cup*
Pears, 1 medium	*Sliced medium thin*	*1 cup*
Pecans, 1 cup broken meats	*Coarsely chopped*	*1 cup*
	Finely chopped	*1¼ cups*

FOOD AND AMOUNT	HOW PROCESSED	EQUIVALENT YIELD
Peppers, sweet, 1 medium green or red	Coarsely or moderately coarsely chopped	1 cup
	Minced	¾ cup
	Sliced	1¼ cups
Pineapple, 1 medium, trimmed and cored	Moderately coarsely chopped	3½ cups
	Sliced medium thin	4 cups
Pine Nuts, Pistachios, 1 cup, whole	Coarsely chopped	1 cup
	Finely chopped	1¼ cups
Pork (see Beef)		
Potatoes, Irish or sweet, 1 medium	Coarsely chopped	¾ cup
	Sliced medium thin	¾ cup
	Shredded	½ cup
Purées: 1 cup cooked, drained vegetable	Puréed	½ cup
1 cup berries or other juicy fruit	Puréed	½ cup
Scallions, 6 medium, trimmed	Coarsely chopped	⅓ cup
	Minced	¼ cup
Shallots, 6 medium	Minced	¼ cup

FOOD AND AMOUNT	HOW PROCESSED	EQUIVALENT YIELD
Squash, summer, 1 medium	*Coarsely chopped*	*1¼ cups*
	Finely chopped	*1 cup*
	Sliced medium thin	*1½ cups*
	Shredded	*1 cup*
Tomatoes, 1 medium	*Coarsely chopped*	*1 cup*
Turkey (see Chicken)		
Turnips, 1 medium	*Coarsely chopped*	*⅔ cup*
	Finely chopped	*½ to ⅔ cup*
	Sliced medium thin	*⅔ to 1 cup*
	Shredded	*½ cup*
	Puréed (cooked)	*⅓ cup*
Veal (raw or cooked), ½ pound, boneless well trimmed	*Ground or chopped*	*1 cup*
	Sliced medium thin	*1½ cups, loosely packed*
Walnuts, 1 cup broken meats	*Coarsely chopped*	*1 cup*
	Finely chopped	*1¼ cups*
Watercress (see Parsley)		
Zucchini (see Squash, summer)		

Using the Processor to Stock the Freezer, Refrigerator & Pantry, Plus Basic Recipes

As EVERY GOOD COOK KNOWS, the ultimate in efficiency is to lay in a supply of homemade broths and stocks and sauces, purées and flavored butters, bread crumbs, even freshly grated Parmesan, so that when you set out to make a recipe, you're a jump ahead of those who must begin from scratch or fall back on canned or packaged foods.

There's nothing new about this. What *is* new is that the food processor makes it all possible. And easy. And quick—so *very* quick.

Consider, for example, the hours of mincing and slicing and chopping required to prepare a good, sturdy beef stock the old-fashioned way. The processor not only attends to it all lickety-split, it also cuts the vegetables more finely than you're apt to do, which means that every last smidgen of flavor will be extracted from them. The processor, to be sure, does nothing to shortcut cooking time, but you don't have to watch the pot. The stocks simmer themselves into savory richness, then all that's left for you to do is skim, strain and freeze in pint or quart containers (the amounts most often called for in recipes). With the processor to assist you, you could cook up a half-year's supply of stock in just one morning.

I also like to whip up flavored butters in the processor, roll them into logs, foil-wrap and freeze them so that all I need do is slice off a pat or two whenever I need them and return the balance to the freezer. (Is there an easier way to dress up broiled steaks, chops or fish?) And I make a point of buzzing up batches of bread and cracker crumbs (it's such a bore when you have to stop mid-recipe to prepare a cup or so of crumbs for a casserole topping or a meat loaf). With the processor, I can fill up a quart jar with fine crumbs in no time at all. Moreover, if they are tightly covered and stored in the refrigerator, they remain fresh and fluffy for two weeks or more.

Because I never seem to have enough Parmesan, I buy it by the 2-pound wedge, then processor-grate it and store it in snugly covered quart jars in the refrigerator. (The Parmesan that you grate yourself will be infinitely fresher after one month's cold storage than the commercial brands are on the day you buy them.)

Pickles . . . relishes . . . marmalades . . . preserves. No recipes use the processor to better advantage. Anyone with a processor and access to farm- or orchard-fresh produce is both a spendthrift and missing a rare pleasure not to set aside a few summer mornings to put up some additive-free jars of pickles and preserves.

In the pages that follow you will find almost four dozen basic recipes—handy staples to have on hand and pastries and sauces that are integral to recipes in the second part of the book. All demonstrate what a whiz the processor is and how much time and tedium it spares you.

Stocks

Beef Stock

Makes about 3 quarts

Usually, when making a stock, you simply slice or chunk the vegetables. But if you processor-mince them instead, they will release far more of their flavor into the stock, producing a richer "brew."

3 pounds marrow bones, cracked
2 pounds beef shinbones, cracked
2 large yellow onions, peeled and cut into slim wedges
4 large leeks, trimmed, washed carefully and cut into 1-inch lengths

3 medium-size celery ribs, trimmed, washed and cut into 1-inch
  lengths
3 medium-size carrots, peeled and cut into 1-inch lengths
4 parsley branches, washed
8 peppercorns
2 bay leaves, crumbled
5 quarts cold water
1 tablespoon salt (or to taste)

Trim a little fat from the bones, dice it, then melt it in a large heavy soup kettle set over high heat. Brown the bones lightly on all sides in the kettle, then turn heat to low and let stand while you prepare the vegetables. In a food processor equipped with the metal chopping blade, mince the onions fine by pulsing or switching the motor on and off 5 or 6 times. Add to kettle. Now fine-mince the leeks and celery ribs together the same way and add to kettle. Mince the carrots, also, by letting the motor run nonstop for about 30 seconds. Add to kettle along with all remaining ingredients. Raise heat to moderate, bringing mixture to a boil; this is just to precipitate a scum that can be skimmed off. When you have removed as much scum as possible, turn heat to low, cover the kettle, and simmer very slowly for about 5 hours, or until the stock has a robust, beefy flavor. Very carefully skim off as much fat as possible. Line a large sieve with several thicknesses of cheesecloth and set over a second large kettle. Pour in the stock and let it drip through undisturbed. If you try to force it through the sieve, you'll press through some of the solids and the stock will cloud.

While the stock drains, quickly wash and dry the soup kettle. Pour in the strained stock and bring to a boil over moderately high heat. Allow to boil, uncovered, until the stock has reduced to about 3 quarts. Taste for salt and add more if needed. Chill the stock until the fat rises to the top and solidifies. Lift off the layer of fat, then skim up any recalcitrant bits. The stock is now ready to use in soups, sauces, stews. If you like, ladle into 1-pint or 1-quart freezer containers, date and label and store in the freezer. The stock will keep well in the refrigerator for about 2 weeks, in the freezer for about 1 year.

Glace de Viande

Makes ⅓ cup

This is nothing more than Beef Stock cooked down, down, down to a rich brown glaze that can be used, a teaspoon or so at a time, to heighten the flavor and color of soups and sauces. It's what we buy in the supermarket as "gravy browner" or "beef extract." The homemade, not surprisingly, is infinitely superior because it contains no ersatz flavorings, preservatives or stabilizers. Simply begin with 1 cup of Beef Stock and simmer in a small, heavy, open saucepan over moderate heat until mixture is rich and brown and glistening and reduced by two thirds. Ladle into a jar, cover tightly, and store in the refrigerator. *Glace de Viande* will keep well under refrigeration for about one month.

Rich Chicken Broth

Makes about 2 quarts

Often, when I stew a hen or a capon (as when making Cold Molded Chicken-and-Walnut Loaf—see Index for recipe page number), I will boil the leftover chicken stock and carcass down into this rich broth to use in making soups, stews, casseroles—dozens of different recipes. So that the broth will be as robust as possible, I processor-mince the vegetables that simmer in it, instead of slicing them, because the greater the surface area of the vegetable, the more flavor it will impart to the broth.

> 3 quarts chicken stock (left over from cooking a capon or a hen; do not strain or remove vegetables and seasonings that cooked in the stock along with the fowl)
> The capon or hen carcass
> 2 medium-size yellow onions, peeled and cut into slim wedges
> 3 medium-size celery ribs, washed, trimmed and cut into 1-inch lengths
> 2 medium-size carrots, peeled and cut into 1-inch lengths
> 8 peppercorns
> 1 bay leaf

3 large parsley branches, washed
Salt and freshly ground black pepper to taste

Place the chicken stock and carcass in a large, heavy kettle and set, uncovered, over moderate heat. Meanwhile, mince the onions in a food processor fitted with the metal chopping blade by pulsing or switching the motor on and off 5 or 6 times; add onions to kettle. Fine-mince the celery the same way and add to kettle. Now chop the carrots quite fine by letting the processor motor run nonstop for 20 to 30 seconds. Add carrots to kettle, drop in peppercorns, bay leaf and parsley branches. Adjust heat under kettle so that liquid boils gently, then simmer uncovered for 3 to 3½ hours, or until liquid has reduced by about one third and the broth has a rich chicken flavor. Strain broth through a large, fine sieve (discard bones, vegetables and seasonings), then season to taste with salt and pepper. Cool the broth, skim off the fat that has floated to the top, and freeze in 1-pint or 1-quart freezer containers. Don't forget to label and date each container.

Rich Court Bouillon

Makes about 2½ quarts

This is another basic stock that every cook should have on hand. Use it as a base for fish soups, sauces, mousses, soufflés, aspics. To extract as much flavor from the vegetables as possible, I thin-slice them in the processor rather than chunking them.

1 pound fish trimmings, heads, bones (I like to use the bones of flounder, pike, haddock, scrod or cod or a mixture of any of these.)
2 quarts cold water
1 large yellow onion, peeled and halved lengthwise
1 large carrot, peeled and cut into 4-inch lengths
1 large celery rib, washed and cut into 4-inch lengths
1 garlic clove, peeled
3 large parsley branches, washed
1 large branch of thyme, washed, or ½ teaspoon crumbled leaf thyme
1 large branch of chervil, washed, or ½ teaspoon crumbled leaf chervil

8 peppercorns
2 cups dry white wine
1 teaspoon salt (or to taste)

Simmer the fish trimmings in the water in a large, covered enamel or stainless-steel kettle for 25 minutes. Meanwhile, prepare the vegetables. Thin-slice the onion in a food processor fitted with the slicing disc by pushing it down the feed tube with light pressure. Now thin-slice the carrot and celery the same way; add to kettle along with all remaining ingredients. Cover and cook at a gentle simmer for 45 minutes.

Set a very large sieve over a large, heatproof bowl and line the sieve with several thicknesses of cheesecloth. Pour in the *court bouillon* and allow to drain through undisturbed. The *court bouillon* is now ready to use. Taste for salt and add more, if needed. Pour into 1-pint freezer containers, cool to room temperature, snap on the lids, label, date, then quick-freeze. The *court bouillon* will keep well in the freezer for about 6 months, in the refrigerator for about 1 week.

Vegetable Stock
Makes about 2 quarts

Handy to have on hand as a base for soups and sauces. The processor minces and chops the vegetables in jig time, and to such a degree of fineness that the stock's flavor is unusually rich and well balanced.

1 very large Spanish onion, peeled and cut into 1-inch chunks (I
*   prefer a Spanish onion to a yellow onion for vegetable stock,*
*   because its flavor is more delicate and less apt to turn bitter after*
*   hours of slow simmering.)*
4 large leeks, trimmed, washed very carefully and cut into 1-inch
*   chunks*
4 large celery ribs, trimmed, washed and cut into 1-inch chunks
4 large carrots, peeled and cut into 1-inch chunks
2 medium-size white turnips, trimmed, peeled and cut into 1-inch
*   chunks*
2 large, fully ripe tomatoes, washed, cored and cut into slim wedges
*   (no need to peel)*

½ *pound medium-size mushrooms, wiped clean, stemmed and*
   quartered (reserve stems)
6 *large parsley branches, washed*
8 *peppercorns*
2 *bay leaves, crumbled*
4 *quarts cold water*
1 *tablespoon salt (or to taste)*

In a food processor fitted with the metal chopping blade, mince the onion, one half of it at a time, by pulsing or snapping the motor on and off 5 or 6 times; empty into a very large soup kettle. Mince the remaining onion the same way and add to kettle. Now fine-mince the leeks with the celery, again using 5 or 6 pulses or on-offs of the motor; add to kettle. Mince the carrots, then the turnips, using one 30-second churning of the motor for each. Add to kettle. Reduce the tomatoes to mush in the processor—work with only two tomatoes at a time, as the full amount will overflow the work bowl—and let the motor run nonstop 10 to 15 seconds for each batch. Add all tomatoes to the kettle. Now chop the mushrooms fine, first the caps, then the stems, by pulsing or snapping the motor on and off 6 or 7 times. Add mushrooms to kettle, also all remaining ingredients. Cover and simmer slowly for 3 hours. Set a large sieve over a second large kettle and line the sieve with several thicknesses of cheesecloth. Pour in the contents of the first kettle and allow to drain undisturbed until all of the liquid has trickled through—do not force or press the strained-out solids to extract extra liquid, because doing so will cloud the stock.

While the mixture drains, wash and dry the soup kettle. Return the strained stock to the kettle, set over moderate heat and allow to boil, uncovered, until the liquid has reduced to 2 quarts. (Here's a trick: Mark the inside of the kettle at the 2-quart level—I usually make a tiny nick or scratch there—so that you'll know at a glance when the stock has reduced sufficiently.) Taste the stock for salt and add more, if needed. Ladle into 1-pint freezer containers, cool to room temperature, snap on the lids, label and date, then quick-freeze. The stock will keep well for about 1 year in the freezer.

Processor Sauces

Processor Hollandaise
Makes about 1½ cups

Almost as buttery and rich as the real thing. And it takes less than 2 minutes to prepare. Serve over steamed asparagus, broccoli, cauliflower or green beans.

Juice of ½ lemon
1 very large (jumbo) egg
Pinch of salt
Pinch of white pepper
½ cup melted butter
½ cup corn oil or peanut oil

Place lemon juice, egg, salt and pepper in the work bowl of a food processor fitted with the metal chopping blade and pulse once or twice to blend. With the motor running, drizzle the butter, then the corn oil, down the feed tube in a very fine stream. Let motor run nonstop for about 20 seconds after all of the butter and oil have been incorporated.

VARIATIONS:

Mousseline Sauce: Prepare the Processor Hollandaise as directed and fold in ½ cup heavy cream that has been beaten to stiff peaks. Delicious over seafood as well as any of the vegetables that are good with hollandaise.

Figaro Sauce: Prepare the Processor Hollandaise as directed and blend in 2 tablespoons of tomato purée and 1 tablespoon minced fresh parsley. Delicious with grilled fish.

Mustard Hollandaise: Prepare the Processor Hollandaise as directed, then blend in 2 tablespoons Dijon mustard. Serve with seafood or green vegetables.

Maltaise Sauce: Prepare the Processor Hollandaise as directed, then stir in ½ teaspoon very finely grated orange rind. Serve with boiled fish or vegetables.

Processor Béarnaise
Makes about 1½ cups

Leaves from 3 nice sprigs of tarragon (about 2 tablespoons)
   or ¾ teaspoon crumbled leaf tarragon
2 tablespoons fresh chervil leaves or ¾ teaspoon crumbled leaf
   chervil
1 tablespoon minced shallot
¼ cup tarragon vinegar
2 tablespoons dry white wine
1 very large egg
¼ teaspoon salt
Several grindings of black pepper
½ cup melted butter
½ cup corn oil or peanut oil

In a small, covered saucepan, boil the tarragon, chervil, shallot, vinegar and wine about 3 minutes, or until herbs are wilted; uncover and boil until liquid reduces to about 2 tablespoons. Empty into a food processor fitted with the metal chopping blade and cool 5 minutes. Break the egg into the work bowl, add salt and pepper, cover and pulse quickly once or twice to blend. Now, with the motor running, drizzle first the butter, then the corn oil, down the feed tube in a very fine stream. Beat the mixture for about 20 seconds nonstop after all of the butter and oil have been incorporated. Serve over broiled steaks, chops or fish.

Sauce Soubise
Makes about 4 cups

Approximately a half-and-half mix of puréed onions and Béchamel, *Sauce Soubise* is one of the great French classics. It is traditionally served with poached sweetbreads or brains, or with poultry or fish. It's also good over boiled potatoes or steamed green beans.

4 medium-size yellow onions, peeled and cut into slim wedges
1¾ cups chicken stock, in all
¾ cup water
7 tablespoons unsalted butter, in all
4 tablespoons flour
¾ teaspoon salt (or to taste)
⅛ teaspoon white pepper (or to taste)
⅛ teaspoon ground nutmeg
Pinch of crumbled leaf thyme
1 cup milk

In a food processor fitted with the metal chopping blade, coarsely chop the onions, two at a time, using 3 or 4 pulses or on-offs of the motor. Empty onions into a heavy saucepan, add ¾ cup of the chicken stock, all of the water and 3 tablespoons of the butter. Set over moderate heat, cover and simmer about 45 minutes, or until onions are mushy. Uncover, raise heat so that the pan liquid boils vigorously, then cook until the liquid is reduced to about 1 cup. Dump the saucepan contents into the food processor (still fitted with the chopping blade—no need to wash it or the work bowl) and purée by running the motor 10 to 15 seconds nonstop. Set aside.

For efficiency's sake, you can make the Béchamel sauce while the onions cook. Melt the remaining 4 tablespoons of butter in the top part of a double boiler over moderate heat, blend in the flour, salt, pepper, nutmeg and thyme, and heat, stirring constantly, 2 to 3 minutes. Whisk in the milk and the remaining 1 cup of chicken stock and heat, stirring all the while, until thickened and smooth—about 3 to 5 minutes. Now set the double-boiler top over simmering water, cover and simmer the Béchamel for about 45 minutes, stirring from time to time with a rubber spatula. Blend in the onion purée, heat 1 to 2 minutes longer, then serve.

Processor Mayonnaises

One-Minute Mayonnaise

Makes about 2 cups

This mayonnaise is slightly thinner than the commercial mayonnaises we've all become accustomed to, but then, it has no artificial stabilizers or emulsifiers either. It will keep well in the refrigerator for about five days.

> 2 egg yolks
> 1 egg
> Juice of 1 lemon
> 2 tablespoons white wine vinegar
> ½ teaspoon dry mustard
> ½ teaspoon salt
> ¼ teaspoon white pepper
> 1 cup olive oil (best quality)
> 1 cup of corn oil or peanut oil

In a food processor fitted with the metal chopping blade, blend the egg yolks, egg, lemon juice, vinegar, mustard, salt and pepper, using 2 pulses or on-offs of the motor. Combine the olive oil and the corn oil in a 1-pint measure, then, with the processor motor running, trickle them down the feed tube in a very fine stream. After all of the oil has been incorporated, buzz for 10 seconds longer. Spoon into a 1-pint jar, cover and keep well refrigerated until ready to use.

Aïoli

(Provençal Garlic Mayonnaise)

Makes about 1½ cups

As it is made in Provence, *Aïoli* contains almost a whole bud of garlic, or as one wit remarked, "enough to blow a safe." I've reduced the amount slightly, because processor-minced garlic is more potent than the hand-minced. *Aïoli* is the traditional topping for *bourride* (Provençal fish soup) and for steamed salt cod. And I know people who like to stir it into gazpacho.

> *1 slice firm-textured white bread, trimmed of crusts and torn into*
>   *small pieces*
> *5 medium-size garlic cloves, peeled*
> *2 egg yolks*
> *Juice of ½ lemon*
> *¼ teaspoon salt*
> *Pinch of white pepper*
> *1 cup olive oil (top quality)*
> *3 to 4 tablespoons light cream*

Place bread, garlic, egg yolks, lemon juice, salt and pepper in a food processor fitted with the metal chopping blade; turn motor on and let run nonstop for 10 seconds. Scrape down the sides of the work bowl with a rubber spatula, re-cover and buzz 5 seconds longer. With the motor running, pour the olive oil down the feed tube in a very fine stream. The mixture will emulsify and become quite thick. After all of the olive oil has been incorporated, let the motor run 5 seconds longer. Add 3 tablespoons of the light cream, buzz a few seconds, and if mixture still seems unduly thick (it should be about the consistency of a thick mayonnaise), whir in the remaining tablespoon of cream.

Green Mayonnaise

Makes about 2 cups

Here's another of those formerly tedious recipes that becomes a one-step, one-minute operation with the food processor. The green mayonnaise keeps well in the refrigerator for four to five days. Use to dress cold steamed salmon, lobster, shrimp or scallops. It's also delicious stirred into cold mixed cooked vegetables.

> *⅔ cup loosely packed parsley sprigs, washed and patted very dry on*
>   *paper toweling*
> *⅔ cup loosely packed young and tender spinach leaves, washed and*
>   *patted very dry on paper toweling*

⅓ cup loosely packed young watercress leaves, washed and patted
  very dry on paper toweling
¼ cup loosely packed (1-inch lengths) of chives; the easiest way to
  prepare these is simply to grab a small handful of chives and snip
  directly into the measuring cup
2 cups mayonnaise
1 tablespoon lemon juice
½ teaspoon salt (or to taste)
⅛ teaspoon cayenne papper

Dump all ingredients into a food processor fitted with the metal chopping blade, turn motor on and let run continuously for 45 to 60 seconds, or until mixture is creamy-smooth. Pour into a bowl, taste for salt and add more, if needed, then cover and refrigerate several hours before serving.

Curry Mayonnaise
Makes about 1¼ cups

Delicious with cold fish, shellfish, ham or chicken.

1 small yellow onion, peeled and quartered
2 tablespoons butter
1 tablespoon curry powder
1 egg
1 egg yolk
Juice of ½ lemon
1 tablespoon tarragon vinegar
¼ teaspoon dry mustard
¼ teaspoon salt
⅛ teaspoon white pepper
1 cup corn oil or peanut oil

Mince the onion fine in a food processor fitted with the metal chopping blade, using 5 or 6 pulses or on-offs of the motor. Empty into a small skillet in which you have already melted the butter. Set over moderate heat and sauté 5 to 8 minutes until limp and golden, but not brown. Blend in the curry powder, reduce heat to low and let the curry powder mellow 2 to 3 minutes, or until there is no longer a raw curry taste; cool. Dump the skillet mixture into the processor work bowl, still fitted with the metal chopping blade, and add all remaining ingredients except the oil. Blend, using 2 or 3 pulses or on-offs of the motor. Then, with the motor running, drizzle the oil down the feed tube in a very fine stream. Beat a few seconds longer until fluffy-smooth. If mayonnaise seems too thick, thin with 1 or 2 tablespoons light cream. Refrigerate until ready to serve.

Flavored Butters

Maître d'Hôtel Butter
(Parsley-Lemon Butter)

Makes about 1½ cups

This is such a versatile all-purpose butter (equally delicious with fish, shellfish, broiled chicken, steaks and chops, not to mention such vegetables as carrots, broccoli, beets and green beans) that I like to make it in quantity, shape it in rolls about 1½ inches in diameter, then wrap it in foil and keep it in the freezer. Whenever I want to serve *maître d'hôtel* butter, I simply slice off as many pats of it as I need, then return the balance to the freezer.

1 cup loosely packed parsley sprigs, washed and patted dry on paper toweling
1½ cups (3 sticks) unsalted butter, at room temperature
Juice of ½ lemon
¾ teaspoon salt
¼ teaspoon white pepper

In a food processor fitted with the metal chopping blade, mince the parsley fairly fine by using two or three 5-second churnings of the motor. Add all remaining ingredients and cream until smooth by letting the processor run 30 seconds nonstop. Uncover the work bowl, remove the chopping blade, scrape the plastic spatula down along the sides and bottom of the bowl, lifting up any bits the chopping blade may have missed (because butter is so slick, the blades are not as effective at dealing with it as they are with other foods). Replace the metal chopping blade and work-bowl cover, turn the motor on and let run nonstop for another 15 to 20 seconds. Scrape the butter onto a large square of foil, chill until firm enough to shape, then roll into three logs about 1½ inches in diameter. Wrap each snugly in heavy-duty aluminum foil and freeze until firm.

Anchovy Butter
Makes about ¾ cup

6 anchovy fillets, drained
1 teaspoon lemon juice
⅛ teaspoon cayenne pepper
¾ cup (1½ sticks) unsalted butter, at room temperature

In a food processor equipped with the metal chopping blade, whir the anchovies with the lemon juice and cayenne until finely minced—using about two 5-second churnings of the motor (scrape down the work bowl between churnings). Add the butter and buzz until uniformly creamy, using two or three 10-second churnings of the motor. Spread on broiled steaks, chops or fish.

Garlic-Cheese Butter
Makes about ¾ cup

1 large garlic clove, peeled and halved
¼ cup freshly grated Parmesan cheese
¼ teaspoon salt
Pinch of freshly ground black pepper
¾ cup (1½ sticks) unsalted butter, at room temperature

In a food processor equipped with the metal chopping blade, churn the garlic with the Parmesan, salt and pepper until finely minced—about three or four 5-second whirrings of the motor should do the job. Add the butter and blend until uniformly creamy, using two 10-second churnings of the motor and scraping down the work bowl between each. Use in making garlic bread or serve with broiled chops, chicken or fish.

Horseradish Butter

Makes about ¾ cup

¾ cup (1½ sticks) unsalted butter, at room temperature
2 tablespoons prepared horseradish
½ teaspoon salt
⅛ teaspoon white pepper

Place all ingredients in a food processor fitted with the metal chopping blade and whir until creamy, using 3 or 4 pulses or on-offs of the motor. Serve with broiled steaks or chops or with boiled beef.

Mustard Butter

Makes about ¾ cup

¾ cup (1½ sticks) unsalted butter, at room temperature
2 tablespoons Dijon mustard

Whir both ingredients in a food processor fitted with the metal chopping blade until creamy-smooth—about 4 pulses or on-offs of the motor. Use to dress broiled steaks, chops, fish, chicken, or such steamed vegetables as broccoli, cauliflower or asparagus.

Stuffings & Crumb Toppings

Sage and Onion Stuffing for Poultry
Makes about 2 quarts, enough to stuff a 12-pound turkey

This recipe demonstrates how easily and quickly the processor can cope with the basics of poultry stuffing: It crumbs the bread, minces the parsley, chops the onion and celery. Experiment with this recipe, if you like—it takes well to improvisation, and the processor is there to serve you: If you chop a cup of nuts—peanuts, pecans, walnuts, hazelnuts, almonds—all will be at the perfect degree of fineness after two 5-second churnings of the metal chopping blade; to mince a pound of mushrooms, do only about one third of them at a time and switch the processor motor on and off quickly several times until the mushrooms are moderately coarsely minced; if you decide to chop some tart, green, cored and quartered apples, there will be no need to peel them—again a couple of pulses or fast on-offs will do the job. Or, simply use the chopping times and techniques described here as a guide in preparing your own favorite poultry stuffing in the processor.

> 1 cup loosely packed parsley sprigs, washed and patted very dry on paper toweling
> 16 slices firm-textured white bread, torn into small pieces
> 2 large yellow onions, peeled and cut into 1-inch chunks
> ⅔ cup melted butter
> 3 medium-size celery ribs, trimmed, washed and cut into 1-inch lengths
> 2 teaspoons crumbled leaf sage
> ½ teaspoon crumbled leaf thyme
> ¼ teaspoon crumbled leaf marjoram
> ¼ teaspoon freshly ground black pepper
> 1½ teaspoons salt
> 1 egg, lightly beaten
> ⅓ cup chicken broth or water (optional—this will give you a much moister stuffing)

In a food processor fitted with the metal chopping blade, mince the parsley with about one fourth of the bread (you'll be crumbing it as you mince the parsley) by using three 5-second churnings of the motor. Empty into a very large mixing bowl. Now crumb the remaining bread in three separate batches, using two 5-second bursts of speed for each; empty into bowl. Fine-mince the onions, one at a time, using 5 or 6 pulses or on-offs of the motor. Place 3 tablespoons of the melted butter and all of the onions in a large, heavy skillet. Mince the celery just as you did the onions, and add to skillet. Sauté the celery and onions slowly over moderately low heat about 10 minutes, until limp and golden. Add to the bowl of crumbs along with the remaining melted butter and all remaining ingredients except the chicken broth. Toss lightly to mix. If you prefer a wetter stuffing, mix in the chicken broth. The stuffing is now ready to use. NOTE: *To bake the stuffing en casserole, spoon into a well-buttered 2½-quart baking dish, cover with foil and bake for 30 minutes in a moderately slow oven (325° F.); uncover and bake at the same temperature for 30 minutes longer, or until tipped with brown.*

Spinach, Mushroom and Pine-Nut Stuffing

Makes enough to stuff a 5-pound roasting chicken

½ *pound tender young spinach, washed and sorted*
½ *cup loosely packed parsley sprigs, washed and patted very dry on paper toweling*
½ *pound medium-size mushrooms, wiped clean and stemmed (reserve stems)*
2 *tablespoons butter*
1 *medium-size yellow onion, peeled and cut into slim wedges*
1 *medium-size garlic clove, peeled and crushed*
½ *cup pignoli (pine nuts)*
¼ *cup freshly grated Parmesan cheese*
1 *cup cooked unseasoned rice or wild rice*
1½ *teaspoons salt*
Several grindings of black pepper
Pinch of ground nutmeg
1 *egg lightly beaten*

Pile the spinach in a large saucepan, add no water, cover and set over moderate heat for about 2 minutes—just until spinach wilts. Meanwhile, dump the parsley into a processor fitted with the metal chopping blade and mince by giving the motor a couple of fast whirls or pulses. Empty into a large mixing bowl. Drain the spinach very dry in a strainer, pressing out as much liquid as possible. Dump spinach into the food processor (still fitted with the metal chopping blade) and, with a couple of pulses or on-offs of the motor, chop moderately fine. Empty into mixing bowl. Add half of the mushrooms to the work bowl and chop moderately coarsely with a few pulses or on-offs of the motor; empty into a large, heavy skillet in which you have already melted the butter. Chop the remaining mushrooms and the reserved stems the same way and add to skillet. Now coarsely chop the onion with 3 or 4 bursts of the processor motor. Add to skillet along with the garlic, set over moderate heat and allow to sauté while you chop the *pignoli*. Dump the nuts into the processor and give the motor a few fast pulses or whirs; add chopped nuts to mixing bowl. When onions and mushrooms have sautéed for about 10 minutes, or until limp, add to bowl and toss well to mix. Add the Parmesan, rice, salt, pepper, nutmeg and egg and toss well again. The stuffing is now ready to use.

Cracker-Crumb Topping

Makes about 2 cups

If you make casseroles often, you may want to make up a batch of this topping to keep on hand in the refrigerator. This amount is enough for four average-size casseroles. It will keep well in the refrigerator for about two weeks.

4 dozen saltines (the 2-inch-square size)
¼ cup melted butter

Place half of the crackers in a food processor fitted with the metal chopping blade and buzz to moderately coarse crumbs by letting the motor run nonstop for 10 to 15 seconds. With the motor still running, drizzle 2 tablespoons of the melted butter down the feed tube and buzz for about 5 seconds longer. Empty crumbs into a 1-pint preserving jar.

Buzz the remaining crackers the same way and add the butter as before. Add to jar, screw the lid down tight and store in the refrigerator.

VARIATIONS:

Cheese-Crumb Topping: Prepare as directed, then mix in ¼ cup freshly grated Parmesan cheese.

Herbed Crumb Topping: Prepare as directed, then mix in ½ teaspoon crumbled leaf thyme, marjoram, oregano, sage or savory.

Bread-Crumb Topping
Makes about 2 cups

Soft bread crumbs, like cracker crumbs, can be buzzed up with melted butter, then stored in the refrigerator for about 2 weeks. Make them with white bread, with whole-wheat, even with a light rye bread. They are convenient to have on hand and make far fresher casserole toppings than anything that comes "prepared."

4 slices firm-textured white, whole-wheat or light rye bread
2 tablespoons melted butter

Equip the processor with the metal chopping blade. Tear the bread into small pieces and drop into the processor work bowl. For moderately coarse crumbs (best for casserole toppings), pulse or snap the motor on and off about 3 times, then with the motor running, pour the melted butter down the feed tube. The instant the butter has been incorporated, snap the motor off. Empty the crumb topping into a 1-pint preserving jar, screw the lid down tight and store in the refrigerator.

VARIATION:

Italian-Style Bread-Crumb Topping: Place torn pieces of white bread into processor work bowl as directed, add 2 tablespoons freshly grated Parmesan or Romano cheese, ½ teaspoon crumbled leaf oregano or marjoram and ¼ teaspoon crumbled leaf basil. Whir to crumbs as directed, then with the processor motor running, drizzle 2 tablespoons top-quality olive oil down the feed tube. Store airtight in the refrigerator.

Pastries & Crumb Crusts

Flaky Pie Crust

Makes enough for one 8- or 9-inch single-crust pie

It *is* possible to make a light and tender pastry in the food processor, but you must follow these instructions explicitly. Also, do not attempt to do a double batch of this recipe at one fell swoop for a two-crust pie. The processor can't cope with the double load and the pie crust will be tough. Manipulation is the key, and because of the processor's powerful action, you must keep a watchful eye on the pastry at all times and stop mixing the minute the proper texture or consistency is achieved (each is described in the method below).

1¼ cups sifted all-purpose flour
½ teaspoon salt
3 tablespoons ice-cold vegetable shortening
2 tablespoons ice-cold butter
¼ cup ice-cold water

Place the flour and salt in a food processor fitted with the metal chopping blade. Cut the shortening and butter into small cubes and distribute evenly over the surface of the flour. Now "knead" the fats into the flour in the processor by using four or five 1-second bursts of speed—when it reaches the proper texture, the mixture will be fine and crumbly, about like moderately finely chopped nuts. Uncover the work bowl and drizzle about one third of the water over the surface of the mixture; re-cover and blend with 2 pulses or on-offs of the motor. Add another one third of the water the same way, again scattering it over the surface, and pulse or snap the motor on and off twice. Now add the final one third of the water and give the motor 2 additional pulses or on-offs. The mixture will just begin to cling together. Don't worry if it still seems crumbly—overmixing at this point will result in a tough pie crust. Scoop the pastry onto a square of wax paper, pat into a flat round about 5 inches in diameter and chill 20 to 30 minutes before rolling.

Turn the pastry onto a lightly floured pastry cloth and roll with a lightly floured stockinette-covered rolling pin into a circle 3 inches larger in diameter than the pan you intend to use. Lay the rolling pin across the center of the rolled-out circle of pastry, lop half of the pastry over the rolling pin, then lift and ease into the pie pan. Trim the overhang so that it is about 1 inch larger than the pan all around. Roll the overhang under on top of the rim and flute or crimp. The pie shell is now ready to fill and bake as individual recipes specify.

For a top crust: Simply make a second batch of pastry exactly the same way, then chill and roll as directed. Ease the pastry into place on top of the filled pie shell, then trim the top- and bottom-crust overhangs so that they are 1 inch larger than the pan all around. Roll the two together up on top of the pie-pan rim and flute or crimp.

Pâte Sablée
(Sweet Pastry)

Makes enough for one single-crust 9- or 10-inch pie

One of the miracles of the food processor is that it simplifies and short-cuts the making of almost the entire repertoire of pesky French pastries. The machine neatly cuts the butter into the flour in seconds, eliminating the tedium of rubbing it in by hand. It even incorporates the water and egg, whirling the whole into a soft, manageable dough. *Pâté Sablée*, a fragile sweet pastry used in making open-faced fruit tarts, can be buzzed up in the processor in about five seconds. It is important—imperative—that the butter be icy cold and sliced very thin before it is added to the processor work bowl. The powerful metal chopping blade will reduce the butter to golden flecks and distribute them evenly among the dry ingredients—the secret of a tender, flaky pastry.

1⅓ cups sifted all-purpose flour
3 tablespoons sugar
¼ teaspoon salt
½ cup (1 stick) icy-cold butter, sliced into ½-inch pats
1 egg yolk
4 to 5 tablespoons ice-cold water

In a food processor fitted with the metal chopping blade, whir the flour with the sugar and salt, using 2 or 3 pulses or on-offs of the motor. The result will be perfectly sifted dry ingredients. Distribute the pats of butter as evenly as possible over the bed of dry ingredients, then, with about three 1-second bursts of speed, cut the butter in. Remove the work-bowl lid at this point and examine the mixture. It should be crumbly, about the texture of oatmeal flakes. If not, pulse or snap the motor on and off a couple of times—no more. If the mixture is not crumbly, the pastry will not be flaky. Drop in the egg yolk and with 1 or 2 bursts of speed, incorporate. The mixture will still be crumbly. Have at hand a measuring cup and in it the 5 tablespoons of ice water. Turn the processor on and immediately begin pouring the ice water down the feed tube in a thin stream with the motor running. Watch the mixture like a hawk, and the minute it churns into a ball and begins to ride up the chopping-blade spindle, stop adding water and snap the motor off. The pastry is ready. This is the critical mixing point. If you overmix at this stage—even so much as a second—the pastry will toughen. When you uncover the work bowl, you may notice that some of the crumbly mixture in the bottom of the bowl has not been incorporated. No matter. You will work it in as you knead the pastry.

Turn the pastry onto a lightly floured board with lightly floured hands. Shape into a pone (a thick disc), then knead lightly and briskly for 45 to 60 seconds, just until it holds together nicely and responds smoothly to your touch. Wrap in wax paper and chill several hours before rolling.

Roll the pastry on a lightly floured pastry cloth with a lightly floured stockinette-covered rolling pin into a circle 3 inches larger in diameter than the pan or flan ring you will use. The French way, of course, is to bake the crust in a flan ring—a shallow, straight-sided metal ring that is set on a baking sheet. (You can buy flan rings at specialty kitchen shops, also in the housewares departments of many large stores.) Lay the rolling pin smack across the center of the rolled-out circle of pastry, lop half of the pastry over the rolling pin, then lift and lay across the center of the pie pan or flan ring. Gently unfold the pastry and ease it into the pan or flan ring so that it overhangs evenly all around. With a sharp knife, trim the overhang so that it is about 1 inch, then carefully press the pastry against the contours of the pan or ring. Roll the overhang over on top of the rim and flute or crimp with the tines of a fork.

For most fresh-fruit tarts, the pastry should be partially baked before it is filled, so that the bottom crust does not become soggy. You must, however, weight the pastry down, otherwise it will shrink from the sides of the pan and billow across the bottom—and shatter the minute you fill the crust. The best trick, I've found, is to butter the shiny side of a large square of lightweight aluminum foil, then to press it gently—buttered-side down—so that it conforms to the contours of the pastry. Now fill the foil liner with uncooked rice or dried beans. These, by the way, can be used over and over again to weight crusts, and they can also be cooked later as you would any rice or dried beans (they will have a wonderfully toasty flavor).

Bake the pastry in a hot oven (425° F.) for 10 minutes. Remove from oven and lift out the liner of rice or beans. Prick the bottom and sides of the crust evenly with a fork (this is to allow steam to escape and to prevent the crust from buckling or bubbling as it finishes baking). Return the pastry to the oven and bake 3 to 4 minutes longer, just until it begins to color. Remove from oven and cool thoroughly before filling. As an extra safeguard against a soggy bottom crust, brush the pastry lightly with frothily beaten egg white. Let dry before filling.

The crust is now ready to fill and bake as individual tart or pie recipes direct.

Pâte Brisée

Makes enough for one single-crust 9- or 10-inch pie

Another of the rich, short French pastries that the food processor makes so well. This one is savory rather than sweet and is a good choice for pie shells, quiches, pot pie toppings, turnovers and *Piroshki* (see Index for recipe page number).

  2 cups sifted all-purpose flour
  1 teaspoon baking powder

½ teaspoon salt
¼ cup (½ stick) refrigerator-cold unsalted butter, cut into thin pats
⅓ cup refrigerator-cold lard or vegetable shortening, cut into small chunks
2 egg yolks, lightly beaten
2 teaspoons lemon juice
⅓ cup cold water

In a food processor fitted with the metal chopping blade, place the flour, baking powder and salt; pulse or snap the motor on and off 2 or 3 times to combine the dry ingredients. Add the butter and lard to the work bowl, distributing them as evenly as possible over the surface of the dry ingredients, then cut the fats into the flour, using two or three 1-second churnings of the motor. The mixture should be quite coarse and crumbly, about the texture of uncooked oatmeal. In a small bowl combine the egg yolks, lemon juice and water, whisking lightly with a fork. With the work-bowl cover off, pour the combined liquids into the work bowl, distributing them as evenly as possible over the surface of the fat-flour mixture. Re-cover the work bowl, switch the motor on and let run 5 or 6 seconds nonstop, just until the pastry forms into a ball that rides up on the chopping blade's central spindle. Snap the motor off immediately so that you don't risk overmixing the pastry.

Place pastry on a lightly floured bread board and knead briskly with your hands 4 or 5 times; wrap in wax paper and refrigerate at least 3 hours before rolling. For directions on rolling the pastry and shaping into a pie shell or flan ring, see the preceding recipe for *Pâte Sablée*.

Graham-Cracker Crust

Makes one 9-inch pie shell

24 graham crackers (the 2⅜-inch-square size)
⅓ cup sugar
Pinch of ground cinnamon (optional)
Pinch of ground nutmeg (optional)
⅓ cup melted butter

Place half of the crackers in a food processor fitted with the metal chopping blade and buzz to fine crumbs by letting the motor run nonstop for about 60 seconds. Add the remaining crackers and buzz for another 60 seconds, or until uniformly fine. Add the sugar and, if you like, the spices, and pulse or snap the motor on and off a couple of times to blend. Uncover the processor and drizzle the melted butter over the surface of the crumbs. Re-cover, turn the motor on and run 1 minute nonstop. Stop the processor, uncover, and with the plastic spatula, stir crumb mixture, digging down to the bottom of the work bowl and lifting the bottom layer of crumbs up to the top; work carefully, because the cutting blades are razor sharp. Re-cover work bowl, turn motor on and buzz about 10 to 15 seconds longer, or until butter is well mixed throughout the crumbs.

Spoon the crumb mixture into a 9-inch pie pan or springform pan, and pat firmly against the bottom and sides, using the back of a spoon. Bake, uncovered, in a moderate oven (350° F.) for 10 minutes. Remove from oven and cool thoroughly before filling.

Vanilla-Wafer-Crumb Crust
Makes one 9-inch pie shell

36 vanilla wafers
⅓ cup melted butter
1 tablespoon light brown sugar
Pinch of ground nutmeg or mace (optional)

Place half of the vanilla wafers in a food processor fitted with the metal chopping blade and buzz to fine crumbs, using four 5-second churnings of the motor. Empty crumbs into a mixing bowl, pulverize the remaining wafers the same way and add to the original batch of crumbs. Drizzle in the melted butter, add the sugar and, if you like, the nutmeg, and toss all briskly with a fork until well blended. Spoon the mixture into a 9-inch pie pan or springform pan and pat firmly against the bottom and sides, using the back of a spoon. Bake, uncovered, in a moderate oven (350° F.) for 10 minutes. Cool to room temperature before filling.

VARIATIONS:

Gingersnap-Crumb Crust: Prepare as directed, but substitute 36 gingersnaps for the vanilla wafers.

Lemon-Wafer-Crumb Crust: Prepare as directed, but use 36 lemon wafers instead of vanilla wafers; omit the optional nutmeg and add ¼ teaspoon finely grated lemon rind.

Chocolate-Crumb Crust
Makes one 9-inch pie shell

24 thin chocolate wafers (those that are 2 inches in diameter)
2 tablespoons sugar
⅓ cup melted butter

Place half of the cookies and 1 tablespoon of the sugar in a food processor fitted with the metal chopping blade and buzz to fine crumbs by using four 5-second bursts of speed. Empty the crumbs into a mixing bowl, reduce the remaining wafers to crumbs the same way with the remaining tablespoon of sugar and add to the first batch along with the melted butter. Toss well with a fork to mix. Spoon the crumb mixture into a 9-inch pie pan or springform pan, and pat firmly against the bottom and sides, using the back of a spoon. Bake uncovered in a moderate oven (350° F.) for 10 minutes. Cool to room temperature before filling.

Nut-Crumb Crust
Makes one 9-inch pie shell

½ cup pecan or walnut meats or shelled unblanched almonds
24 vanilla wafers
Pinch of salt
¼ cup melted butter

Place the nuts, wafers and salt in a food processor fitted with the metal chopping blade and, with three or four 5-second churnings of the motor, reduce to crumbs. Now, with the processor motor running, slowly pour the melted butter down the feed tube. Once all of the butter has been incorporated, stop the machine and inspect the texture of the crumb mixture. It should be quite fine. If not, pulse the machine or snap the motor on and off several times until the crumbs are about the texture of cornmeal. Dump the crumb mixture into a 9-inch pie pan or springform pan, and pat firmly against the bottom and sides, using the back of a spoon. Bake, uncovered, in a moderate oven (350° F.) for 10 minutes. Cool to room temperature before filling.

VARIATION:

Chocolate-Nut-Crumb Crust: Substitute 18 thin chocolate wafers (those that are about 2 inches in diameter) for the 24 vanilla wafers. Buzz the ½ cup of nuts, half of the chocolate wafers and the salt to crumbs, using the above times as a guide, then dump into a mixing bowl. Crumb the remaining chocolate wafers the same way, add to bowl, blend in the ¼ cup melted butter, then shape and bake as directed above.

Pickles & Preserves

Sweet Yellow Squash Pickles
Makes 6 to 8 pints

Some years ago, when I was developing recipes for *The Green Thumb Preserving Guide* (also published by William Morrow & Company, Inc.), it was this one recipe that spurred me into buying a food processor. For days I had been slicing, chopping, mincing, grinding and puréeing, and one look at the ingredients in this old Southern specialty—one dozen squash, *three* dozen small onions, all to be sliced thin—convinced me that the time had come to invest in a processor. And considering the hundreds of hours of work it has saved me, it is unquestionably one of the wisest investments I ever made. This recipe was published in *The Green Thumb Preserving Guide*, but because I have had so many raves about it from readers, I offer it once again here. Few recipes use the food processor to better advantage. **NOTE:** *To speed up the peeling of the onions used in this recipe, blanch them*

20 to 30 seconds in boiling water—just as you would peaches or to-matoes. The skins will slip right off.

12 medium-size tender young straight-neck yellow squash, washed,
   trimmed and cut into 4-inch lengths
3 dozen small silverskin (white) onions, peeled
½ cup pickling salt
6 cups cracked ice cubes
3½ cups sugar
1 quart white vinegar
1¾ teaspoons ground turmeric
1¾ teaspoons celery seeds
1¾ teaspoons white mustard seeds

Equip the food processor with the slicing disc—the medium-slicing disc, if you have one. In the feed tube, stand as many pieces of squash as will fit fairly snugly. Press down firmly on the pusher, turn motor on or depress the Pulse button and push squash through the slicer. Continue until work bowl fills up, then empty squash slices into a large bowl. Repeat until all squash is sliced. Slice the onions the same way and empty into a second large bowl. Now layer the sliced squash and onions alternately into a third very large mixing bowl, sprinkling with pickling salt as you go. Pile cracked ice on top and let stand, uncovered, at room temperature for 3 hours. Drain, place in a colander and rinse well with cool water. Drain well again, pressing out as much liquid as possible.

Meanwhile, wash and rinse eight 1-pint preserving jars and their closures; keep hot in separate kettles of simmering water until you are ready to use them.

Bring sugar, vinegar, turmeric, celery and mustard seeds to a rolling boil over high heat in a large, heavy enamel or stainless-steel kettle. Add squash and onions and stir gently. Bring just to the boiling point, then, using a wide-mouth canning funnel, pack into hot preserving jars, filling to within ¼-inch of the top. Make sure squash and onions are covered with pickling liquid. Run a thin-bladed knife around the inside of each jar to release any trapped air bubbles.

Wipe jar rims and seal jars. Process 10 minutes in a boiling bath (212° F.). Remove jars from water bath, complete seals if necessary and cool to room temperature. Check seals, label jars and store in a cool, dark, dry place.

Sweet Pickle Relish

Makes 5 to 6 half pints

This recipe demonstrates what a whiz the processor is at chopping ingredients for pickle relishes—the whole repertoire of them.

> 2 pounds firm, green tomatoes, washed and quartered (do not peel or core)
> 1 large sweet red pepper, washed, cored, seeded and cut into 1-inch squares
> 1 large sweet green pepper, washed, cored, seeded and cut into 1-inch squares
> 4 medium-size pickling cucumbers, washed, halved, seeded and cut into 1-inch chunks. (Pickling cucumbers are about half the size of regular cucumbers; they are firmer and have fewer seeds; moreover, they are less likely to have been waxed. Since the cucumbers for this recipe are not peeled, make sure that the ones you choose are not waxed.)
> 1 large yellow onion, peeled and cut into 1-inch chunks
> 1⅔ cups cider vinegar
> 1¼ cups sugar
> 1½ teaspoons mustard seeds
> 1 teaspoon celery seeds
> ½ teaspoon ground allspice
> 1 teaspoon salt

You will need, first of all, a large, deep enamel or stainless-steel kettle in which to cook the relish (an aluminum kettle may give the relish an unpleasant metallic taste). Equip the food processor with the metal chopping blade, then coarsely chop the vegetables this way, adding each to the kettle as soon as it is chopped: green tomatoes (do one fourth of the total amount at a time, allowing 3 or 4 quick bursts of speed for each batch); red and green peppers (mince each separately, using 2 or 3 pulses or on-offs of the processor motor for each); cucumbers (do one half of the total amount at a time, allowing 4 pulses or fast churnings of the motor for each batch—on-off, on-off, etc.); and finally, the onion (3 or 4 pulses or on-offs of the motor). Stir vegetables in the kettle, add all remaining ingredients, place over moderately low heat, set the lid on the kettle askew, and boil slowly for 30 minutes, stirring occasionally. Ladle into hot, half-pint preserving jars, filling each to within ⅛ inch of the top. Wipe the jar rims and seal. Label jars, then store in a cool, dark, dry place for about one month before serving.

Jerusalem Artichoke Pickle Relish
Makes 10 to 12 half pints

Few people bother to make this crisp, tart relish anymore, even in the South, where it's a great favorite. Preparing the artichokes simply takes too much time and energy. You must still scrape them by hand, removing blemished parts (they're almost impossible to peel because of their knobbiness). But be thankful that you don't have to hand-chop them—or the onions or sweet peppers. These tasks the food processor performs with stunning speed.

> *5 pounds Jerusalem artichokes (sold in some stores as Sunchokes), washed in cool water, scraped with a sharp paring knife and cut into 1½-inch chunks*
> *4 large sweet red peppers, washed, cored, seeded and cut into 1-inch squares*
> *5 large yellow onions, peeled and cut into slim wedges*
> *2 gallons cold water mixed with 2 cups pickling salt (brine)*
> *2½ cups sugar*
> *5 cups cider vinegar*
> *3 tablespoons mustard seeds*
> *2 tablespoons ground turmeric*

Place about 2 cups artichoke chunks in the food processor fitted with the metal chopping blade, and with 2 to 3 pulses or fast bursts of speed, chop coarsely. Empty into a very large enamel or stainless-steel kettle. Continue machine-chopping the artichokes, doing no more than 2 cups at a time, until all are done; as each batch is chopped, add to the kettle. Now machine-chop the red peppers and onions the same way, doing no more than 2 cups at a time. Add to kettle. Pour in the brine, cover kettle and allow to soak for 3 hours. Line a very large colander with a clean dish towel, ladle in about a fourth of the artichoke mixture, bundle up in the towel and twist and squeeze to extract as much liquid as possible; place drained mixture in a second large kettle. Repeat until all of the mixture has been drained and squeezed dry.

Immerse 12 spanking-clean preserving jars and their closures in a large kettle of simmering water and keep them there until you are ready to fill the jars.

Combine the sugar, vinegar, mustard seeds and turmeric in a medium-size, heavy enamel or stainless-steel kettle, set over moderate heat and boil, uncovered, for 2 minutes. Pour this over the relish mixture and stir well to mix. Pack into hot preserving jars (a wide-mouth funnel makes the job easier), leaving ¼ inch of head space at the top of each jar. Run a thin-bladed knife around the inside of each jar to remove air bubbles, wipe jar rims and seal. Process the jars of relish for 10 minutes in a boiling water bath (212° F.). Remove jars from the water bath and cool to room temperature. Check the seals, label the jars and store in a cool, dark, dry place. Allow the relish to mellow for 3 to 4 weeks before serving.

Mango Chutney
Makes about 5 pints

Food processors should lead to a renaissance in pickling and preserving. To prove the point again, I've added this chutney recipe, for which 4 pounds of green mangoes must be coarsely chopped.

> 4 pounds green mangoes or peaches, peeled, pitted and cut into 1-inch chunks
> 1 large sweet red pepper, washed, cored, seeded and cut into 1-inch pieces
> 1 large yellow onion, peeled and cut into slim wedges
> 2 large garlic cloves, peeled
> 3 cubes (about 1 inch each) peeled fresh ginger
> 1 pound sultana raisins
> 1 pound dried currants
> 1 pound granulated sugar
> 1 pound light brown sugar
> 1 quart (4 cups) cider vinegar
> 1 tablespoon ground cinnamon

1 teaspoon ground cloves
1 tablespoon dry mustard
1½ teaspoons salt
¼ teaspoon crushed dried red chili peppers

For this recipe you will need a deep, heavy enamel or stainless-steel kettle in which you can both soak and cook the chopped fruits. (An aluminum kettle will give a metallic taste to the chutney.) Equip the food processor with the metal chopping blade, then chop the mango chunks, 2 cups of them at a time, by pulsing or snapping the motor on and off 3 or 4 times. As each batch is chopped, dump it into the enamel kettle. Now processor-mince the sweet pepper, using 5 or 6 pulses or on-offs of the motor; add to kettle. Mince the onion the same way and add it to kettle. Now place the garlic and ginger in the processor and mince quite fine by letting the motor run nonstop for about 5 seconds; scrape from the work bowl into the kettle. Add all remaining ingredients to kettle, stir well, set in a cool spot, cover and let stand undisturbed for 8 hours, or overnight.

Next day, set the kettle over moderate heat and bring slowly to a boil. Adjust heat so that mixture boils slowly and cook, uncovered, about 1½ to 2 hours, or until glossy and thick. Ladle into hot preserving jars, filling to within ¼ inch of the tops. Wipe jar rims and seal. Process the jars of chutney for 10 minutes in a boiling water bath (212° F.), then remove from the water bath and cool to room temperature. Check the seal on each jar, then label and store in a cool, dark, dry place. The chutney will have better flavor if you allow it to mellow on the shelf for about a month before opening it.

Grapefruit-Orange Marmalade
Makes about 4 half pints

If you've ever spent hours laboriously slicing orange and grapefruit rinds into thinnest strips for marmalade, you'll be delighted to know that you can chop them with the processor's metal chopping blade in about one minute. The rinds' texture will be a coarse chop rather than a shred, but in view of all the time saved, I think you'll agree that a slight change of texture is small sacrifice indeed. The marmalade's flavor remains the same, of course—in this case, bitingly tart.

1 large grapefruit (a thick-skinned variety), halved
2 large juice oranges, halved
1 large lemon, halved
2 cups water
3½ to 4 cups sugar

Section the grapefruit (save the sections to eat later). Turn the grapefruit rinds inside out, then peel off all the inner membranes and pith—it's easy if you start at the top or center of each grapefruit half, then peel the membranes down toward the cut edge. Now scrape the white inner rind with a spoon to remove any recalcitrant bits of membrane; cut the rind into 1-inch pieces and set aside for the moment. Now juice the oranges and lemon, strain the combined juices and pour into a large, heavy saucepan (preferably an enameled pan so that the marmalade won't take on a metallic taste). Turn the orange and lemon rinds inside out and peel off all inner membranes and pith—just as you did with the grapefruit. Cut the rinds into 1-inch pieces.

In a processor fitted with the metal chopping blade, chop the grapefruit rind moderately coarsely, using two 10-second churnings of the motor, then 2 or 3 pulses or on-offs. Dump rind into saucepan. Now chop orange and lemon rinds together the same way and add to pan. Stir in the water, set over moderately high heat, bring to a simmer, and cook, uncovered, for 10 minutes. Remove from heat, cover and let stand 4 hours.

Measure the rind mixture carefully (include all liquid), then add to it an equal measure of sugar—that is, if you have 3½ cups of rind and liquid, add 3½ cups of sugar. Return the mixture to the pan in which you soaked the rind, insert a candy thermometer and set over moderate heat. Bring to the boil, then cook, uncovered, at a slow boil for 2 to 2½ hours, or until thermometer registers 220° F. The marmalade will be glossy and thick. The old-fashioned way to test for consistency—and as foolproof a method today as it was in our grandmothers' day—is to spoon a little of the hot mixture onto a cold saucer, to let it cool briefly, then to tilt the saucer. If the drops of marmalade slide together in a jelly-like sheet, the marmalade is done.

Remove pan from the heat and let it stand 1 to 2 minutes. Skim off froth, then, with the aid of a wide-mouth canning funnel, ladle the marmalade into four hot, sterilized half-pint preserving jars, filling each to within ¼ inch of the top. Wipe jar rims and seal. Cool to room temperature, check seals, then label jars and store on a cool, dark, dry shelf. The marmalade will have better flavor if you allow it to mellow on the shelf for about 4 weeks before using.

Some Specialties
for the Processor

Homemade Peanut Butter
Makes about 1 cup

I am not convinced that peanut butter made in a food processor is superior to the top commercial brands, but it will *not* contain artificial additives. If you are going to the trouble of making peanut butter, don't waste time and money with the canned, salted cocktail peanuts, which invariably taste stale. Start with the freshest unblanched raw peanuts you can find, then proceed according to this recipe.

2 cups shelled but unblanched raw peanuts
2 quarts boiling water
2 quarts peanut oil
4 teaspoons butter, at room temperature
¼ teaspoon salt

Blanch the peanuts in the boiling water for 1 minute; drain, then slip off the skins. Spread the peanuts out on several thicknesses of paper toweling and let dry 30 minutes. Heat the oil in a large, heavy skillet over moderately high heat until a nut, dropped into the oil, will sizzle vigorously. Add the peanuts and stir-fry 3 to 4 minutes, just until a light golden tan—the nuts will continue to cook after they are out of the oil. With a slotted spoon, transfer peanuts to several thicknesses of paper toweling and cool to room temperature.

Place half of the nuts in a food processor fitted with the metal chopping blade and let the motor run for 1 minute nonstop. Uncover the work bowl, scrape down the sides of the bowl with a rubber spatula and also scrape nuts up from the bottom of the bowl. Re-cover and churn for 60 seconds longer. Again scrape up nuts from bottom of work bowl—they will by now be turning into a thick paste. Re-cover and buzz 60 seconds longer. Add half of the butter and salt and churn 60 seconds longer; scrape into a jar and set aside. Grind the remaining peanuts into peanut butter precisely the same way and add to the original batch. Do not refrigerate. The peanut butter will keep about ten days (perhaps half that in hot, muggy weather).

Almond Paste

Makes about 1¼ cups

Unlike marzipan, which is blended with egg white and sugar, almond paste is nothing more than blanched almonds ground to paste with enough cold water to make it malleable. Use in recipes calling for commercial almond paste, or use to make Old-Fashioned Macaroons (see Index for recipe page number).

1¼ cups whole, shelled, unblanched almonds
3 cups boiling water
¼ cup cold water

Blanch the almonds in the boiling water for 1 minute; drain and slip off the skins. Do not dry the almonds. Place them immediately in a food processor fitted with the metal chopping blade and grind very fine by letting the motor run nonstop for 60 seconds. Add 1 tablespoon of the cold water and grind for 60 seconds; add a second tablespoon of cold water and grind for 60 seconds longer; finally, add the remaining 2 tablespoons of cold water and grind for 60 seconds, or until smooth and paste-like. Wrap the almond paste snugly in plastic food wrap and refrigerate until ready to use. It will keep well in the refrigerator for about two weeks.

Coconut Cream
Makes about 1 quart

Coconut cream is integral to many recipes—Brazilian, East Indian, Indonesian. It not only lends a subtle flavor, but also serves as a medium in which shrimp, delicate white fish or chicken can be simmered. Canned or bottled coconut cream is available in many Spanish or Latin American groceries. You can also make your own coconut cream easily with the food processor, and in my opinion, it is far superior. Homemade coconut cream keeps well in the refrigerator for a week to ten days. NOTE: *For directions on how to open a fresh coconut and prepare it for the processor, see* **Coconut** *in* A Dictionary of Foods & How to Process Them *(consult Index for page number).*

Meat of ½ medium-size fresh coconut, peeled and cut into 1-inch
chunks.
2 cups milk
2 cups light cream

Place about half of the coconut chunks in a food processor fitted with the metal chopping blade, and with 5 or 6 pulses or short bursts of speed, begin grinding the coconut. If mixture seems dry and machine is laboring, add about ¼ cup of the milk. Let processor run for about a minute more, just until coconut is finely grated. Transfer to a large, heavy saucepan. Grind the remaining coconut the same way and add to saucepan along with the remaining milk and the cream. Set lid on the saucepan askew, and simmer very slowly for 35 to 40 minutes. Place 2 cups of the mixture—no more—in the processor work bowl, still fitted with the metal chopping blade, and buzz 60 seconds nonstop. Empty into a large, fine sieve set over a large, heatproof bowl. Continue puréeing the mixture as before. Put all through the sieve, pressing with a wooden spoon to extract as much liquid as possible. Pour coconut cream into a 1-quart jar and refrigerate until ready to use.

Oven-Dried Shrimp
Makes about 1 cup

Asian and Latin American recipes often call for dried shrimp as well as fresh ones, the dried shrimp being puréed into a sauce in which the fresh shrimp are simmered or served (one such recipe is the magnificent Brazilian *Vatapá* included elsewhere in this book; see Index for recipe page number). Dried shrimp can be bought at most Oriental groceries and at many specialty food shops. If, however, you are unable to obtain them (or if you object to their almost fertilizer-strong smell), you can machine-mince fresh shrimp in your food processor, then dry them in your own oven. I've done it often and find that I prefer the flavor of the shrimp I dry myself to that of the commercially dried shrimp.

You will need 1 pound of raw, shelled and deveined shrimp altogether. Place half of them in the food processor fitted with the metal chopping blade and mince very fine with about 10 seconds of nonstop churning. Transfer to a small bowl and machine-mince the remaining shrimp the same way. They will be almost paste-like. Spread the shrimp out on a *very lightly* oiled baking sheet, set, uncovered, in a very slow oven (275° to 300° F.) and let dry 3½ to 4 hours, stirring now and then. In the beginning, considerable juices will ooze out of the shrimp. Drain them off and save to add to soups, sauces or seafood casseroles. When the shrimp are rosy-pink and crunchy, they are sufficiently dry. Bundle them into a plastic bag and store in the freezer. Or use at once in any recipe calling for dried shrimp.

Duxelles
(Minced Sautéed Mushrooms)

Makes about 1½ cups

No French cook worth her salt would be without a supply of *duxelles*, which can be used to season soups, sauces and stuffings. The recipe below will keep well in the refrigerator for about two weeks—or, better still, freeze it. You can dip into the mixture, removing only what you need for a particular recipe and returning the balance to the freezer.

2 large shallots, peeled
3 tablespoons butter
1 pound fresh mushrooms, wiped clean, stemmed and quartered
(reserve stems)

¼ teaspoon salt
Pinch of freshly ground black pepper

Equip the food processor with the metal chopping blade, snap the motor on, drop the shallots down the feed tube into the spinning blade, then mince fine by letting the motor run for 3 seconds nonstop. Empty shallots into a large, heavy skillet in which you have already melted the butter, set over low heat and allow to sauté while you mince the mushrooms. Pile about one third of the mushrooms into the processor work bowl and, with four or five 1-second churnings of the motor, mince very fine. After about two churnings, stop the motor, uncover the work bowl and scrape down the sides. When mushrooms are finely chopped, empty onto a large, clean, dry dish towel. Chop the remaining mushrooms the same way in two batches (mince the stems, too) and add to towel. Bundle mushrooms up inside of the towel, then, working over a large bowl, squeeze and massage the mushrooms to extract as much liquid as possible (this liquid may be saved and added to soups or stews).

Add mushrooms to the skillet and sauté over moderate heat, stirring often, 10 to 12 minutes until mixture cooks down to a paste. Mix in the salt and pepper, transfer to a storage jar and refrigerate or freeze until ready to use.

Asparagus-Stem Purée
Makes 1½ to 2 cups

In the long run, a food processor will save you considerable money because it enables you to use parings and trimmings that would normally be tossed out. Asparagus stems illustrate the point. Cook them, processor-purée them, then use as a base for asparagus soup or soufflé (see Index for recipe page numbers). The purée, moreover, keeps well for about six months in the freezer.

Stems from 2 pounds of fresh asparagus
2 cups water
2 tablespoons butter, at room temperature

2 teaspoons salt
Pinch of freshly ground black pepper

Trim the truly tough and woody portions from the stems and discard. Scrub remaining stems well and cut into 1-inch lengths. Boil in the water in a covered saucepan for 35 to 40 minutes, or until very tender. Drain well, return pan to heat and shake gently to drive off excess moisture. Add butter, salt and pepper, toss lightly, then dump all into a food processor fitted with the metal chopping blade. Reduce to a fine and silky purée by letting the motor run nonstop for 20 seconds. Stop the motor, scrape down the work bowl, then purée for another 5 to 10 seconds. Pack the purée in a 1- or 1½-pint freezer container, snap on the lid, label and quick-freeze.

Part Two

270 RECIPES DEVELOPED ESPECIALLY FOR THE PROCESSOR

Appetizers & Hors d'Oeuvre

Tarragon-Tomato Granité
Makes 4 to 6 servings

Here's a different sort of first course—a tarragon-spiked blend of tomato juice and beef broth that's been partially frozen, then buzzed up in the processor to snowy fineness. For a showy presentation (and to help keep the *granité* from melting at table before it's eaten), bed each portion in a bowl of crushed ice.

1 envelope plain gelatin
1½ cups vegetable or tomato juice
1½ cups beef broth
1 bay leaf, crumbled
1 teaspoon crumbled leaf tarragon

Sprinkle the gelatin over the vegetable juice and let stand 5 minutes. Pour into a medium-size saucepan, add all remaining ingredients and heat, stirring constantly, over moderate heat about 5 minutes, or until the gelatin dissolves. Turn heat to lowest point and let mixture steep 5 minutes. Pour through a fine sieve, then divide the mixture between two ice-cube trays (not plastic because the frozen cubes will stick to the plastic and be difficult to remove). Freeze 2 to 3 hours or until not quite hard.

Dump 1 tray of cubes into the work bowl of a food processor fitted with the metal chopping blade and, with 3 or 4 pulses or on-offs of the motor, buzz until fluffy. Quickly spoon into a 1-quart plastic container and return to freezer. Buzz up the remaining cubes the same way, add to plastic container and snap on the lid. (You can keep the *granité* this way for about an hour; do not try to hold it longer, however, or it will freeze hard and be difficult to spoon out.) When serving, sprig, if you like, with fresh tarragon or garnish with slim lime wedges.

Oysters Bienville
Makes 6 first-course servings; 4 main-course servings

An incomparable old Gulf Coast recipe that can be served as either a first course or a main dish. There's considerable chopping and mincing involved, but the processor does it all in jig time.

SAUCE:

2 large shallots, peeled, or 6 scallions, trimmed, washed and cut into
    1-inch lengths (use white part only)
8 medium-size mushrooms, wiped clean and stemmed (reserve stems)
3 tablespoons butter
6 medium-size shelled and deveined raw shrimp
3 tablespoons flour
⅓ cup fish stock, bottled clam juice or chicken broth
⅓ cup dry vermouth
½ cup light cream
1 egg yolk, lightly beaten
¼ teaspoon salt
⅛ teaspoon cayenne pepper

OYSTERS:

8 cups rock salt
24 large oysters on the half shell

TOPPING:

2 slices firm-textured white bread, broken into small pieces
2 tablespoons freshly grated Parmesan cheese
½ teaspoon paprika

Prepare the sauce first: In a food processor fitted with the metal chopping blade, mince the shallots moderately fine with the mushroom caps and stems by letting the motor run nonstop for 5 or 6 seconds. Melt the butter in a medium-size, heavy skillet over moderate heat, add the minced shallots and mushrooms and stir-fry 3 to 5 minutes until limp. Set mixture off the heat for the moment. Add the raw shrimp to the processor and mince moderately fine, using three or four 2-second bursts of speed. Add shrimp to skillet and stir-fry 1 to 2 minutes, just until pink. Blend in the flour, then the fish stock, vermouth and cream and heat, stirring constantly, until thickened and smooth— about 3 minutes (do not allow to boil or mixture may curdle). Set off the heat. Whisk a little of the hot mixture into the egg yolk, blend back into skillet and mix in well along with the salt and cayenne pepper. Set aside for the moment.

Now prepare the oysters: Divide the rock salt between two 13x9x2-inch baking pans. Sprinkle the salt lightly with water, then set in a very hot oven (450° F.) and heat, uncovered, for 5 minutes. Remove pans from oven and arrange 12 oysters in each pan, anchoring the shells in the salt so that they will not tilt and spacing the oysters equidistantly.

Now quickly buzz up the topping: Place the bread in a clean, dry work bowl fitted with a clean, dry metal chopping blade and reduce to fine crumbs by using three 5-second buzzings of the motor. Uncover work bowl, add Parmesan and paprika, re-cover and buzz quickly once or twice to blend.

To finish the dish: Spoon the sauce on top of the oysters, dividing the total amount as evenly as possible, then scatter with topping, again dividing the amount evenly. Bake, uncovered, in a very hot oven (450° F.) for 7 to 8 minutes, or until bubbly. Serve at once.

Baked Stuffed Clams with Mushrooms

Makes 4 first-course servings; 2 main-course servings

2 slices firm-textured white bread, broken into small pieces
2 tablespoons melted butter
*½ cup loosely packed parsley sprigs, washed and patted very dry on
    paper toweling*
1 small yellow onion, peeled and quartered
*1 medium-size celery rib, trimmed, washed and cut into 1-inch
    chunks*
¼ cup butter

¼ *pound medium-size mushrooms, wiped clean and stemmed*
  (reserve stems)
2 *tablespoons flour*
½ *teaspoon salt*
⅛ *teaspoon freshly ground black pepper*
12 *large clams on the half shell*
4 *cups rock salt*

In a food processor fitted with the metal chopping blade, buzz the bread to moderately fine crumbs, using two or three 5-second churnings of the motor; empty into a bowl, drizzle the butter in and toss lightly to mix; set aside. Place parsley in processor work bowl and mince quite fine, using two or three 5-second whirrings of the motor; empty onto a piece of wax paper and set aside. Now processor-chop the onion and celery together, using 5 or 6 pulses or on-offs of the motor. Dump into a skillet in which you have already melted the ¼ cup of butter. Quickly machine-mince the mushrooms and their stems, again using about 5 or 6 pulses or quick bursts of speed. Add to skillet and sauté 5 to 8 minutes over moderate heat until onion and celery are pale golden and mushrooms have surrendered their juices. Continue to cook and stir until most of the juices evaporate.

Now scoop the clams from their shells into the processor work bowl (still equipped with the metal chopping blade); also add any juice from the clam shells. Pulse or turn the motor on and off quickly 4 or 5 times, or until clams are moderately coarsely chopped. Leave in the work bowl for the moment.

Blend the flour, salt and pepper into the skillet. Now add the minced parsley and the chopped clams. Heat, stirring briskly, until thickened—about 3 minutes. Butter each clam shell, spoon in the clam mixture, mounding it up, then top each with a scattering of the buttered bread crumbs.

Make a bed of rock salt in a 9x9x2-inch baking pan, sprinkle lightly with water, and anchor the stuffed clams in the salt. Bake, uncovered, in a hot oven (425° F.) for 10 to 12 minutes, or until lightly browned. Serve at once.

VARIATION:

Deviled Clams: Prepare as directed, but to the minced clam mixture add 1 tablespoon Dijon mustard and 2 teaspoons each Worcestershire sauce and chili sauce. Fill and bake the clams as directed.

Brandade de Morue

Makes about 3 cups, enough for 10 to 12 cocktail servings

Few recipes are more tedious to prepare the old-fashioned way than this fluffy salt-cod spread from the south of France. The preliminaries are easy enough—soaking the board-stiff slabs of salt cod, then cooking them to tenderness. But the puréeing—still done in Provence and the Languedoc with a mortar and pestle—is something else again. Imagine the energy (not to mention the hours) needed to pound them to velvet, with no flakes or strands of cod discernible. Here again the food processor performs miracles. NOTE: *The* brandade *can be made well ahead of time, refrigerated, then reheated shortly before serving in the top of a double boiler over simmering water. Fluff the mixture with a fork as it heats and, if necessary to soften it, beat in 1 to 2 tablespoons additional heavy cream.*

1 pound boneless dried salt cod
Cold water
1 large garlic clove, peeled and quartered
Juice of ½ lemon
Finely grated rind of ½ lemon
½ cup plus 3 tablespoons heavy cream, at room temperature
½ cup plus 3 tablespoons olive oil (use a fine and fragrant French oil)
⅛ teaspoon white pepper

Soak the dried salt cod overnight, in the refrigerator, in enough cold water to cover. Next day, drain and rinse the cod, then simmer 15 minutes in enough water to cover, just until the cod flakes easily at the touch of a fork. Drain very dry. Break the cod into smallish chunks and place in the food-processor work bowl fitted with the metal chopping blade. Add the garlic, lemon juice and rind, ½ cup each of the heavy cream and olive oil, and the white pepper. Turn the machine on and purée 30 seconds. With machine still on, remove pusher from feed tube, then add, alternately and 1 tablespoon at a time, the remaining 3 tablespoons of heavy cream and olive oil. When both are incorporated, blend about 10 seconds longer until *brandade* is fluffy—about like mashed potatoes. Serve while warm with thin slices of French bread, which have been brushed with a half-and-half mixture of melted butter and olive oil, then toasted 30 minutes in a slow (300° F.) oven. For one loaf of French bread, you'll need about ¼ cup melted butter and ¼ cup olive oil.

Caponata
(Sicilian Eggplant Appetizer)

Makes about 1 quart

There's nothing very difficult about making *caponata*, but without a food processor to do all of the slicing and mincing, it's a long and boring process. *Caponata* keeps well in the refrigerator for several weeks. Serve at room temperature as a spread for crackers or melba toast.

1 small eggplant, washed, stemmed and cut into chunks about the height and width of the food processor feed tube (do not peel the eggplant)
4 tablespoons olive oil (top quality)
1 large yellow onion, peeled and halved lengthwise
2 large celery ribs, washed, trimmed and cut into 4-inch lengths
1 small sweet red or green pepper, washed, cored, halved lengthwise and seeded
½ cup pitted ripe olives or pimiento-stuffed green olives
5 anchovy fillets, rinsed very well and patted dry on paper toweling
1 can (8 ounces) tomato sauce
2 tablespoons red wine vinegar
1 bay leaf
½ teaspoon crumbled leaf basil
¼ teaspoon crumbled leaf thyme
⅛ teaspoon freshly ground black pepper
1 tablespoon sugar
⅓ cup loosely packed parsley sprigs, patted very dry on paper toweling
3 tablespoons drained small capers

In a food processor fitted with the French-fry cutter (or failing that, the medium-slicing disc), stand a chunk of eggplant with the skin side toward the blade. Turn motor on or depress the Pulse button and push eggplant through by exerting firm pressure on the pusher. Repeat until all eggplant is cut. Heat the olive oil in a large, heavy kettle over moderate heat until quite hot, dump in the eggplant, and allow to sauté while you prepare the remaining ingredients. Reduce heat under kettle slightly and give the eggplant a brisk stir now and then to keep it from burning.

Remove French-fry cutter from food processor (if used) and fit the slicing disc into place. Thin-slice the onion, then the celery and red pepper by pushing each down the feed tube with light pressure. Add all to kettle, stir well, and continue to sauté.

Remove the slicing disc from the food processor and set the metal chopping blade into place. Add the olives and, with 3 pulses or on-offs of the motor, chop moderately coarsely; add to kettle. Now place the anchovy fillets in the work bowl and mince fairly fine by letting the chopping blade run for about 1 second; scrape anchovies from the work bowl into the kettle. Mix in along with the tomato sauce, vinegar, bay leaf, basil, thyme, pepper and sugar. Cover, reduce heat to low, and simmer for 1 hour; uncover and simmer 45 minutes to 1 hour longer, or until juices have cooked down and mixture is quite thick. Remove bay leaf.

Wash and dry the processor work bowl and chopping blade; reassemble. Add the parsley and mince fairly coarsely by pulsing or snapping the motor on and off 5 or 6 times. Stir parsley and capers into the *caponata,* and simmer about 10 minutes longer. Remove from heat and cool to room temperature before serving.

Patlican Salatasi
(Turkish Eggplant Caviar)

Makes 6 to 8 cocktail servings

A "poor man's caviar" popular in Turkey that is served during that seemingly endless parade of hors d'oeuvre called *mezze.* The Turkish way to eat it is as a dip or spread for bite-size wedges of *pita* bread.

2 large eggplants, halved lengthwise but not peeled
4 tablespoons sesame seed oil
½ cup parsley sprigs, washed and patted very dry on paper toweling
2 tablespoons olive oil

Juice of ½ lemon
2 small garlic cloves, peeled and crushed
1 teaspoon salt (or to taste)
¼ teaspoon freshly ground black pepper

Arrange the eggplants cut sides up on a baking sheet; brush each well with sesame oil, then bake in a very hot oven (425° F.) for 45 minutes to 1 hour, or until nicely browned and quite soft. Remove from the oven and cool until easy to handle. Meanwhile, pile parsley sprigs in a food-processor work bowl fitted with the metal chopping blade, and with 1 quick pulse or on-off of the motor, chop very coarsely. Leave in the work bowl. Scoop eggplant flesh into the work bowl; discard skins. Add all remaining ingredients and purée until creamy—2 or 3 bursts of speed is sufficient. Transfer to a small bowl, cover and chill several hours before serving. Bring to room temperature, arrange in a serving bowl, garnish if you like with tomato wedges, black olives and a ruff of parsley, then pass as a cocktail dip.

Hummus

Makes about 1½ cups

This creamy Middle Eastern cocktail dip made of puréed chick peas, *tahini* (sesame seed paste), lemon and plenty of garlic was hell to make before food processors came along. Even a blender couldn't cope with the mass successfully, so everything had to be puréed by hand. Today you can buzz the mixture up in about 3 minutes—start to finish. I've tried this recipe with both canned chick peas and with the dried (soaked overnight, then boiled several hours until mushy), and for once I'm convinced that the results are better when canned chick peas are used (the pressure canning softens the chick peas more than mere cooking ever could). If you're planning a large party and want more *hummus* than the following recipe yields, simply prepare two separate batches of it. Don't try to double the recipe, because the sturdiest food processor can't manage a double load.

2 medium-size garlic cloves, peeled
1 can (1 pound, 14 ounces) chick peas, well drained

1 cup tahini *(sesame seed paste, available in Middle Eastern groceries or specialty food shops)*
Juice of 1 large lemon
⅓ *cup water*
¾ *teaspoon salt (or to taste)*
¼ *teaspoon freshly ground black pepper (or to taste)*

Place all ingredients in food-processor work bowl fitted with the metal chopping blade, then purée for 1½ to 2 minutes until smooth and creamy. Empty *hummus* into a mixing bowl, taste for salt and pepper and add more if needed. Cover and chill several hours before serving. About 30 minutes before serving, set *hummus* out on the counter so that it will soften to spreading consistency. As an accompaniment, serve triangles of *pita* bread.

Tapenade

Makes about 1½ cups

It's incredible how easy this garlicky anchovy and olive mayonnaise is to make in the food processor. Serve as a dip for such crisp raw vegetables as finocchio, zucchini and carrot sticks, flowerets of broccoli and cauliflower.

¼ *cup loosely packed parsley sprigs, washed and patted very dry on paper toweling*
5 *anchovy fillets, rinsed well and patted dry on paper toweling*
6 *pitted ripe olives, preferably the glistening black Greek ones*
1 *large garlic clove, peeled*
2 *tablespoons drained small capers*
Juice of ½ lemon
1 *slice firm-textured white bread, broken into small pieces*
⅛ *teaspoon freshly ground black pepper*
1 *large egg*
1 *cup olive oil (top quality)*

Place parsley, anchovies, olives, garlic, capers, lemon juice, bread and pepper in food processor fitted with the metal chopping blade, then churn for 10 seconds nonstop. Uncover the work bowl, scrape down sides with the plastic spatula, re-cover and buzz for 5 seconds nonstop. Uncover work bowl and scrape down once again, then re-cover and churn for 5 seconds longer, or until mixture is a smooth thick paste. Break the egg into the work bowl and buzz for 3 seconds nonstop. Now, with the motor running, drizzle the olive oil down the feed tube in a very fine stream. Continue beating the *tapenade* for about 30 seconds after all of the oil has been incorporated. Store in the refrigerator, but let stand at room temperature for at least 30 minutes before serving. The *tapenade* will keep well for about 5 days in the refrigerator.

Guacamole
Makes about 2 cups

It took me two or three tries to come up with a good processor *guacamole*, good meaning lumpy rather than soupy. The secret, I find, is adding the avocado at the last minute, spooning it in large chunks directly from the avocado half into the work bowl, then buzzing in quick bursts.

1 small yellow onion, peeled and quartered
Juice of ½ lemon
⅓ cup mayonnaise (see Index for recipe page number)
½ teaspoon crushed dried red chili peppers
½ teaspoon salt
2 small ripe avocados, halved and pitted

In a food processor fitted with the metal chopping blade, place the onion, lemon juice, mayonnaise, chili peppers and salt. Turn the motor on and let run for 10 seconds nonstop—this will mince the onion and blend the ingredients. Now, using a tablespoon, scoop large chunks of avocado into the work bowl, cleaning out each avocado shell as thoroughly as possible. Distribute the chunks of avocado around the chopping blade, then with two or three 1-second bursts of speed, churn just until lumpy—about the texture of a curded cottage cheese. Spoon into a small bowl and serve with corn chips. NOTE: *If you make the* guacamole *more than 30 minutes ahead of time, it will darken into an unattractive khaki color.*

Taramasalata

(Greek Carp-Roe Dip)

Makes about 1 cup

Tarama (coral-colored carp roe) is the foundation of this creamy appetizer. Most Greek and Middle Eastern groceries stock it, but if you are unable to locate it in your community, substitute red caviar.

3 slices firm-textured white bread, trimmed of crusts
⅓ cup cold water
1 very small yellow onion, peeled and quartered
¼ cup tarama or red caviar
Juice of ½ large lemon
⅔ cup olive oil (best quality)

Soak the bread in the water 10 minutes, then squeeze bread dry and set aside. Place onion in the work bowl of a food processor fitted with the metal chopping blade and mince fine, using 5 or 6 pulses or on-offs of the motor. Add the bread, *tarama* and lemon juice, turn the motor on and run nonstop for 5 seconds—just until mixture is uniformly creamy. With the motor running, drizzle the olive oil down the feed tube in a thin stream, then after all of the oil has been incorporated, let the processor run for about 10 seconds longer, or until mixture is thick and smooth. Serve as an appetizer with small crusty chunks of bread.

Terrine of Pork with Cognac and Juniper Berries

Makes one 9x5x3-inch loaf

The processor should open up the whole world of *pâtés* and *terrines* because it simplifies beyond belief what were once tiresome and messy recipes to prepare. How much neater it is to mince raw liver in an enclosed processor work bowl than to push it through a meat grinder— twice. And how much faster it is to "grind" raw pork with the processor. If you plan your sequence of chopping and mincing correctly (as I have in the recipe below), you won't even have to wash the processor work bowl or chopping blade until the finished *terrine* is in the oven.

Since you have been dealing with raw pork, scald all component parts of the processor before running them through the dishwasher.

5 slices firm-textured white bread, broken into small pieces
½ cup loosely packed parsley sprigs, washed and patted very dry on paper toweling
½ cup light cream
½ teaspoon salt
¼ teaspoon freshly ground black pepper
2 tablespoons bacon or ham drippings
1 medium-size yellow onion, peeled and cut into slim wedges
1 large garlic clove, peeled
4 juniper berries (make sure they are nice and fresh, not dried up, which happens when spices stand too long on the cupboard shelf)
½ teaspoon crumbled leaf thyme
Pinch of ground nutmeg
Pinch of ground cloves
1 pound pork or calf's liver, trimmed of veins and sinew and cut into 1-inch chunks (I personally prefer the milder calf's liver.)
1 pound boneless fresh pork loin or shoulder, trimmed of sinew and cut into 1-inch chunks (do not trim away the fat, as it's needed to give the terrine a spreadable consistency)
½ pound boneless smoked ham, cut into 1-inch chunks
2 large eggs
¼ cup cognac
5 large sheets of barding fat (You will need these to line the mold in which you bake the terrine; ask your butcher to cut fresh pork fat—that surrounding the loin is best—and have him slice the sheets about ⅛ inch thick.)

In a food processor fitted with the metal chopping blade, crumb the bread and mince the parsley together by using three 5-second churnings of the motor (the two buzz up nicely together and this saves a separate step in the recipe's preparation). Empty the bread crumbs and parsley into a large mixing bowl and drizzle the cream on top. Add the salt and pepper, fork lightly to mix and let stand at room temperature while you proceed with the recipe.

Melt the bacon drippings in a medium-size skillet over moderate heat. And at the same time, churn the onion, garlic and juniper berries to paste in the processor by using three 5-second churnings of the motor. Scrape this mixture into the skillet, turn heat to low and allow to sauté 10 minutes until limp and golden. Add the thyme, nutmeg and cloves and allow to mellow another 10 minutes on very low heat.

Place half of the liver in the processor (still fitted with the metal chopping blade) and mince quite fine by letting the motor run 5 seconds nonstop; add to crumb mixture in bowl. Mince the remaining liver the same way and add to bowl. Now "grind" the pork, half of the total amount at a time, by letting the processor run 10 seconds nonstop; add to bowl. Chop the ham moderately coarsely by running the processor 8 seconds nonstop. Add to the bowl along with the sautéed onion mixture. Stir well with a wooden spoon. Add the eggs and mix well again, then pour in the cognac and stir well once again until all ingredients are uniformly blended.

Many *terrines* are baked in showy earthernware casseroles (usually rectangular or oval in shape), but I find that a standard 9x5x3-inch ovenproof glass baking dish works well (you can even use a standard bread pan, although technically speaking, a *terrine* should be baked in an earthenware dish of some sort—its name, in fact, derives from the Latin word *terra*, meaning *ground* or *earth*). The easiest way to line the baking dish with barding fat is to cut a paper pattern first—I use typing paper, stand the pan on the paper and trace around the outline of the sides, ends, and bottom. Once the paper patterns are made, it's a simple matter to lay them on top of the barding fat and to cut around them with a sharp knife. Oil the pan lightly, then fit the barding fat into place—first the bottom, then the sides and ends. Now pack the *terrine* mixture in firmly, cover with several thicknesses of foil, then weight the mixture down with a brick or a heavy container that is more or less the size of the *terrine* mold. Some people use cans of food— risky business, I think, because there is the danger of a can's exploding in the oven.

Now set a large, shallow baking pan on the middle oven rack and pour in enough water to half fill the pan. Set the weighted *terrine* in the middle of the water bath and bake in a moderate oven (350° F.) for 2½ hours. Remove from the oven, and from the water bath, lift off the weight and the foil and examine the terrine closely. If it has pulled from the sides of the mold (as it certainly should have by now), you may be sure that it is done—it's the same look that a well-done meat loaf has. If, by some chance, the *terrine* is not done, re-cover, reweight and bake 15 to 30 minutes longer.

When finally the *terrine* is done, remove the weight and the foil and cool to room temperature. Re-cover the pan with foil and chill at least 12 hours before unmolding. To unmold, loosen the *terrine* around the edges with a thin-bladed knife or spatula, lay a small platter on top, then invert. Let the mold stand inverted until the *terrine* drops out of its own accord—this may take as long as an hour, because the barding fat must loosen and soften.

Serve the *terrine* as you would a *pâté*—with cocktails or as a first course, with crisp slices of melba toast.

Danish Liver Pâté
Makes 6 to 8 servings

A moist, marvelously spreadable calf's-liver *pâté* seasoned with parsley, dill, thyme, allspice, ginger and cardamom. It requires only one pound of calf's liver and is stretched to the *n*th by soft, fresh bread crumbs. The processor, of course, accounts for the *pâté's* exquisite texture. Serve as a cocktail spread or as a first course, with dark Danish pumpernickel bread or melba toast.

6 slices firm-textured white bread, torn into small pieces
½ cup loosely packed parsley sprigs, washed and patted very dry on paper toweling
⅓ cup loosely packed dill fronds, washed and patted very dry on paper toweling
¼ pound refrigerator-cold salt pork, cut into 1-inch cubes
1 medium-size Spanish onion, peeled and cut into 1-inch chunks
1 pound sliced calf's liver, trimmed of veins and connective tissue
½ teaspoon crumbled leaf thyme
¼ teaspoon ground allspice
¼ teaspoon ground ginger
¼ teaspoon ground cardamom
¼ teaspoon salt
⅛ teaspoon freshly ground black pepper
¾ cup beef stock or broth
¾ cup heavy cream
2 large eggs, lightly beaten

Place half of the bread with the parsley and the dill in a food processor fitted with the metal chopping blade and buzz until uniformly fine and crumbly, using two or three 5-second churnings of the motor; empty into a large mixing bowl. Crumb the remaining bread the same way and add to bowl. Now mince the salt pork fairly fine by pulsing or snapping the motor on and off 3 or 4 times; place salt pork in a large, heavy skillet, set over moderate heat and allow to sauté while you mince the onion. Place the onion chunks in the processor (still fitted with the metal chopping blade—no need to wash the blade or the work bowl) and mince moderately fine, using 4 or 5 pulses or on-offs of the motor. Set aside for the moment.

Continue to sauté the salt pork 10 to 15 minutes over moderate heat until almost all of the fat has melted and the solids have cooked down to crisp brown bits; scoop these into the bowl with the bread crumbs. Add the minced onions to the salt-pork drippings and stir-fry about 10 minutes until golden and touched with brown. Push onions to one side of skillet, add the liver, raise heat to moderately high and brown the liver quickly on both sides. Reduce heat, add thyme, allspice, ginger, cardamom, salt and pepper and warm 2 to 3 minutes.

Now empty half of the skillet mixture into the processor (again no need to wash the blade or work bowl) and churn for 10 seconds non-stop. Open the work bowl, scrape down the sides, then buzz for 20 seconds nonstop or until smooth and creamy; add to bowl of crumbs. Purée the remaining skillet mixture the same way and add to crumbs. Also add the beef stock, cream and eggs and stir all lightly but thoroughly to mix. Spoon into a well-buttered *pâté* pan measuring 10 inches long, 2¾ inches wide and 3 inches deep (the kind with a re-movable bottom—these are available in specialty kitchen shops) or, if you have no such pan, in a buttered 8½x4½x2½-inch loaf pan. Set pan of *pâté* in a large, shallow baking pan, pour water into baking pan to a depth of about 1½ inches, then bake, uncovered, in a moderately hot oven (375° F.) for 1 hour.

Remove the *pâté* from the oven (and from the water bath) and cool to room temperature. Cover and chill until firm, then carefully loosen *pâté* around the edges and unmold onto a serving platter.

Creamy Chicken-Liver Pâté with Cognac
Makes about 5 cups

1 large yellow onion, peeled and cut into slim wedges
2 tablespoons unsalted butter
1 small garlic clove, peeled and crushed
2 pounds chicken livers, halved at the natural separation and trimmed of connective tissue
⅛ teaspoon ground allspice
⅛ teaspoon ground nutmeg or mace
¼ teaspoon freshly ground black pepper
½ teaspoon salt (or to taste)
½ cup cognac
2 packages (8 ounces each) cream cheese (cut cheese into 1-inch chunks)
¼ cup minced parsley (for an amount this small, I prefer to hand-mince)
2 tablespoons snipped fresh chives

Pile onion wedges in food-processor work bowl fitted with the metal chopping blade; chop coarsely with about 2 pulses or on-off bursts. Sauté in the butter in a very large, heavy skillet (not cast iron) with the garlic over moderate heat about 8 minutes, just until golden but not brown. Add the chicken livers and sauté, stirring often, until just barely pinkish (about 10 minutes). Add allspice, nutmeg, pepper, salt and stir to mix. Pour cognac on top (do not stir), warm 2 to 3 minutes, then blaze with a match and allow flames to subside. Ladle about one third of the chicken-liver mixture into the work bowl fitted with the metal chopping blade, add about one third of the cheese and purée, using 10 to 12 pulses or on-off bursts, or until creamy. Transfer to a large mixing bowl, then repeat the process until all chicken livers and cheese are puréed. Add parsley and chives and beat well with a wooden spoon. Taste for salt and add more, if needed. Cover and chill several hours before serving as a spread for melba toast.

Pork and Mushroom Piroshki

Makes about 3½ dozen

These bite-size Russian meat pies are perfect for a cocktail party when you need something fairly substantial in the way of finger food. Both the *piroshki* pastry and filling can be buzzed up in the processor. The *piroshki* can, in fact, be made a day ahead of time, then baked at the very last minute. This particular recipe utilizes leftover roast pork, but you could easily substitute beef, lamb, chicken or turkey. The filling can also be used to stuff larger meat pies or turnovers, or to make cabbage rolls, and it can be baked inside hollowed-out tomatoes or onions (the onions should be parboiled until crisp-tender before they are hollowed out and stuffed).

THE PASTRY:

1 recipe Pâte Brisée *(see Index for recipe page number)*

THE PORK AND MUSHROOM FILLING:

1 small yellow onion, peeled and cut into slim wedges
3 medium-size mushrooms, wiped clean, stemmed and quartered
   (reserve stems)
4 smallish sprigs of parsley, washed and patted very dry on paper
   toweling
4 small fronds of fresh dill, washed and patted very dry on paper
   toweling or ¼ teaspoon dill weed
2 tablespoons butter
1 tablespoon flour
½ teaspoon salt
Several heft grindings of black pepper
¼ cup cold water
¼ pound cold roast pork, cut into 1-inch chunks
1 small hard-cooked egg, peeled and halved lengthwise

THE EGG GLAZE:

2 egg yolks blended with 2 tablespoons cold water

For the pastry: Prepare the *Pâte Brisée* as the recipe directs, then wrap and chill for 3 hours.

Meanwhile, make the filling: In a food processor fitted with the metal chopping blade, fine-mince the onion together with the mushrooms, parsley and dill, using two 5-second churnings of the motor (scrape the work-bowl sides down after the first 5 seconds). Melt the butter in a medium-size, heavy skillet over moderately low heat, add the onion mixture and allow to sauté for 10 minutes, or until mixture is quite soft. Blend in the flour, salt and pepper to make a thick paste, then pour in the water. Heat, stirring constantly, until thickened and smooth—about 3 minutes. Turn the burner heat to its lowest setting and allow the mixture to mellow while you proceed with the recipe. Place the pork chunks in the processor work bowl (still fitted with the metal chopping blade—no need to wash it or the work bowl) and grind quite fine, using two 5-second churnings of the motor. Add the pork to the skillet; now mince the egg, using 3 pulses or on-offs of the motor, and add to the skillet also. Blend the skillet mixture well, then refrigerate until you are ready to make the *piroshki.*

To shape and fill the piroshki: Divide the *Pâte Brisée* in half and keep one half refrigerated while you roll the other half. Lightly flour a pastry cloth, also a stockinette-covered rolling pin, then roll the pastry into a large, thin circle, working from the center outward and using short, quick strokes—the rolled-out pastry should be a shade thinner than pie crust. Cut into rounds with a 3-inch, floured biscuit cutter and space the rounds about 2 inches apart on ungreased baking sheets. Now, using the ¼ teaspoon of a measuring spoon set, drop a small mound of the filling in the center of each pastry circle. Dampen the edges of each pastry circle lightly (I use a small cotton swab dipped in cold water), then fold the pastries in half, enclosing the filling and forming mini half-moons. Crimp the pastry edges with the tines of a fork, then brush each pastry lightly with the Egg Glaze. Shape and fill the remaining *piroshki* the same way until you have used up all the filling and pastry. The pastry scraps can be rerolled and cut, but they will not be as flaky and tender as the first rolling.

To bake the piroshki: Set a single baking sheet of *piroshki* on the middle rack of a moderately hot oven (375° F.) and bake for 12 to 15 minutes, or until nicely browned. Remove from the oven and serve hot. Bake the remaining *piroshki* the same way. NOTE: *Baked, cooled piroshki can be frozen, then reheated briefly in a moderately slow oven (325° F.) for 8 to 10 minutes, but they should stand at room temperature 20 minutes before they go into the oven, so that they have a chance to thaw slightly.*

Potted Shrimp

Makes about 1¼ cups

The processor, I predict, will reintroduce us to a lot of the old-fashioned recipes that we've considered too fussy to prepare of late—potted shrimp, for example, a perfectly delicious, spicy *pâté*. Serve with homemade melba toast.

> *½ pound shelled and deveined raw shrimp*
> *2 cups boiling water*
> *5 anchovy fillets, rinsed well in cool water and patted dry on paper toweling*
> *Juice of ½ lemon*
> *¼ cup unsalted butter, at room temperature*
> *⅛ teaspoon white pepper*
> *Pinch of cayenne pepper*
> *Pinch of ground cloves*
> *Salt, if needed, to taste (you're not likely to need any salt at all, because of the brininess of the anchovies)*

Cook the shrimp in the boiling water 3 to 4 minutes—just until they turn pink and curl slightly. Drain at once. Place the shrimp in the work bowl of a food processor equipped with the metal chopping blade and mince quite fine by letting the motor run nonstop for 5 seconds. Add all remaining ingredients and purée until silky-smooth by letting the motor run 30 seconds nonstop. Uncover the work bowl, scrape down the sides, then buzz or pulse mixture quickly once or twice. Pack the potted shrimp into a crock or bowl and refrigerate until ready to serve. This will keep well for about a week in the refrigerator.

Curried Egg Spread

Makes about 2 cups

> *1 medium-size yellow onion, peeled and cut into slim wedges*
> *⅓ cup melted butter*
> *1 tablespoon curry powder*
> *5 hard-cooked eggs, peeled and halved lengthwise*

1 tablespoon minced fresh dill
1 tablespoon minced fresh parsley
2 teaspoons Dijon mustard
1 tablespoon tarragon vinegar
½ teaspoon salt
Several hefty grindings of black pepper

In a food processor fitted with the metal chopping blade, mince the onion fine by pulsing or snapping the motor on and off about 6 times. Place 2 tablespoons of the butter in a small skillet, add the onion, set over moderate heat and stir-fry 5 to 6 minutes until onion is limp and golden. Blend in the curry powder and let mellow over low heat about 2 minutes, or until no raw curry flavor remains. Place half of the eggs in the processor, still fitted with the chopping blade, and mince quite fine, using 4 or 5 quick pulses or on-offs of the motor. Empty into a mixing bowl. Chop the remaining eggs the same way and add to bowl. Add the curry-onion mixture, the remaining melted butter and all remaining ingredients. Beat briskly with a fork to blend. Cover and refrigerate until about 20 minutes before serving as a spread for pumpernickel, crackers or melba toast.

Chèvre au Poivre
Goat Cheese with Pepper

Makes one 6x3x1-inch loaf

Here's a nippy cheese spread that couldn't be easier to make. Spread on French, Italian or sourdough bread or, if you prefer, upon crisp, unsalted crackers.

6 ounces ripe chèvre *(goat cheese), cut into slim pats*
8 ounces cream cheese, cut into slim pats
1 tablespoon coarsely ground black pepper
⅛ to ¼ teaspoon cayenne pepper (depending upon how "hot" you
  like things)

Place all ingredients in the work bowl of a food processor fitted with the metal chopping blade, then cream by churning 20 seconds nonstop. Scrape the sides of the work bowl down and churn another 20 seconds nonstop. Scrape the mixture onto a piece of aluminum foil and chill until firm enough to shape (about 45 minutes in the freezer and 2 to 3 hours in the refrigerator). Shape into a small loaf about 6 inches long, 3 inches wide and 1 inch high, wrap in foil and let season at least 24 hours before serving. Unwrap the *Chèvre au Poivre,* center on a small plate, then let stand at room temperature 30 minutes so that it reaches a good spreading consistency and its flavors heighten.

Homemade "Boursin" Cheese
Makes about 1 cup

1 medium-size clove garlic, peeled
3 tablespoons unsalted butter, at room temperature
½ teaspoon crumbled leaf marjoram
⅛ teaspoon crumbled leaf thyme
1 teaspoon coarsely ground black pepper
⅛ teaspoon cayenne pepper
2 packages (8 ounces each) cream cheese, cut into slim pats

Equip the processor with the metal chopping blade, snap the motor on, then drop the garlic down the feed tube into the spinning blade; buzz 2 seconds nonstop, scrape down the sides of the work bowl, buzz 2 seconds longer. Add the butter, marjoram, thyme, black pepper and cayenne to the work bowl. Buzz 5 seconds nonstop; scrape down the work bowl sides and buzz 5 seconds more. Now add the pats of cream cheese, buzz 10 seconds nonstop, scrape the work bowl sides down, buzz 10 seconds more, then scrape once again and buzz 10 seconds longer.

Scoop the cheese mixture into a small bowl and chill until firm enough to shape (about 30 minutes in the freezer, 1 hour in the refrigerator). Shape into a small round loaf or pone, then wrap in foil and allow to season overnight in the refrigerator. Unwrap the cheese, arrange it on a small plate, then let stand at room temperature 30 minutes. Serve with crisp crackers as a cocktail spread.

Liptauer Cheese

Makes about 1½ cups

With a food processor, this sharp Hungarian cheese spread is virtually a one-minute production. Serve with dark pumpernickel.

1 small scallion, washed, trimmed and cut into 1-inch lengths (use
    white part only)
2 tablespoons snipped chives
1 tablespoon drained capers
1 tablespoon paprika (preferably the Hungarian sweet rose paprika)
1 teaspoon caraway seeds
1 teaspoon dry mustard
¼ teaspoon salt
Several hefty grindings of black pepper
1 package (8 ounces) cream cheese, at room temperature
⅓ cup unsalted butter, at room temperature

In a food processor fitted with the metal chopping blade, place the scallion, chives, capers, paprika, caraway seeds, mustard, salt and pepper. Turn motor on and let run nonstop for 15 seconds, or until ingredients are reduced to a thick paste. Add the cream cheese and butter and let the motor run nonstop for 20 seconds. Uncover work bowl, scrape down the sides, re-cover and churn the creamed mixture for 15 to 20 seconds longer, until uniformly smooth.

Fresh Sage and Cheddar Spread

Makes about 2 cups

You must use fresh sage in making this fragrant spread, not the dried, which lacks the proper delicacy.

1 large shallot, peeled
12 young and tender sage leaves, rinsed and patted very dry on
    paper toweling
1 tablespoon unsalted butter, at room temperature
1 tablespoon Dijon mustard

½ pound sharp Cheddar cheese, cut into columns the height and
  width of the processor feed tube
¼ cup dry white wine
¼ teaspoon cayenne pepper
1 package (8 ounces) cream cheese, cut into slim pats

Equip the processor with the metal chopping blade, snap the motor on, then drop the shallot down the feed tube into the spinning blade; buzz 2 seconds nonstop. Add the sage leaves and buzz 5 seconds nonstop. Scrape the work bowl down, add the butter and mustard and buzz 10 seconds nonstop. Remove the chopping blade and set aside; equip the processor with the medium-shredding disc, then shred the Cheddar cheese directly into the mustard mixture by pushing down the feed tube with moderate pressure. Remove the shredding disc, set the metal chopping blade back into place. Add the white wine and cayenne and buzz nonstop 10 seconds; scrape the work bowl down and buzz 10 seconds longer. Add the cream cheese, buzz 20 seconds nonstop, scrape the work bowl down and buzz 20 seconds longer until creamy.

Scoop into a bowl, cover and season several hours in the refrigerator. Let stand at room temperature 30 minutes, then serve as a cocktail spread with crisp crackers or slices of French bread.

Malty Cheddar Spread
Makes about 3 cups

When Cheddar or other semi-hard cheese is to be creamed in a food processor, it is imperative that the cheese be at room temperature, also that it be cut into small cubes—I have found ½-inch cubes a workable size. Otherwise, the cheese will not cream up to silky smoothness and there is also the risk of stalling the machine. This particular spread is a nippy one, an excellent choice for cocktails. It's best spread on crackers or on crisp buttery rounds of melba toast.

1 small yellow onion, peeled and cut into slim wedges
1 small garlic clove, peeled
2 tablespoons Dijon mustard
2 tablespoons tomato catsup

1 tablespoon prepared horseradish
3 ounces cream cheese, at room temperature
¾ pound sharp, well-aged Cheddar, cut into ½-inch cubes and at
room temperature
½ cup flat beer

In a food processor fitted with the metal chopping blade, place the onion, garlic, mustard, catsup, horseradish, cream cheese, one third of the Cheddar and one half of the beer. Turn motor on and let run 30 seconds nonstop; stop the motor, scrape down the sides of the processor bowl and lid, re-cover and run 10 seconds longer. Add the remaining beer with another one third of the cheese and buzz for 60 seconds nonstop. Add the remaining cheese, again scrape down sides of bowl and lid, then whir for 60 seconds longer. Inspect the texture of the mixture and if it is not creamy-smooth, buzz for another 30 seconds or so. Empty into a bowl, cover and let ripen in the refrigerator for several hours. Let stand at room temperature 30 minutes before serving, or until of a good spreading consistency.

Pimiento Cheese Spread
Makes about 3 cups

¾ cup sharp, well-aged Cheddar cheese, cut into ½-inch cubes and
at room temperature
¾ cup mayonnaise (see Index for recipe page number)
1 tablespoon pimiento liquid (drained from jar of pimientos)
6 whole canned pimientos, drained well

Place one half of the Cheddar with the mayonnaise and the pimiento liquid in a food processor fitted with the metal chopping blade. Buzz for 1 minute nonstop. Add the remaining cheese with 4 of the pimientos, which have been cut into 1-inch squares, and churn for 1 minute more. If not creamy-smooth, buzz for an additional 30 seconds or so. Empty mixture into a bowl. Hand-mince the remaining 2 pimientos and stir into the cheese. (These are for color—the machine does such a good job of puréeing that unless you hold back 2 of the pimientos to hand-mince, there will be no flecks of red discernible in the cheese spread at all.)

Deviled Ham Spread

Makes about 1½ cups

Good in sandwiches or as a cocktail spread. And you can make it in less than 2 minutes.

> *1 small yellow onion, peeled and quartered*
> *½ pound cooked smoked ham, cut into 1-inch cubes*
> *2 tablespoons Dijon mustard*
> *3 tablespoons mayonnaise (see Index for recipe page number)*
> *2 tablespoons milk or light cream*
> *¼ teaspoon cayenne pepper*

Place all ingredients in a food processor fitted with the metal chopping blade, turn the motor on and let run for 15 seconds nonstop. Uncover the work bowl, scrape the sides of the bowl down with a rubber spatula, re-cover and buzz for 15 seconds longer or until uniformly smooth and creamy. Scoop into a small bowl, cover and refrigerate until ready to use.

Parslied Ham-Salad Sandwich Spread

Makes about 4 cups

> *1 cup loosely packed parsley springs, washed and patted very dry on*
>   *paper toweling*
> *2 medium-size celery ribs, trimmed, washed and cut into 1-inch*
>   *chunks*
> *1 medium-size yellow onion, peeled and cut into slim wedges*
> *1 pound cooked smoked ham, cut into 1-inch cubes*
> *½ cup mayonnaise (see Index for recipe page number)*
> *¼ cup India relish*
> *2 tablespoons light cream*
> *Pinch of freshly ground black pepper*
> *Salt, if needed (this will depend upon the saltiness of the ham)*

In the work bowl of a food processor fitted with the metal chopping blade, mince the parsley very fine, using about three 5-second churnings of the motor. Empty into a mixing bowl. Mince the celery fine by letting the motor run for 5 seconds; add to bowl. Now mince the onion fine with 5 or 6 pulses or on-offs of the motor. Add to bowl. Place half of the ham in the processor and chop moderately fine by letting the motor run nonstop for about 8 seconds. Add to bowl. Chop the remaining ham the same way and add to bowl along with all remaining ingredients. Mix thoroughly, cover and let flavors blend together in the refrigerator 2 to 3 hours before serving.

Curried Chutney Dip
Makes about 2 cups

The next time you serve *crudités* (crisp raw cauliflowerets, carrots, zucchini, celery and *finocchio* sticks, radishes) as an appetizer, put out a bowl of this nippy sweet-sour dip to accompany. You can buzz it up in a food processor in less than a minute.

1 medium-size yellow onion, peeled and cut into slim wedges
1 medium-size garlic clove, peeled
2 tablespoons butter
1 tablespoon curry powder
8 ounces cream cheese, cut into 1-inch cubes
⅓ cup chutney
2 tablespoons light cream
¼ teaspoon salt
Several generous grindings of black pepper

Finely mince the onion and the garlic in a food processor fitted with the metal chopping blade, using 5 or 6 pulses or on-offs of the motor. Scrape mixture into a small skillet in which you have already melted the butter and sauté over moderate heat about 5 minutes, until limp and golden. Blend in the curry powder and mellow 2 to 3 minutes over moderate heat. Scrape skillet mixture into the processor work bowl, still equipped with the metal chopping blade, add remaining ingredients and cream until smooth by letting the motor run nonstop for 15 seconds. Serve straightaway or refrigerate until about 30 minutes before serving time.

Soups

Cream of Almond Soup
Makes 6 servings

1 cup whole blanched almonds
4 large leeks, trimmed, washed well and cut into 4-inch lengths
2 medium-size celery ribs, trimmed, washed and cut into 4-inch lengths
3 tablespoons butter
4 cups chicken broth
½ teaspoon salt (or to taste)
⅛ teaspoon white pepper
¼ teaspoon ground mace
2 cups light cream
¼ cup freshly snipped chives or minced parsley

In a food processor fitted with the metal chopping blade, buzz the almonds to fine crumbs—this will take about 15 seconds with the motor running nonstop. Inspect the texture of the almonds at this point and, if they are not uniformly fine, buzz for another 5 seconds. Empty onto a piece of wax paper and set aside. Remove the chopping blade from the processor and slip the slicing disc into place. Thin-slice the leeks, then the celery ribs, by pushing through the feed tube with light pressure. Empty into a large, heavy saucepan in which you have already melted the butter, then sauté about 5 minutes over moderate heat, just until leeks and celery are golden. Add the ground almonds, chicken broth, salt, pepper and mace, then cover and simmer 40 to 45 minutes, stirring now and then. Remove from the heat and let the saucepan stand, covered, at room temperature for 1 hour.

Set a large fine sieve over a large bowl and pour in the soup mixture. Remove the slicing disc from the food processor and slip the metal chopping blade back into place (no need to wash it or the work bowl). Dump in the strained-out soup solids with ⅔ cup of the soup and purée the mixture by buzzing for about 10 seconds nonstop. Stop the machine and examine the purée. It should be absolutely smooth. If not, buzz for another 5 seconds or so. Return the purée to the saucepan, along with the strained soup, then stir in the cream and bring just to serving temperature, stirring now and again. This will take about 5 minutes. Taste for salt and add more, if needed. Ladle into soup bowls and top each serving with a sprinkling of fresh chives or parsley. Or, if you prefer, chill the soup and serve icy cold, topped with chives or parsley.

Potage aux Asperges

(Asparagus Soup)

Makes 4 to 6 servings

If you have saved and puréed tough, trimmed-off asparagus stems (as suggested in the collection of basic recipes in Part One), here's a good way to utilize the purée.

4 large leeks, trimmed, washed carefully and cut into 4-inch lengths
3 tablespoons butter
2 cups chicken stock or broth
1 recipe Asparagus-Stem Purée, thawed (see Index for recipe page number)
2 cups light cream
3 egg yolks, lightly beaten
Salt and white pepper to season

Thin-slice the leeks in a food processor fitted with the slicing disc by pushing them gently down the feed tube. Melt the butter in a large, heavy saucepan over moderately low heat, add the leeks and sauté slowly for 10 minutes until very soft and golden but not brown. Add chicken stock and asparagus purée and heat, stirring now and then, about 5 minutes—do not allow to boil. Combine the cream and the egg yolks, ladle in a little of the hot soup, then stir back into pan and turn burner heat to lowest point. Cook slowly, stirring constantly, for about 2 minutes, or until slightly thickened. Remove from heat and season to taste with salt and white pepper. Serve hot, or chill well and serve cold.

Curried Avocado Soup

Makes 4 to 6 servings

Equally good hot or cold.

1 medium-size yellow onion, peeled and cut into slim wedges
1 medium-size garlic clove, peeled and crushed
3 tablespoons butter
1 large celery rib, washed, trimmed and cut into 1-inch chunks
1 tablespoon curry powder
2 tablespoons flour
2 cups chicken stock or broth
1 large, very ripe avocado, halved and pitted
Juice of ½ lemon
2 cups light cream
1 teaspoon salt (or to taste)
Pinch of white pepper
Pinch of ground mace or nutmeg

In a food processor fitted with the metal chopping blade, chop the onion fine, using 5 or 6 pulses or on-offs of the motor. Add to a large, heavy saucepan in which you have already placed the garlic and butter. Finely mince the celery, using 5 or 6 pulses or on-offs of the processor motor, and add to pan. Set over moderate heat and sauté, stirring now and then, 5 to 8 minutes until limp and golden. Blend in curry powder and flour and let mellow 2 to 3 minutes over moderate heat. Add chicken broth and heat, stirring constantly, 3 to 5 minutes until slightly thickened and smooth. Turn heat to lowest point and let mixture mellow while you purée the avocado.

With a tablespoon, scoop chunks of avocado into the processor work bowl, still fitted with the metal chopping blade; clean out each avocado half as well as possible. Distribute the avocado chunks around the processor blades, then sprinkle with lemon juice. Turn the motor on and let it run nonstop for 8 to 10 seconds. Examine the texture of the purée and, if it is not absolutely creamy-smooth, give the motor two or three 1-second churnings. Blend the purée into the soup along with the cream, salt, pepper and mace. Heat and stir 3 to 5 minutes longer— just until soup reaches serving temperature. Taste for salt and add more, if needed, then ladle into soup bowls and serve. Or, if you prefer, chill well and serve cold.

Belgian Endive Velouté

Makes 6 servings

6 large Belgian endives, washed
2 large leeks, trimmed, washed very well and cut into 4-inch lengths
3 tablespoons butter
3 cups chicken stock or broth
Pinch of ground mace
1½ cups heavy cream
3 egg yolks, lightly beaten
Salt and white pepper to season

In the feed tube of a food processor fitted with the slicing disc, stand a stalk of endive. It may protrude above the top of the feed tube, but no matter. Once you turn the motor on, it will inch down through the tube. Thin-slice all the endive in the processor, then the leeks. Add to a large, heavy saucepan in which you have already melted the butter, set over moderately low heat and sauté about 10 minutes, or until endive is limp and golden. Add the chicken stock and mace, then cover and simmer 10 to 15 minutes until the endive is very tender.

Set a large, fine sieve over a large, heatproof bowl and pour in the soup. Remove the slicing disc from the food processor and slip the metal chopping blade into place (no need to wash the work bowl). Dump the strained-out soup solids into the work bowl and purée until silky by letting the motor run nonstop for 10 to 12 seconds. Empty the purée into the saucepan, add the strained liquid and set over low heat. Whisk the heavy cream and egg yolks together, then ladle in about 1 cup of the hot soup and mix well. Stir back into the saucepan and cook, stirring constantly, over low heat, about 5 minutes, or until slightly thickened. Do not allow to boil. Season to taste with salt and pepper and serve.

Cream of Broccoli Soup

Makes 6 servings

*1 large bunch of broccoli, trimmed, washed and cut into small
    flowerets (include some of the more tender stalks, cutting them*

into ½-inch cubes, and some of the younger leaves to lend
pungency to the soup)
2 large garlic cloves, peeled and quartered
2 tablespoons butter
1 tablespoon olive oil
3 cups beef stock or broth
1½ cups light cream
3 egg yolks, lightly beaten
Salt and white pepper to taste

Stir-fry the broccoli and garlic in the butter and olive oil in a large heavy kettle over moderate heat about 10 to 12 minutes, just until the broccoli is golden and slightly limp. Add the beef stock, cover and cook about 20 minutes until broccoli is very tender.

Set a large, fine sieve over a large, heatproof bowl and pour in the soup. Dump the broccoli and garlic into the work bowl of a food processor fitted with the metal chopping blade. Purée until fine and smooth—about 15 seconds with the motor running nonstop. If the mixture is not uniformly silky after this period of puréeing, buzz about 5 seconds longer. Empty the purée into the kettle and stir in the strained soup. Whisk the cream and egg yolks together until well blended, ladle in about 1 cup of the hot soup, then stir into kettle. Cook and stir over lowest heat about 5 minutes, or until slightly thickened. Do not allow mixture to boil. Season to taste with salt and pepper and serve.

Potage Crécy
(Cream of Carrot Soup)

Makes 6 servings

6 medium-size carrots, peeled, trimmed and cut into 4-inch lengths
3 tablespoons butter
2 medium-size leeks, trimmed, washed very well and cut into 4-inch
    lengths
3 cups chicken broth
1½ cups heavy cream
3 egg yolks, lightly beaten
Salt and white pepper to taste

¼ cup very finely shredded carrot, minced parsley or snipped chives
(for garnish)

In a food processor fitted with the slicing disc, thin-slice the carrots by pushing them down the feed tube with almost no pressure. Empty into a large, heavy saucepan in which you have already melted the butter. Thin-slice the leeks the same way and add to the pan. Set over moderately low heat and stir-fry about 10 minutes, or until limp and golden. Add the chicken broth, cover and simmer about 30 minutes, or until carrots are mushy-tender. Set a large, fine sieve over a heatproof bowl and pour in the soup.

Remove the slicing disc from the food processor and slip the metal chopping blade into place (no need to wash the work bowl). Put in the strained-out solids and purée by letting the motor run nonstop for about 10 seconds. Examine the texture of the purée; it should be silky-smooth. If it is not, buzz for another 5 seconds. Empty the purée into the saucepan and add the strained soup. Whisk the cream and egg yolks together in a mixing bowl, ladle in about 1 cup of the hot soup and mix briskly; stir into saucepan. Set over low heat and heat and stir about 3 minutes, just until thickened. Do not allow to boil, or mixture may curdle. Season to taste with salt and pepper. Ladle into soup bowls and scatter shredded carrots, minced parsley or snipped chives over each portion.

Cream of Cauliflower Soup
Makes 6 servings

Silky-smooth and subtly flavored, this soup is equally good hot or cold.

1 medium-size cauliflower, trimmed and divided into flowerets
1 quart lightly salted water
1 tablespoon butter
2 cups chicken stock or broth
1 cup light cream
1 cup milk
Pinch of ground mace
Several grindings of black pepper

Salt to taste
¼ cup freshly snipped chives

Cook the cauliflower in the salted water in a covered saucepan about 25 minutes, or until very tender. Drain well. Put half the cauliflower and half the butter into a food processor fitted with the metal chopping blade, and purée until smooth by letting the motor run nonstop for about 10 seconds; spoon purée into the saucepan in which you cooked the cauliflower. Purée the rest of the cauliflower and the butter in the same way and add to saucepan. Mix in all remaining ingredients, set over moderate heat and warm about 3 to 5 minutes, stirring now and then. Serve hot or chill well and serve cold.

Curried Cream of Celery Soup
Makes 6 servings

6 large celery ribs, trimmed, washed and cut into 4-inch lengths
2 medium-size yellow onions, peeled and halved lengthwise
2 tablespoons butter
2 tablespoons curry powder
1 quart good strong beef stock or broth
2 cups light cream
Salt and freshly ground black pepper to taste

In the feed tube of a food processor fitted with the slicing disc, stand as many pieces of celery as needed for a fairly snug fit; turn motor on or depress the Pulse button and thin-slice the celery, using gentle pressure with the pusher. Repeat until all celery is sliced, then thin-slice the onions the same way. Put celery and onions into a large, heavy saucepan in which you have already melted the butter, set over moderate heat and sauté about 10 minutes until celery and onions are golden and lightly browned. Stir in the curry powder until smoothly incorporated and let mellow 2 to 3 minutes over moderate heat. Pour in the beef stock, cover and simmer 30 to 40 minutes, or until celery is very tender.

Set a large, fine sieve over a large, heatproof bowl and pour in saucepan's contents. Remove slicing disc from food processor and slip the metal chopping blade into place. Dump the strained-out celery and onions into the food processor, then add ½ cup of the beef stock. Purée by letting processor motor run nonstop for about 5 seconds. When mixture is uniformly smooth, pour back into saucepan. Add the strained beef stock and the light cream. Bring slowly to serving temperature, stirring occasionally. Taste for salt and pepper and add to suit your taste. Serve hot or chill well and serve cold.

Potage aux Marrons

(Chestnut Soup)

Makes 6 to 8 servings

For making this soup I use the dried Italian chestnuts, which have already been shelled and blanched. To reconstitute them, simply bring to a boil, then cover, set off the heat and let stand in the water for about 4 hours. Once reconstituted, the dried chestnuts can be substituted for the fresh in almost any recipe and are as easy to deal with as dried peas or beans. The best places to find dried Italian chestnuts are Italian, Middle Eastern or specialty groceries. Lest the supply run short, I lay in a big stock of them (5 pounds or more) and store them in half-gallon preserving jars where ants and weevils can't get at them.

> 2 cups dried, shelled and blanched chestnuts, washed and sorted
> 4 cups cold water
> 2 medium-size yellow onions, peeled and cut into slim wedges
> 2 medium-size celery ribs, trimmed, washed and cut into 1-inch chunks
> ¼ cup butter
> 4 cups chicken broth
> 2 cups light cream
> Salt and pepper to taste

Bring the chestnuts and water to a boil in a large, heavy saucepan, remove from heat, cover and let stand at room temperature for 4 hours. Drain the chestnuts in a colander, then pick over carefully to remove the inevitable bits of clinging skin. If you've ever tried to skin *fresh* chestnuts, you know how tenaciously the skin sticks to the nut, especially about the furrows. This is easier, though, and it helps to break the chestnuts in half with your hands, then to remove the skin from the crevices—usually it slips right out.

In a food processor fitted with the metal chopping blade, fine-mince the onions and celery together, using 5 or 6 pulses or on-offs of the motor. Melt the butter in the saucepan in which you soaked the chestnuts (no need to wash it), add the minced onions and celery and sauté over moderate heat about 10 minutes until limp and golden—do not allow to brown. Add the chestnuts and chicken broth, cover and simmer about 1 hour, or until chestnuts are very soft.

While chestnuts cook, wash and dry processor work bowl and chopping blade and reassemble. When chestnuts are very soft, purée about one fourth of the saucepan contents at a time in the processor by letting the motor run nonstop for 25 seconds, or until mixture is silky-smooth. As each batch is puréed, pour into a second large heavy saucepan. Then blend in the cream, taste and add salt and white pepper as needed. Set the soup over low heat and bring just to serving temperature or, if you prefer, chill well and serve cold, topped by snippets of fresh chives. Make the portions small; this soup is uncommonly rich.

Sopa de Palmito
(Creamed Hearts-of-Palm Soup)

Makes 6 servings

Hearts of palm are the tender young shoots of the palmetto tree, stripped of their coarse outer layers. The palmetto grows throughout much of the southern United States (South Carolina is, in fact, known as "The Palmetto State"), but oddly, most of the canned hearts of palm available in specialty groceries and supermarkets come from Brazil. The following soup is a great favorite not only among Brazilians but also among visitors to Brazil. Its flavor is both subtle and tart, and the soup is equally delicious hot or cold.

2 cans (14 ounces each) hearts of palm
2 tablespoons butter
1 teaspoon finely grated yellow onion
Pinch of ground mace
¾ cup hearts-of-palm liquid (drained from cans) plus enough
*   chicken broth to total 1 quart*

1 teaspoon lemon juice
1 cup heavy cream
3 egg yolks, lightly beaten
Salt and white pepper to taste

Drain the hearts of palm, reserving ¾ cup liquid. Equip the food processor with the slicing disc (the thin-slicing disc if you have one), then stand as many hearts of palm in the feed tube as will fit; slice thin. Continue until all hearts of palm are sliced. Save out about ½ cup of the sliced hearts of palm to garnish each portion of soup. Sauté the rest in the butter with the onion and mace in a large saucepan over moderate heat for about 5 minutes. Add the combined hearts-of-palm liquid and chicken broth and simmer, uncovered, for 20 minutes.

Set a large, fine sieve over a large, heatproof mixing bowl and pour in the saucepan mixture. Remove the slicing disc from the food processor and slip the metal chopping blade into place. Dump the contents of the strainer into the processor work bowl and also add 1 cup of the broth mixture. Buzz about 30 seconds nonstop until uniformly smooth. Scrape the purée into the saucepan, mix in the reserved liquid and the lemon juice.

Combine the cream and beaten yolks, beating briskly with a fork, then whisk a little of the hot soup into the yolk mixture; stir back into saucepan. Set over lowest heat and cook and stir 3 to 5 minutes, just until slightly thickened. Do not allow to boil, lest the soup curdle. Serve hot, or if you prefer, chill well and serve cold, topping each portion with a scattering of the reserved hearts-of-palm slices. The soup may thicken somewhat on chilling, so thin if necessary with a little additional chicken broth.

Puréed Lentil Soup

Makes 6 servings

2 bacon strips, snipped crosswise in julienne strips
2 medium-size yellow onions, peeled and cut into slim wedges
2 medium-size carrots, peeled and cut into 1-inch chunks
6 cups water
1 cup lentils, washed and sorted
2 large parsley sprigs

1 bay leaf
½ teaspoon crumbled leaf thyme
1 teaspoon salt (or to taste)
Several hefty grindings of black pepper

Sauté bacon in a large, heavy kettle over moderately high heat until crisp and brown; reduce heat to moderate. In a food processor fitted with the metal chopping blade, coarsely chop the onions, using about 4 pulses or on-offs of the motor. Empty into kettle with bacon. Add carrots to processor and chop moderately coarsely by letting the chopping blade run nonstop for 10 to 12 seconds; empty into kettle. Stir-fry onions and carrots about 10 minutes over moderate heat until limp and golden. Add all remaining ingredients, cover and simmer about 1 hour and 15 minutes, or until lentils are very soft. Remove parsley sprigs and bay leaf and discard.

Dump the kettle contents into a large, fine sieve set over a large, heatproof bowl. Purée the strained-out solids, about one third of them at a time with ½ cup of the strained soup liquid, until smooth—3 or 4 fast pulses or on-offs of the metal chopping blade will be sufficient. Return purée to soup kettle along with the strained liquid, taste for salt and add more if needed, then bring to serving temperature and ladle into soup bowls.

Cream of Fresh Mushroom Soup

Makes 6 servings

1 pound medium-size fresh mushrooms, wiped clean and stemmed
   (reserve stems)
4 tablespoons butter
1 large yellow onion, peeled and cut into slim wedges
3 cups beef stock or broth
¼ teaspoon crumbled leaf thyme
Pinch of ground nutmeg or mace
1 cup light cream
½ cup heavy cream
3 egg yolks, lightly beaten
Salt and freshly ground black pepper to taste

In the feed tube of a food processor equipped with the slicing disc, stand as many mushroom caps on their sides as will fit fairly snugly. Thin-slice the mushrooms by pushing them through the feed tube with almost no pressure. Repeat until all mushrooms are sliced. Empty into a large, heavy saucepan in which you have already melted the butter. Remove the slicing disc from the processor and slip the metal chopping blade into place. Dump in the mushroom stems and, with 3 or 4 fast pulses or bursts of speed, chop fairly coarsely. Add to saucepan. Now chop the onion the same way and add to pan. Set over moderate heat and sauté for 10 to 12 minutes, until mushrooms are golden and their juices have cooked down. Add beef stock, thyme and mace, cover and simmer 10 to 15 minutes until mushrooms are very tender.

Set a large, fine sieve over a heatproof bowl and pour in the soup. Dump the strained-out solids into the processor work bowl (still fitted with the chopping blade) and purée by letting the motor run nonstop for about 10 seconds. Check the consistency of the purée, and if it is not velvety smooth, buzz for about 5 seconds longer.

Empty the purée into the saucepan and add the strained soup. Combine the light and heavy creams with the egg yolks in a small bowl, whisking briskly. Ladle about 1 cup of the hot soup into the cream mixture, stir vigorously, then mix into soup. Set over low heat and cook, stirring constantly, just until mixture thickens slightly—4 to 5 minutes. Do not allow the soup to boil, or it may curdle. Add salt and pepper to season, then ladle into soup bowls and serve.

Green Pea Soup with Mint

Makes 6 servings

1 medium-size yellow onion, peeled and cut into slim wedges
¼ cup loosely packed tender young mint leaves, washed and patted
*   dry on paper toweling*
4 or 5 fresh rosemary leaves, washed and patted dry on paper
*   toweling or ¼ teaspoon crumbled leaf rosemary*
2 tablespoons butter
3 packages (10 ounces each) frozen green peas
2 cups light cream
1 cup milk

1 teaspoon salt (or to taste)
⅛ teaspoon white pepper

Finely mince the onion, mint and rosemary together in a food processor fitted with the metal chopping blade—5 or 6 fast pulses or bursts of speed should do the job. Empty the mixture into a very large, heavy saucepan in which you have already melted the butter, set over moderate heat and sauté about 5 minutes, just until onion is golden but not brown. Add the peas, cover and cook about 30 minutes, or until peas are very tender. From time to time, uncover the pan and break up frozen clumps of peas. Also watch them to see that they are not boiling dry; if so, add a bit of water, though this usually is not necessary because water accumulates as the peas thaw.

When peas are done, dump saucepan contents into the processor, still fitted with the chopping blade, turn motor on and let run 5 seconds. Examine the peas and if they seem dry, add about ¼ cup of the light cream. Continue to purée until uniformly smooth. Pour the pea purée back into the saucepan, add remaining ingredients, set, uncovered, over low heat and bring just to serving temperature, stirring now and then. This will take 3 to 4 minutes. Taste for salt and add more, if needed. Serve hot or chill well and serve cold.

Potage Parmentier
(Cream of Potato and Leek Soup)

Makes 4 to 6 servings

The best potatoes, I find, for making creamed soups are the so-called Idahos or baking potatoes (Russet Burbanks, to give them their proper name). The flavor is superior, and because they lack the glutinous quality of new or all-purpose potatoes, they can be puréed with a little liquid in the food processor without becoming gummy. This soup is delicious hot—or cold with additional cream, in which case it's known as Vichyssoise.

2 large baking potatoes, peeled and halved lengthwise
4 large leeks, washed well, trimmed of coarse tops and cut into 4-
*   inch lengths*

1 medium-size celery rib, washed and trimmed and cut into 4-inch lengths
3 cups chicken broth
1 pint light cream
Salt and white pepper to taste
2 tablespoons snipped fresh chives (for garnish)

Thin-slice the potatoes in the food processor, then the leeks and celery (no need to empty work bowl until all the vegetables are sliced). Transfer sliced vegetables to a large, heavy saucepan, add chicken broth and bring to a simmer over moderate heat; cover and cook 20 to 25 minutes, or until vegetables are very tender. Meanwhile, rinse out work bowl, return to processor and fit with metal chopping blade. With a small strainer, scoop potatoes, leeks and celery from broth and place in processor work bowl. Add ½ cup hot broth and with 3 or 4 short pulses or on-off bursts of the motor, purée vegetables until smooth and creamy. Stir back into broth in saucepan and add light cream. Heat slowly to serving temperature, stirring now and then, and season to taste with salt and pepper. Ladle into soup bowls and scatter snipped chives on top of each portion.

To serve cold (Vichyssoise): Dilute finished soup with 1 cup light cream, or for a more tart flavor, with 1 cup sour cream. Cover and chill several hours before serving. Garnish each portion with the snipped fresh chives.

Potage Germiny
(Fresh Sorrel Soup)

Makes 6 servings

Something food writers and processor manufacturers have yet to point out is that the processor's fast, powerful chopping blades sometimes alter the flavor of foods. Garlic, for example, becomes more pungent when machine-minced (as mechanically pressed garlic is also more powerful than the hand-minced). But fresh sorrel, on the contrary, loses in processing the biting tartness essential to a proper *potage germiny*. To find the best way of preserving the lemony sourness of sorrel, I've tried different ways of machine-mincing it. Mincing the raw leaves produces a flat, grassy taste. Steaming them before chopping leaches out the flavor.

The best method, I've found, is to warm the sorrel briefly in a nubbin of butter (for this recipe, I simply add it to the butter-sautéed onion), *then* to machine-mince it; the butterfat seems to hold and heighten the sorrel's original tartness.

1 quart chicken broth
1 medium-size yellow onion, peeled and cut into slim wedges
3 tablespoons unsalted butter
3 egg yolks, lightly beaten
1 cup heavy cream
¼ teaspoon cayenne pepper
Pinch of white pepper
½ teaspoon salt (or to taste)
1 pound fresh sorrel leaves, trimmed of coarse stems and wilted
*   leaves, washed well in cool water, then patted as dry as possible*
*   between layers of paper toweling*
1 to 2 tablespoons lemon juice (if needed to increase the tartness of
*   the soup)*

Gently boil chicken broth in a medium-size saucepan, uncovered, about 30 minutes, or until reduced by about one fourth. Machine-chop the onion in a food processor fitted with the metal chopping blade—2 or 3 pulses or bursts of speed is all you need. Sauté the onion in the butter in a very large, heavy skillet over moderate heat until limp and golden, about 5 minutes; reduce heat under skillet to lowest point and allow onion to mellow while you proceed with the recipe.

Whisk together egg yolks and cream, ladle in a little of the reduced hot broth, blend well, then stir back into saucepan. Add cayenne, white pepper and salt. Heat and stir over lowest heat about 5 minutes, until slightly thickened and smooth, then remove from heat and allow to stand while you prepare the sorrel.

Pile the sorrel into the skillet with the onion, cover and warm about 30 seconds; stir well, re-cover and warm 30 seconds longer, or just until sorrel is wilted. Machine-chop the sorrel and onion in the food processor fitted with the metal chopping blade—on-off—that's all. Stir sorrel mixture into soup and return saucepan to low heat just long enough to bring the soup to serving temperature—3 to 5 minutes— stirring occasionally. Taste for seasonings and add more salt, if needed—also 1 to 2 tablespoons of lemon juice, if the soup is not tart enough to suit you. Serve hot, or chill well and serve cold.

Cream of Fresh Tomato Soup
Makes 4 to 6 servings

Unless you have access to honest-to-goodness vine-ripened tomatoes, don't waste your time making this soup. Hothouse tomatoes, which have all the flavor and character of Styrofoam, will produce a virtually tasteless, colorless soup. A cheering note: Because the food processor reduces the tomato skins to pulp, you needn't peel the tomatoes when making this soup. Indeed, the pulverized skins add body and color.

> *2 medium-size yellow onions, peeled and cut into 1-inch chunks*
> *1 medium-size celery rib, washed and cut into 1-inch chunks*
> *4 tablespoons unsalted butter, in all*
> *¼ teaspoon crumbled leaf basil*
> *Pinch of crumbled leaf thyme*
> *2 tablespoons sugar*
> *2 large fully ripe tomatoes, washed, cored and cut into 1-inch chunks*
> *1¼ cups good strong beef stock*
> *3 tablespoons flour*
> *2 cups milk*
> *1 cup light or heavy cream*
> *Salt and freshly ground pepper to taste*

In a food processor fitted with the metal chopping blade, mince the onions and celery together, using 5 or 6 pulses or on-offs of the motor. Melt 2 tablespoons of the butter in a heavy saucepan over moderate heat, add the minced onions and celery and sauté 8 to 10 minutes until golden. Mix in the basil, thyme and sugar and set off the heat for the moment. Add the tomato chunks to the processor work bowl (still fitted with the metal chopping blade) and reduce to juice by letting the motor run nonstop for 60 seconds. Add to saucepan along with the beef stock, return to moderate heat and simmer, uncovered, for about 30 minutes, or until mixture has been reduced by about one half.

Meanwhile, make a white sauce by melting the remaining 2 tablespoons of butter over moderate heat in a second heavy saucepan, blending in the flour, then adding the milk and cream and cooking and stirring until mixture is thickened and smooth—3 to 5 minutes. Turn heat to lowest point, lay a flame-tamer on top of the burner, then set the saucepan on top and let stand while you finish preparing the tomato mixture. Stir the sauce from time to time so that a "skin" doesn't form on the surface.

When the tomato mixture has boiled down to about half of its original volume, pour into a large, fine sieve set over a heatproof bowl. Turn the strained-out solids into the food processor (still fitted with the metal chopping blade—no need to wash it or the work bowl) and churn for 30 seconds nonstop or until absolutely smooth. Blend the tomato purée into the white sauce—add it slowly, whisking all the while, lest the acid of the tomatoes curdle the sauce. Finally, mix in the strained stock mixture. Taste for salt and pepper and season as needed. Warm briefly over low heat—just to serving temperature. But keep your eye on the pot, keep stirring the soup, and don't let it bubble up—even for an instant. You're dealing with an unstable (easily curdled) mixture and too much heat will precipitate the curdling.

Ladle into soup bowls and serve, topped, if you like, with fresh snipped chives or dill.

Cream of Turnip Soup
Makes 6 servings

Turnips are one of the vegetables most maligned by Americans, and yet, properly prepared, they are perfectly delicious, as this lovely French soup readily proves. Also try the delicate Shaker Turnip Pudding included elsewhere in this book (see Index for recipe page number).

4 large white turnips, peeled and halved lengthwise
2 medium-size yellow onions, peeled and halved lengthwise
1 large Irish potato, peeled and halved lengthwise
3 tablespoons unsalted butter
6 cups chicken stock
1 cup light cream
Salt and white pepper to taste
¼ cup minced fresh parsley (for an amount this small, I prefer to do the mincing by hand)

In a food processor fitted with the slicing disc, thin-slice the turnip halves by pushing them down the feed tube with gentle pressure.

Thin-slice the onions and potato the same way. Melt the butter in a large, heavy saucepan, add the sliced vegetables and stir-fry over moderate heat about 10 minutes, or until golden. Add the chicken stock, cover and simmer 1 hour, or until vegetables are very soft. Set a large, fine sieve over a large, heatproof bowl, and dump in the kettle's contents.

Remove the slicing disc from the food processor and slip the metal chopping blade into place. Churn the strained-out soup vegetables to a purée, doing about one third of the total amount at a time and adding just enough of the strained liquid to facilitate puréeing—about ½ cup for each batch. For timing, use about three 10-second churnings of the motor for each batch of vegetables. Return the purée to the saucepan with the rest of the strained liquid. Smooth in the cream and heat slowly, stirring now and then, for about 10 minutes. Add salt and pepper to season, then ladle into soup bowls. Top each portion with a scattering of minced parsley. This soup, by the way, is also very good cold.

Potage aux Légumes
(Puréed Vegetable Soup)

Makes 6 to 8 servings

> *2 large yellow onions, peeled and halved lengthwise*
> *3 tablespoons unsalted butter*
> *3 medium-size carrots, peeled and cut into 4-inch lengths*
> *3 medium-size turnips, peeled and halved*
> *3 medium-size potatoes, peeled and halved*
> *6 cups chicken stock or broth*
> *2 parsley sprigs, washed*
> *½ teaspoon crumbled leaf thyme*
> *⅛ teaspoon freshly ground black pepper*
> *Salt to taste (whether you need any at all will depend upon the*
> *   saltiness of the chicken stock)*

Thin-slice the onions in a food processor fitted with the slicing disc by pushing them down the feed tube with minimal pressure. Dump into a large heavy kettle in which you have already melted the butter. Set over moderate heat and allow to sauté while you thin-slice the remaining vegetables, but keep an eye on the kettle and give the onions a quick stir now and again. Stand as many carrot pieces in the feed tube as will fit fairly snugly, then slice thin by pushing them gently down the tube. Thin-slice the turnips and potatoes the same way—the work bowl will be big enough to accommodate all of the vegetables at one time.

When onions are limp and golden—after 8 to 10 minutes of sautéing—add all of the other vegetables and stir-fry about 5 minutes over moderate heat. Pour in the chicken stock, add parsley, thyme and pepper, cover and simmer about 45 minutes, or until vegetables are very tender. Set a large fine sieve over a very large heatproof bowl and pour in the kettle's contents. Purée the strained-out solids—half of them at a time with ½ cup of chicken stock—in the food processor, now fitted with the metal chopping blade (no need to wash the work bowl). It will take about three 5-second churnings of the motor to purée each batch of vegetables. Return both the puréed vegetables and the strained stock to the soup kettle, set over moderately low heat and simmer, uncovered, for about 1 hour, or until reduced slightly. Taste for salt and season as needed. Ladle into soup bowls and serve. Add a piece of butter to each serving if you wish.

Velouté Cressonière
(Cream of Watercress Soup)

Makes 6 to 8 servings

When I was testing this recipe, I discovered another of the food processor's miracles. Just as I was ready to serve the soup, I was called to the phone, and even though I'd turned the heat under the kettle to low, I was dismayed to find, on returning to the stove, that the soup had curdled. Miserably. I should have known better than to take chances with an egg-thickened soup, for as every cook is aware, it doesn't take much to curdle an egg. The old dodge, of course, is to strain out the curds and serve the soup anyway. So I dumped the lot into a large, fine sieve. And then it occurred to me. Why not buzz the curds up in the processor? If it can grind raw meat, surely it could pulverize those curds to velvet. It did, magically, with just 60 seconds of nonstop churning of the metal chopping blade. I then stirred the puréed curds into the soup, served it, and no one was any the wiser.

1 *large bunch of watercress, washed well and patted dry on paper*
   toweling
3 *tablespoons butter*
1 *medium-size yellow onion, peeled and cut into slim wedges*
2 *large baking potatoes, peeled and halved lengthwise*
5 *cups chicken broth*
3 *large eggs*
1 *cup light cream*
¾ *teaspoon salt (or to taste)*
⅛ *teaspoon white pepper*

For this soup you will want only the tender young sprigs of watercress, not the coarse stems, so pick over the bunch carefully. Also set aside 1 cup of stemmed leaves to stir into the soup just before serving (measure them loosely packed). Place the watercress sprigs in a food processor fitted with the metal chopping blade and, with 3 or 4 pulses or on-offs of the motor, chop moderately coarsely. Empty into a large, heavy kettle in which you have already melted the butter. Coarsely chop the onion the same way and add to kettle. Set over moderate heat and sauté 3 to 4 minutes, just until onion and watercress are limp.

Remove metal chopping blade from the processor and slip the slicing disc into place. Thin-slice the potatoes by pushing them down the feed tube with very little pressure. Add potatoes to kettle along with the chicken broth. Cover and simmer about 35 minutes, or until the potatoes are very tender. Set a large fine sieve over a large, heatproof bowl and pour in the soup mixture. Re-equip the food processor with the metal chopping blade (no need to wash it or the work bowl). Place about one third of the strained-out solids into the work bowl along with ⅔ cup of the strained soup. (The reason for working with such small batches and for adding this much liquid when puréeing these soup solids is that potatoes tend to become gluey when churned at such high speed. This is also the reason that I have chosen to use baking potatoes for this recipe instead of all-purpose or boiling potatoes, which are far waxier and much more likely to gum up.) Purée each batch of potatoes, onion and watercress by letting the chopping blade run nonstop for 10 seconds. When all are puréed, return to the kettle along with the strained soup.

In a small bowl, whisk the eggs until frothy. Blend in the cream, salt and pepper, then ladle a little of the hot soup into the egg mixture, beating all the while. Stir into soup along with the reserved watercress leaves, set over moderately low heat and cook, stirring constantly, for 4 to 5 minutes, or until slightly thickened. Taste for salt and add more, if needed. Ladle into bowls and serve hot. or chill well and serve cold.

Portuguese Onion Soup
Makes 6 to 8 servings

Those accustomed to French onion soup will find this one completely different. It's thickened with egg yolks and spiked with either Port or Madeira.

1 large Spanish onion, peeled and cut into wedges slim enough to fit the food-processor feed tube
4 large yellow onions, peeled and quartered
2 tablespoons olive oil
2 tablespoons butter
¼ teaspoon ground coriander
Pinch of ground mace
1½ quarts (6 cups) good strong beef broth
2 tablespoons Madeira or Port
3 egg yolks, lightly beaten
Salt and freshly ground black pepper to taste

Equip the food processor with the slicing disc, then stand in the feed tube as many Spanish onion wedges as will fit snugly. Turn machine on and push the onions gently through the tube. Repeat until all the Spanish onion is sliced. Slice the yellow onions the same way. You may have to stop midway through and empty the work bowl if it threatens to overflow; if so, simply dump onions into a medium-size heavy kettle to which you have already added the olive oil and butter. When all onions are sliced, add to kettle, set over moderate heat and sauté about 15 minutes until limp and lightly touched with brown. (The browning is important for flavor.) Blend in the coriander and mace and allow to mellow 2 to 3 minutes. Add the broth, turn heat to low and simmer, uncovered, about 45 minutes, or until onions are very soft and flavors well blended; stir in the wine and simmer 5 minutes longer. Whisk a little of the hot soup into the egg yolks, mix back into kettle and heat and stir 2 to 3 minutes, just until soup thickens ever so slightly. Do not allow to boil or the soup may curdle. Season to taste with salt and pepper, ladle into small soup bowls and serve.

Sopa de Feijão Preto
(Brazilian Black Bean Soup)

Makes 6 servings

Much as I've always liked this recipe, I'll admit that it was no picnic to make when I had to force the black beans through a food mill, bit by bit. Now that I have a food processor, I make the soup often—it's cheap, spicy and good. What distinguishes it from the more familiar Spanish black bean soup is the subtle addition of orange rind and cinnamon.

1 cup dried black beans, washed and sorted
2 cups cold water
1 large carrot, peeled and cut into 1-inch chunks
1 large garlic clove, peeled
2 tablespoons olive oil
1 large celery rib, washed and cut into 1-inch chunks
2 large yellow onions, peeled and cut into slim wedges
½ teaspoon ground coriander
Pinch of ground cinnamon
¼ teaspoon finely grated orange rind
⅛ teaspoon freshly ground black pepper
⅛ teaspoon cayenne pepper
¼ pound salt pork, scored deeply crisscross fashion
1 quart good strong beef stock or broth
1 cup loosely packed parsley sprigs, washed and patted very dry on
  paper toweling
½ teaspoon salt (or to taste)
¼ cup Tawny Port or Madeira

GARNISHES:

2 hard-cooked eggs, peeled and halved lengthwise
Minced parsley

Place beans in a mixing bowl, add water and allow to soak overnight. Next day, place the carrot chunks and garlic in the food processor fitted with the metal chopping blade and buzz 30 seconds nonstop until carrot is finely chopped. Empty into a medium-size, heavy kettle to which you have already added the olive oil. Coarsely machine-chop the celery with 1 or 2 quick pulses or bursts of speed and add to kettle. Machine-chop the onions the same way, doing about half of them at a time; add onions to kettle. Set kettle over moderate heat and sauté, stirring occasionally, 10 to 12 minutes until onions are limp and ever-so-slightly browned. Mix in the coriander, cinnamon, orange rind, black pepper and cayenne and warm about 2 minutes, just long enough to mellow the flavors. Add the beans and their soaking water, the salt pork and beef stock. Cover and simmer gently until beans are very soft, about 2½ hours. Remove salt pork and discard.

Place a very large fine sieve over a large heatproof bowl and pour in the soup mixture. Spoon about half of the solids in the sieve into the processor work bowl (still fitted with the metal chopping blade), then turn the motor on and let it run about 1 minute. Examine the purée— it should be absolutely smooth; if it is not, let the processor run another 30 seconds or so. Empty purée into the soup kettle. Purée the remaining strained-out solids the same way and add to kettle; also add the soup liquids that drained through the sieve into the bowl. Set kettle over low heat and simmer, uncovered, for about 1 hour, or until the consistency of a medium gravy.

Meanwhile, wash and dry all parts of the food processor and reassemble. Dump the parsley sprigs into the work bowl and, with about 2 fast pulses or bursts of speed, chop fairly coarsely. Reserve half of the chopped parsley to use as a garnish; add the rest to the soup along with the salt and wine. Simmer, uncovered, for 25 to 30 minutes longer, just until flavors are well blended. Taste for salt and add more, if needed. Just before serving, place all the hard-cooked eggs in the processor work bowl, pulse or turn the motor on, then off, then on, then off—zip, zip—until eggs are coarsely chopped. Ladle soup into large shallow bowls and scatter chopped eggs and chopped parsley on top of each portion.

Tuscan Navy Bean Soup

Makes 8 servings

1 pound dried navy beans, washed and sorted
2½ quarts (10 cups) cold water (about)
4 leeks, trimmed of green tops, washed well and cut into 1-inch
  chunks
½ cup olive oil
1 medium-size garlic clove, peeled and minced
1 medium-size yellow onion, peeled and cut into slim wedges
2 medium-size carrots, peeled and cut into 1-inch chunks
1 teaspoon crumbled leaf sage
½ teaspoon crumbled leaf thyme
2 medium-size juicily ripe tomatoes, washed, cored and cut into slim
  wedges (no need to peel)
1 tablespoon salt (or to taste)
¼ teaspoon freshly ground black pepper
¼ cup minced parsley (for an amount this small, I prefer to hand-
  mince)

Soak the beans overnight in 2 quarts of the cold water. Next day, drain beans; reserve and measure soaking water, and add just enough cold water to total 2 quarts. Cook the beans in the 2 quarts water in a large, covered kettle over moderate heat about 2 hours, or until quite soft.

Meanwhile, coarsely chop the leeks in a food processor fitted with the metal chopping blade, using 2 or 3 pulses or bursts of speed; empty into a second large, heavy kettle in which you have already placed the olive oil and garlic. Machine-chop the onion the same way and add to kettle. Now mince the carrots, letting the processor run nonstop for about 30 seconds; add carrots to kettle along with sage and thyme. Set over moderate heat and sauté, stirring occasionally, 10 to 12 minutes, just until onions and leeks are limp and golden. Purée tomatoes in the processor (still fitted with the metal chopping blade—this will take 10 to 15 seconds) and add to onion mixture. Turn heat as low as it will go and allow this mixture to mellow while the beans finish cooking.

When beans are done, ladle 2 cups of them into the vegetable mixture. Purée the remainder with the cooking water, 2 cups at a time, in food processor—5 or 6 powerful pulses or bursts of the chopping blade should be about right. As you purée the beans, add to vegetable mixture. Stir in salt, pepper and parsley and heat, stirring occasionally, 15 to 20 minutes longer to mellow the flavors. Taste for salt, add more if necessary, then serve.

Lentil, Leek and Escarole Soup
Makes 8 servings

1 pound lentils, washed and sorted
2 quarts chicken stock or broth
6 large leeks, trimmed of tops, washed and cut into 4-inch lengths
1 medium-size yellow onion, peeled and halved lengthwise
¼ cup olive oil
1 medium-size garlic clove, peeled and crushed
4 large celery ribs, washed, trimmed and cut into 4-inch lengths
2 medium-size carrots, peeled and cut into 4-inch lengths
1 cup loosely packed parsley sprigs, washed and patted very dry on paper toweling
1 cup loosely packed fresh basil leaves washed and patted very dry on paper toweling
3 cups loosely packed escarole leaves, washed and patted very dry on paper toweling
2 medium-size very ripe tomatoes, washed, cored and cut into slim wedges (no need to peel)
Juice of ½ lemon
¼ cup uncooked rice
Salt and freshly ground pepper to taste

Cook the lentils in the chicken broth, covered, in a large heavy kettle over moderate heat for 45 minutes to 1 hour, or until very soft. Meanwhile, thin-slice the leeks in a food processor fitted with the slicing disc by pushing them through the feed tube with minimal pressure. Thin-slice the onion halves the same way; add leeks and onion to a second large, heavy kettle in which you have already placed the olive oil and garlic. Thin-slice the celery and carrots and add to leeks and onion. Remove slicing disc from processor and slip metal chopping blade into place. Pile parsley and basil in work bowl and with 2 or 3 quick pulses or on-offs of the motor, chop moderately coarsely; add to leek mixture and sauté over low heat, stirring now and then, about 15 minutes, or until leeks and onion are limp and golden but not brown. Dump escarole into processor (still fitted with the chopping blade) and chop coarsely, using 3 or 4 fast pulses or bursts of the motor; add to sautéed vegetables. Finally, purée the tomatoes in the processor by letting the chopping blade run steadily for 10 to 15 seconds; add to sautéed vegetables, reduce heat to lowest point and let the tomatoes reduce slowly while the lentils finish cooking.

When the lentils are done, ladle 2 cups of them into the tomato mixture. Drain the remainder, reserving the cooking water. Measure out 2 cups of the cooking water to use in puréeing the lentils; add the remainder to the tomato mixture along with the lemon juice and rice; bring to a boil, cover and cook about 20 minutes, or until rice is tender.

While the rice cooks, purée the reserved lentils in the food processor fitted with the metal chopping blade by letting the motor run nonstop for about 60 seconds. The machine will only be able to cope with about 2 cups of lentils and ⅓ to ½ cup of the cooking water at a time. When all lentils are puréed, smooth into the soup, season to taste with salt and pepper, then cook and stir about 5 minutes longer before serving.

Soupe au Pistou
(Provençal Vegetable Soup
with Garlic-Tomato-Basil Sauce)

Makes 10 to 12 servings

Pistou is to Provence what *pesto* is to Genoa—a thick garlic-basil sauce. In the South of France, however, tomato paste is blended into the mix, and the resulting sauce is stirred into soup rather than being used to dress pasta, which is the Italian way.

> *1 cup dried navy or pea beans, marrowfat or baby lima beans, washed and sorted*
> *3 quarts cold water (about)*
> *½ cup loosely packed parsley sprigs, washed and patted very dry on paper toweling*

2 large yellow onions, peeled and halved lengthwise
5 tablespoons olive oil
4 medium-size carrots, peeled and cut into 4-inch lengths
4 large leeks, washed, trimmed and cut into 4-inch lengths
3 medium-size celery ribs, washed and cut into 4-inch lengths
3 medium-size potatoes, peeled and quartered lengthwise
4 large very ripe tomatoes, washed, cored and cut into slim wedges
   (no need to peel)
½ teaspoon crumbled leaf thyme
3 to 4 strands saffron mixed with 1 tablespoon warm water
3 medium-size zucchini, washed and cut into 4-inch lengths
½ pound tender young green beans, tipped, washed and cut into 1-
   inch lengths (this you will have to do by hand, but it's fast work if
   you bundle about 6 to 8 beans together and slice across them at
   one time)
4 teaspoons salt (or to taste)
¼ teaspoon freshly ground black pepper (or to taste)
Handful of thin (No. 9) spaghetti, broken into about 2-inch lengths

PISTOU:

1 cup loosely packed tender young basil leaves, washed and patted
   very dry on paper toweling
4 large garlic cloves, peeled
1 slice firm-textured white bread, torn into small chunks
1 tablespoon tomato paste
½ cup freshly grated Parmesan cheese
⅓ cup olive oil (best quality)

Soak the dried beans in 2 cups of the cold water overnight. Next day, drain the beans, place in a heavy saucepan, add 1 quart of the cold water, bring to a simmer, cover and cook over moderate heat about 1 hour, or until beans are almost tender. Set off the heat but do not drain.

Meanwhile, begin preparing the vegetables for the soup. In a food processor fitted with the metal chopping blade, mince the parsley fairly fine, using two or three 5-second churnings of the motor. Empty onto a piece of wax paper and set aside. Remove the chopping blade from the processor and slip the slicing disc into place (no need to wash the processor work bowl). Thin-slice the onions by pushing them through the feed tube with gentle pressure. Heat the olive oil in a very large, heavy kettle over moderate heat until it issues a nice olive aroma, dump in the onions and let sauté, stirring now and then, while you slice the remaining vegetables.

Thin-slice the carrots, then the leeks, celery and potatoes, by pushing them gently through the feed tube. If work bowl threatens to fill up before you've sliced the potatoes, simply dump the bowl's contents into the kettle with the onions and move on to slicing the potatoes. Add these to the kettle, too, as soon as they're sliced. Also add the minced parsley and stir well. Let the combined vegetables sauté lazily for about 20 minutes, or until richly golden.

Now remove the slicing disc from the processor and fit the metal chopping blade back into place (again no need to wash the work bowl). Coarsley chop the tomatoes, two at a time, using 2 or 3 pulses or on-offs of the motor; add each batch of tomatoes to the kettle as it is chopped. Also add the beans and their cooking water, the remaining 6 cups of water, the thyme and saffron. Stir well, cover and allow the soup to simmer slowly for 2 hours, or until vegetables are tender and flavors nicely blended.

Meanwhile wash and dry the processor work bowl and the slicing blade; reassemble. Thin-slice the zucchini by pushing them lightly down the feed tube. Add to the soup along with the green beans, salt and pepper. If soup seems quite thick, add a cup or two of additional water and when all comes to a boil, toss in the spaghetti. Cover and cook about 40 minutes longer, or until zucchini, beans and spaghetti are tender.

It's time now to prepare the *pistou:* Place the basil, garlic, bread and tomato paste in the processor, now fitted with the metal chopping blade. Turn the motor on and let run for 15 seconds nonstop. Uncover work bowl, scrape down the lid and sides, re-cover and let motor run for 5 seconds longer, or until the ingredients have been reduced to a thick paste. Add the grated Parmesan and pulse or snap the motor on and off a couple of times to blend, then, with the motor running, drizzle the oil down the feed tube in a fine stream. Beat the sauce for about 10 seconds after all of the oil is incorporated.

When the soup has cooked for the last allotted 40 minutes, add one third of the *pistou* and stir well to mix. Taste the soup for seasonings and add more salt and pepper, if needed. Ladle into large soup plates and pass the remaining *pistou* with plenty of freshly grated Parmesan so that everyone can add as much of each as he likes to his soup. NOTE: *This soup keeps well in the refrigerator for about a week. It can also be frozen.*

Caldo Verde

(Portuguese Green Soup)

Makes 8 to 10 servings

½ *pound* chorizo, pepperoni *or other garlicky dry sausage, cut into 4-inch lengths*
5 *medium-size potatoes, peeled and halved lengthwise*
4 *medium-size yellow onions, peeled and halved lengthwise*
2 *quarts chicken stock*
2 *tablespoons olive oil*
¼ *pound tender young kale, washed and trimmed, or ¼ of a medium-size green cabbage, cored and cut into columns about the size of the processor feed tube*
1 *tablespoon salt (about)*
¼ *teaspoon freshly ground black pepper*

Thin-slice the sausage by pushing it gently through the feed tube of a food processor fitted with the slicing disc; empty the slices into a medium-size skillet, set over moderately low heat and allow to sauté while you slice the potatoes and onions. Thin-slice the potatoes just as you did the sausage and add to a large heavy kettle, then thin-slice the onions and add to kettle along with the chicken stock. Set over moderate heat, cover and simmer about 40 minutes, or until potatoes are mushy. Meanwhile, remove sausage from the heat, cover and keep warm.

When potatoes are mushy-tender, pour the kettle mixture into a very large, fine sieve set over a large, heatproof bowl. Remove the slicing disc from the food processor and set the metal chopping blade into place. Now purée the strained-out potatoes and onions in four batches, using ½ cup of the strained chicken stock for each (this is to keep the potatoes from becoming gummy). A couple of pulses or fast on-offs of the processor motor will do the job—you do not want an absolutely creamy purée, but rather a lumpy one. Return the purée to the soup kettle with the rest of the strained chicken stock. Add the sausages and any skillet drippings, with the olive oil; cover and set over low heat.

Quickly wash and dry the processor work bowl as well as the slicing disc, and reassemble. Stack 3 or 4 kale leaves together, then roll them up jelly-roll style into a snug bundle slightly smaller than the feed tube. Stand the bundle of leaves in the feed tube and slice as thin as possible by using minimal pressure on the pusher. Repeat until all kale has been sliced. If you are using cabbage instead, simply push the columns of cabbage down the feed tube, one after another.

Add the kale or cabbage to the kettle with the salt and pepper; re-cover and simmer slowly for 10 to 15 minutes, just until kale or cab-bage is crisp-tender. Taste for salt and add more, if needed. Ladle into soup bowls and serve. This soup, by the way, is husky enough to serve as a main course and needs only crusty chunks of bread and a crisp green salad to accompany.

Old-Fashioned Yankee Vegetable Chowder
Makes 6 to 8 servings

⅛ pound salt pork (a piece about the height and width of the food-processor feed tube and partially frozen so that it is firm enough to stand upright in the feed tube and to offer enough resistance to the cutting blade—the processor will not cut the salt pork into neat slices if it is too soft)
1 large Spanish onion (about 4 inches in diameter), peeled and quartered lengthwise
2 medium-size white turnips, peeled and halved lengthwise
2 medium-size parsnips, peeled and cut into 4-inch lengths
2 medium-size carrots, peeled and cut into 4-inch lengths
4 medium-size potatoes, peeled and halved lengthwise
3 cups water
1 quart milk
2 cups light cream
2 teaspoons salt
¼ teaspoon freshly ground black pepper
2 cups crumbled common crackers or water biscuits, softened in ¾ cup milk

¼ cup minced fresh parsley (for an amount this small, I prefer to hand-mince)

In a food processor fitted with the slicing disc, thin-slice the salt pork by pushing it down the feed tube with minimal pressure. Empty into a large heavy kettle, set over moderately high heat and brown the salt pork—this will take about 10 minutes. With a slotted spoon, lift the crisp brown bits of salt pork onto paper toweling to drain. Set the kettle off the heat.

Thin-slice the onion, then the turnips, parsnips, carrots and potatoes in the processor, emptying the work-bowl contents into the kettle each time it fills up. When all vegetables are sliced, stir-fry in the salt-pork drippings over moderate heat about 15 minutes, or until limp and golden. Pour in the water, cover and simmer 40 to 45 minutes, or until vegetables are tender. Check the kettle from time to time and, if the liquid seems to be boiling away too fast, add a little extra water. When vegetables are tender, add the milk, cream, salt, pepper and reserved salt pork, and bring just to the simmering point—do not allow the mixture to boil or it may curdle. Stir in the softened crackers and parsley, heat 1 to 2 minutes longer, then ladle into large soup plates and serve.

New England Fish Chowder
Makes 6 to 8 servings

⅛ pound salt pork (a piece the height and width of the food-processor feed tube and partially frozen, so that it is firm enough to stand upright in the tube and to offer enough resistance to the cutting blade)
1 large Spanish onion (about 4 inches in diameter), peeled and quartered lengthwise
4 medium-size Irish potatoes, peeled and halved lengthwise
2½ cups cold water
2 pounds cod, scrod, flounder or haddock fillets
3 cups milk
1 cup heavy cream
2 tablespoons butter

Salt and white pepper to taste

¼ cup minced fresh parsley (for an amount this small, I prefer to hand-mince)

In a food processor fitted with the slicing disc, thin-slice the salt pork by pushing it down the feed tube with gentle pressure. Dump into a large heavy kettle, set over moderately high heat and fry until the pieces of salt pork are crisp and brown; then, with a slotted spoon, lift them onto paper toweling to drain, and reserve them. Set the kettle off the heat for the moment.

Thin-slice the onion, then the potatoes, in the food processor and add to the drippings in the kettle. Set over moderate heat and stir-fry about 10 minutes, or until onion is limp and golden. Pour in the water, cover and simmer 10 to 15 minutes, or until potatoes are almost tender. Lay the fish fillets on top of the potatoes and onion, re-cover kettle and simmer 10 to 15 minutes, or until fish flakes at the touch of a fork—it will break apart as it cooks, which is as it should be. Add the milk, cream, butter, salt, pepper and reserved pieces of salt pork, and bring just to serving temperature—do *not* cover the kettle at this point. Ladle the chowder into large soup plates and top each portion with a sprinkling of minced parsley.

Lobster Stew

Makes 4 to 6 servings

The only thing difficult about making this elegant lobster stew is mincing the lobster meat extra fine. The processor does it to perfection.

1 pound cooked, shelled lobster meat
4 tablespoons unsalted butter
1 quart milk
1½ teaspoons salt
⅛ teaspoon cayenne pepper

Place half the lobster meat in the food processor fitted with the metal chopping blade, turn motor on and let run steadily for 3 or 4 seconds. Examine texture of lobster—it should be quite fine. If it is not, give the motor a couple of quick bursts of speed. Add the lobster to a large, heavy saucepan in which you have already melted the butter, Chop the remaining lobster meat the same way and add to saucepan. Set over gentle heat and sauté the lobster in the butter about 5 minutes, just until golden. Add remaining ingredients and heat slowly about 5 minutes, just until steam rises from the pan. Remove stew from heat immediately, cool 15 minutes, then set in the refrigerator, uncovered, and let stand until shortly before serving time. Reheat mixture slowly—again just until steam rises from the pan. Do not allow to boil. Ladle into soup bowls and serve.

Consommé Madrilène

Makes 6 servings

Few of us have tasted a *consommé madrilène* that doesn't come out of a can. That's too bad, for the flavors are far more delicate when a homemade beef stock and sun-ripened, full-flavored tomatoes are used.

> *2 large, dead-ripe tomatoes, washed, peeled, cored and cut into 1-*
> *inch chunks*
> *1 quart Beef Stock (see Index for recipe page number)*
> *1 tablespoon freshly snipped chives*
> *1 tablespoon hand-minced fresh parsley*
> *⅛ teaspoon cayenne pepper*
> *¼ cup dry Madeira (Sercial), dry Port or sherry*

In a food processor fitted with the metal chopping blade, reduce the tomatoes to juice by running the motor nonstop for 10 to 12 seconds. Empty into a large, heavy enamel or stainless-steel saucepan. Add the stock, chives, parsley and cayenne, bring to a simmer, cover and cook slowly for 45 minutes. Set a very large, fine cheesecloth-lined sieve over a second large enamel or stainless-steel saucepan. Pour in the *madrilène* and allow to drip through unattended (if you stir the strained-out solids or press them, you will not have a sparklingly clear *madrilène*, which is your aim). When all of the *madrilène* has dripped through, set the saucepan over moderate heat and bring just to a simmer. Stir in the Madeira and serve.

Gazpacho

Makes 6 to 8 servings

There is little point in making this cold Spanish vegetable soup unless you have vine-ripened tomatoes full of fresh tomato bouquet. The soup itself may be prepared in the processor, and some of the garnishes, too (the sliced scallions, minced parsley and green pepper). But the rest of the garnishes you must do by hand—the croutons, the diced cucumber and tomato—because the machine will cut them too fine.

1 medium-size Spanish onion, peeled and cut into 1-inch chunks
1 medium-size garlic clove, peeled
1 medium-size green pepper, washed, cored, seeded and cut into 1-inch pieces
1 medium-size cucumber, peeled, seeded and cut into 1-inch chunks
4 fully ripe tomatoes, peeled, cored and cut into 1-inch chunks
2 eggs
¼ cup tarragon vinegar
1 slice firm-textured white bread, broken into small pieces
1 tablespoon honey
½ teaspoon salt
⅛ teaspoon freshly ground black pepper
⅛ teaspoon cayenne pepper
⅔ cup olive oil

GARNISHES:

1 cup loosely packed fresh parsley sprigs, washed and patted very dry on paper toweling
1 medium-size green pepper, washed, cored, seeded and cut into 1-inch chunks
8 scallions, trimmed, washed and cut into 4-inch chunks
1 medium-size fully ripe tomato, peeled, cored, seeded, juiced and diced by hand
1 medium-size cucumber, peeled, seeded and diced by hand
6 slices firm-textured white bread, trimmed of crust, cut into ½-inch cubes and fried in a little olive oil until crisp and golden brown

In a food processor fitted with the metal chopping blade, reduce the onion and garlic to juice by letting the motor run nonstop for 30 seconds; empty into a large bowl. Buzz the green pepper and cucumber to juice the same way and add to bowl, then purée the tomatoes, two at a time, allowing 30 seconds of nonstop churning for each batch; add to bowl. Place eggs, vinegar, bread, honey, salt, black and cayenne pepper in the processor and combine by letting the motor run nonstop for 10 seconds. Now, with the motor running, drizzle the olive oil down the feed tube in a fine stream and allow motor to run 10 seconds after all of the oil has been incorporated. Mix into the puréed vegetables. Cover and chill several hours so that flavors have a chance to mellow. Stir well just before serving.

For the garnishes: Equip a clean processor bowl with a clean metal chopping blade, add the parsley and mince fairly fine, using two or three 5-second churnings of the motor. Empty into a small bowl. Now mince the green pepper, using 3 or 4 pulses or on-offs of the motor; arrange in a separate small bowl. Remove metal chopping blade from processor and slip the slicing disc into place; thin-slice the scallions by stacking them all in the feed tube, then pushing them through the slicing disc with gentle pressure. Place in a third bowl. Set out all the hand-cut garnishes in their bowls so that everyone may sprinkle as much of each over his *gazpacho* as he likes.

Minestrone
Makes 6 to 8 servings

What I like about this soup is that I can set a huge, heavy kettle on the stove, then dice or chop or mince the various ingredients in the order listed, dumping them directly from the processor work bowl into the kettle. Timing isn't important, so you can work at your own pace. Once the basics are in the pot, turn the heat to its lowest point, clap the lid on the kettle, then go about your business. The soup can simmer the better part of the day—in fact, I think it's better if it does. Just make sure that the burner heat is as low as it can go—the soup should never boil.

> *¼ pound partially frozen salt pork, cut into 1-inch chunks (If the salt pork is not partially frozen, the processor's chopping blade will reduce it to mush. What you want is a coarse chop that approximates diced salt pork.)*

2 *large yellow onions, peeled and cut into 1-inch chunks*
2 *large garlic cloves, peeled and crushed*
2 *large celery ribs, trimmed, washed and cut into 1-inch chunks*
3 *large leeks trimmed, carefully washed to remove grit and sand and*
  cut into 1-inch chunks
2 *large carrots, peeled and cut into 1-inch chunks*
1 *large Irish potato, peeled and cut into 1-inch chunks*
4 *large juicily ripe tomatoes, cored and cut into 1-inch chunks (no*
  need to peel)
1 *quart (4 cups) good strong beef stock or broth*
1 *bay leaf, crumbled*
½ *teaspoon crumbled leaf thyme*
½ *teaspoon crumbled leaf basil*
¼ *teaspoon crumbled leaf marjoram*
2 *tablespoons sugar*
2 *young zucchini, washed, trimmed and quartered lengthwise*
¼ *pound tender young green beans, washed, tipped and cut into 1-*
  inch lengths (This you have to do by hand because the food
  processor slices the beans too thin.)
¼ *small cabbage, cored and cut into columns about the height and*
  width of the food-processor feed tube
Salt and freshly ground black pepper to season

In a food processor fitted with the metal chopping blade, coarsely chop the salt pork by pulsing or snapping the motor on and off about 5 times. Empty into a large heavy kettle and set over moderate heat. While the salt pork crisps and browns—this will take 12 to 15 minutes—you can begin preparing the vegetables for the processor. I find that by the time I've washed, trimmed and pared them, the salt pork has cooked down to crisp brown bits, leaving lots of rich drippings in which to sauté the vegetables. Skim the crisp brown bits from the kettle with a slotted spoon, spread out on paper toweling to drain and reserve.

Mince the onion fairly fine in the processor (still fitted with the metal chopping blade—no need to wash it or the work bowl) using 5 or 6 pulses or on-offs of the motor. Dump into the kettle along with the crushed garlic, stir, then allow to sauté while you mince the celery and leeks together—they will need 5 or 6 pulses or on-offs of the motor, too. Dump into kettle. Now coarsely chop the carrots by letting the processor run nonstop for 10 seconds. Add carrots to kettle. Coarsely chop the potato by pulsing or snapping the motor on and off 3 or 4 times (it doesn't matter if the pieces are irregularly cut) and add to kettle. Stir kettle mixture well, then take about a 20-minute break while the vegetables sauté lazily—they should be tender and golden but not brown.

Chop the tomatoes quite fine, doing about one third of the total amount at a time and adding each batch to the kettle as it is chopped— simply let the processor, fitted with the metal chopping blade, run nonstop for 5 to 8 seconds each time. When all of the tomatoes are in the kettle, add the beef stock, bay leaf, thyme, basil, marjoram and sugar. Bring to a gentle simmer, cover and cook very slowly for 5 to 6 hours.

Meanwhile wash the processor work bowl and equip with the slicing disc. About 2 hours before time to serve, stand the zucchini quarters in the feed tube and thin-slice by pushing them through with gentle pressure. Add to kettle along with the green beans, then thin-slice the columns of cabbage by pushing them lightly down the feed tube. Add to kettle, cover and simmer slowly for 1½ to 2 hours, or until cabbage, beans and zucchini are quite tender and flavors are well blended. Taste for salt and pepper and add as needed, then ladle into large soup plates and scatter a few of the reserved crisp, brown bits of salt pork into each portion. Serve with crusty chunks of Italian bread. NOTE: *This soup keeps well in the refrigerator for about 1 week; it also freezes well.*

Root Soup
Makes 8 to 10 servings

This is one of those robust, slow-simmering soups to which you can add almost any vegetable—turnips, beets, parsnips, carrots, potatoes, cabbage, celery, tomatoes. Improvise with whatever vegetables you fancy, but let the food processor do all of the chopping and slicing for you. This soup, like many others, actually improves in flavor after a day or two in the refrigerator.

½ pound lean boneless chuck, cut into 1-inch cubes, trimmed of sinew and chilled well
1 tablespoon butter, olive oil or vegetable oil

3 medium-size yellow onions, peeled and cut into slim wedges
1 garlic clove, peeled
4 medium-size carrots, peeled and cut into 1-inch lengths
4 medium-size parsnips, peeled and cut into 1-inch lengths
4 celery ribs, washed, trimmed of tops, and cut into 4-inch lengths
4 medium-size beets, peeled, trimmed of stems and root ends, and
    quartered
4 medium-size white turnips, peeled, trimmed of stems and root
    ends, and quartered
2 cups canned tomatoes
2 cups beef broth or stock
2 cups water
½ cup dry white wine
1 bay leaf, crumbled
½ teaspoon leaf basil, crumbled
¼ teaspoon leaf rosemary, crumbled
¼ teaspoon leaf thyme, crumbled
¼ teaspoon leaf marjoram, crumbled
1 small cabbage, trimmed of coarse outer leaves, quartered, cored,
    then cut into wedges slim enough to fit in the food-processor feed
    tube
¼ cup minced fresh parsley (I prefer to do an amount this small by
    hand)
Salt and freshly ground black pepper to taste

Fit chopping blade into processor work bowl, set lid in place and, with the motor running, drop in about 4 cubes of beef. **NOTE:** *Although manufacturers of food processors insist that it is possible to grind as much as half a pound of beef at a time, I have had machines stall under the load and find it better to chop tougher cuts this way.* Pulse or turn the machine on, off, on, off—using 3 or 4 short bursts—until the beef is coarsely chopped. With the machine off, transfer beef to a very large, heavy kettle. Repeat until all beef is coarsely chopped. Add the butter or oil to the kettle, set over moderate heat and allow beef to sauté slowly while you prepare the vegetables.

ᐧ Place half of the onion wedges and the garlic in the processor work bowl fitted with the metal chopping blade, then chop coarsely with 3 or 4 fast pulses or on-offs. With the machine off, scoop contents into soup kettle; chop remaining onion the same way and add to kettle. Coarsely chop the carrots (10 to 15 seconds of nonstop chopping should do it). Add carrots to kettle, then chop the parsnips the same way and add to kettle.

The remaining vegetables will be sliced, so remove chopping blade from processor and fit slicing disc into place. Slice first the celery, then the beets and turnips (the work bowl should be large enough to accommodate them all, but if it seems to be filling up, turn motor off, scrape vegetables into kettle, then slice remaining vegetables). Add all remaining ingredients to kettle except for cabbage, parsley, salt and pepper. Bring mixture to a simmer, cover and cook slowly for 2 to 3 hours. If the heat under the kettle is low enough, it doesn't much matter how long you simmer the soup—I've sometimes let it laze along for the better part of a day. About ½ hour before serving, thin-slice the cabbage wedges in the processor and add to the soup along with the minced parsley. Season to taste with salt and pepper, re-cover and simmer 30 to 40 minutes longer, just until cabbage is tender and flavors are well blended.

Italian Meatball-and-Vegetable Soup
Makes 8 to 10 servings

What a boon the food processor is when it comes to making this long-winded recipe! It will spare you an hour or more of slicing and mincing and grinding. You'll note that in the list of meatball ingredients, I call for dry bread crumbs and freshly grated Parmesan cheese instead of telling at this point how to prepare them in the processor. These are the kinds of staples that are handy to have on hand to begin with. For directions on how to grate the Parmesan and make the bread crumbs in the food processor, refer to A *Dictionary of Foods & How to Process Them.*

1 meaty beef shank, about 4 inches long
2 quarts water
1 tablespoon salt (or to taste)
¼ teaspoon freshly ground black pepper
½ small rutabaga, peeled and cut into columns about the height of
*   the processor feed tube and 1-inch square*
1 large baking potato, peeled and halved lengthwise
2 medium-size carrots, peeled and cut into 4-inch lengths

2 large celery ribs, trimmed, washed and cut into 4-inch lengths
2 medium-size yellow onions, peeled and cut into slim wedges
½ small sweet green pepper, washed, cored and seeded
¼ small cabbage, cored and cut into 1½-inch chunks
3 juicily ripe medium-size tomatoes, washed, cored and cut into slim
    wedges (no need to peel)
1 to 2 tablespoons light brown sugar (if needed to mellow the
    tartness of the tomatoes)

MEATBALLS:

½ pound boneless beef chuck, trimmed of sinew, cut into 1-inch
    cubes and chilled well
1 small yellow onion, peeled and cut into 1-inch cubes
¼ cup fine dry bread crumbs
¼ cup freshly grated Parmesan cheese
1 small garlic clove, peeled and crushed
½ teaspoon salt
⅛ teaspoon freshly ground black pepper
3 to 4 tablespoons cold water (just enough to bind the meatballs)

Simmer the beef shank in the water with the salt and pepper in a large heavy kettle for 30 minutes.

Meanwhile, prepare the meatballs: Fit the food processor with the metal chopping blade; add the beef and onion cubes and, with three or four 5-second bursts of speed, grind quite fine (the moisture in the onion makes it possible to grind the beef all at once instead of bit by bit as in the preceding recipe). If after this amount of processing the texture still seems coarse, pulse or turn the motor on and off several more times until mixture is velvety. Empty into a bowl and mix well with all the remaining meatball ingredients, adding only enough of the cold water to bind the mixture together. Shape into ½-inch balls and set aside for the time being.

Remove the metal chopping blade from the processor, wash and dry and set aside. Slip the slicing disc into place (no need to wash the work bowl at this point), then thin-slice the rutabaga by pushing it through the slicer with gentle pressure. Add to soup kettle. Thin-slice the potato the same way and add to kettle along with all of the meatballs. Cover and simmer for 1 hour, stirring from time to time. Meanwhile, wash and dry the processor work bowl and slicing disc. Reassemble, and thin-slice the carrots, celery, onions and green pepper. Add all to soup kettle.

Remove the slicing disc from the processor and slip the metal chopping blade back into place. Put about 2 cups of cabbage chunks into the work bowl and, with 5 to 7 quick pulses or bursts of power, chop the cabbage moderately fine; empty into soup kettle; repeat until all cabbage is chopped, adding each batch to the kettle as it is done. Cover and simmer 20 minutes. Put half of the tomatoes in the processor and chop fairly coarsely with 1 or 2 pulses or quick on-offs of the motor; add to kettle. Repeat with remaining tomatoes and add to kettle. Cover and simmer 30 minutes longer. Taste soup and, if it seems tart, stir in 1 to 2 tablespoons light brown sugar. Also add more salt, if needed. Ladle into soup bowls and serve. This soup, by the way, keeps well in the refrigerator for 4 to 5 days. It also freezes well.

Lamb and Lima Bean Soup
with Turnips and Parsnips
Makes 6 to 8 servings

2 medium-size yellow onions, peeled and halved lengthwise
2 large celery ribs, trimmed, washed and cut into 4-inch lengths
2 tablespoons any meat drippings or cooking oil
2 medium-size carrots, peeled and cut into 1-inch chunks
2 medium-size parsnips, peeled and cut into 1-inch chunks
2 medium-size turnips, peeled and cut into 1-inch chunks
1 cup dried whole green peas, washed, sorted and soaked overnight
    in just enough cold water to cover
½ cup medium pearl barley, washed
2½ quarts water
1 tablespoon salt (or to taste)
¼ teaspoon freshly ground black pepper
1 lamb shank, cracked
1 cup dried baby lima beans, washed, sorted and soaked overnight
    in just enough cold water to cover
1 cup loosely packed parsley sprigs, washed and patted very dry on
    paper toweling

In a food processor fitted with the slicing disc, thin-slice the onion halves, two at a time, by pushing them through the feed tube with a light touch. Thin-slice the celery the same way. Dump onions and celery into a very large, heavy kettle; add meat drippings or oil, set over moderate heat and stir-fry 8 to 10 minutes until golden. Remove slicing disc from processor and slip the metal chopping blade into place. Add the carrots and chop quite fine by letting the motor run nonstop for 25 to 30 seconds; add to kettle. Chop the parsnips, then the turnips the same way. (The turnips will only require 10 to 20 seconds of chopping, because they are softer and moister than the carrots or parsnips.) Add to the kettle along with the soaked and drained green peas, the barley, water, salt, pepper and lamb shank. Cover and simmer 1 hour.

Meanwhile wash and dry the processor work bowl and chopping blade and reassemble (you'll use it later to mince the parsley). When the soup has cooked for the allotted hour, stir in the soaked and drained baby limas, re-cover and simmer 1 hour longer. Pile the parsley into the food processor and with a couple of fast pulses or whirs, mince moderately coarsely. Stir into soup. Fish the lamb shank from the soup, cut all meat from the bone and return the meat to the kettle. Recover and simmer 10 minutes longer. Ladle into large soup bowls and serve. To accompany, you'll need nothing more than crusty chunks of French bread and a crisp green salad.

Meats

Wiener (Viennese) Goulash

Makes 8 to 10 servings

Whenever special guests were coming to dinner, my mother would take down her wooden recipe box and pull out a card written in an angular German script. I have that card today, and although I understand very little German, I keep the Wiener Goulash recipe to remind me of the days when Mother and I would sit down to a morning of chopping onions and slicing mushrooms. It was tiresome work, but Mother always eased the tedium (if not the tears) by telling me of the wonderful year that she and my father had spent in Vienna as newlyweds. It was there that she was given the goulash recipe, by her Viennese landlady, if I remember correctly. As I prepare the recipe today, I wonder what that old-fashioned Austrian cook would think of speed-slicing the onions and mushrooms in a food processor. I suspect that she would be delighted. And I know that my mother would be.

6 pounds boned lean beef chuck, cut into 1½-inch cubes
1 cup all-purpose flour (unsifted)
⅓ to ½ cup unsalted butter
6 large yellow onions, peeled and cut into wedges slim enough to fit
  into the feed tube of a food processor
2 garlic cloves, peeled and crushed
2 pounds medium-size mushrooms, wiped clean with a damp cloth
  (trim stems so that mushrooms will fit sideways in feed tube of a
  food processor)
¼ cup paprika (preferably the Hungarian sweet rose paprika)
½ teaspoon leaf thyme, crumbled
Pinch of ground nutmeg or mace
1 pint strong beef stock
½ cup dry red wine
1 teaspoon salt (or to taste)

¼ teaspoon freshly ground black pepper (or to taste)
1 cup sour cream, at room temperature

Dredge the beef, 8 to 10 cubes at a time, by shaking in the flour in a heavy paper bag, then brown well on all sides in the butter in a very large heavy kettle over moderately high heat. Begin with about 4 table-spoons butter and about a fourth of the beef; as you continue browning the beef, add butter as needed to keep beef from sticking. Drain browned beef on paper toweling. Slice onion wedges crosswise in a food processor fitted with a slicing disc (the fine-slicing disc, if you have one). NOTE: *Although the original goulash recipe calls for coarsely chopped onions, I find slicing both simpler and faster—a one-step operation because the onion wedges can be added to the feed tube as fast as the processor can slice them. Not so with chopping: you can successfully coarse-chop only two onions at a time; then you must stop the machine and empty the work bowl before proceeding. Since the onions used merely cook down into a rich brown gravy, it's immaterial whether they're sliced or chopped.*

Melt remaining butter in the kettle (there should be about 2 table-spoons left), then dump in sliced onions and garlic and let sauté over moderately low heat while you thin-slice the mushrooms in the processor. Add mushrooms to kettle and stir-fry 8 to 10 minutes, just until golden. Return beef to kettle, sprinkle with paprika, thyme and nutmeg; cover and simmer 5 minutes. Add beef stock and wine, stir well, bring to a simmer, adjust heat so that kettle liquid barely ripples, re-cover and cook slowly 3 to 4 hours, or until beef is fork-tender.

Season to taste with salt and pepper. If goulash seems too liquid at this point, simmer, uncovered, about 20 minutes, or until juices thicken slightly. Smooth in sour cream, then bring goulash to serving temperature, but do not allow to boil, lest the cream curdle. Ladle over hot buttered noodles or *nockerln* or boiled new potatoes. (*Nockerln* are now packaged like noodles and sold in many specialty food shops.)

Carbonnade Flamande

(Flemish Beef and Onion Stew with Beer)

Makes 8 servings

Any recipe calling for eight thinly sliced onions is bound to be a tearful one, unless, of course, you have a food processor to do the slicing for you.

8 medium-size yellow onions, peeled and halved lengthwise
4 tablespoons unsalted butter (about)
2 medium-size garlic cloves, peeled and crushed
4 pounds of lean, boneless beef chuck, cut into 1½-inch cubes and trimmed of excess fat
⅔ cup unsifted all-purpose flour
1 teaspoon salt (or to taste)
¼ teaspoon crumbled leaf thyme
Several hefty grindings of black pepper
Pinch of freshly ground nutmeg
2 cans (12 ounces each) light lager beer

In a food processor fitted with the slicing disc, thin-slice the onion halves by pushing them down the feed tube with minimal pressure. Melt 2 tablespoons of the butter in a large heavy kettle over moderate heat, add the onions and garlic and stir-fry about 10 minutes until limp and golden; lift with a slotted spoon to paper toweling to drain. Add the remaining 2 tablespoons of butter to the kettle and let it melt while you dredge the beef.

Shake the beef, a few cubes at a time, in the flour in a heavy brown paper bag to dredge; then brown in the butter, again a few cubes at a time, over moderately high heat. As the beef browns, lift to paper toweling to drain. Continue until all beef is browned, adding a bit of additional butter if necessary. Return all of the beef to the kettle with the onions and the garlic; sprinkle with salt, thyme, pepper and nutmeg. Pour in the beer, adjust heat so that mixture simmers slowly, then cover and cook about 2 hours until you can pierce a cube of beef easily with a fork.

Turn the heat off, cool to room temperature, then cover and refrigerate for at least 8 hours. Uncover, skim off and discard as much fat as possible, then set, uncovered, over low heat and bring slowly to serving temperature. Taste for salt and pepper and add more if necessary. Serve with small new potatoes boiled in their skins, a crisp green salad and frosty glasses of beer.

Beef Stroganoff
Makes 4 servings

What most of us think of as Stroganoff—a sort of beef and mushroom stew awash with sour cream—isn't Stroganoff at all. The real thing contains no sliced mushrooms, very little sour cream, and it is made not with stew beef but with tenderloin, which the French-fry cutter (an extra available for some food processors) cuts precisely the right size. **NOTE:** *Before using the French-fry cutter to cut the meat, read the warning under* **Beef, Raw: To Shred,** *in* A Dictionary of Foods & How to Process Them. (If you haven't a machine with this attachment, you can processor-slice the tenderloin with the serrated slicing disc [preferably a thick-slicing one], but *do* exert firm pressure on the pusher as you guide the tenderloin down the feed tube so that the slices will have some substance to them. The texture of the Stroganoff will be more like that of a Chinese stir-fried wok dish, but the flavor will nevertheless be decidedly Russian.) **NOTE:** *Although an authentic Stroganoff does not contain mushrooms, I sometimes add a couple of tablespoons of Duxelles, which, I think, enriches the flavor.*

> 2 pounds well-trimmed beef tenderloin, sliced 1 inch thick and
>   trimmed of any connective tissue
> 1 large Spanish onion, peeled and cut vertically into chunks that will
>   fit into the food-processor feed tube
> ½ teaspoon salt (or to taste)
> ¼ teaspoon freshly ground black pepper
> 5 tablespoons unsalted butter
> 3 tablespoons flour
> 1½ cups beef stock or broth
> 1 tablespoon Dijon mustard
> 1 tablespoon tomato paste
> 2 tablespoons Duxelles (optional; see Index for recipe page number)
> ½ cup sour cream, at room temperature

Arrange the slices of tenderloin between sheets of wax paper and set in the freezer until firm enough to cut neatly with the processor—about 1½ hours. Equip a food processor with the slicing disc and thin-slice the onion by pushing the chunks lightly down the feed tube, one at a time. Empty onto a piece of wax paper and set aside. If you do not have the French-fry-cutting disc, slice the beef this way: Stand a semi-frozen slice of tenderloin on end in the feed tube, turn the motor on and push the meat through with firm, steady pressure. Repeat until all meat is sliced. The technique is precisely the same for the French-fry-cutting disc.

Put the cut meat on a large sheet of wax paper, sprinkle with salt and pepper and toss well with your hands to mix. Now spread the meat out on the wax paper and blanket with the onion slices. Let stand at room temperature for 2 hours so the tenderloin will absorb a good bit of the onion flavor. Remove the onions from the beef and save to use in a soup or stew. (You won't need them again for the Stroganoff.)

Melt 2 tablespoons of the butter in a large heavy skillet over moderate heat, blend in the flour and heat about 2 minutes, stirring constantly, until you have a smooth golden roux. Pour in the stock and cook, stirring all the while, about 3 minutes, until thickened and smooth. Blend in the mustard, tomato paste, and if you like, the *Duxelles*, turn heat to lowest point and allow sauce to mellow while you brown the beef.

Melt the remaining 3 tablespoons of butter in a second large heavy skillet over high heat, add the tenderloin and stir-fry quickly until brown. Add the tenderloin and all its drippings to the first skillet, stir well, raise heat to moderate, cover and simmer 10 minutes, stirring once or twice. Remove the skillet from the heat and smooth in the sour cream. Taste for salt, add more if needed and serve. Accompany with buttered wide noodles, if you like, but remember that this particular Stroganoff has very little gravy.

Ukrainian Borsch with Beef and Pork

Makes 10 to 12 servings

1 pound lean, boneless beef chuck, cut into 1-inch cubes
4 tablespoons butter or bacon drippings

1 pound boneless pork shoulder, cut into 1-inch cubes

4 medium-size yellow onions, peeled and halved lengthwise

4 large carrots, peeled and cut into 4-inch lengths

4 medium-size celery ribs, washed, trimmed and cut into 4-inch
  lengths

6 large leeks, trimmed, washed very well to remove bits of grit and
  sand and cut into 4-inch lengths

8 large beets, trimmed, washed, peeled and halved lengthwise

4 large ripe tomatoes, washed, cored and cut into slim wedges (no
  need to peel)

3 quarts water

2 tablespoons cider vinegar

2 large parsley branches

1 teaspoon crumbled leaf thyme

½ teaspoon crumbled leaf chervil

1 small cabbage, trimmed, cored and cut into columns about the
  height and width of the food-processor feed tube

2 tablespoons salt (or to taste)

¼ teaspoon freshly ground black pepper

1 cup sour cream

⅓ cup snipped fresh dill

Brown the beef in the butter in a very large heavy kettle set over high heat; push to one side of kettle, add pork and brown also. Reduce heat to moderately low and let the beef and pork continue to cook while you prepare the vegetables. In a food processor fitted with the slicing disc, thin-slice the onions by pushing them lightly down the feed tube. Add to kettle, stir well, and allow to sauté while you slice the carrots, celery and leeks—push them down the feed tube lightly, as you did the onions, then dump all into kettle. Now thin-slice 6 of the beets and add to kettle (the remaining 2 will be shredded later and added to the borsch shortly before serving to impart their rich, red color). Sauté vegetables, stirring, 12 to 15 minutes.

Remove the slicing disc from the processor and slip the metal chopping blade into place (no need to wash the work bowl). Add about half of the tomato wedges and chop moderately coarsely by pulsing or snapping the motor on and off 4 to 5 times; add to kettle. Chop remaining tomatoes the same way and add to the kettle also. Now pour in the water, add the vinegar, parsley branches, thyme and chervil and bring to a gentle simmer. Cover the kettle and cook 2½ to 3 hours, or until meats are very tender and flavors well blended. Remove the parsley branches and discard.

In a clean processor work bowl fitted with a clean slicing disc, thin-slice the columns of cabbage, one at a time, by pushing them down the feed tube with almost no pressure. Add cabbage to soup, re-cover the kettle and cook for 30 minutes. Now remove the slicing disc from the processor and fit the shredding disc in place (no need to wash or rinse the work bowl). Shred the remaining 2 beets, add to kettle, stir well to mix, then simmer the borsch for about 30 to 45 minutes, or until cabbage and shredded beets are quite tender. Add the salt and pepper, taste and add a little more of each, if needed.

Ladle into large soup bowls and serve, topping each portion with a drift of sour cream and a sprinkling of snipped fresh dill. NOTE: *The borsch keeps well in the refrigerator for about a week; it also freezes well.*

Chili
Makes 8 to 10 servings

This chili has a beefier flavor than most, because it's made with lean chunks of chuck that have been coarsely ground in the food processor, instead of with conventional hamburger.

> *1 pound dried red kidney beans, washed and sorted*
> *2 quarts cold water*
> *4 large yellow onions, peeled and cut into slim wedges*
> *2 large garlic cloves, peeled and crushed*
> *3 tablespoons butter*
> *2 pounds very lean beef chuck, cut into 1-inch cubes, trimmed of*
>   *sinew and chilled well*
> *⅓ cup chili powder*
> *1 bay leaf, crumbled*
> *½ teaspoon crumbled leaf thyme*
> *¼ teaspoon crumbled leaf marjoram*
> *1½ teaspoons salt (or to taste)*
> *¼ teaspoon freshly ground black pepper*
> *1 pound vine-ripened tomatoes (preferably Italian plum tomatoes,*
>   *which have a more mellow flavor), washed (no need to peel)*

Soak the beans in the water in a large heavy kettle overnight. Next day, drain the beans, reserving the soaking water, Measure soaking water and add enough cold water to total 1 quart. Return beans and water to the kettle, set over moderate heat, cover and simmer about 1 hour, or until beans are firm-tender.

Meanwhile, coarsely chop the onions in the food processor fitted with the metal chopping blade. You'll only be able to chop about one third of the total amount of onions at a time; use 2 or 3 pulses or fast bursts of speed for each batch. As you chop the onions, dump them into a very large heavy kettle to which you have already added the garlic and butter. Sauté the onions over moderate heat about 10 minutes until limp and golden. **NOTE:** *Before chopping the beef, read the notes under* **Beef** *in* A Dictionary of Foods & How to Process Them *(consult Index for page number).* Machine-chop the beef coarsely, as directed, then add to kettle. Stir-fry 10 to 12 minutes, just until beef is no longer pink—the point is not to brown it, merely to take the raw edge off. Sprinkle chili powder over surface of beef, add bay leaf, thyme and marjoram and heat and stir about 5 minutes to mellow the seasonings.

Drain the kidney beans well, reserving the cooking water, and add to kettle along with 1 cup of the bean-cooking water, the salt and pepper. If you are using the Italian plum tomatoes, you won't have to core them, but do halve them lengthwise; if you're using the regular garden variety of tomatoes, cut out the cores, then divide each tomato into slim wedges. Place about half the tomatoes in the processor work bowl (still fitted with the metal chopping blade) and, with 10 to 15 seconds of nonstop buzzing, reduce to a purée. Add to chili mixture, purée remaining tomatoes the same way and add also.

Reduce heat underneath chili to low, set lid on kettle askew, and simmer 1 to 1½ hours, or until beans are tender and flavors are well blended. If at any time the mixture seems too thick, thin with a little additional reserved bean-cooking water. Taste the chili for salt and add more, if needed. Ladle into soup bowls and serve.

Szechwan Shredded Beef and Carrots

Makes 4 servings

Szechwan cooking might be considered the "Tex-Mex" of China because it is loaded with hot peppers. This particular dish is less incendiary than most, which is one reason I like it. The authentic version calls for five-spice powder, a blend of finely ground cloves, hot peppers, cinnamon, fennel and star anise. Because five-spice powder is not widely available across the country, I have taken the liberty of using the component spices, then grinding them up in the processor. If you are unable to obtain star anise (most Chinese groceries stock it), substitute ⅛ teaspoon regular anise seeds or ground anise. If you have the five-spice powder on hand or are able to obtain it, use ¾ teaspoon of it in place of the individual spices and heighten the pepperiness to taste with cayenne; then buzz it up in the marinade as the recipe directs.

You'll note that I call for beef tenderloin for preparing this recipe, which may seem extravagant. But it is the one cut of beef that shreds easily with the French-fry cutter (an extra available for some food processors). I have experimented with beef chuck, which is so full of sinew that it is easier to hand-cut it then to remove all the gristle and connective tissue preparatory to using the processor. The same goes for rump and flank. Moreover, these cuts are not suitable for stir-frying because they need slow, moist cooking if they are to become succulent and tender. **NOTE:** *Before using the French-fry cutter to shred the beef, read the warning under* **Beef, Raw**: To Shred, *in* A Dictionary of Foods & How to Process Them.

MARINADE:

1 *large garlic clove, peeled*
2 *cubes (about 1 inch each) of fresh ginger root, peeled*
¼ *teaspoon ground cloves*
¼ *teaspoon ground cinnamon*
¼ *teaspoon fennel seeds*
1 *small star anise or ⅛ teaspoon anise seeds or ground anise*
⅛ *teaspoon crushed red chili peppers (use ¼ teaspoon for a really "hot" dish)*
3 *tablespoons dry sherry*
3 *tablespoons dark soy sauce*
1 *tablespoon sesame oil*

1 pound trimmed beef tenderloin, sliced 1 inch thick (The pieces of
    tenderloin should be about the right size to stand on end in the
    feed tube of the processor.)
2 medium-size carrots, peeled and cut into 4-inch lengths
2 medium-size celery ribs, trimmed, washed and cut into 4-inch
    lengths
6 medium-size scallions, trimmed, washed and cut into 4-inch
    lengths (include some green tops)
3 tablespoons peanut oil (about)

Prepare the marinade first: Place all ingredients in the work bowl of a
food processor fitted with the metal chopping blade and churn for 60
seconds nonstop. Scrape down the work-bowl lid and sides, re-cover
and churn 60 seconds longer (mixture will splatter considerably, so
keep the pusher in the feed tube). Pour into a large shallow mixing
bowl and let stand until you are ready to use. Wash and dry the processor work bowl, lid, pusher and chopping blade. Reassemble, insert-
ing the French-fry cutter this time.

Place the slices of beef between two pieces of wax paper and set in
the freezer until partially frozen—about 1½ hours. This is to firm the
beef up sufficiently so that it will cut into neat shreds rather than be
mashed to pulp by the cutting blade's fierce action. When the beef is
firm, stand a slice on end in the feed tube of the processor, snap the
motor on or depress the Pulse button and push through, exerting
steady, moderately heavy pressure on the pusher. Repeat until all beef
is shredded. Empty at once into the marinade, toss well to mix, then
let stand at room temperature 1 hour. Again quickly wash and dry the
processor parts; reassemble, putting in the shredding disc this time.

About 5 minutes before you are ready to cook the dish, shred the
carrots and empty onto a piece of wax paper. Remove the shredding
disc and slip the slicing disc into place. Now thin-slice the celery and
scallions together (the feed tube should be large enough to accommodate them all at once) by pushing them through the slicer with light
pressure.

Heat 2 tablespoons of the peanut oil in a wok or in a large, heavy
skillet set over high heat until a slice of scallion will sizzle; dump in the
scallions and celery with the shredded carrots and stir-fry about 3 minutes, just until limp. Quickly add 1 to 2 additional tablespoons of oil,
also the beef and any remaining marinade, and stir-fry 2 to 3 minutes,

just until beef is no longer red—it will not brown in the conventional way because of the moisture in the wok. Serve at once with fluffy boiled rice.

Sukiyaki
Makes 4 servings

If the processor is to cut the beef into gossamer slices, you must partially freeze it so that it offers some resistance to the cutting blade and will stand up against the machine's force rather than being reduced to pulp. At many Japanese restaurants, *sukiyaki* is prepared at table. You can do this, too, if you have an electric wok.

1 pound well-trimmed beef tenderloin
1 small Spanish onion, peeled and halved lenghwise
8 medium-size scallions, trimmed, washed and cut into 4-inch
    lengths (include some green tops)
½ pound medium-size mushrooms, wiped clean and stemmed
    (reserve stems to use in another recipe later)
2 tablespoons peanut oil
¼ pound trimmed and washed tender young spinach leaves
1 can (8 ounces) shirataki *noodles, drained (these cellophane-like*
    noodles are stocked by most Oriental groceries and by the
    "gourmet" sections of better supermarkets)
1 can (8 ounces) sliced bamboo shoots, drained
2 cakes of tofu *(bean curd), drained and cut into 1-inch cubes*
⅓ cup Japanese soy sauce
⅓ cup mirin *(sweet rice wine), dry sherry or Port*
2 tablespoons sugar

Slice the tenderloin 1 inch thick, lay slices between two pieces of wax paper and set in the freezer for about 1½ hours, or until fairly firm but not brick-hard. About 30 minutes before you are ready to serve, thin-slice the onion and scallions in a food processor fitted with the slicing disc; dump onto a piece of wax paper and set aside. Stand as many mushrooms on their sides in the feed tube of the processor as needed for a fairly tight fit, turn the motor on or depress the Pulse button and push them through the slicing disc with gentle pressure. Repeat until all mushrooms are thin-sliced, then empty onto a piece of wax paper and set aside. Now stand a slice of beef tenderloin on end in the feed tube, turn the motor on or depress the Pulse button and push the beef through, using firm pressure on the pusher. Repeat until all beef has been sliced; empty onto a piece of wax paper and set aside also.

Heat the peanut oil in a wok or in a large, heavy skillet over moderately high heat until a piece of onion, dropped into the oil, will sizzle. Dump in the sliced onion and scallions and stir-fry about 2 minutes. Now add the spinach, *shirataki* and bamboo shoots and stir-fry about 2 minutes, just until spinach is wilted. Add the beef and stir-fry 2 minutes, then add the bean curd. Quickly mix together the soy sauce, *mirin* and sugar and dump into the wok. Heat and stir the *sukiyaki* 2 minutes longer, just until steaming hot. Serve at once with fluffy boiled rice.

NOTE: *If you are going to cook the* sukiyaki *at table, arrange all of the ingredients as artfully as possible on a large platter, more or less beginning with the bean curd and beef, then working backward up the ingredient list to the scallions and onion—this is to make certain that the ingredients to be cooked first are on top and easily accessible. Pour the peanut oil into a small ramekin; also, combine the soy sauce,* mirin *and sugar in a cruet. Set the electric wok on the table, then group the* sukiyaki *ingredients and any utensils you will need in such a way that you can get at them easily. The procedure for cooking the* sukiyaki *at table is exactly the same as described above.*

Steak Tartare

Makes 2 servings

For Steak Tartare you should go to a trusted butcher and buy from him the very best tenderloin he has. The meat, as you know, is ground and eaten raw, and there is nothing in the recipe that can mask inferior quality. So that I can avoid washing the processor work bowl in the course of preparing the recipe, I mince the herbs first, then the onion, and finally the beef. It's not only an efficient sequence, it also means that any residual herb or onion flavor in the work bowl will be absorbed by the beef. I like to vary the herbs I serve with Steak Tartare, depending upon which of my kitchen herbs needs trimming. Tarragon is a particular favorite, also fresh chervil and dill. I usually add a few fronds of one or the other to the work bowl along with the parsley and mince the two together.

½ cup loosely packed parsley springs, washed and patted very dry on paper toweling
2 to 3 sprigs of fresh tarragon, chervil or dill, washed and patted very dry on paper toweling
1 small Spanish onion, peeled and cut into 1-inch chunks
1 pound well-trimmed beef tenderloin, cut into 1-inch chunks and chilled well
2 raw egg yolks
¼ cup drained small capers
Salt and freshly ground pepper to taste

In a food processor fitted with the metal chopping blade, mince the parsley and tarragon quite fine by using two or three 5-second churnings of the motor; empty onto a piece of wax paper and set aside. Fine-mince the onion, using 5 or 6 pulses or on-offs of the motor; dump onto a piece of wax paper and set aside. Now grind the tenderloin quite fine, doing only one half of the total amount at a time and using two 5-second churnings of the motor for each.

Shape the ground tenderloin into two patties, place each on a luncheon plate and make a depression in the center of each. Ease an egg yolk into the hollow in each patty, then sprinkle both with the minced parsley-herb mixture. Place the chopped onion and capers in separate small bowls so that each person can help himself to as much of each as he wants. Also set out the salt shaker and pepper mill. Other popular accompaniments for steak Tartare: buttered melba toast, minced anchovies, watercress, lemon wedges and Worcestershire or steak sauce.

Émincé de Veau à la Zürichoise
(Minced Veal Zurich Style)

Makes 4 servings

"Minced" here does not mean "ground," but thinly cut strips of veal, approximately 1½ inches long and ¼ inch wide. I've found that the

French-fry cutter (an extra available for some food processors) cuts the veal precisely the right size *if* you use only the tenderest, milk-fed baby veal (sold as *"Plume de Veau"* or *"Provimi Delft Blue"* in most parts of the country), *if* you use top round (scaloppine also comes from this cut), *if* you cut the meat into columns about the height and width of the food-processor feed tube, *if* you trim each piece of veal of all sinew and connective tissue, and finally, *if* you freeze each just long enough so that it will stand upright in the food-processor feed tube and offer some resistance to the cutting blade. Lots of *ifs*, but it works. NOTE: *Before using the French-fry cutter to cut the veal, read the warning under* Beef, Raw: To Shred, *in* A Dictionary of Foods & How to Process Them.

Émincé de Veau is a favorite throughout Switzerland and the traditional accompaniment is *Rösti,* a crisp-crusted grated-potato pancake. (The recipe is included elsewhere; see Index for page number.) Each Swiss canton has a slightly different way of preparing an *émincé* and the Zurich way is to add sliced morels. Because fresh morels are rarely available in this country, I have substituted the more conventional "supermarket" mushrooms. And very good they are, too.

1½ pounds top round of baby veal (Have the butcher cut one chunk
*   of top round about 1½ inches thick.)*
5 tablespoons unsalted butter
1 large shallot, peeled and minced
½ pound fresh medium-size mushrooms, wiped clean and stemmed
*   (reserve stems)*
½ cup dry white wine
1½ cups heavy cream
½ teaspoon salt
Several grindings of black pepper

Cut the veal into pieces about the height and width of the food-processor feed tube, trim each of connective tissue, wrap in plastic food wrap and freeze several hours—just until meat firms up (it should not be frozen brick-hard). Equip the food processor with the French-fry disc, stand a piece of veal in the feed tube, turn the motor on or depress the Pulse button and push the veal down the feed tube, using steady pressure. Repeat until all veal has been cut into thin strips. NOTE: *If the processor balks, it probably means that you have not removed all sinew and connective tissue. Turn the motor off, disassem-*

ble the machine and clean any bits of connective tissue from the cutting disc. Reassemble the processor and proceed.

Heat one half of the butter in a large heavy skillet over moderately high heat until frothy, add half of the veal and stir-fry quickly until lightly browned; transfer to a bowl with a slotted spoon. Add the remaining butter and stir-fry the remaining veal the same way; add to bowl. Add the minced shallot to the skillet and let sauté while you slice the mushrooms.

Remove the French-fry cutter from the food processor and slip the slicing disc into place (no need to wash the work bowl). Thin-slice the mushrooms by standing the caps on their sides in the feed tube (as many at a time as needed for a snug fit) and pushing them through with gentle pressure. Thin-slice the stems also. Add all mushrooms to the skillet and sauté 8 to 10 minutes until limp and lightly browned. Add the white wine, raise the heat to high, and boil until the wine has been reduced, leaving a rich brown glaze over the mushrooms. Reduce heat to moderate, add the cream, salt and pepper and cook, stirring constantly, until cream has reduced by about one third. Return the veal to the skillet, also any drippings in its bowl, and cook and stir 2 to 3 minutes longer, just until the veal is heated through and nicely glazed with cream. Serve at once.

Veal Birds Stuffed with Leeks and Liver Sausage
Makes 4 servings

STUFFING:

3 leeks, washed well, trimmed and cut into 4-inch lengths
2 tablespoons butter
1 hard-cooked egg, peeled and halved lengthwise
¼ pound soft liver sausage, sliced thin

1½ pounds veal round, sliced ¼ inch thick and pounded thin as for scaloppine
1½ teaspoons salt
¼ teaspoons freshly ground black pepper
2 tablespoons butter
¾ cup beef stock or broth

¼ cup tomato purée
1 tablespoon prepared mild yellow mustard

Prepare the stuffing first: In a food processor equipped with the slicing disc, thin-slice the leeks by pushing them down the feed tube with very little pressure. Melt the butter in a heavy saucepan, add leeks and stir-fry about 5 minutes over moderate heat until limp and golden. Remove the slicing disc from the food processor and slip the metal chopping blade into place (no need to wash the work bowl). Add the egg and chop fine, using 3 or 4 pulses or on-offs of the motor. Add the sautéed leeks and liver sausage. Pulse or snap the motor on and off 3 or 4 times until mixture begins to cream, then let run steadily for 5 seconds. Examine the mixture and, if it is not creamy-smooth, buzz for 5 seconds more.

Sprinkle one side of each veal slice with salt and pepper, then place a dab of stuffing on each. Roll up jelly-roll style and secure with wooden toothpicks. Brown the veal rolls, half of them at a time, in the butter in a large, heavy skillet, allowing 8 to 10 minutes for each batch. Return the first batch to the skillet, combine the beef stock, tomato purée and mustard and add to skillet. Cover and simmer 20 to 25 minutes, or until veal is tender. Serve topped with the pan juices.

Escalopes de Veau Chasseur
(Sautéed Veal Scallops Hunter's Style)

Makes 4 servings

½ pound medium-size mushrooms, wiped clean and stemmed
  (reserve stems)
4 shallots, peeled
1 small garlic clove, peeled
2 medium-size firm-ripe tomatoes, peeled, cored and cut into slim
  wedges
1½ pounds veal round, sliced ¼ inch thick and pounded thin as for
  scaloppine
2 tablespoons butter
1 tablespoon cooking oil
½ teaspoon salt
⅛ teaspoon freshly ground black pepper

1 tablespoon minced fresh tarragon or ½ teaspoon crumbled leaf
   tarragon
⅓ cup dry vermouth
½ cup beef stock or broth
1 tablespoon cornstarch blended with 2 tablespoons cold water
2 tablespoons minced fresh parsley

Into the feed tube of a food processor equipped with the slicing disc
stand as many mushroom caps on their sides as will fit fairly snugly.
Turn machine on or depress the Pulse button and thin-slice the mushrooms. Repeat until all mushrooms are sliced. Empty into a bowl and
set aside. Remove slicing disc from food processor, slip the metal chopping blade into place, add mushroom stems and, with 2 or 3 pulses or
whirs of the motor, mince fairly coarsely. Add to mushrooms in bowl.
Now add shallots and garlic to the work bowl and with 3 or 4 pulses or
on-offs, mince relatively fine. Scoop onto a piece of wax paper and
reserve. Now place tomatoes in the machine and chop coarsely with 3
or 4 fast pulses of the motor. Leave tomatoes in the work bowl.

Pat the veal scallops dry on paper toweling; heat the butter and oil in
a large, heavy skillet over moderately high heat until a cube of bread
will sizzle in it. Brown the veal, a few pieces at a time, 1 to 2 minutes
on each side. Drain on paper toweling, sprinkle with salt and pepper
and keep warm at the back of the stove. Add sliced mushroom caps
and chopped stems to the skillet and stir-fry in the drippings about 5
minutes over moderate heat; add shallots and garlic and stir-fry about 5
minutes longer. Add chopped tomatoes and tarragon, then cover and
simmer 5 minutes. Add vermouth, beef stock and cornstarch paste and
cook and stir 5 to 10 minutes, or until sauce has reduced and is the
consistency of gravy. Taste for salt and pepper, and add more, if
needed. Return the veal scallops to the skillet and warm 2 to 3 minutes, basting with the sauce. Sprinkle with parsley and serve.

Spadini alla Siciliana

(Skewered Ham-and-Caper-Stuffed Veal Rolls
Sicilian Style)

Makes 8 servings

For years I've been enjoying this dish at one of New York City's fine little neighborhood restaurants—Sal Anthony's, on Irving Place a few blocks south of Gramercy Park. But it wasn't until I bought a food processor that I attempted to make *spadini* for myself. I hadn't the nerve to ask the chef for his secret recipe, but have come up with something fairly close to it. *Spadini* is an excellent party dish because it can be made several hours ahead of time—all but the finishing touches. And the food processor magically simplifies the preparation. Make the stuffing first and chop the ingredients in the food processor in the order listed; that way you won't have to wash and dry the work bowl several times along the way.

STUFFING:

½ cup loosely packed parsley sprigs, washed and patted very dry on
    paper toweling
4 slices firm-textured white bread, torn into 1½-inch pieces
½ pound fully cooked smoked ham, trimmed of sinew and cut into 1-
    inch cubes
¼ cup freshly grated Parmesan cheese
2 tablespoons well-drained small capers
¾ teaspoon crumbled leaf sage
¼ teaspoon crumbled leaf thyme
⅛ teaspoon freshly ground black pepper
1 small garlic clove, peeled and crushed
½ cup light cream (about)
Salt (if needed to taste)

SPADINI:

2 pounds veal scaloppine, pounded very thin and cut into rectangles
    about 6 inches long and 4 inches wide
½ pound prosciutto, sliced tissue-thin
2 large Spanish onions, peeled and cut into eighths
Olive oil (for brushing onion wedges)

2 pounds medium-size mushrooms, wiped clean and trimmed of stems
6 tablespoons butter
6 garlic cloves, peeled
⅔ cup dry white wine
Salt and freshly ground black pepper to taste

For the stuffing: In a food processor fitted with the metal chopping blade, mince the parsley quite fine, using 7 to 8 pulses or bursts of speed; empty into a mixing bowl. Buzz the bread to soft, moderately fine crumbs the same way, with 5 or 6 pulses or on-offs of the motor. Empty into bowl with parsley. Now grind the ham very fine—three or four 5-second whirs of the chopping blade should be about right. Add to mixing bowl along with all remaining stuffing ingredients. Mix well with your hands to combine, and if mixture seems too dry or crumbly, stir in another tablespoon or so of cream. Taste for salt and add if necessary. (Whether or not you will need salt will depend upon the saltiness of the ham.)

For the spadini: Spoon about 1 heaping teaspoon of the stuffing onto one end of each piece of scaloppine; you will roll these up the long way, jelly-roll style, so shape the stuffing into a small mound across the narrow, 4-inch width of veal. Roll veal up snugly, then wrap each roll in a slice of prosciutto so that both the veal and the stuffing are completely enclosed. You won't need to use toothpicks to secure the veal rolls: the prosciutto is virtually self-sealing. Thread the *spadini* on long metal skewers, allowing 4 to each skewer and spacing the rolls about 1 inch apart. Place on a large metal tray, cover loosely and refrigerate until about 20 minutes before serving. When ready to proceed, separate the onion wedges so that you have crescents of onion, each about 2 layers (or 2 plies) thick. Thread the onions onto 4 long metal skewers and brush them liberally with olive oil. Set aside for the time being.

For the sauce: Wash and dry the food-processor bowl and equip it with the slicing disc. Stack enough mushrooms on their sides in the feed tube for a fairly tight fit, then thin-slice by pushing the mushrooms through the slicing disc with minimal pressure. Repeat until all mushrooms have been sliced. You'll have to do this in two batches—that is, slice half the mushrooms, then dump them into a very large heavy skillet in which you have placed the butter and the 6 garlic cloves. When all mushrooms are sliced, set the skillet over moderate heat and sauté about 10 minutes or until mushrooms are golden and their juices have cooked down. Add the white wine and allow to cook about 5 minutes longer, or until liquid is reduced by about one half. Season to taste with salt and pepper.

Broil the spadini: While the mushrooms are sautéing, broil the skewers of *spadini* about 6 inches from the flame, allowing 5 to 8 minutes per side—just until lightly browned.

Remove the skewers from the broiler and, with a wooden spoon, push the *spadini* into the skillet with the sauce. Spoon mushrooms on top, cover skillet and reduce burner heat to lowest point. Now broil the skewers of onion, also 6 inches from the flame, allowing about 5 minutes per side until onions are browned here and there. Remove skewers from broiler and, with the wooden spoon, push the onions, too, into the skillet. Stir lightly to mix, then serve, allowing 3 veal rolls per person, and top the *spadini* with a generous ladling of the mushroom-onion-garlic sauce.

Osso Buco

Makes 6 servings

Try to track down fresh basil, marjoram and rosemary for making this recipe—the flavor will be deliciously fresh and fragrant. The herbs may be processor-minced together, but each must be washed and patted bone dry first on paper toweling. For me the easiest way is to wash the herbs the night before, then to bundle them up tight in super-absorbent paper toweling and to refrigerate them until I'm ready for them.

6 veal shanks, each about 4 inches in diameter and 2½ inches thick
1 cup flour
3 tablespoons unsalted butter
2 tablespoons olive oil, in all
1½ teaspoons salt (or to taste)
¼ teaspoon freshly ground black pepper
1 large Spanish onion, peeled and cut into 1½-inch chunks
1 medium-size celery rib, washed and cut into 1-inch lengths

1 large garlic clove, peeled

2 medium-size carrots, peeled and cut into 1-inch lengths

¼ cup loosely packed Italian parsley leaves, washed and patted very
  dry on paper toweling

⅓ cup loosely packed basil leaves, washed and patted very dry on
  paper toweling or 1 teaspoon crumbled leaf basil

1 tablespoon marjoram leaves, washed and patted very dry on paper
  toweling or ½ teaspoon crumbled leaf marjoram

1 teaspoon rosemary leaves, washed and patted very dry on paper
  toweling or ¼ teaspoon crumbled leaf rosemary

2 strips (each about 1½ inches long) lemon peel (the yellow part
  only, not the bitter white rind underneath)

2 medium-size very ripe tomatoes, washed, cored and cut into slim
  wedges (no need to peel)

2 cups dry white wine

Dredge veal shanks well on all sides in the flour, then brown well in
the 3 tablespoons butter and 1 tablespoon of the oil in a large heavy
kettle over fairly high heat. You'll only be able to brown about half the
shanks at a time. Add the remaining tablespoon of olive oil when
browning second batch. As shanks brown, transfer to paper toweling to
drain. Salt and pepper each well on all sides.

In a food processor fitted with the metal chopping blade, coarsely
mince half of the onion chunks with 2 or 3 pulses or quick on-offs of the
motor; add to kettle in which you browned the veal. Repeat with remaining onion and add to kettle. Coarsely chop the celery the same
way and add to kettle. Place garlic and carrots in processor and chop
moderately fine, letting the motor run for about 10 to 15 seconds nonstop; add to kettle. Pile all fresh herbs into processor and, with a couple of pulses or quick bursts of speed, coarsely chop; mix into kettle
along with lemon peel.

Set kettle over low heat and sauté the vegetable mixture, stirring
often, about 20 minutes, or until very soft *but not brown*. Dump tomatoes into processor and reduce to juice—about 30 seconds of buzzing will do it. Add to kettle along with the wine and stir well to mix.
Return veal shanks to the kettle, pushing them down into the vegetable mixture; cover and simmer very slowly 3½ to 4 hours, or until the
meat all but falls from the bones. Remove the lemon peel, taste for salt
and add more, if needed. Serve with fluffy boiled rice.

Veal Sandwich Roast with Roquefort-Pecan Filling

Makes 6 servings

Here's a showy dish that's bound to impress.

3 medium-size carrots, peeled and cut into 1-inch chunks
¼ cup butter
1 large yellow onion, peeled and cut into slim wedges
One 3-pound boned and rolled veal loin or rump roast (Ask the
    butcher to prepare the roast carefully and tie it tightly so that
    later the slices will hold their shape.)
⅓ cup beef stock or broth
⅓ cup dry white wine
2 parsley sprigs
2 bay leaves, crumbled
¼ cup heavy cream

FILLING:

¾ cup pecans
¼ cup Roquefort cheese, softened to room temperature
3 to 4 tablespoons veal cooking liquid

In a food processor fitted with the metal chopping blade, chop the carrots moderately fine by letting the motor run nonstop for about 20 seconds. Dump into a large heavy kettle in which you have already melted the butter. Coarsely chop the onion in the processor with 2 or 3 pulses or quick bursts of speed. Add to kettle. Stir-fry the carrots and onion over moderately high heat about 5 minutes until golden; push to one side of kettle, add roast and brown it lightly on all sides. Add beef stock, wine, parsley and bay leaves, cover and simmer slowly for 1½ hours. Cool roast to room temperature; strain and reserve the cooking liquid.

Meanwhile, make the filling: Wash and dry the processor work bowl and metal chopping blade; reassemble. Place the pecans in the work bowl and, with 3 or 4 pulses or on-offs of the motor, chop. Examine the texture, and if it is still fairly coarse, let the machine run about 3 seconds longer. Your aim is to reduce the nuts to the texture of cracker meal. If they are still too coarse, whir the motor another 2 or 3 seconds. Now add the cheese and 3 tablespoons of the veal cooking liquid and whir about 10 seconds nonstop, just until mixture is creamy-smooth. If too thick (it should be about the consistency of a commercial cheese spread), add the additional tablespoon of cooking liquid and whir briefly again. Empty filling into a bowl and set aside for the time being.

With a very sharp carving knife, cut the roast into slices ¼ inch thick, making the slices as uniform as you can and arranging them on the counter in the order that you slice them so that you can reassemble the roast. Spread both sides of each slice lightly with the filling, reshaping the roast as you go. Tie securely with string, both around the roast and end to end to hold the slices firmly in place. Return roast to kettle, add the reserved cooking liquid, cover and simmer 1 hour longer.

Transfer the roast to a heatproof platter. Remove the strings carefully so as not to dislodge the slices, then drizzle with the heavy cream and brown quickly under the broiler. Strain the cooking liquid again, skim off fat, and pass the cooking liquid as gravy.

Vitello Tonnato
(Veal with Tuna Sauce)

Makes 8 servings

This Italian classic is such a workhouse of a recipe that few of us bothered to make it before food processors came along and trimmed the chopping and mincing time to minutes.

*1 boned and rolled veal rump roast weighing about 4 pounds (Make
   sure that the butcher rolls the roast tightly and ties it around at
   about 1½-inch intervals.)*
3 tablespoons olive oil
2 medium-size yellow onions, peeled and cut into slim wedges
2 medium-size celery ribs, washed and cut into 1-inch lengths
2 carrots, peeled and cut into 1-inch lengths
2 large parsley branches, washed
2 large garlic cloves, peeled
5 anchovy fillets, rinsed and patted dry on paper toweling
1 can (7 ounces) white tuna, drained well
1 cup dry white wine
Juice of ½ lemon

½ teaspoon crumbled leaf thyme
¼ teaspoon freshly ground black pepper
1 bay leaf

SAUCE:

The kettle mixture in which you cooked the veal
1½ cups mayonnaise (see Index for recipe page number)
Juice of ½ lemon
¼ cup drained small capers
¼ cup minced parsley (for an amount this small, I prefer to do the
  mincing by hand)

Brown the veal roast lightly on all sides in the oil in a large heavy kettle over high heat. Reduce heat to moderate and let veal continue sautéing while you mince the vegetables.

Equip the food processor with the metal chopping blade and, with 4 or 5 pulses or on-offs of the motor, mince the onions fairly fine. Add to the kettle. Mince the celery the same way and add it to the kettle, then chop the carrots by letting the processor run nonstop for about 15 seconds. Add carrots to kettle along with the parsley branches. Stir-fry the mixture over moderate heat about 10 minutes until onion and celery are limp and golden but not brown. Reduce heat to low.

Place garlic cloves and anchovy fillets in the processor, still fitted with the metal chopping blade, and mince together by letting the motor run nonstop for 5 seconds. Scrape down the work bowl, add the drained tuna, breaking it into large chunks, and flake moderately fine, using 3 pulses or on-offs of the motor. Add the tuna-garlic-anchovy mixture to the kettle and stir into the sautéed vegetables. Also mix in the wine, lemon juice, thyme and pepper; drop in the bay leaf. Cover and simmer 2 to 2½ hours, or until veal is fork-tender. Meanwhile, wash and dry the food-processor work bowl and chopping blade and reassemble.

When veal is tender, set off the heat and allow to cool for 30 minutes. Remove and discard the bay leaf and parsley branches and lift the veal to a mixing bowl. Then purée the kettle mixture, about one third of it at a time, in the food processor by letting the motor run nonstop for about 1 minute. Pour the purée over the veal, cover with plastic food wrap and marinate in the refrigerator for 24 hours, turning the veal in the purée once or twice.

Remove from the refrigerator, lift the veal from the purée and set it on a slicing board. Scrape as much of the purée from the surface of the veal as possible and place in a clean processor work bowl equipped with the metal chopping blade (also clean). Add about one third of the remaining purée to the work bowl with one third of the mayonnaise and all of the lemon juice. Let processor motor run nonstop for 1 minute; empty sauce into a medium-size mixing bowl. Buzz the remaining vegetable purée the same way in two batches, adding ½ cup of mayonnaise to each, then combine with the first batch. Mix in the capers and parsley.

Now remove the strings from the veal roast and discard; cut the roast into slices about ¼ inch thick, keeping them in the order in which you carved them. Arrange the slices slightly overlapping on a large platter, spooning some of the sauce over each one as you set it in place. When all slices have been arranged on the platter, spoon some additional sauce on top. Cover loosely with plastic food wrap and refrigerate several hours. Remove from the refrigerator and let stand at room temperature for about 30 minutes before serving. Uncover and, if you like, sprinkle a few additional capers on top of the *vitello tonnato*, sprig with parsley and garnish with wedges of lemon. Pour the remaining sauce into a sauceboat and pass it, so that everyone can help himself to additional sauce.

Kibbeh
(Lebanese Lamb and Bulgur Pie)

Makes 10 servings

When I visited Lebanon some years ago, I watched village women pounding lamb, onions and bulgur to paste in stone mortars, slowly, rhythmically. They were making *kibbeh,* and the preparation required the better part of a day. I tried *kibbeh* once the old-fashioned way and was so exhausted by the time I finished that I could scarcely enjoy it. Today, of course, I make it in a fraction of the time in the food processor. I won't say that *kibbeh* is a snap even with the processor, but it does spare you hours of hand-grinding and puréeing and chopping— and the results are simply superb.

2 cups bulgur wheat
3 cups boiling water

⅓ cup loosely packed fresh mint leaves, washed and patted very dry
on paper toweling
2 large yellow onions, peeled and cut into 1-inch chunks
2 tablespoons olive oil
1 large garlic clove, peeled and crushed
2 pounds boneless leg of lamb, cut into ½-inch cubes, trimmed of fat
and sinew, and chilled well
2½ teaspoons salt
¾ teaspoon ground cinnamon
¼ teaspoon crumbled leaf thyme
¼ teaspoon freshly ground black pepper
½ cup pine nuts
½ cup walnut meats
⅔ cup dried currants
½ cup melted butter
1 pint of yogurt, at room temperature (topping)

Place the bulgur wheat in a large heatproof bowl, pour in the boiling water and let stand 30 minutes. Meanwhile, mince the mint leaves in a food processor fitted with the metal chopping blade, using two or three 5-second bursts of the motor; empty onto a piece of wax paper and set aside. Mince the onions, one at a time, using 5 or 6 pulses or on-offs of the motor. Empty half of the onions into a large heavy skillet in which you have already placed the olive oil and garlic; scrape the remaining onions onto a piece of wax paper and reserve.

Divide the lamb into two equal parts (they are to be ground to different degrees of fineness). Place half of one batch of the lamb in the processor, still fitted with the metal chopping blade, and grind very fine by letting the motor run nonstop for about 10 seconds. Empty onto a piece of wax paper; grind the remaining half of that batch the same way and add to the already ground lamb. Set this lamb aside for the time being. Now place half of the second batch of lamb in the processor and with 5 to 6 pulses or on-offs of the motor, grind moderately coarsely; scrape into the skillet. Grind the remaining lamb the same way and add to skillet. Set the skillet over moderate heat and sauté the lamb, onions and garlic about 10 minutes, or until onion is limp and golden and the lamb is no longer pink. As the lamb cooks, break up any clumps with a wooden spoon. Now mix into the skillet 1 teaspoon of the salt, all of the cinnamon and thyme and half of the pepper. Turn heat under skillet to low and let mixture mellow while you proceed with the recipe.

Quickly wash the processor work bowl and chopping blade and re-assemble. Add the pine nuts and, with a few fast whirs of the motor, chop moderately fine; add to skillet. Chop the walnuts the same way and add to skillet along with the currants and reserved chopped mint. Remove skillet from the heat, cover and keep warm. This will be the filling for the *kibbeh*.

The next step is to prepare the mixture for top and bottom layers. Place the reserved minced onions and one half of the finely ground lamb in the processor, still fitted with the metal chopping blade, and grind again to a paste by letting the motor run nonstop for 10 seconds. Add the remaining lamb and grind 10 seconds longer. Empty this mixture into a large bowl.

Dump the bulgur into a large fine sieve and drain well. Now grind it to a stiff paste, 2 cups at a time, in the food processor fitted with the metal chopping blade by letting the motor run nonstop for 15 seconds. When the bulgur is the right consistency, it will form into a ball and ride up on the chopping blade spindle. As each batch is ground, add to the lamb-onion paste. Add the remaining 1½ teaspoons of salt and ⅛ teaspoon of pepper. Knead the bulgur mixture thoroughly with your hands until absolutely uniform—no pink streaks of ground lamb should show. The mixture will be quite stiff—about like a sugar cookie dough. If it seems unworkably stiff, knead in 1 to 2 tablespoons of warm water.

Grease the bottom and sides of a 13x9x2-inch pan with butter. Moisten your hands with warm water and pat half of the bulgur mixture into the bottom of the pan, pressing it down to make as smooth a layer as possible. You'll find the mixture easier to work with (it is extremely sticky) if you dip your hands into warm water again from time to time as you shape and pat it into the pan.

Spoon all of the skillet mixture into the pan on top of the bulgur layer and smooth out with a wooden spoon. Press gently so that this layer adheres to the bulgur one underneath. Now pat the remaining bulgur mixture on top, again moistening your hands with warm water to facilitate handling. When the layer is uniformly smooth, press firmly with the palms of your hands so that all three layers of the *kibbeh* will stick to one another.

With a sharp knife, score the top of the *kibbeh* in a diamond or harlequin pattern, making parallel cuts about 1½ inches apart. Pour the melted butter evenly on top.

Bake the *kibbeh* uncovered in a moderate oven (350° F.) for 40 to 45 minutes, or until lightly browned. You'll note that there is a pool of melted butter on top—don't worry, it will seep in as the *kibbeh* cools. Remove the *kibbeh* from the oven and cool 20 minutes, then cut into large squares and serve with plenty of yogurt to spoon on top.

What does one serve with *kibbeh?* A raw spinach and mushroom salad would be perfect.

Kofta (Meatball) Curry

Makes 4 to 6 servings

Curry as the women of southern India make it.

KOFTA:

1 medium-size garlic clove, peeled
One 1-inch cube fresh ginger root, peeled
¼ teaspoon coriander seeds
⅛ to ¼ teaspoon crushed dried red chili peppers (depending upon how "hot" you like things)
1 pound boneless leg of lamb, trimmed of fat and sinew, cut into 1-inch cubes, and chilled well
1 medium-size yellow onion, peeled and cut into slim wedges
⅛ teaspoon ground cinnamon
Pinch of ground cloves
1 teaspoon salt
1 teaspoon lime juice
2½ cups peanut oil (for frying the kofta)

CURRY SAUCE:

2 medium-size yellow onions, peeled and cut into slim wedges
5 tablespoons ghee (melted unsalted butter poured off from its milk solids)
2 very large sweet and ripe tomatoes, cored and cut into slim wedges (no need to peel)
2 medium-size garlic cloves, peeled
One 1-inch cube fresh ginger root, peeled
½ teaspoon ground turmeric

*¼ to ½ teaspoon crushed dried red chili peppers (depending upon
   your tolerance for pepper)*
½ teaspoon poppy seeds
¼ teaspoon coriander seeds
¼ teaspoon cumin seeds
⅛ teaspoon ground cinnamon
Pinch of ground cloves
1½ cups water
2 teaspoons salt (or to taste)
*1 to 2 tablespoons light brown sugar (to mellow the tartness of the
   tomatoes, if needed)*

Prepare the kofta: In a food processor fitted with the metal chopping
blade, grind the garlic, ginger root, coriander seeds and chili peppers
to a paste—about 60 seconds of nonstop buzzing. Scrape into a mixing
bowl and reserve. Place half of the lamb chunks in the work bowl, still
fitted with the metal chopping blade, and grind quite fine with 10 to 15
seconds of grinding, but stop the motor and inspect the texture a couple of times en route. Add to mixing bowl, then grind the remaining
lamb the same way; add to bowl. Now machine-chop the onion very
fine (no need to wash the work bowl or metal chopping blade) using 5
or 6 pulses or quick bursts of speed. Add to lamb mixture along with all
remaining *kofta* ingredients except, of course, the peanut oil in which
you will fry them. Mix thoroughly with your hands, then shape into 1-
inch balls; arrange the *kofta* one layer deep on a baking sheet and chill
1 to 2 hours.

Prepare the curry sauce: For this you'll need a pristine work bowl
and metal chopping blade, so wash and dry each carefully, then reassemble. Place onion wedges in processor work bowl and mince fairly
fine, using 4 or 5 pulses or quick on-offs. Spoon 3 tablespoons of the
ghee into a very large heavy skillet, add the onions, set over moderate
heat and sauté 12 to 15 minutes, stirring now and then, until soft and
lightly browned.

Meanwhile, purée together in the processor (still fitted with the
metal chopping blade) one of the tomatoes, the remaining *ghee*, the
garlic, ginger root, turmeric, chili peppers, poppy, coriander and
cumin seeds, cinnamon and cloves—about a minute of buzzing should
do it. Pour into a bowl and set aside. Purée the remaining tomato the
same way and add to bowl; stir to combine.

Pour tomato mixture into skillet over the onions; also add water and salt. Cover, reduce heat to low and simmer slowly for about 1 hour and 20 minutes. Taste for seasoning, and if not salty enough, add a bit more salt. If too tart, blend in 1 to 2 tablespoons of light brown sugar. Uncover and let sauce simmer slowly, stirring now and then, while you cook the *kofta*.

Fry the kofta: Heat the peanut oil to 360°F. on a deep-fat thermometer, in a second large heavy skillet over high heat. Add about half of the meatballs and deep-fry until nicely browned on all sides. Remove with a slotted spoon to paper toweling to drain; brown the remaining meatballs the same way and drain well. Add the *kofta* to the sauce, spoon sauce over all, then cover and simmer over low heat for 10 to 15 minutes—just long enough for the *kofta* to absorb the flavor of the sauce. Serve ladled over hot boiled rice.

Albanian Lamb Balls with Mint

Makes 4 servings

2 slices firm-textured white bread, torn into small chunks
1 pound boneless lamb shoulder, cut into 1-inch cubes, trimmed of
*   fat and sinew and chilled well*
1 medium-size yellow onion, peeled and cut into slim wedges
1 medium-size garlic clove, peeled and crushed
2 eggs, lightly beaten
3 tablespoons minced fresh mint
½ teaspoon ground cinnamon
1½ teaspoons salt
⅛ teaspoon freshly ground black pepper
1 tablespoon flour
2 quarts vegetable oil (for deep-fat frying)

In a food processor fitted with the metal chopping blade, buzz the bread to moderately fine crumbs with 5 to 6 pulses or on-offs of the motor; empty crumbs into a mixing bowl. Place half of the lamb cubes in the processor and grind fairly fine, using two or three 5-second bursts of speed. Add to crumbs and grind the remaining lamb the same way; add to crumbs also. Now mince the onion fine, using 5 or 6 pulses or on-offs of the motor. Add to bowl along with all remaining ingredients except, of course, the vegetable oil. Roll into 1-inch balls and chill 30 minutes.

Heat the oil in a deep-fat fryer until a fat thermometer registers 325° F. Fry the lamb balls, 5 or 6 at a time, until richly browned all over—about 2 to 3 minutes. Adjust heat as needed to keep the temperature of the oil as close to 325° F. as possible. Drain the lamb balls on paper toweling and serve with rice, pilaf or bulgur wheat.

Lamb and Eggplant Loaf
Makes 6 to 8 servings

Eggplant is not something we think of chopping and adding to meat loaf, and yet it imparts a rare moistness and delicacy of flavor. The processor, as usual, chops the eggplant, lamb and onion to perfection and buzzes the bread to feathery crumbs.

> *4 slices firm-textured white bread, torn into small chunks*
> *1 small eggplant, peeled and cut into 1-inch cubes*
> *2 tablespoons olive oil*
> *1½ pounds boneless lamb shoulder, cut into 1-inch cubes, trimmed*
> *   of all sinew and chilled well*
> *1 medium-size yellow onion, peeled and cut into slim wedges*
> *1 large garlic clove, peeled and minced*
> *¼ cup tomato paste*
> *2 large eggs*
> *1½ teaspoons salt*
> *¼ teaspoon crumbled leaf oregano*
> *¼ teaspoon crumbled leaf thyme*
> *Several hefty grindings of black pepper*

In a food processor fitted with the metal chopping blade, whir the pieces of bread to soft fine crumbs by using two or three 5-second bursts of speed. Empty into a large mixing bowl and set aside. Place half of the eggplant cubes in the work bowl, still fitted with the metal chopping blade, and with 5 or 6 pulses or on-offs of the motor, chop fairly coarsely; add to a large, heavy skillet in which you have already placed the olive oil. Machine-chop the remaining eggplant the same way and add to skillet.

Place one fourth of the lamb cubes in the processor and chop moderately fine—two or three 5-second churnings will be enough; empty the lamb into the mixing bowl with the bread crumbs. Chop the remaining lamb the same way, adding each batch to the bowl as it is chopped.

Now coarsely machine-chop the onion with 2 to 3 pulses or quick surges of power. Empty the onion into the skillet along with the garlic. Set over moderate heat and stir-fry 8 to 10 minutes until onion and eggplant are golden. Remove from heat and cool to room temperature. Then add to lamb and bread crumbs along with all remaining ingredients and mix thoroughly with your hands.

Pack the mixture into a well-greased 9x5x3-inch loaf pan and bake uncovered in a moderate oven (350° F.) for 1 hour and 20 minutes, or until loaf has pulled slightly from sides of pan and is nicely browned. Remove from oven, pour off any pan drippings, then let the loaf stand upright in its pan on a wire rack for 15 to 20 minutes before turning out (this is to allow the juices to settle and the loaf to firm up). Invert the loaf onto a platter and carve into slices about ⅜ inch thick.

Spicy Lamb and Tomato Stew with Juniper Berries
Makes 8 servings

4 pounds boned lamb shoulder, trimmed of excess fat and cut into 1-inch cubes
6 medium-size carrots, peeled and cut into 4-inch lengths
3 medium-size yellow onions, peeled and cut into slim wedges
6 shallots, peeled
2 medium-size garlic cloves peeled
12 juniper berries, crushed
12 peppercorns
2 whole allspice
2 bay leaves, crumbled
4 medium-size tomatoes, washed, cored and cut into slim wedges (no need to peel)

1¾ cups good strong chicken stock or broth
1 cup dry red wine
6 medium-size boiled new potatoes, cooled, peeled and quartered
Salt to taste

Brown the lamb, a few pieces at a time, in a large heavy kettle over moderately high heat; as the lamb browns, transfer the pieces to paper toweling to drain.

In a food processor fitted with the slicing disc, thin-slice the carrots by pushing them through the feed tube with minimal pressure. Add to kettle. Remove slicing disc from processor and slip the metal chopping blade into place. Chop the onions fairly coarsely, doing about half of the total amount at one time and using 2 to 3 pulses or fast on-offs of the motor. Add onions to kettle as they are chopped. Now mince the shallots and garlic in the processor, using two or three 5-second bursts of the motor. Add to kettle and now also add the browned lamb. Tie the juniper berries, peppercorns, allspice and bay leaves in a piece of cheesecloth and add to kettle. Coarsely machine-chop the tomatoes, about half of them at a time, using a few quick bursts of speed. Add to kettle along with chicken stock and wine.

Cover and simmer 1 hour. Uncover and simmer 30 to 40 minutes longer, or until lamb is nearly tender. Add potatoes, pushing them down well into the stew, and simmer uncovered about 30 minutes longer. Remove cheesecloth bag of seasonings. Add salt to taste, and serve.

Venisonburgers
Makes 6 servings

If you have a hunter in the family (or someone in the neighborhood who shares his quarry with you), you may be interested in knowing how to deal with those less-than-tender cuts of venison (shoulder, leg, neck trimmings, etc.). They make superb burgers if you mix the venison about half-and-half with ground beef—the venison is too lean to make a juicy burger on its own.

1 pound boneless venison, cut into 1-inch cubes, trimmed of sinew
and chilled well

1 pound boneless beef chuck, cut into 1-inch cubes, trimmed of
  sinew and chilled well
1 small yellow onion, peeled and quartered
1½ teaspoons salt
¼ teaspoon freshly ground black pepper
2 tablespoons dry red wine (optional)
2 tablespoons butter

Before grinding the venison and beef, read the notes under **Beef** in *A Dictionary of Foods & How to Process Them* (consult Index for page number). Machine-grind the venison, then the beef as directed and combine the two in a large mixing bowl. Add onion to processor, still fitted with the metal chopping blade, and mince very fine—let the motor run nonstop for about 5 seconds. Add to meats along with salt, pepper and, if you like, the dry red wine. Mix thoroughly with your hands, then shape into 6 large, flat patties. Brown in the butter in a very large, heavy skillet over moderately high heat, allowing 4 to 5 minutes per side for rare burgers and 7 to 8 minutes for well done. Serve as is or in buns, with as many or as few condiments as you like.

Venison Mincemeat
Makes about 2 quarts

Few of us know that mincemeat descended from American Indian pemmican, a sort of early K-ration made of dried venison or other game. Mincemeats today rarely contain meat (certainly most commercial varieties do not), and if they do contain any, it is more likely to be beef than venison. If you have access to fresh venison, by all means try this recipe for your next Thanksgiving pie. Or make it with lean beef chuck—almost as delicious. The food processor does yeoman service grinding the venison, the suet and the apples.

2 quarts apple cider
1½ pounds tart green apples, quartered, cored and peeled
¼ pound suet, cut into ½-inch cubes and chilled well
1 pound seedless raisins
½ pound dried currants
½ cup honey

2 pounds boneless venison shoulder or rump, trimmed of sinew, cut
   into 1-inch cubes (or substitute 2 pounds lean beef chuck) and
   chilled well
2 teaspoons salt
1 tablespoon ground cinnamon
2 teaspoons ground ginger
1 teaspoon ground cloves
1 teaspoon ground nutmeg
½ teaspoon ground allspice

Boil the cider, uncovered, in a large, heavy kettle until reduced by one half. Meanwhile, equip the food processor with the metal chopping blade. Place about one fourth of the apple quarters in the work bowl and with 3 or 4 pulses or bursts of the motor, chop fairly coarsely. Empty into a large bowl and repeat with remaining apples; add these to the bowl also. Place suet in the work bowl, still fitted with the metal chopping blade; turn the motor on and let run for about 1 minute nonstop. Examine the texture of the suet—it should be crumbly and fairly fine, about the texture of oatmeal. If not, buzz for another 30 to 60 seconds, then empty into the bowl with the apples.

When the cider has cooked down to about half of its original volume, add to it the apples, suet, raisins, currants and honey, cover the kettle and cook over lowest heat for 1 hour, stirring occasionally. Meanwhile, grind the venison in the food processor with the metal chopping blade, doing only about one fourth of the total amount at a time and letting the motor run nonstop about 5 seconds for each batch, or until the texture of twice-ground hamburger.

When the kettle mixture has simmered for the allotted hour, add the ground venison along with all remaining ingredients. Simmer, uncovered, for 1½ to 2 hours, stirring now and then. Check the level of the liquid occasionally, and add a little more cider or water if dry; mixture should be quite thick.

This quantity of mincemeat will fill two 9-inch pies. Keep refrigerated until ready to use.

Rôti de Porc à la Boulangère
(Roast Pork in the Manner of the Baker's Wife)

Makes 8 to 10 servings

A simple oven meal (pork loin bedded on a blanket of potatoes and onions) that the old-time French baker's wife would pop into the brick oven to roast on residual heat once her husband's loaves of bread had been baked. The roasting is simple, to be sure, but not the endless cutting of potatoes and onions into see-through-thin slices. Although this has long been a favorite dish of mine (and of my dinner guests), I rarely served it more than once a year because of the tedious hours of preparation required. Now I make it as often as I like, grateful that I have a food processor to slice through those mountains of potatoes and onions quick as a greased streak. Few recipes demonstrate a food processor's prowess better.

1 bone-in pork loin weighing about 8 pounds (Have the butcher crack the backbone along the ribs to facilitate carving.)
3 garlic cloves, peeled and crushed
2 teaspoons crumbled leaf sage
½ teaspoon crumbled leaf thyme
2 teaspoons salt
¾ teaspoon freshly ground black pepper
1 cup parsley sprigs, washed and patted very dry between several thicknesses of paper toweling
12 large baking potatoes, peeled and halved lengthwise
12 medium-size yellow onions, peeled and halved lengthwise
½ cup melted butter

Rub the pork loin well all over with the following mixture: the crushed garlic cloves, sage and thyme, 1 teaspoon of the salt and ½ teaspoon of the pepper. Place in a very large, shallow roasting pan (the pork should rest on the rib ends) and let stand at room temperature 30 minutes. Set pork in a very hot oven (450° F.) and roast, uncovered, for 30 minutes; reduce heat to moderate (350° F.) and roast for 2 hours longer. Remove pork from oven and drain off all drippings. (These may be saved, if you like, for pan-frying potatoes later.)

Transfer pork to a large wire rack to rest while you mince the parsley and slice the potatoes and onions. Pile the parsley in a food processor fitted with the metal chopping blade, then, with 6 to 7 pulses or quick bursts of speed, mince fairly fine. Empty parsley into the roasting pan. Fit the slicing disc into the processor work bowl (the thin-slicing disc, if you have one), set the cover in place, then fit 2 potato halves snugly into the feed tube. Turn the machine on or depress the Pulse button and, with the pusher, ease the potatoes through the slicer. Continue until the work bowl is full, then stop the machine and scrape the potatoes into the roasting pan. Repeat until all of the potatoes have been sliced. Next, slice the onions the same way and add to roasting pan. Sprinkle mixture with the remaining 1 teaspoon of salt and ¼ teaspoon of pepper, drizzle with the melted butter, then toss well as you would a green salad.

Center the roast on the bed of potatoes and onions, raise oven temperature to hot (400° F.) and roast, uncovered, for 1 to 2½ hours, until potatoes are tender and nicely browned. You will have to stir the potato mixture from time to time to keep those on top from drying too much and those underneath from overcooking. To serve, carve the roast down along the ribs into chops and spoon a hefty portion of potatoes and onions onto each plate.

Chinese Pork and Peppers
Makes 4 servings

The best cut of pork to use for the stir-fried Chinese dishes, at least when you are processor-slicing the meat, is loin that has been boned and rolled. This cut contains virtually no connective tissue to jam the cutting blade; its shape, when sliced fairly thick, seems tailor-made for the processor feed tube; and, finally, it is a basically tender cut that does not demand long, slow cooking in the presence of moisture in order to become succulent.

1 pound well-trimmed, boned and rolled pork loin, cut into 1-inch
*   slices (remove all strings)*
1 large garlic clove, peeled
One 1-inch cube fresh ginger, peeled
1 tablespoon light brown sugar
¼ cup dark soy sauce
3 tablespoons dry sherry

⅛ teaspoon crushed dried red chili peppers
1 medium-size Spanish onion, peeled and quartered
2 medium-size sweet green peppers, washed, cored, quartered and
seeded (if you prefer, use one red and one green pepper)
3 tablespoons peanut oil

Place the slices of pork between sheets of wax paper and set in the freezer until firm enough to slice neatly in the food processor—about 1½ hours. Meanwhile, equip the processor with the metal chopping blade; add the garlic, ginger, brown sugar, soy sauce, sherry and chili peppers, and churn for 1 minute nonstop; pour into a small bowl and reserve. Remove the chopping blade and slip the *serrated* slicing disc into place.

Stand a slice of pork on end in the processor feed tube, snap the motor on or depress the Pulse button and push the pork down the tube, using firm pressure. Repeat until all the pork is sliced; empty onto a piece of wax paper and reserve. Now thin-slice the onion quarters, one at a time, by pushing lightly down the feed tube. Fit the quarters of green pepper together spoon-fashion, stand in the processor feed tube, then thin-slice by using gentle pressure on the pusher.

Heat the oil in a wok or in a large heavy skillet over high heat until a piece of pork will sizzle vigorously in it; dump in all of the pork and stir-fry 4 to 5 minutes until lightly browned. Add the onions and peppers and stir-fry 3 minutes, or just until onions start to become translucent. Pour in the soy mixture and stir-fry 3 minutes longer. Turn heat to lowest point, clap on the lid and cook for 1 minute exactly. Serve over fluffy boiled rice. **NOTE:** *Because the slices of pork are so thin, the pork will be thoroughly cooked in the length of time it takes to prepare this recipe if you follow the instructions exactly.*

Jambon Persillé
(Parslied Ham)

Makes about 12 servings

This elegant creation of Burgundy (the traditional Easter ham in that French province) is far more than a "parslied ham." It is a showy gelatin mold, beribboned with pink layers of minced ham and green layers of chopped parsley and scallions, all delicately held in place by a wine-scented aspic. The recipe is a natural for the processor since every-thing, almost, must be minced or chopped.

> 1 bone-in, shank-end, semi-cooked smoked half ham weighing 6½ to
>   7 pounds
> 1 fifth dry white wine
> 3 quarts cold water
> 4 sprigs of fresh tarragon
>   or ½ teaspoon crumbled leaf tarragon
> 2 springs of fresh thyme
>   or ¼ teaspoon crumbled leaf thyme
> 3 large branches of fresh parsley
> 2 large garlic cloves, peeled
> 2 medium-size yellow onions, peeled and cut into slim wedges
> 2 medium-size carrots, peeled and cut into 1-inch chunks
> 2 medium-size celery ribs, washed, trimmed and cut into 1-inch
>   chunks
> 8 peppercorns
> 4 whole cloves

THE WINE ASPIC:

> 5 cups of the wine-and-ham stock (used for cooking the ham),
>   strained through several thicknesses of dampened cheesecloth
> 2 envelopes plain gelatin

THE PARSLEY ASPIC:

> 2 cups loosely packed parsley sprigs, washed and patted very dry on
>   paper toweling
> ½ cup loosely packed fresh tarragon leaves, washed and patted very
>   dry on paper toweling
>   or 2 teaspoons crumbled leaf tarragon
> 6 scallions, washed, trimmed and cut into 1-inch chunks
> 2½ cups of the wine aspic (above)

Place the ham in a large, deep kettle, add wine, water, tarragon, thyme, parsley and garlic; set over moderate heat and bring to a sim-mer. Meanwhile, chop the onions fairly fine in a food processor fitted with the metal chopping blade by pulsing or snapping the motor on and off 5 or 6 times. Empty into kettle. Now chop the carrots by running the processor 10 seconds nonstop; add to kettle. And finally, mince the celery with 5 or 6 pulses or quick on-offs of the motor. Add to kettle also along with peppercorns and cloves. Cover and simmer slowly for 2½ hours, or until ham is very tender. Cool to room temperature.

Lift ham from the kettle, remove and discard the rind, then trim off as much fat as possible. Set the ham in the refrigerator for the time being. Also chill the ham stock until the fat rises to the top and solidifies. Lift off the layer of fat, then blot up any remaining fat globules with paper toweling. Place the stock in a clean kettle and boil, uncovered, for about 1 hour, or until reduced in volume by about one third. For this recipe you will need 5 cups of the stock, carefully strained. Pour the remainder into freezer containers and freeze to use later in soups, stews or aspics.

For the wine aspic: Cool the 5 cups of reserved, strained stock to room temperature, place in a medium-size heavy saucepan and sprinkle the gelatin over the surface. Set over moderate heat, and heat and stir about 3 minutes or until gelatin dissolves. Cool to room temperature.

For the parsley aspic: Place the parsley, tarragon and scallions in a food processor fitted with the metal chopping blade (both the work bowl and the blade should be clean) and mince quite fine, using two or three 5-second churnings of the motor. Empty into a mixing bowl and stir in the wine aspic. Refrigerate until mixture is syrupy *but not set.*

Assembling the jambon persillé: You will need, first of all, a bowl that can serve as a mold. I use a 2½-quart, round-bottomed, flameproof glass casserole dish and I oil the inside lightly to facilitate removing the finished *jambon persillé.*

The next step is to mince the ham. Remove all ham from the bones, trim off and discard the fat, then cut the ham into 1-inch chunks. In the processor (still fitted with the metal chopping blade—no need to wash the blade or work bowl), mince the ham moderately coarsely, 2 cups of the cubes at a time, by pulsing or switching the motor on and off 3 or 4 times. Empty each batch of ham into a large mixing bowl as soon as it is minced.

Pour about ¾ cup of the wine aspic into the bowl you will be using as a mold; set it in the freezer or refrigerator to quick-chill just until gelatin is tacky. Stir the remaining wine aspic into the minced ham. Remove the bowl from the freezer or refrigerator, cover the tacky layer of wine aspic with about 1 inch of the ham mixture and smooth the surface. Now ladle about half of the parsley aspic on top and quick-chill until gelatin is tacky. (The reason for the quick-chilling is that the layers will not be well defined if you simply pour one liquid aspic on top of another; moreover, the layers will adhere to one another far better if the gelatin begins to set before successive layers are added.) Now add a second layer of ham (again about 1 inch thick) and top with the remaining parsley aspic. Chill once again until tacky, then top with the remaining ham mixture. Cover with several thicknesses of foil, cut to fit, then refrigerate 1 hour. Remove from refrigerator, set a heavy plate on top of the foil, then weight down with a brick or a heavy pan. (This is to compress and firm up the mold so that it will slice more neatly.) Refrigerate for at least 12 hours.

To unmold, remove the foil cover, place a large round platter on top of the bowl, then invert. The mold should slide right out. If it seems to stick, turn bowl upright again, then dip quickly in warm—*not hot*—water and invert once again. To serve, cut in wedges as you would a cake.

Eastern Shore Stuffed Ham

Makes 6 to 8 servings

An old Maryland recipe—ham scored and stuffed with a mince of spinach, parsley, watercress and scallions—and a natural for the food processor. The only tedious part of the recipe is stuffing the slits cut into the surface of the ham. The rest is a snap.

STUFFING:

  ¼ pound tender young spinach, trimmed of coarse stems, washed in several changes of tepid water to remove grit and sand and patted very dry on paper toweling
  1 cup loosely packed parsley sprigs, washed and patted very dry on paper toweling
  ¼ cup loosely packed young watercress leaves, washed and patted very dry on paper toweling

*4 medium-size scallions, trimmed, washed and cut into 1-inch
  lengths
Several hefty grindings of black pepper*

Ham:

*1 fully cooked, shank-end half ham weighing 6 to 7 pounds
1½ cups dry white wine (for basting)*

Place half of the spinach in a food processor fitted with the metal chopping blade, pushing the spinach down firmly in the work bowl, then mince quite fine by letting the motor run nonstop for 10 seconds. Empty into a mixing bowl. Mince the remaining spinach the same way and add to bowl. Now place parsley, watercress and scallions in the processor and mince by running the motor for 10 seconds nonstop. Add to spinach along with the black pepper; stir well to mix.

If ham has a coarse rind, remove and discard. Trim the outer covering of fat so that it is a uniform ¼ inch thick. Now, with a very sharp knife, make deep X-shaped cuts over the surface of the ham, spacing them about 1½ inches apart. Each prong of the X should be about 1½ inches long and each cut as deep as you can make it. Cover the counter top with wax paper, then begin stuffing the ham, working on top of the paper. (The stuffing mixture spatters about as you work with it, so you'll be glad you protected the counter top.) Pack the mixture into the X-cuts as firmly as possible. When the ham is fully stuffed, wipe the surface well with damp paper toweling. (You will have made a mess of it, but the excess stuffing wipes right off.)

Place the ham in a shallow, open roasting pan and pour about ½ cup of the wine evenly over the ham. Bake, uncovered, in a moderately slow oven (325° F.) for 2½ hours, basting every half hour or so with additional wine. Remove ham from oven and let stand at room temperature 30 minutes before carving. (This is to allow the stuffing and the juices inside the ham to settle and to make slicing easier.)

Glazed Ham-and-Zucchini Loaf

Makes 6 to 8 servings

One of the distinct benefits of owning a food processor is that you can grind your own ham and pork, which many butchers are now forbidden to do by state laws. A word of caution, however: Be especially meticulous about the cleaning of all parts of the food processor after grinding raw pork or any ham that is not fully cooked. I routinely scald all parts in simmering water before loading them into the dishwasher, and unless the temperature of your hot tap water is well above 140° F. (the temperature needed to kill the organism that causes trichinosis), I recommend that you do the same.

3 slices firm-textured white bread, torn into large chunks
2 pounds boneless smoked ham, cut into 1-inch cubes and trimmed
    of any connective tissue
1 pound boneless pork shoulder, cut into 1-inch cubes, trimmed of
    any connective tissue and chilled well
2 medium-size yellow onions, peeled and cut into slim wedges
1 medium-size zucchini, washed and cut into 1-inch chunks
2 eggs
½ teaspoon crumbled leaf marjoram
⅛ teaspoon ground cloves
⅛ teaspoon ground ginger
⅛ teaspoon ground allspice
2 tablespoons Dijon mustard
⅛ teaspoon freshly ground black pepper
⅓ cup sour milk or buttermilk

GLAZE:

4 tablespoons light brown sugar

In a food processor fitted with the metal chopping blade, buzz chunks of bread to moderately fine crumbs—5 or 6 pulses or quick on-offs will do it. Empty into a large mixing bowl. With the same blade, chop ham to a finely ground texture, doing only about one fourth of the total amount at a time. (Each batch will take about 20 seconds nonstop.) Add to mixing bowl. Grind remaining ham the same way, then the pork, doing only half of the full amount at a time. Add to mixing bowl. Next, coarsely chop the onions with the same chopping blade—a couple of pulses or a quick on-off or two will be sufficient; add to bowl. Finally, chop the zucchini moderately coarsely—3 to 5 seconds with the same blade. Add to bowl. Add all remaining ingredients to bowl (except glaze) and mix well with your hands.

Pat brown-sugar glaze over the bottom of a well-greased 9x5x3-inch loaf pan, then pack ham mixture firmly on top. Bake, uncovered, in a moderate oven (350° F.) for 1 hour and 45 minutes. Remove ham loaf from oven and let stand upright at room temperature for 30 minutes before serving. (This is to allow the juices to settle and the loaf to firm up.) Drain off accumulated juices (save, if you like, for a gravy, sauce or soup later), then turn loaf out on a platter and carve into slices about ⅜ inch thick.

Smoked Ham Soufflé with Madeira
Makes 4 to 6 servings

I can think of few more delicious way to use up leftover baked ham.

½ cup loosely packed parsley sprigs, washed and patted very dry on
  paper toweling
1 medium-size yellow onion, peeled and cut into slim wedges
6 tablespoons unsalted butter
½ pound fully cooked smoked ham, trimmed of fat and cut into 1-
  inch cubes
6 tablespoons flour
2 tablespoons Dijon mustard
¼ teaspoon salt
⅛ teaspoon freshly ground black pepper
1½ cups milk
5 tablespoons Madeira
6 eggs, separated
Pinch of cream of tartar

In a food processor fitted with the metal chopping blade, mince the parsley quite fine by using three 5-second churnings of the motor; scrape the sides of the work bowl down between each churning. Empty parsley onto a piece of wax paper and reserve. Fine-mince the onion in the processor by pulsing or snapping the motor on and off 5 or 6 times. Melt the butter in a medium-size heavy saucepan over moderate heat, add the onion and allow to sauté while you "grind" the ham.

Place the ham cubes in the processor work bowl and chop quite fine, using three 5-second churnings of the motor. Empty ham onto a piece of wax paper and set aside. Continue sautéing the onion until limp and golden but not brown—this will take about 10 minutes altogether. Blend in the flour and heat, stirring, until you have a thick, golden roux—about 3 minutes. Blend in the mustard, salt and pepper and allow to mellow 2 to 3 minutes. Add the milk slowly, whisking the roux vigorously all the while. Continue to whisk until mixture thickens— about 3 minutes. Mix in the Madeira, 1 tablespoon at a time.

Lightly beat the egg yolks, spoon a little of the hot sauce into the yolks, mix well, then stir back into pan. Turn burner heat to its lowest setting and whisk the sauce 1 minute longer. Remove from the heat, mix in the reserved minced parsley and ham, then transfer to a large bowl and cool to room temperature. Whisk the sauce from time to time as it cools to prevent a "skin" from forming on the surface.

Place the egg whites in a large bowl, sprinkle in the cream of tartar, then beat with a rotary beater or whisk until the whites mound softly when the beater is withdrawn. Spoon about 1 cup of the beaten whites into the ham mixture and fold in gently (this is to lighten the base sauce so that the bulk of beaten whites can more easily be folded in). Pour the remaining beaten whites on top of the ham mixture, then fold in gently but thoroughly with a rubber spatula until no streaks of pink or white remain.

Pour the soufflé mixture into an ungreased 10-cup (2½-quart) soufflé dish, set on the middle rack of a moderate oven (350° F.), and bake, uncovered, for 45 to 50 minutes, or until soufflé is nicely puffed and browned. Rush the soufflé to the table and serve.

Curried Cold Ham Mousse
with Sour Cream-Caper Sauce

Makes 6 servings

1 medium-size yellow onion, peeled and cut into slim wedges
1 tablespoon butter
1 tablespoon curry powder
1⅔ cups chicken broth
2 tablespoons dry Port or sherry
1 envelope plain gelatin
3 tablespoons chutney

½ pound smoked cooked ham, cut into ½-inch cubes
¼ cup milk
1 cup refrigerator-cold heavy cream

In a food processor fitted with the metal chopping blade, mince the onion fine, using 5 or 6 pulses or on-offs of the motor. Empty into a small skillet in which you have already melted the butter, and sauté over moderate heat about 5 minutes until limp and golden. Blend in the curry powder and let mellow over moderate heat 2 or 3 minutes, stirring occasionally. Remove from heat and cool.

Meanwhile, pour the chicken broth into a small saucepan, stir in the Port and sprinkle the gelatin over the surface. Let stand about 2 minutes, then set over moderate heat and cook and stir about 5 minutes (do not allow mixture to boil), until gelatin is thoroughly dissolved. Remove from heat and cool.

Dump the curry-onion mixture into the processor work bowl, still fitted with the metal chopping blade, add the chutney and purée, using several fast bursts of speed. Add half of the ham cubes and all of the milk, turn the motor on and let run nonstop for 10 seconds. Scrape down the sides of the processor bowl with a rubber spatula, re-cover, and purée for 10 seconds longer. Add the remaining ham and purée with two 10-second bursts of speed. Empty all into a large bowl and blend in the gelatin mixture.

Now whip the cream softly in the processor, using three or four 5-second churnings of the motor. Inspect the consistency of the cream closely after each 5-second churning and, as soon as it peaks softly, fold into the ham mixture.

Spoon the ham mixture into a lightly oiled 5- or 6-cup decorative mold and chill for 8 hours, or overnight, until firm. To unmold, dip quickly in hot water, then invert mousse onto a platter. Garnish with orange slices and watercress sprigs. Serve with Sour Cream-Caper Sauce (recipe follows).

Sour Cream-Caper Sauce
Makes about 1½ cups

1 cup sour cream, at room temperature
½ cup mayonnaise (see Index for recipe page number)

1 tablespoon Dijon mustard
¼ cup drained small capers

Place all ingredients in the work bowl of a food processor fitted with the metal chopping blade and blend, using 3 or 4 pulses or on-offs of the motor. The object is not to purée the capers into the mixture, only to blend all ingredients quickly. Spoon into a sauceboat and serve.

Yam and Sausage Casserole
Makes 6 servings

There *are* ways to prepare yams and sweet potatoes other than candying them or mashing them and mixing with marshmallows. They needn't be *sweet* to be good, as this savory casserole readily proves. This recipe comes from the coastal plains of North Carolina—"Yam Country"—where cooks still shred the yams the old-fashioned way by hand. The processor, of course, does the job better and faster.

½ pound bulk sausage meat
1 large yellow onion, peeled and cut into slim wedges
1 medium-size celery rib, washed, trimmed and cut into 1-inch
*   lengths*
¼ cup minced parsley (for an amount this small I prefer to hand-
*   mince)*
½ teaspoon crumbled leaf sage
¼ teaspoon crumbled leaf thyme
1 teaspoon salt
⅛ teaspoon freshly ground black pepper
4 large yams or sweet potatoes, peeled and halved lengthwise
Juice of ½ lemon

TOPPING:

2 slices firm-textured white bread, torn into small pieces
2 tablespoons melted butter

Stir-fry the sausage in a large, heavy skillet over moderate heat about 5 minutes, just until sausage is no longer pink. Quickly chop the onion and celery in a food processor fitted with the metal chopping blade—4 or 5 pulses or on-offs of the motor should be about right. Add to skillet and stir-fry about 10 minutes until onion and celery are limp. Turn heat to lowest point, mix in parsley, sage, thyme, salt and pepper and let mixture mellow while you shred the yams.

Remove the metal chopping blade from the processor and slip the shredding disc into place (the medium-shredding disc, if you have one), then shred the yams by pushing them through the feed tube with gentle pressure. If work bowl threatens to overflow, simply dump shredded yams into a large mixing bowl, then shred the remainder. Add these to the bowl, also the skillet mixture and the lemon juice. Toss well to mix. Spoon into a well-buttered 1-quart casserole, pack the mixture down with the back of a spoon, cover and bake in a moderately slow oven (325° F.) for 2½ hours. From time to time, uncover the casserole and stir the mixture up from the bottom.

Meanwhile, prepare the topping: Wash the work bowl and metal chopping blade and reassemble. Add the pieces of bread and, with a few fast pulses or whirs of the motor, buzz to moderately coarse crumbs. Empty into a bowl and toss lightly with the melted butter.

When the casserole has baked the allotted 2½ hours, remove from oven, stir well, then scatter topping over the surface. Return to the oven and bake, uncovered, for 1 hour longer.

Homemade Pork Sausage
Makes 2 pounds

One of the greatest advantages of having a food processor is that you can make your own nitrite-free sausage, shape it into patties and freeze them (the patties will keep well for about three months at 0° F.). You can also make Old-Fashioned Scrapple (see Index for recipe page number). NOTE: *Because of the danger of trichinosis (the disease caused by a microscopic parasite present in much of America's fresh pork), be especially meticulous about the cleaning of all parts of your food processor after grinding raw pork. I always make a point of scalding whatever blade or disc I've used—also the work bowl, lid and pusher—before I run them through the dishwasher.*

1½ pounds lean pork shoulder, trimmed of fat and sinew, cut into 1-inch chunks and chilled well

½ pound fresh pork jowl, cheek or fat trimmings, trimmed of sinew, cut into 1-inch chunks and chilled well

2 teaspoons salt

½ teaspoon freshly ground black pepper

1 teaspoon crumbled leaf sage

½ teaspoon crumbled leaf thyme

Place ½ pound of the lean pork chunks and about one third of the jowl in a food processor fitted with the metal chopping blade and grind together until quite fine by using two or three 5-second churnings of the motor. Empty into a mixing bowl. Grind the remaining lean and fat pork the same way, in two separate batches. Add to bowl along with all remaining ingredients and mix thoroughly with your hands. Shape into patties, wrap individually and quick-freeze. Cook as you would any uncooked sausage patties, making certain that they are cooked through—and well done—before you serve them.

Boudin Blanc

(White Sausage)

Makes 8 to 10 sausages measuring about 4 inches long and 1½ inches in diameter, enough for 6 servings

These delicate sausages are made of fresh pork, chicken and/or veal and bound together with both egg white and bread paste *(panade)*. The processor crumbs the bread, grinds the meat, chops the onions, then churns the whole into a *quenelle*-smooth forcemeat that can be stuffed into sausage casings or wrapped snugly in cheesecloth and poached. If you use cheesecloth, be sure to use the old-fashioned woven type, not the miserable new knitted stuff that stretches out of shape. If you use sausage casings (they are sold by the yard and a good butcher can obtain them for you), you will need a sausage-stuffing attachment for your meat grinder or electric mixer. I find that the cheesecloth method works very well, and that's the one I used in developing this recipe for the processor.

3 slices firm-textured white bread, torn into small pieces
1 cup milk
¼ pound chilled fresh, snowy pork fat (Fat from the loin is
    particularly fine-grained and delicate.)
3 large yellow onions, peeled and cut into 1-inch chunks
¼ teaspoon white pepper
¼ teaspoon crumbled leaf thyme
¼ teaspoon fennel seeds
Pinch of ground mace
Pinch of ground allspice
Pinch of ground cardamom
1 large, plump chicken breast, boned, skinned, cut into 1-inch cubes
    and chilled well
1½ teaspoons salt
¾ pound boneless, well-trimmed fresh pork loin, cut into 1-inch
    cubes and chilled well
3 large eggs whites
½ cup heavy cream

In a food processor fitted with the metal chopping blade, buzz the bread to fine crumbs, using about two 5-second churnings of the motor. Empty into a heavy saucepan, stir in the milk, set over very low heat and cook slowly about 30 minutes, or until mixture has a thick paste-like consistency. Stir the mixture from time to time and watch closely so that it does not scorch on the bottom.

Meanwhile, grind the pork fat quite fine, using two 3-second churnings of the motor. Scrape half of the ground fat onto a piece of wax paper and set aside; place the remainder in a large heavy skillet and set over low heat to melt. Mince half of the onion chunks in the processor (no need to wash the work bowl or chopping blade yet) by pulsing or snapping the motor on and off 5 or 6 times; add to skillet. Chop the remaining onion the same way and add to skillet also. Sauté very slowly about 10 minutes until soft and golden, but not brown; mix in the pepper, thyme, fennel, mace, allspice and cardamom and let mellow over lowest heat for another 10 minutes.

While the onions cook, grind the remaining meat. Place the chicken and salt in the processor work bowl (again no need to wash it or the chopping blade) and grind quite fine by letting the motor run nonstop for 3 or 4 seconds. Empty into a mixing bowl. Now grind the pork, one third of the total amount at a time, by running the processor motor 5 seconds nonstop. Add each batch to the bowl as it is chopped. Also add the reserved ground fat, the sautéed onion mixture and the bread paste; stir well to mix. Add the egg whites, one at a time, and beat hard with a wooden spatula after each addition.

Now pile all of this mixture in the processor work bowl (still fitted with the chopping blade). It may seem like too much, but though the mixture is very soft and delicate, it is solid enough not to overflow the work bowl. Snap the motor on and let run nonstop for 10 seconds. With the motor still running, slowly drizzle the heavy cream down the feed tube; snap the motor off as soon as all of it has been incorporated.

Empty the sausage mixture back into the mixing bowl, cover and chill several hours until firm enough to shape. For shaping the sausages, you will need 10 double thicknesses of cheesecloth, each about 7 inches square. You will also need 20 pieces of string, each about 4 inches long, a pastry brush and a small ramekin of vegetable oil (for oiling the squares of cheesecloth before the sausage mixture is added).

Wet the cheesecloth well with cold water, then wring each square as dry as possible. On a counter top covered with wax paper (this is to simplify cleanup and to help prevent the raw pork from getting into any counter-top crevices), spread out a cheesecloth square. Brush the surface lightly with oil. Now spoon onto the center of the square about 2½ heaping tablespoons of the sausage mixture, shaping it with the spoon into a log about 4 inches long and 1½ inches in diameter. Lift up the cheesecloth, holding by the two sides so that it cradles the sausage like a hammock, and shake very lightly to settle and firm the sausage. Return to the counter, then roll the sausage up tight in the cheesecloth. Tie one end securely, then pick up by the *untied* end and shake lightly to pack the sausage into the cheesecloth casing. Now tie the loose end securely, too. Shape the remaining sausage mixture the same way.

Arrange the rolls of sausage one layer deep on a baking sheet, cover loosely and refrigerate 8 hours, or overnight, before cooking. The *boudins* must be cooked twice, poached the first time around, then pan-fried or baked or broiled.

To poach: Bring a large kettle of lightly salted water to a boil, drop in the cheesecloth-wrapped *boudins,* adjust heat so that water simmers gently, then cover and simmer for 30 minutes. NOTE: *In Wisconsin, where a great many Scandinavians settled in the mid-1800s, boudins are poached in beer, which I'm told gives them a deliciously malty flavor. I haven't tried it, but by all means do if you have the beer on* *hand.* When the *boudins* are done, drain well, cool to room temperature, then cover and refrigerate about 8 hours before proceeding—this is to allow the flavors a chance to mellow and the sausages time to firm up. When you are ready for the final cooking, remove each *boudin* carefully from its cheesecloth wrapper.

To finish cooking: My favorite way is to slice the *boudins* about 1 inch thick, then to brown them slowly in butter, allowing about 5 minutes per side. Some people like to dip the whole *boudins* in crumbs (you'll have to press the crumbs into the sausage to make them stick), then to bake in a slow oven (300° F.) for about 30 minutes, basting frequently with butter. Still others like to crumb the *boudins,* drizzle them with butter, then set them about 6 inches below the broiler unit and broil them slowly, turning them often and basting frequently until nicely browned all over.

NOTE: *The poached* boudins *will keep well in the refrigerator for about 4 days, but they should first be removed from their cheesecloth wrappers. They also freeze well. Again remove the cheesecloth, then wrap each* boudin *separately in aluminum foil, smoothing out any air pockets. Set directly on the freezer's freezing surface to quick-freeze (the faster ground meats are frozen, the better), then, if you like, bundle all of the individually wrapped* boudins *into a single package. Keeping time in the freezer: about 4 months.*

Old-Fashioned Scrapple

Makes 6 servings

This isn't a processor recipe, except for the Homemade Pork Sausage that is an integral ingredient.

½ pound Homemade Pork Sausage (see Index for recipe page number)
¾ teaspoon poultry seasoning
2½ cups chicken stock
1 cup cornmeal
¼ cup bacon drippings (for frying the scrapple)

In a large heavy skillet set over moderate heat, stir-fry the sausage about 5 minutes, breaking up any large clumps of it with a wooden spoon. Blend in the poultry seasoning and chicken stock and bring to a boil. Very slowly add the cornmeal, beating vigorously all the while with the spoon to keep the mixture from lumping. Turn the heat to the lowest setting, cover the skillet and let the scrapple cook very slowly for 15 minutes. Uncover the skillet 2 or 3 times as the scrapple cooks and stir well. Spoon the scrapple into a greased loaf pan measuring 8½x4½x2½ inches, pressing mixture down firmly, lay a piece of foil on top, press down firmly again, then chill 8 hours or overnight until firm. Unmold the scrapple, slice about ⅜ inch thick, then fry in the bacon drippings over moderately high heat until nicely browned on both sides. Eat as is, or top with hot maple syrup.

Poultry

Malabari Chicken Piri
(Mild Chicken Curry with Ground Coconut Balls)

Makes 6 to 8 servings

A delicate East Indian chicken-and-coconut curry with a unique flavor, not one that we usually associate with curry. Turmeric and cumin, two of the components of commercial curry powders, predominate. The coconut balls, instead of being light and fluffy like dumplings, are more akin to the Italian *gnocchi* in texture. They must be made with fresh coconut, but the food processor, praised be, grinds it to feathery perfection in minutes. **NOTE:** *For directions on how to open a fresh coconut and prepare it for the processor, see* A Dictionary of Foods — How to Process Them *(consult Index for page number).*

1 broiler-fryer (about 3 pounds), disjointed
1 teaspoon ground turmeric
½ teaspoon freshly ground black pepper
2 cubes (each about ¾ inch) fresh ginger root, peeled
Meat of 1 fresh coconut, peeled and cut into 1-inch chunks (reserve coconut liquid)
1 large yellow onion, peeled and cut into slim wedges
1 garlic clove, peeled
½ teaspoon cumin seeds
3 tablespoons ghee (melted unsalted butter poured off from its milk solids)
2 teaspoons salt (or to taste)
¼ teaspoon ground cinnamon
¼ teaspoon ground coriander
⅛ teaspoon ground cloves
Reserved coconut liquid
1 cup rice flour (available at health-food stores and Oriental groceries)

1 cut hot water
1 quart (4 cups) cold water
1 tablespoon lime juice

Spread pieces of chicken out on a large sheet of wax paper, then rub well all over with turmeric and black pepper. Let marinate at room temperature about half an hour.

Meanwhile, grind the ginger root to a paste in the food processor fitted with the metal chopping blade—about 5 seconds of nonstop churning should be all that's needed. Scrape the ginger-root paste from the work bowl onto a piece of wax paper and set aside. No need to rinse the work bowl at this point.

Place about one fourth of the coconut chunks in the work bowl, still fitted with the metal chopping blade, and grind quite fine by using three 10-second churnings of the motor. Scrape down the sides of the work bowl after each 10-second churning so that the coconut is as uniformly fine as possible. Empty ground coconut into a large mixing bowl. Mince the remaining coconut the same way, in three batches, and combine with coconut in bowl. Now place the onion, garlic and cumin seeds in the work bowl (still no need to wash it) and mince quite fine using 5 or 6 pulses or on-offs of the motor. Empty into the bowl with the coconut and mix in thoroughly.

Measure out half of the coconut mixture and drain very dry in a large fine sieve set over a bowl. Press hard with a spoon to extract as much liquid as possible. The drained coconut is to be used in making the coconut balls, the extracted liquid for cooking the chicken. The remaining undrained coconut mixture will also be used for cooking the chicken.

Heat the *ghee* in a large heavy kettle over moderately high heat and brown the pieces of chicken well on all sides. Reduce heat to low. Add any of the turmeric and black pepper remaining on the sheet of wax paper on which the chicken marinated; also add the reserved ginger-root paste. Heat and stir about 5 minutes, just until ginger turns a rich gold. Now add 1 teaspoon of the salt, the cinnamon, coriander, cloves, liquid reserved from the coconut, the undrained coconut mixture and the liquid extracted from the ground coconut. Stir well to mix, cover kettle and simmer over very low heat about 45 minutes, or until chicken is tender.

Meanwhile, prepare the coconut balls, Place the rice flour in a large, heavy saucepan and heat over low heat about 15 minutes, stirring now and then, just to mellow the flavor somewhat. The flour will not brown. Transfer to a small bowl to cool slightly. Mix in the remaining 1 teaspoon of salt, then add the hot water, about ¼ cup at a time, tossing lightly with a fork, just until dough holds together. It should be quite stiff, almost crumbly. Mix in the well-drained coconut mixture and if too soft to shape, quick-chill for 10 to 15 minutes in the freezer. Roll into small balls about the size of marbles. Arrange the coconut balls on a large baking sheet and refrigerate until ready to cook them.

As soon as chicken is tender, remove from the cooking liquid, shaking off as much of the coconut mixture as possible, and set aside on a large plate. Add the cold water and the lime juice to the kettle mixture and bring quickly to a boil. Drop the coconut balls in one by one, spacing as evenly as possible; adjust heat so that mixture just simmers, cover and cook coconut balls for 10 minutes. Return chicken to kettle, pushing pieces down and around the coconut balls, re-cover and cook 10 to 15 minutes longer. Taste for salt and add more if needed.

To serve, place chicken on beds of hot, fluffy boiled rice and ladle kettle gravy and coconut balls on top.

Country Captain

Makes 8 to 10 servings

This mild chicken curry is an old Southern favorite. Almost every cook has a favorite version, and this one is mine (or rather my mother's). The recipe has a hidden asset—after stewing the capon, you'll end up with about three quarts of good chicken stock, which you can freeze to use later on in making soups and stews.

> 1 capon or stewing hen weighing about 6 pounds
> 4 quarts water
> 2 large celery ribs, cut into 1-inch chunks
> 2 medium-size carrots, cut into 1-inch chunks
> 5 medium-size yellow onions, peeled and cut into slim wedges
> 4 tablespoons butter
> 1 medium-size sweet green pepper, washed, cored, seeded and cut
>   into 1-inch squares

*1 medium-size sweet red pepper, washed, cored, seeded and cut into
    1-inch squares*
2 large garlic cloves, peeled and crushed
2 tablespoons curry powder
*1 cup loosely packed parsley sprigs, washed and patted very dry on
    paper toweling*
1 bay leaf, crumbled
2 cups reserved chicken stock
6 medium-size tomatoes, washed and cored (no need to peel)
1 cup dried currants or raisins
2 teaspoons salt (about)
¼ teaspoon freshly ground black pepper
1½ cups blanched, toasted whole almonds

Place the capon and water in a large heavy kettle, cover and set over moderate heat. Coarsely chop the celery in a food processor equipped with the metal chopping blade by pulsing or snapping the motor on and off 2 or 3 times; add celery to kettle. Coarsely chop the carrots in the processor with 2 or 3 pulses or on-offs; add carrots to kettle. Now coarsely chop 2 of the onions—3 or 4 pulses or on-offs of the motor will be sufficient. Add onions to kettle, re-cover and simmer slowly about 2 hours, or until capon is very tender. Remove from kettle and cool until easy to handle. Strain the stock, reserving both the stock and the strained-out solids.

Coarsely chop the remaining 3 onions in two batches in the food processor, still fitted with the metal chopping blade—3 or 4 pulses or on-offs of the motor will be about right—and add to a second large heavy kettle in which you have already melted the butter. Now mince the green and red peppers using 6 pulses or on-offs of the motor; add to kettle along with the garlic. Stir-fry the onions, peppers and garlic over moderate heat 10 to 12 minutes, or until golden and very limp. Blend in the curry powder and let mellow 2 to 3 minutes. Now purée the solids strained out from the chicken stock by running the processor nonstop for 30 seconds; add purée to kettle.

At this point, quickly wash and dry the processor work bowl and metal chopping blade; reassemble. Mince the parsley moderately fine, using two or three 5-second churnings of the motor. Add to kettle along with the bay leaf and 2 cups of the reserved chicken stock (cool the remaining stock and pour it into 1-quart containers, leaving ½ inch of head space, and freeze to use later on).

Processor-chop the tomatoes, two at a time, with 3 or 4 pulses or quick on-offs of the motor and add each batch to the kettle as it is chopped. Stir raisins, salt and pepper into kettle, set over moderately low heat and simmer, uncovered, for 30 to 40 minutes, stirring occasionally, until flavors are well blended.

Skin the capon, remove bones, cut or tear meat into 1½- to 2-inch chunks and add to kettle. Cover and simmer 30 to 40 minutes longer.

Once again, wash and dry the food-processor work bowl and chopping blade and reassemble. Add the almonds and chop coarsely, using several pulses or quick bursts of the motor. Empty nuts onto a piece of wax paper and set aside.

Taste the Country Captain for seasoning and add more salt if needed. Ladle over fluffy boiled rice and top each portion with a scattering of chopped almonds.

Gingered Chicken and Cucumbers

Makes 4 servings

2 tablespoons cornstarch
¼ cup plus 1 tablespoon dry sherry
1 egg white, beaten until frothy
⅛ teaspoon salt
3 boned and skinned chicken breasts, cut into 1-inch cubes
1 large garlic clove, peeled
2 cubes (1 inch each) peeled fresh ginger
⅓ cup dark soy sauce
⅛ teaspoon crushed dried red chili peppers
2 medium-size yellow onions, peeled and halved lengthwise
2 medium-size celery ribs, trimmed, washed and cut into 4-inch lengths
6 scallions, trimmed, washed and cut into 4-inch lengths (include some green tops)
2 medium-size cucumbers, peeled, halved lengthwise, seeded and cut into 4-inch lengths
4 tablespoons peanut oil

In a medium-size mixing bowl, combine the cornstarch, 1 tablespoon of the sherry, the egg white and the salt. Add the chicken cubes, toss well to mix, then let stand at room temperature 30 minutes. Meanwhile, place the remaining ¼ cup of sherry, the garlic, ginger, soy sauce and chili peppers in a food processor fitted with the metal chopping blade and churn for 60 seconds nonstop to blend. Empty into a small bowl and reserve.

Shortly before you are ready to serve, remove the chopping blade from the work bowl and slip the slicing disc into place. (There really is no need to wash the work bowl despite the fact that the residual soy sauce will make it look unappetizing.) Thin-slice the onions, then the celery and scallions, by pushing each down the feed tube with gentle pressure. Empty onto a piece of wax paper and set aside. Now fit the lengths of cucumber together spoon-fashion and stand enough of them in the food-processor feed tube for a snug fit; snap the motor on and push through with fairly firm pressure. Repeat until all cucumbers have been sliced. Empty these onto wax paper, too.

Heat the peanut oil in a wok or in a large heavy skillet set over high heat until a piece of the chicken will sizzle in it. Dump in the chicken mixture and stir-fry, breaking up the clumps, until richly golden brown—about 3 minutes. Remove the chicken to paper toweling to drain; also skim off and discard 2 tablespoons of the oil remaining in the wok. Dump in the sliced onions, celery and scallions and stir-fry 2 minutes. Pour in the soy-sauce mixture, put the chicken back in the wok and boil vigorously 2 minutes to reduce liquid slightly. Dump in the cucumbers, stir-fry 1 minute, turn heat to low, cover for 1 minute to allow the flavors to penetrate the cucumber, then serve with fluffy boiled rice.

Fricassee of Chicken, Mushrooms and Onions in Sweet Cream

Makes 4 servings

2 whole chicken breasts, split in half
½ cup all-purpose flour (unsifted)
4 tablespoons unsalted butter
2 tablespoons peanut oil or corn oil
4 medium-size yellow onions, peeled and halved vertically
1½ pounds medium-size mushrooms, wiped clean with a damp cloth

(*Trim stems so that you can fit mushrooms into processor feed tube sideways.*)
¼ *teaspoon crumbled leaf thyme*
⅛ *teaspoon crumbled leaf sage*
2 *teaspoons paprika*
¾ *teaspoon salt (or to taste)*
⅛ *teaspoon white pepper (or to taste)*
1 *cup light cream, at room temperature*

Dredge each piece of chicken by shaking in the flour in a heavy paper bag. In a large heavy skillet, heat 2 tablespoons of the butter and all of the oil over moderately high heat until a piece of chicken will sizzle in it. Brown chicken well on both sides, then drain on paper toweling. Pour drippings from skillet and discard; add remaining 2 tablespoons butter and warm slowly over moderately low heat. Slice onion halves in a food processor fitted with a slicing disc (the medium-slicing disc, if you have one). Add onions to skillet and allow to sauté while you thin-slice the mushrooms in the processor. Add mushrooms to skillet and stir-fry about 10 minutes until lightly browned. Return chicken breasts to skillet, spoon mushrooms and onions over each, sprinkle with thyme, sage, paprika, salt and pepper, cover skillet and simmer 35 to 45 minutes, or until chicken is fork-tender. Uncover skillet, stir in cream and simmer, uncovered, stirring now and then, until cream and juices cook down into a medium-thick sauce—about 15 minutes. Taste for salt and pepper and adjust if necessary. Serve with rice or wild rice.

Golden Crusty-Crumbed Baked Chicken

Makes 4 to 6 servings

I've been making this recipe for years, long before the commercial crumb-coating mixtures came on the market. With the processor to crumb the bread, grate the Parmesan and mince the parsley, the recipe is a snap. And it bakes virtually unattended.

8 *slices* stale and dry *firm-textured white bread, broken into small chunks*
¼ *pound Parmesan cheese, cut into 1-inch cubes*

½ cup loosely packed parsley sprigs, washed well and patted very
   dry on paper toweling
½ teaspoon crumbled leaf thyme
½ teaspoon crumbled leaf marjoram
1½ teaspoons salt
¼ teaspoon freshly ground black pepper
1 cup melted butter
1 medium-size garlic clove, crushed
2 broiler-fryers (about 3 pounds each), cut up for frying

Put half the bread chunks in a food processor fitted with the metal chopping blade and buzz to moderately fine crumbs by pulsing or snapping the motor on and off 5 or 6 times. Empty into a large, shallow bowl. Crumb the remaining bread the same way and add to bowl. Now grate the Parmesan in the processor, still fitted with the metal chopping blade, by letting the motor run nonstop for 1 minute (you want the cheese to be fine and feathery). Add to crumbs. Pile the parsley in the work bowl and chop fairly fine with 5 or 6 pulses or on-offs of the motor. Add to crumbs along with thyme, marjoram, salt and pepper. Toss well to mix and let stand at room temperature for about 2 hours. Combine the butter and garlic in a second bowl. Dip each piece of chicken into garlic butter, then into the crumb mixture to coat well. Arrange in a shallow roasting pan, pour any remaining garlic butter over chicken and bake, uncovered, for 1 hour in a moderate oven (350° F.) until nicely browned. Do not turn the chicken as it bakes, but do baste occasionally with pan drippings.

Chicken, Mushroom and Irish Bake
Makes 6 servings

Here's an imaginative way to rejuvenate leftover chicken and Irish potatoes. You can substitute leftover roast turkey, if you like, and of course you can slip in other leftover vegetables—as much as 1 cup of green peas or diced carrots or whole-kernel corn or green beans. Much as I would like to say that you can cube the potatoes in the food processor, you can't. Nor can you, as I tried in vain to do in retesting this recipe, slice them in the processor. Machine-sliced *cooked* potatoes are limp and gluey. You can, of course, machine-slice the mushrooms, onion and celery. And you can machine-chop the chicken or turkey.

1 pound medium-size mushrooms, wiped clean and stemmed (reserve stems to mince)
1 large yellow onion, peeled and halved lengthwise
2 medium-size celery ribs, trimmed, washed and cut into 4-inch lengths
6 tablespoons butter
4 tablespoons flour
2 cups milk
1¼ teaspoons salt
1 teaspoon crumbled leaf sage
¼ teaspoon crumbled leaf thyme
⅛ teaspoon freshly ground black pepper
3 cups 1-inch chunks of boned and skinned leftover chicken or turkey
4 medium-size cold boiled potatoes, peeled and cut into ½-inch cubes

In the feed tube of a food processor fitted with the slicing disc, stand as many mushrooms on their sides as will fit fairly snugly; turn machine on and push the mushrooms through, using gentle pressure on the pusher. Repeat until all mushrooms are sliced. Thin-slice the onion halves and celery the same way; add all to a large, heavy skillet in which you have already melted 2 tablespoons of the butter. Stir-fry mushrooms, onion and celery over moderately high heat about 5 minutes until limp and golden. Set aside. In a small saucepan, melt the remaining 4 tablespoons of butter. Blend in flour, then whisk in milk and heat, stirring constantly, until thickened and smooth—about 3 minutes. Mix in salt, sage, thyme and pepper, reduce heat to lowest point and allow sauce to mellow while you proceed with the recipe.

Remove the slicing disc from the processor and slip the metal chopping blade into place. Add the reserved mushroom stems and, with a few bursts of speed, chop fairly coarsely. Add chopped mushrooms to the skillet and sauté 5 minutes, stirring now and then. Mix in the sauce, turn heat to lowest point and let stand while you chop the chicken.

Add half of the chicken to the processor and, with 2 or 3 fast pulses or on-offs, chop fairly coarsely; add to skillet. Chop remaining chicken the same way and add to skillet along with the cubed potatoes. Toss gently to mix, spoon into a buttered 6-cup casserole and bake, uncovered, in a moderate oven (350° F.) for 40 to 45 minutes, or until bubbling and lightly browned.

Circassian Chicken
Makes 8 servings

I'll never forget the first time I made this Turkish chicken classic without benefit of a food processor. It took very nearly a whole day and dirtied almost everything in the kitchen. Delicious as the dish was, and impressed as my friends were, I vowed never to make it again. And I didn't until I decided to put the food processor to the test with it. The biggest challenge was grinding the walnuts to paste; the blender was never able to cope with more than a handful of nuts at a time and never ground them fine enough. The processor, I'm pleased to report, works like a charm and reduced the recipe preparation time to about two hours—and most of this for simmering the chicken in an unwatched pot.

Now a bit about the recipe itself. It is Turkish, as I said—chunks of chicken layered together with a sauce of puréed walnuts, vegetables and bread. Because the dish is served cold, it can be made one day and served the next—in fact, the flavors improve after a stint in the refrigerator. Circassian Chicken is an ideal buffet dish—everything is boneless, bite-size and easily managed with a fork.

5 large whole chicken breasts, split (or 10 large half-breasts)
1 large yellow onion, peeled and halved lengthwise
2 medium-size carrots, peeled and cut into 4-inch lengths
2 medium-size celery ribs, washed and cut into 4-inch lengths
2 large garlic cloves, peeled
2 large bay leaves
8 peppercorns
4 whole cloves
2 teaspoons salt (or to taste)
3 cups water
2½ cups walnuts meats
3 slices firm-textured white bread, broken into small pieces

Place the chicken breasts in a large heavy kettle. In a food processor equipped with the slicing disc, thin-slice the onion halves by pushing them through with gentle pressure. Thin-slice the carrots and celery ribs the same way. Add all to the kettle along with the garlic, bay leaves, peppercorns, cloves, salt and water. Set over moderate heat, cover and simmer about 45 minutes, or until chicken is tender. Remove chicken from the kettle and cool. Also remove the bay leaves and cloves and discard. Then boil the kettle's contents, uncovered, for 15 to 20 minutes, or until reduced to 2½ cups (this includes the solids as well as the liquid).

Remove the slicing disc from the processor and slip the metal chopping blade into place. Dump in the walnuts and grind very fine by letting the motor run nonstop for 30 seconds. Place the walnuts in a mixing bowl. Now buzz the chunks of bread to fine crumbs using two 5-second churnings; add to walnuts. Pour the 2½ cups of kettle mixture into the processor and purée, using two 10-second bursts of speed. Mix into the walnuts and crumbs.

Now return half of this mixture to the processor work bowl and churn until ivory-hued and the consistency of mayonnaise—about 60 seconds of nonstop churning will be about right. Pour into a clean bowl; purée the remaining walnut mixture the same way and combine with the original batch. Taste for salt and add more if needed. Set aside for the moment.

Skin the chicken breasts, then pull the meat from the bones in as large chunks as possible—you should be able to lift out most of it intact. Slice the breast meat crosswise and slightly on the diagonal at ½-inch intervals so that you have strips of meat about 2 to 3 inches long and ½ inch wide. Cover the bottom of a medium-size platter with a layer of chicken (use about half of the total amount), spread generously with half of the walnut sauce, top with the remaining chicken, then "frost" with the remaining walnut sauce so that all of the chicken is covered. Cover with plastic food wrap and refrigerate until about 40 minutes before serving. Garnish, if you like, with a blush of paprika, sprigs of parsley and wedges of lemon.

Cold Molded Chicken-and-Walnut Loaf

Makes 8 to 10 servings

1 capon weighing 6 to 6½ pounds
1 gallon (4 quarts) cold water
3 medium-size yellow onions, peeled and halved lengthwise
5 medium-size celery ribs, washed and trimmed (Cut 2 of the ribs
    into 4-inch lengths, the remaining 3 into 1-inch pieces.)
3 medium-size carrots, peeled (Cut 2 of the carrots into 4-inch
    lengths and the remaining one into 1-inch pieces.)
2 large parsley branches, washed
6 peppercorns
4 whole cloves
½ cup loosely packed parsley sprigs, washed and patted very dry on
    paper toweling
⅓ cup loosely packed dill fronds, washed and patted very dry on
    paper toweling
1½ cups walnut meats
2 tablespoons drained small capers
2 envelopes plain gelatin
2 cups chicken stock (from cooking the capon), cooled
1 cup heavy cream
1 cup sour cream
1 cup mayonnaise (see Index for recipe page number)
Juice of ½ lemon
1½ teaspoons salt
¼ teaspoon freshly ground black pepper

Place capon (also neck and giblets) in a large heavy kettle, add water and set over moderate heat. While the kettle heats, thin-slice two of the onions in a food processor fitted with the slicing disc by pushing them through with gentle pressure; add to kettle. Cut the remaining onion into 1-inch chunks and set aside (it will be chopped later). Now thin-slice the 4-inch lengths of celery and carrot by pushing them lightly down the feed tube; add to kettle (the unsliced balance of celery and carrot will be chopped later). Also add the parsley branches, peppercorns and cloves to the kettle. Bring to a simmer, cover, and cook slowly for about 2 hours, or until capon is very tender and meat almost falls from bones. Lift the bird from the stock and cool until easy to handle. Measure out and reserve 2 cups of the stock to use in finishing the recipe. Strain, skim and freeze the remaining stock, or, if you prefer, cook down to make Rich Chicken Broth (see Index for recipe page number).

In a clean processor work bowl fitted with a clean metal chopping blade, mince the parsley, dill and walnuts together until moderately fine—7 or 8 pulses or on-offs of the motor should be sufficient. Empty into a large mixing bowl. Now chop the reserved onion and 1-inch pieces of celery together, using 5 or 6 pulses or quick bursts of speed; add to bowl. Chop the remaining carrot fine by letting the motor run nonstop 10 seconds; add to bowl. Skin the chicken, remove meat from bones and cut into 1-inch chunks. Add about one fourth of the meat to the processor work bowl and chop moderately coarsely, using 5 pulses or on-offs of the motor; add to bowl; chop the remaining chicken the same way in three separate batches; add to the bowl along with the capers.

Sprinkle the gelatin over the chicken stock and let stand 5 minutes. Empty into a medium-size, heavy saucepan, add cream, set over moderately low heat and heat, stirring constantly, about 3 to 5 minutes until gelatin is dissolved. Pour into a second mixing bowl and whisk in the sour cream, mayonnaise, lemon juice, salt and pepper until uniformly smooth. Pour over the chicken mixture, then mix all carefully and thoroughly with an over-and-over folding motion. Spoon into an oiled 3-quart decorative ring mold, cover with plastic food wrap and chill at least 8 hours, or overnight, until firm.

To turn out, dip the mold quickly in warm water, place a plate on top of it, then invert the two together, giving the mold a couple of good hefty shakes to dislodge the chicken-and-walnut loaf. Garnish, if you like, with parsley or watercress, and serve as a main course.

Tomato-Turkey Soufflé

Makes 4 to 6 servings

A processor, I've discovered, encourages me to be more creative about leftovers. I would have hesitated to make this recipe some years back, for example, because it would have meant hauling out the old meat grinder. But with the processor at the ready, grinding the turkey is a neat, 15-second operation. This particular soufflé is equally good made with leftover minced chicken or with flaked white tuna.

*½ cup loosely packed parsley sprigs, washed and patted very dry on
   paper toweling*
1 medium-size yellow onion, peeled and cut into slim wedges
6 tablespoons unsalted butter
*½ pound cold roast turkey, trimmed of skin and fat and cut into 1-
   inch chunks*
2 tablespoons flour
½ teaspoon crumbled leaf sage
¼ teaspoon crumbled leaf thyme
¼ teaspoon crumbled leaf marjoram
2 tablespoons tomato paste
¼ teaspoon salt
⅛ teaspoon freshly ground black pepper
1 cup chicken stock or broth
½ cup milk
¼ cup dry white wine
6 eggs, separated
2 tablespoons freshly grated Parmesan cheese
Pinch of cream of tartar

In a food processor fitted with the metal chopping blade, mince the
parsley quite fine by using three 5-second whirs of the motor; scrape
down the work-bowl sides after each churning. Empty parsley onto a
piece of wax paper and reserve. Mince the onion, using 5 or 6 pulses or
bursts of speed. Melt the butter in a medium-size, heavy saucepan
over moderate heat, add the onion and allow to sauté while you "grind"
the turkey. Place the cubes of turkey in the processor work bowl and
mince fine, using three 5-second churnings of the motor; empty onto a
piece of wax paper and set aside.

Continue sautéing the onion until limp and golden—about 10 minutes in all. Blend in the flour, sage, thyme and marjoram and heat,
stirring, until you have a thick golden roux—about 3 minutes. Mix in
the tomato paste, salt and pepper and allow to mellow 2 to 3 minutes.
Meanwhile, combine the chicken broth and milk, then pour the mixture slowly into the roux, whisking vigorously. Continue heating and
whisking until sauce thickens—about 3 minutes. Add the white wine
slowly, again whisking briskly. Beat the egg yolks lightly with a fork,
mix a little of the hot sauce into the yolks, then stir back into pan. Turn
burner heat to its lowest point, and heat and stir the sauce 1 minute
longer. Remove from the heat, mix in the minced parsley, turkey and

Parmesan cheese. Transfer to a large mixing bowl and cool to room temperature, whisking the sauce occasionally to prevent a "skin" from forming on the surface.

Place the egg whites in a large bowl, sprinkle in the cream of tartar, then beat to soft peaks. Mix about 1 cup of the beaten whites into the turkey mixture, then add the remaining whites and fold in gently but thoroughly with a rubber spatula.

Pour the soufflé mixture into an ungreased 10-cup (2½-quart) soufflé dish, set on the middle rack of a moderate oven (350° F.) and bake, uncovered, for 45 to 50 minutes, or until soufflé is nicely puffed and browned. Serve immediately.

Turkey Hash
Makes 4 servings

Here again, a more or less classic recipe has been altered to accommodate the food processor. The traditional way to start a turkey hash is to dice leftover cooked potatoes for it, but the processor simply transforms them to glue. What I have done instead is to chop the potatoes raw—quite coarsely—then to sauté them slowly with the onion until crisp-tender before adding the chopped turkey. The processor chops turkey nicely if you snap the motor on and off smartly three times only. For hash, the turkey should be in small pieces, not finely ground. Leftover cold chicken works equally well in this recipe (and its variations), as do leftover ham and roast pork.

1 large yellow onion, peeled and cut into slim wedges
3 tablespoons butter
2 medium-size Maine or Eastern potatoes, peeled and cut into 1-inch
  cubes
½ teaspoon salt
Several hefty grindings of black pepper
¼ teaspoon rubbed sage
Pinch of crumbled leaf thyme
Pinch of crumbled leaf rosemary
2 cups 1-inch cubes of leftover cooked turkey
¼ cup chicken stock or water

In a food processor fitted with the metal chopping blade, coarsely chop the onion by pulsing or snapping the motor on and off 2 or 3 times. Melt the butter in a large heavy skillet set over moderate heat, dump in the onion and allow to sauté while you chop the potatoes. Place half of the potato cubes in the processor work bowl, distributing them evenly around the chopping blade, cover, then chop coarsely, using 4 pulses or on-offs of the motor; empty into skillet. Chop the remaining potatoes the same way and add to skillet. Stir-fry the potatoes and onion in the butter over moderately low heat about 10 minutes until limp and golden. Add the salt, pepper, sage, thyme and rosemary and stir lightly to mix. Cover and simmer slowly 10 minutes until potatoes are tender. Add the turkey and the stock and heat, stirring, just to a good serving temperature.

VARIATIONS:

Creamed Hashed Turkey: Prepare exactly as directed, but substitute ½ cup light cream for the ¼ cup chicken stock added at the end. Heat and stir just until steaming hot, then serve.

Curried Turkey Hash: Prepare exactly as directed, but blend 2 teaspoons curry powder into the sautéed potatoes and onion at the same time you mix in the other seasonings. Also substitute ½ cup light cream for the ¼ cup chicken as in Creamed Hashed Turkey above.

Seafood

Fiskpudding
(Norwegian Fish Pudding)

Makes 8 to 10 servings

This elegant, moist and mousse-smooth pudding recipe comes from Norwegian friends who insist that in Norway it is considered everyday fare not fit for company. All I can say is that I have served it to very special company who asked for seconds and then *thirds*. It is perfectly delicious, although not the easiest recipe to prepare, even with a food processor. Without one, it must be torture because you must beat two pounds of fish to a smooth and creamy paste by hand. In Norway, *Fiskpudding* is traditionally topped by a shellfish (usually lobster, shrimp or crab) sauce lightly spiked with sherry (that recipe follows).

> *2 pounds skinned haddock or scrod fillet, cut into 1-inch squares*
> *4 teaspoons salt*
> *2 tablespoons potato starch or cornstarch*
> *2 tablespoons flour*
> *½ teaspoon ground nutmeg*
> *½ cup butter, melted and cooled to room temperature*
> *1½ cups light cream*
> *1 quart milk*
> *¼ teaspoon white pepper*

Pick over fish carefully, removing any fragments of bone. Place one fourth of the total amount of fish in a food processor fitted with the metal chopping blade, add 1 teaspoon of the salt, then turn the motor on and let run continuously for 60 seconds. The fish will cream into a thick and gelatinous paste; scrape into a large mixing bowl. Continue puréeing the remaining fish the same way in three equal batches, adding 1 teaspoon of the salt to each; add to fish in bowl.

With a wooden spoon, work in the potato starch, flour and nutmeg—difficult because the fish is so thick and gummy. Now work in the melted butter a little at a time—the mixture will be quite lumpy, but this is as it should be at this point. Work in the cream, about ¼ cup at a time, beating the mixture well after each addition, then work in the milk the same way, a little bit at a time. This is tiresome business because the mixture is uncommonly stiff and sticky, but it will lighten with subsequent additions of milk and the mixing will become easier. Finally, beat in the pepper. In the end, the mixture should have about the consistency of an angel-food cake batter.

Pour into a well-buttered 3-quart ring mold or angle-food cake pan and set in a large, shallow baking pan. Pour cold water into the baking pan to a depth of about 2 inches, and set in a moderate oven (350° F.). Bake the fish pudding, uncovered, in the water bath for 1 hour. Remove pudding from oven and from the water bath and let stand upright at room temperature for 30 minutes. Invert on a large round platter, cut into wedges and serve with Shellfish Sauce (recipe follows).

Shellfish Sauce for Fiskpudding
Makes about 3 cups

6 tablespoons butter
6 tablespoons flour
1¼ teaspoons salt
⅛ teaspoon white pepper
⅛ teaspoon ground nutmeg or mace
1 cup heavy cream
2 cups milk
1 cup minced cooked lobster, shrimp or crabmeat (for an amount
*   this small, I prefer to hand-mince)*
¼ cup dry sherry

Melt the butter in a heavy saucepan over moderate heat and blend in the flour, salt, pepper and nutmeg. Add the cream and milk and heat, stirring constantly, until thickened and smooth. Add the minced shellfish, reduce heat to lowest point and allow sauce to mellow for 5 to 10 minutes. Mix in the sherry, heat 2 to 3 minutes longer, then ladle over *Fiskpudding.*

Gratinéed Haddock Quenelles

Makes 6 servings

Once considered the province only of the skilled French chef, these soufflé-light fish dumplings can be made by anyone possessing a food processor and a modicum of dexterity. Making the fish base is not a problem, thanks to the processor, but there's still the somewhat pesky business of shaping the *quenelles,* with two tablespoons, into oval dumplings. It's important, first of all, that the basic mixture be refrigerator-cold—about the consistency of cold mashed potatoes. It's also imperative that you keep the two shaping spoons wet so that the *quenelles* don't stick to the spoons. I keep a glass of cold water handy and dip the spoons in each time I shape a *quenelle;* I also replenish the water the instant it becomes cloudy. Once you get the hang of shaping *quenelles,* you'll find that it all goes rather quickly. Basically, the technique is this: With a wet tablespoon, scoop up a small mound of the fish mixture, then, with a second wet tablespoon, smooth and sculpt into a perfect oval dumpling.

One final note: In France, *quenelles* are most often made with fresh pike *(brochet),* but since pike is not widely available throughout the United States, I have specified haddock. Any other fresh white fish with moderately gelatinous flesh (scrod, cod, halibut) will work, but on no account use thawed frozen fish— it is too watery to make successful *quenelles.*

QUENELLES:

1 pound skinned haddock fillets, cut into 1-inch chunks
1½ teaspoons salt
⅛ teaspoon white pepper
Several gratings of nutmeg
1⅔ cups heavy cream
1 large egg
3 quarts lightly salted water

SAUCE:

3 tablespoons butter
1 small shallot, peeled and minced fine
3 tablespoons flour
1 teaspoon salt

⅛ teaspoon white pepper

Pinch of ground nutmeg

Pinch of crumbled leaf thyme

1 cup fish stock or court bouillon (*Here is a good way to use up the frozen* court bouillon *cubes used to make the Cold Fresh Salmon Mousse; see Index for page number. Simply melt the cubes, however many you have left, then add light cream until you have 2 cups of liquid—you will probably need slightly more than the 1 cup of light cream called for just below.*)

1 cup light cream

¼ cup finely shredded Gruyère cheese

¼ cup freshly grated Parmesan cheese

TOPPING:

½ cup freshly grated Parmesan cheese

Prepare the quenelles first: In a food processor fitted with the metal chopping blade, grind the fish, salt, pepper and nutmeg to a paste by letting the motor run nonstop for 30 seconds. Uncover work bowl, scrape down sides and lid, re-cover, then buzz mixture quickly once or twice. Now, with the motor running, drizzle the cream down the feed tube in a fine stream. When all of the cream is incorporated, uncover the work bowl and break the egg into the bowl. Re-cover and pulse or buzz twice—on-off, on-off—to blend (no longer). Transfer the mixture to a metal bowl, cover and chill several hours, or until firm enough to hold a shape.

While the fish mixture chills, place the salted water in a large, heavy, fairly shallow kettle and set on the stove so that it will be ready when you need it. Do not heat it yet, however.

Sauce: When the fish mixture is almost firm enough to shape, begin making the sauce. Melt the butter in a medium-size heavy saucepan over moderate heat, add the shallot and stir-fry about 5 minutes until very limp and golden; do not allow to brown as this will alter the flavor of the sauce. Smooth in the flour, salt, pepper, nutmeg and thyme and mellow over the heat 1 to 2 minutes. Now add the fish stock and the cream and heat, stirring constantly, until thickened and smooth—3 to 5 minutes. Quickly strain the sauce through a fine sieve, return to pan and set over lowest burner heat. Whisk in the Gruyère and Parmesan and heat, stirring, until cheeses are melted and mixture is absolutely smooth. Set off the heat, but keep warm at the back of the stove while you poach the *quenelles*. You will have to whisk the sauce from time to time to keep a "skin" from forming on the surface.

The next step is to bring the salted water to a gentle simmer. The surface of the liquid should ripple faintly; the water should never boil actively as this would break the fragile *quenelles* apart.

Shaping the quenelles: Now, using the technique described in the headnote to this recipe, shape the *quenelles* and slip each one into the salted water as it is done. Poach the *quenelles*, 4 or 5 at a time, allowing 2 to 3 minutes for each batch; drain quickly on paper toweling, then arrange one layer deep in a buttered 9x9x2-inch baking dish. When all *quenelles* are done and in the baking dish, pour the sauce evenly over all, then scatter the ½ cup of grated Parmesan on top. **NOTE:** *You can prepare the recipe up to this point 6 to 8 hours ahead of time, then cover and refrigerate until about 30 minutes before baking. Bring the* quenelles *from the refrigerator and let stand at room temperature for 30 minutes. This is so the ingredients will not be refrigerator-cold and require a longer baking time, which might dry and toughen the* quenelles.

Bake uncovered in a hot oven (425° F.) for 10 minutes, then transfer all to the broiler and broil 6 inches from the heat just until bubbly and dappled with brown—1 to 2 minutes should do it. Serve at once.

Codfish Cakes
Makes 6 servings

This is one of those old American favorites that had become too tedious to prepare of late and which, I suspect, a whole generation of young Americans has never tasted. The processor should reverse the trend because it transforms a formerly tedious recipe into about a 10-minute one (not counting cooking time). **NOTE:** *Normally, it is impossible to mash potatoes in a processor without churning them into glue or using the special technique described in the recipe on page 366. But, I'm happy to report, you can mash them along with the cod and onion, which provide just enough moisture to keep the potatoes fluffy.*

1 pound salt cod
6½ quarts cold water (about)

4 medium-size Maine or Eastern potatoes, peeled and halved
    lengthwise
1 large yellow onion, peeled and cut into slim wedges
½ cup loosely packed parsley sprigs, washed and patted very dry on
    paper toweling
2 tablespoons butter
1 large egg
⅛ teaspoon freshly ground black pepper
2 to 3 tablespoons vegetable oil (for frying the codfish cakes)

Place the salt cod in a large bowl, pour in 2 quarts of the cold water
and soak about 2 hours in the refrigerator; drain off the water, add 2
quarts of fresh water and soak 2 to 3 hours longer; drain once again,
cover with another 2 quarts of cold water and soak 2 to 3 hours longer
in the refrigerator. (All of this is to extract as much salt from the cod as
possible.) Drain the cod well again.

Thin-slice the potatoes by pushing them lightly down the feed tube
of a food processor fitted with the slicing disc; empty the sliced potatoes into a large heavy sacuepan, pouring in the remaining 2 cups of
cold water, then lay the pieces of salt cod on top. Bring to a simmer,
cover and cook 20 to 25 minutes, or until potatoes are very tender.

Meanwhile, remove the slicing disc from the processor and slip the
metal chopping blade into place (no need to wash the work bowl).
Fine-mince the onion and parsley together by pulsing or snapping the
motor on and off 5 or 6 times. Melt the butter in a heavy medium-size
skillet, then stir-fry the onion and parsley over moderately low heat
about 10 minutes, until onion is very soft and golden. Remove from
heat and set aside.

When the cod and potatoes are tender, drain very well. Pick over
the pieces of cod carefully to remove any lurking bits of bone, then
break it into smallish chunks. Place about one third of the cod, one
third of the potatoes, and one third of the sautéed onion in the processor (still fitted with the chopping blade) and chop all together, using
5 or 6 pulses or on-offs of the motor; empty into a mixing bowl. Then
repeat with the remaining cod, potatoes and onion, doing them in two
batches. Add to mixing bowl along with the egg and black pepper. Stir
well to mix, then chill about 1 hour or until the mixture has firmed up
a bit.

To cook, heat 2 tablespoons of the vegetable oil in a large heavy skillet over moderate heat, drop the cod mixture from mounded table-spoonsful and flatten with a spatula into round cakes about ½ inch thick. Brown nicely on both sides, allowing 2 to 3 minutes for each. Continue shaping and cooking the remaining cod mixture the same way, adding more oil to the skillet, if needed.

Fillets of Sole Stuffed and Sauced with Sorrel
Makes 6 servings

I first tasted this dish several Aprils ago at the Ferme Saint-Simeon, an enchanting country inn on the Deauville coast road just west of Honfleur. It's a historic place (a favorite of James McNeill Whistler) and one of the most pleasant places in Normandy to eat. The tables are laid with crisp pink napery and sprigged with fresh flowers, the meals lovingly prepared and served forth on Limoges. At the inn, the recipe is prepared with St. Pierre, a delicate white fish available here. But fillets of sole, I'm pleased to report, work almost as well.

2 tablespoons unsalted butter
1 medium-size yellow onion, peeled and cut into slim wedges
1 pound fresh sorrel leaves, trimmed of coarse stems and wilted
*   leaves, washed well in cool water, then patted very dry on paper*
*   toweling*
1 egg
2 tablespoons flour
1 tablespoon heavy cream
6 medium-size fillets of sole
Fresh Sorrel Sauce (recipe follows)

Melt the butter in a very large heavy saucepan over moderate heat; set aside. Machine-chop the onion in a food processor fitted with the metal chopping blade—4 or 5 pulses or fast bursts of speed will yield moderately finely chopped onion. Empty the onion in the saucepan and sauté in the butter about 5 minutes over moderate heat until limp and golden. Pile the sorrel into the pan, cover and warm 1 minute—just until wilted. Empty all saucepan's contents into the food processor, still fitted with the chopping blade; break in the egg, add the flour and cream and process nonstop for 3 to 5 seconds, just until moderately finely chopped and well blended. Transfer to a small mixing bowl, cover and refrigerate several hours, or until fairly thick.

About 20 minutes before serving, spread the fish fillets out on a wax-paper-covered counter. Spread with the sorrel stuffing, but leave margins of ½ inch all around. Fold the fillets over at the centers (tail ends to head ends), enclosing the stuffing, and secure at the ends with wooden picks. Fit a very large skillet (not iron) with a steamer rack. Pour about 1 inch of boiling water into the skillet, or if you prefer, a half-and-half mixture of water and dry white wine or vermouth. Lay fish on rack, cover skillet and steam for 10 to 12 minutes, just until the fish will flake at the touch of a fork. Remove wooden picks and serve with Fresh Sorrel Sauce.

Fresh Sorrel Sauce

Makes about 2½ cups

3 tablespoons unsalted butter
1 medium-size yellow onion, peeled and cut into slim wedges
2 celery ribs, washed and cut into 1-inch lengths
2 carrots, peeled and cut into 1-inch lengths
3 parsley sprigs
1 quart fish stock or bottled clam juice
⅔ cup dry vermouth
4 egg yolks
2 tablespoons flour
⅛ teaspoon white pepper
1 cup heavy cream
⅓ cup finely minced fresh sorrel (for an amount this small, I prefer to hand-mince)
Salt (if needed to taste)

Melt the butter in a large heavy saucepan over moderate heat. Machine-chop the onion in a food processor fitted with the metal chopping blade—a couple of pulses or on-offs should do the job; empty onion into saucepan. Machine-chop the celery the same way and empty into saucepan. Machine-chop the carrots about 20 seconds nonstop; add to saucepan along with parsley sprigs. Sauté vegetables 10 minutes over moderate heat, stirring now and then, just until limp and golden. Add fish stock and vermouth and simmer, uncovered, 35 to 40 minutes, or until reduced by about one fourth.

Strain the stock, discard vegetables, then return stock to saucepan. Beat egg yolks, flour and pepper just enough to blend; smooth in the cream. Ladle a little of the hot stock into the egg mixture, whisk to blend, then stir back into saucepan. Mix in fresh sorrel and heat and stir over lowest heat about 5 minutes until thickened and smooth. Taste for seasoning and add salt if necessary. Delicious over any steamed or poached delicate white fish.

Parslied Bluefish in Cream
Makes 4 servings

4 fresh bluefish (about 1 pound each), cleaned and boned
1 teaspoon salt
¼ teaspoon freshly ground black pepper
¼ cup unsalted butter
1 cup loosely packed parsley sprigs, washed and patted very dry on
    paper toweling
1 large yellow onion, peeled and cut into slim wedges
1 cup light cream

Sprinkle each fish inside and out with salt and pepper, arrange one layer deep in a shallow roasting pan and dot generously with butter. In a food processor fitted with the metal chopping blade, mince the parsley moderately fine with about two 5-second churnings of the motor; scatter on top of the fish. Now coarsely chop the onion with a couple of pulses or fast whirs of the motor and sprinkle over the fish. Cover pan with foil and bake for 10 minutes in a moderately hot oven (375° F.); uncover and bake 20 minutes longer. Pour the light cream over the fish, bake, uncovered, for 10 minutes and serve.

Salmon-Broccoli Loaf
with Dill and Capers
Makes 6 to 8 servings

For me, one of the unexpected bonuses of having a processor is that I'm learning to utilize trimmings that I formerly would have discarded—coarse broccoli stems, for example. As a matter of fact, it was when I'd planned to serve salmon loaf and fresh broccoli that the idea struck me. Why not chop up the discarded stems and slip them into the salmon loaf? They would add color, texture, flavor and nourishment. It worked beautifully and I'm pleased that friends who sampled the salmon loaf thought it the best they'd ever eaten. **NOTE:** *The broccoli makes the loaf unusually moist and velvety, so it's important to let it stand at room temperature for 30 minutes before slicing. Also, you'll notice that the recipe contains no salt. It doesn't need it. The salmon itself is quite salty and the lemon rind and capers are tart.*

> 1 cup loosely packed parsley sprigs, washed and patted very dry on
>   paper toweling
> 6 slices firm-textured white bread
> 2 cups ½-inch cubes of broccoli stems (This is the amount you'll get
>   from 1 large bunch of broccoli. If you can only manage 1½ or 1¾
>   cups of ½-inch cubes, don't worry; those amounts work well, too.)
> 1 medium-size yellow onion, peeled and cut into slim wedges
> 1¾ pounds cooked or canned boned salmon (remove all dark skin)
> ⅓ cup drained capers (use the small capers)
> ⅔ cup light cream
> 4 eggs
> 2 tablespoons snipped fresh dill or ¾ teaspoon dill weed
> Finely grated rind of ½ lemon
> ⅛ teaspoon freshly ground black pepper

In a food processor fitted with the metal chopping blade, mince the parsley fine, using 7 or 8 pulses or on-offs of the motor; empty into a large mixing bowl. Now crumb the bread, 2 slices at a time, with two or three 5-second churnings of the motor; add to bowl. Dump all of the broccoli stems into the processor and, with about three 5-second bursts of the motor, mince very fine; add to bowl. Processor-mince the onion—3 or 4 pulses or on-offs will do it—and add to bowl. Now flake the salmon in three batches—2 pulses or on-offs of the motor will be enough. Add to the mixing bowl along with all remaining ingredients. Mix very thoroughly, pack mixture firmly into a well-buttered 9x5x3-inch loaf pan and bake in a slow oven (300° F.) for about 1 hour and 40 minutes, or until loaf begins to pull from sides of pan and is firm to the touch. Remove loaf from oven and let it stand upright in its pan on a wire rack for 30 minutes. Carefully loosen the loaf all around with a thin-bladed spatula, then invert gently onto a large serving platter.

Cold Fresh Salmon Mousse with Dill

Makes 6 servings

This is one of those fast-setting gelatin molds made with frozen cubes of *court bouillon*. A couple of zaps in the food processor and the mousse is made. I caution you, however, to serve the mousse as soon as it "sets up" (congeals) because, like other fast-setting molds, it will continue to harden on standing and develop an unpleasant rubbery texture.

> *1 medium-size yellow onion, peeled and cut into slim wedges*
> *1 medium-size celery rib, washed and cut into 1-inch lengths*
> *1 large bunch of parsley, washed*
> *6 large bunches of dill, washed*
> *2 cups cold water*
> *1 cup dry white wine*
> *4 peppercorns*
> *1½ pounds boned and skinned fresh salmon*
> *2 large shallots, peeled*
> *1 tablespoon butter*
> *Juice of 1 large lemon*
> *2 envelopes plain gelatin*
> *⅔ cup boiling court bouillon*
> *¾ cup mayonnaise (see Index for recipe page number)*
> *1¼ cups light cream*
> *12 "ice cubes" court bouillon*
> *1 teaspoon salt*

In a food processor fitted with the metal chopping blade, fine-mince the onion and celery together, using 5 or 6 pulses or on-offs of the motor. Empty into a large heavy skillet (not iron), add the parsley, dill, water, wine and peppercorns and boil, uncovered, for 15 minutes, or until the liquid (*court bouillon*) is reduced by about one half. Lay the salmon in the skillet, reduce heat so that the *court bouillon* barely ripples, cover and cook for 8 minutes exactly. Lift the salmon from the skillet to a plate to cool, then wrap in foil and refrigerate until needed.

Strain the *court bouillon*, discarding the solids. Measure out and reserve ⅔ cup of the *court bouillon*, pour the remainder into a standard ice-cube tray (one that makes 18 cubes) and quick-freeze until firm (this will take about an hour if you have a 0° F. freezer, longer if you do not). There will not be enough *court bouillon* to fill the tray, so you'll not have proper frozen "cubes" but slim wafers—just as well, because the "cubes" would have to be cracked before they could be fed into the food processor; these smaller pieces can be added as is.

As soon as the *court bouillon* is frozen, you can proceed with the recipe. But as a matter of fact, if you want to attend to this part of the recipe the day before, so much the better. From here on out, the mousse can be made in minutes.

In the work bowl of a processor fitted with the metal chopping blade (both the bowl and the blade should be clean and dry), mince the shallots quite fine, using 5 or 6 pulses or bursts of the motor. Scrape into a small saucepan, add the butter, set over moderate heat and sauté about 5 minutes until limp and golden. Scrape back into the processor work bowl (still fitted with the metal chopping blade). Add the lemon juice, gelatin and ⅔ cup boiling *court bouillon*. Turn the motor on and let run 20 seconds nonstop. Break the salmon into small chunks and add it to bowl along with mayonnaise and ¼ cup of the cream; turn motor on and let run 10 seconds nonstop.

The bowl at this point will be quite full, so lift it off the processor base, holding the chopping blade firmly in place to keep the mixture from leaking down the center tube, and pour half of it into a large bowl. Return work bowl to processor base and secure in place; add the remaining 1 cup of cream and whir a couple of times to blend. Now, with the motor running, add the 12 "ice cubes" of *court bouillon* one at a time—allow 1 to 2 seconds between additions. (You will not use all of the frozen cubes, so bundle the remaining 6 in a plastic bag and store in the freezer; they can be added to soups and sauces later.)

When all of the frozen *court bouillon* has been incorporated, combine this salmon mixture at once with the balance in the mixing bowl. Stir in the salt, spoon into an oiled 6-cup decorative mold, cover with plastic food wrap and chill until firm—about 45 minutes to 1 hour, depending upon the coldness of your refrigerator.

Unmold by dipping quickly in warm water, then inverting on a platter. To serve, slice about 1 inch thick. NOTE: *The mousse is quite rich, so accompany with the lightest, crispest green salad in your repertoire.*

Pescado en Escabeche
(Mexican Marinated Fish)

Makes 6 to 8 servings

Here's a refreshing way to serve fish—smothered with thinly sliced carrot, onion, green pepper and an oil-and-vinegar marinade. *Escabeche* is equally good warm or cold. For best results, use a delicate white fish such as flounder or sole—fresh, rather than frozen, because frozen fish is so fragile it will fall apart.

3 pounds flounder fillets
¾ cup unsifted flour
1 teaspoon salt
¼ teaspoon freshly ground black pepper
4 tablespoons vegetable oil
3 tablespoons olive oil
2 small carrots, peeled and cut into 4-inch lengths
⅓ cup water
1 large Spanish onion, peeled and halved lengthwise
1 medium-size sweet green pepper, washed, cored, halved lengthwise and seeded
1 small garlic clove, peeled and minced fine
1 cup loosely packed parsley sprigs, washed and patted very dry on paper toweling
¼ cup loosely packed fresh coriander leaves, washed and patted very dry on paper toweling (You can find fresh coriander in Oriental or Latin-American groceries.)
3 tablespoons cider vinegar

Cut the fish into manageable pieces—about 2 by 4 inches. Mix flour with salt and pepper, then dredge fish lightly in the seasoned flour. Brown the fish in the vegetable oil in a very large, heavy skillet over moderate heat—about 2 minutes per side. As fish browns, transfer to a deep platter. Drain oil from skillet, quickly wipe skillet out, add the olive oil and set skillet aside while you prepare the vegetables.

In a food processor fitted with the slicing disc, thin-slice the carrots by pushing them through the feed tube with as little pressure as possible. Place them in a small saucepan with the water, cover and cook over moderate heat about 10 to 15 minutes until tender; drain well, and set aside. Thin-slice the onion halves in the processor in the same way in which you sliced the carrots, then thin-slice the green-pepper halves. Add onion, green pepper, garlic and cooked carrots to the olive oil in the skillet. Set over moderate heat and stir-fry about 5 minutes, until onion and pepper are limp and golden.

Remove slicing disc from processor and slip the metal chopping blade into place. Dump in the parsley sprigs and coriander leaves and, with 2 or 3 pulses or fast on-offs, mince moderately coarsely. Mix into the vegetables in the skillet along with the vinegar, bring to a simmer, then pour mixture over the fish. Let stand 15 minutes before serving. Or, if you prefer, cover and marinate several hours in the refrigerator and serve cold.

Clamburgers

Makes 4 servings

You may think that the processor's powerful metal chopping blade would reduce clams to paste in no time flat. But, in fact, it does a superb job of mincing them if you control the churning carefully by snapping the motor on and off.

5 slices of firm-textured white bread, broken into small pieces
⅓ cup loosely packed dill fronds, washed and patted very dry on paper toweling
¼ cup loosely packed parsley sprigs, washed and patted very dry on paper toweling
¼ cup snipped fresh chives
1 quart cherrystone or littleneck clams, drained well (reserve juice)

½ cup bottled clam juice
2 eggs, lightly beaten
¼ teaspoon salt
Several hefty grindings of black pepper
2 tablespoons vegetable oil
1 tablespoon butter

Place bread, dill, parsley and chives in a food processor equipped with the metal chopping blade and buzz together until bread is reduced to crumbs and herbs are fairly finely minced—about three 5-second bursts of speed will do the job. Empty into a mixing bowl. Place half of the drained clams in the processor and mince moderately coarsely by pulsing or snapping the motor on and off 5 times. Add to bowl with bread crumbs, mince the remaining clams the same way and add to bowl along with the ½ cup clam juice. (Save the remaining clam juice to add to soups, stews or sauces if you intend to make any such within a day or two. Otherwise, drink the clam juice or discard it.) Add the eggs, salt and pepper to the bowl and stir all well to mix.

Heat the vegetable oil and butter in a large heavy skillet over moderate heat until a drop of the clam mixture will sizzle in it, then spoon in the mixture (about 2 tablespoons per clamburger), smooth out with a spatula into flat cakes about 3 inches in diameter and brown about 3 minutes on each side. Serve at once.

Eastern Shore Deviled Crab and Mushroom Casserole

Makes 6 servings

You will not find lovelier crabs anywhere than the sweet and succulent blue crabs of Chesapeake Bay, although West Coast devotees of the Dungeness will surely argue the point. The meat of either crab is delicious in this particular casserole for which everything, almost, can be processor-chopped, sliced or shredded.

3 slices firm-textured white bread, torn into small pieces
2 tablespoons melted butter
1 medium-size yellow onion, peeled and cut into slim wedges
1 medium-size garlic clove, peeled

1 medium-size celery rib, trimmed, washed and cut into 1-inch
    lengths
½ small green pepper, washed, cored, seeded and cut into 1-inch
    pieces
¼ cup loosely packed fresh parsley sprigs, washed and patted very
    dry on paper toweling
7 tablespoons butter
½ pound medium-size mushrooms, wiped clean and stemmed
    (reserve stems)
½ cup dry sherry
5 tablespoons flour
½ teaspoon dry mustard
2 cups light cream
2 ounces Gruyère cheese (cut into a column about the height and
    width of the food-processor feed tube)
1 teaspoon salt (or to taste)
¼ teaspoon cayenne pepper
1 pound fresh lump or backfin crab meat, well picked over to
    remove bits of shell and cartilage

In a food processor equipped with the metal chopping blade, buzz the bread to moderately fine crumbs, using two or three 5-second churnings of the motor. Empty crumbs into a bowl, add melted butter and toss well to mix. Set aside to use later as the casserole topping.

Now add to the work bowl (still fitted with the metal chopping blade) the onion, garlic, celery, green pepper and parsley, and mince moderately fine by letting the motor run nonstop for 10 seconds. Melt 3 tablespoons of the butter in a large, heavy skillet over moderate heat and dump in all the contents of the processor work bowl. Sauté gently while you prepare the mushrooms. First add all of the stems to the work bowl and mince quite fine, using 5 or 6 pulses or on-offs of the motor; add to skillet. Now remove the metal chopping blade from the processor and slip the slicing disc into place. Thin-slice the mushroom caps by standing as many of them in the feed tube as needed for a snug fit, then pushing them through, using gentle pressure on the pusher. Add to the skillet and sauté, stirring now and then, about 15 minutes, or until the vegetable mixture is lightly browned. Add the sherry and cook, uncovered, until almost all of the liquid has evaporated.

In a small, heavy saucepan set over moderate heat, melt the remaining 4 tablespoons of butter. Blend in the flour and mustard. Add the light cream and heat, stirring, until thickened and smooth and no raw starch flavor remains—about 5 minutes. Mix in the cheese, and season with salt and cayenne pepper. Pour this sauce into the vegetable skillet, add the crab meat, and toss all lightly to mix. Taste for salt and add more, if needed. Spoon into a buttered, shallow 2-quart casserole or *au gratin* dish and scatter the buttered bread crumbs evenly on top. Bake, uncovered, in a moderately hot oven (375° F.) for about 30 minutes, or until bubbling and lightly browned.

Cajun Crawfish (or Crab) Cakes
Makes 4 to 6 servings

The Cajuns say that when they were deported long ago from Acadia (present-day Nova Scotia), lobsters swam south alongside the ships that carried them to Louisiana. By the time the lobsters reached the bayou country where the Cajuns settled, they were so tired and weak they had turned into little crawfish. Apocryphal as the story has to be, it's still true that crawfish are a great Cajun specialty today. Although few people realize it, crawfish (or crayfish, if you prefer) are available over much of the United States. If you should have access to them, by all means prepare them this Cajun way in crisp-crusted patties. Or you can use lump crab meat. The processor does a superb job of mincing the meat of crawfish or crab. But you cannot use it to mash the potatoes that bind the cakes together, since the powerful action of the chopping blade will churn the potatoes to glue in no time.

1 pound cooked and shelled crawfish or 1 pound lump crab meat,
* picked over carefully to remove bits of shell and cartilage*
1 small yellow onion, peeled and halved lengthwise
1 strip (about 1 inch wide) sweet green pepper
1¾ cups unseasoned mashed potatoes (measure firmly packed)
2 eggs, lightly beaten
1½ teaspoons salt
⅛ teaspoon freshly ground black pepper
⅛ teaspoon cayenne pepper
½ cup stone-ground cornmeal (for dredging)
¼ cup lard or vegetable shortening (for frying)

Place one third of the crawfish (halve any that are very large) or pieces of crab meat into a food processor fitted with the metal chopping blade. With 3 or 4 pulses or fast bursts of speed, mince quite fine; empty into a large mixing bowl. Repeat until all crawfish or crab meat is chopped; empty into bowl. Machine-mince the onion and green pepper together by pulsing or snapping the machine on and off 5 or 6 times. Add to crawfish along with mashed potatoes, eggs, salt, black pepper and cayenne. Mix thoroughly, using your hands, then shape into flat patties about ½ inch thick and 2½ inches in diameter. Dredge the patties in cornmeal, then place on a baking sheet lined with wax paper, cover loosely and chill several hours before cooking to allow the patties to firm up.

Heat the lard or shortening in a large heavy skillet over moderate heat until sizzling hot, then brown the cakes well on both sides—3 to 5 minutes per side is about right. Drain on paper toweling and serve.

Mexican Skillet Lobster

Makes 4 to 6 servings

Purists will no doubt scoff at any recipe that gilds the lordly lobster, insisting that the only way to prepare it is to steam it and accompany it with nothing more than ramekins of melted buttter. I agree, certainly, that properly steamed lobster is incomparable. But I am also interested to learn how lobster is prepared in other parts of the world. I happen to think that this Mexican recipe, which I was served not so long ago in Mérida, is both unusual and delicious. It's an easy recipe that processor-chopping makes even easier.

> 2 medium-size sweet green peppers, washed, cored, seeded and cut
>   into 1-inch pieces (or use 1 sweet red one and 1 sweet green
>   pepper)
> ¼ cup vegetable oil, peanut oil or olive oil
> 2 medium-size yellow onions, peeled and cut into slim wedges
> 1 large garlic clove, peeled and hand-minced
> 3 large vine-ripe tomatoes, washed, cored and cut into 1-inch chunks
>   (no need to peel)
> ½ cup dry white wine
> ½ cup fish stock, court bouillon or bottled clam juice (a good way,

*incidentally, to use up the frozen cubes of court bouillon left over
from the Cold Fresh Salmon Mousse recipe; see Index for recipe
page number)*
1½ teaspoons chili powder
¼ teaspoon ground coriander
½ teaspoon salt
⅛ teaspoon cayenne pepper
Pinch of powdered saffron
1 jar (4 ounces) pimientos, drained
1½ pounds cooked lobster meat, cut into small chunks by hand

Mince the sweet peppers in a food processor fitted with the metal
chopping blade by pulsing or snapping the motor on and off 5 or 6
times. Heat the oil in a very large heavy skillet over moderate heat (not
an iron skillet unless it is enameled because the "raw" iron will give the
dish a rusty flavor). Dump in the peppers as soon as they are minced.
Now quickly machine-mince the onions the same way and add to skillet
along with the garlic. Sauté about 10 minutes, or until limp and
golden.

You need not stir the skillet continuously, so use this time to good
advantage by machine-chopping the tomatoes. But first, quickly
squeeze the tomato chunks over the sink to extract the seeds and excess juice. Place half of the tomato chunks in the processor work bowl
(still fitted with the metal chopping blade) and chop moderately
coarsely by pulsing or snapping the motor on and off 2 or 3 times; add
tomatoes to the skillet. Machine-chop the remaining tomato chunks the
same way and add to skillet along with the wine, fish stock, chili
powder, coriander, salt, pepper and saffron. Simmer, uncovered, stirring occasionally, for 30 to 35 minutes, or until mixture has cooked
down into a moderately thick sauce and flavors are well blended.

Wash and dry the processor work bowl and chopping blade and reassemble. Add the pimiento and, with a few pulses or on-offs of the
motor, mince moderately fine. Add pimiento to the skillet. Now add
the lobster, stir to mix, and heat, uncovered, for 10 to 15 minutes,
stirring occasionally just until heated through and flavors "get together." Ladle over boiled rice and serve.

Mousse of Bay Scallops
Makes 6 to 8 servings

A fragile, quivery mousse that can be served hot or cold. I prefer to use bay rather than sea scallops for three reasons: Their flavor is more delicate, their texture more velvety, and their size much smaller so they need not to be cut up before they go into the food processor to be ground.

> 2 pounds bay scallops, well drained
> 4 teaspoons salt
> 3 tablespoons cornstarch
> 3 tablespoons flour
> ¼ cup melted butter
> 3 eggs, lightly beaten
> ½ cup dry white wine
> 2½ cups milk
> 1 cup heavy cream
> ⅛ teaspoon white pepper

In a food processor fitted with the metal chopping blade, grind one fourth of the scallops to a paste with 1 teaspoon of the salt by letting the motor run nonstop for 60 seconds; scrape into a large mixing bowl. Grind the remaining scallops the same way in three batches, adding 1 teaspoon of salt to each; add to bowl.

By hand, blend in the cornstarch and flour with a wooden spoon—slow going, but persist—then mix in the melted butter and eggs. Smooth in the wine, then the milk, adding about ½ cup at a time and beating well after each addition. Finally, blend in the cream and the pepper.

Spoon the mixture into a buttered 2½-quart casserole and set in a large shallow pan. Pour water into the pan to a depth of about 1½ inches, set all in a moderate oven (350° F.) and bake, uncovered, for 1 hour, or until mousse is delicately set. Remove mousse from the oven and from the water bath and cool 15 minutes. Serve directly from the casserole.

Vatapá

Makes about 12 servings

The cuisine most typical of Brazil is the Afro-Brazilian cooking of Bahia, an east-coast state lush with tropical fruits and washed by seas abounding with shrimp. The master Bahian cooks combine the fruits of land and sea in as imaginative an array of dishes as can be found anywhere on earth. *Vatapá*, to name one of the best of them, is a kettle of shrimp bathed in coconut cream, thickened with bread paste and made piquant with red chilis. Like many Bahian recipes, *vatapá* calls for dried shrimp as well as fresh and for an even more exotic ingredient known as *dendê*, the oil of a tropical palm. It can be bought in Spanish or Latin-American groceries. You can also approximate (although not duplicate) its unique flavor and orange color by mixing together olive oil, sesame oil, paprika and a dab of grated lemon rind (proportions are given below).

Vatapá is a superb choice for a large buffet. It can be made—all but the finishing touches—a day ahead of time. It's easy to handle, filling, and can be stretched over a lot of servings by being ladled over rice. The perfect accompaniment would be a salad of avocado crescents and grapefruit sections or, if you prefer, a tartly dressed, crisp green salad.

½ cup Oven-Dried Shrimp (see Index for recipe page number)
1 cup cold water
1 medium-size loaf French bread (It should measure about 14 inches long and 3 inches wide when trimmed of crusts; save these to buzz into crumbs to store for other uses.)
2 cups milk
1 large Spanish onion, peeled and cut into slim wedges
1 large garlic clove, peeled and crushed
3 tablespoons olive oil
1 medium-size sweet green pepper, washed, cored, seeded and cut into 1-inch squares
2 large very ripe beefsteak tomatoes, cored and cut into slim wedges (no need to peel)
1 to 2 teaspoons sugar (if needed to mellow the tartness of the tomatoes)
¾ teaspoon ground coriander
1 teaspoon crushed dried red chili peppers

Cold water to soak dried shrimp, plus enough cold water to total 2½
   cups
2 cups Coconut Cream (see Index for recipe page number)
2½ pounds raw shelled and deveined shrimp
1 cup roasted cashew nuts (preferably unsalted)
3 tablespoons dendê oil or 3 tablespoons olive oil mixed with ½
   teaspoon sesame oil, ½ teaspoon paprika and ⅛ teaspoon very
   finely grated lemon rind
1 teaspoon salt (or to taste)
⅛ teaspoon freshly ground black pepper
1½ cups parsley sprigs, washed and patted very dry on paper
   toweling
8 scallions (include some green tops), washed, trimmed and cut into
   1-inch lengths

Soak the dried shrimp for 2 hours in enough cold water to cover them.
Also break the French bread into small chunks, soak them in the milk,
and coarsely chop the onion in a food processor fitted with the metal
chopping blade. You'll only be able to do about half the onion at a time
if it is a truly big one—2 or 3 pulses or quick bursts of speed should
do it.

Empty onion into a large heavy kettle to which you have already
added the garlic and olive oil. Set over moderate heat and stir-fry 10
minutes. Drain the soaked, dried shrimp (reserve the soaking water)
and stir them into the kettle. Coarsely chop the green pepper in the
food processor—a couple of pulses or fast on-offs will do it—and add to
kettle. Put half the tomatoes into the food processor (still fitted with the
metal chopping blade) and buzz 10 to 15 seconds nonstop—just until
nicely puréed. Add to kettle, purée remaining tomatoes the same way
and add to kettle also. Taste tomatoes and if they seem tart, add 1 to 2
teaspoons sugar along with the coriander and chili peppers. Heat and
stir over fairly high heat 10 to 15 minutes, or until the juices have
cooked down and are fairly thick. Then add the reserved shrimp-soak-
ing water, which has been diluted with enough cold water to total 2½
cups, and simmer, uncovered, for 20 minutes, stirring occasionally.

Remove the kettle from the heat. Measure out 2 cups of the kettle
mixture, place in the food processor (still fitted with the metal chopping blade) and buzz 60 seconds nonstop to purée. Empty into a large
bowl. Repeat until all of the kettle mixture is puréed. Return purée to

the kettle. Empty the soaked bread into the processor and buzz 10 seconds to purée; mix into kettle. Simmer very slowly, uncovered, for 45 minutes, stirring often to prevent mixture from sticking.

Now add the coconut cream and the raw shrimp. Dump cashews into processor work bowl and, with 4 or 5 pulses or bursts of speed, mince quite fine. Stir these into the shrimp mixture, then beat in the *dendê* oil, 1 tablespoon at a time. Add the salt and simmer slowly for 8 to 10 minutes, just until the shrimp turn pink. Taste for salt and add more if needed; also mix in the black pepper.

Note: *The* vatapá *can be prepared up to this point as much as 24 hours before serving. Cool to room temperature, cover, then refrigerate. About 20 minutes before you are ready to serve, set the kettle of* vatapá *over low heat and bring slowly to serving temperature, stirring frequently.*

For mincing the parsley and scallions, you will need a clean, dry work bowl and metal chopping blade. Place the parsley in the work bowl, then buzz once or twice to mince fairly coarsely. Stir into the *vatapá*, then machine-mince the scallions, using pulses or 4 or 5 bursts of power. Mix into *vatapá*, then simmer all together very slowly for 10 to 15 minutes, stirring frequently. Serve over fluffy boiled rice, and take a bow.

Curried Shrimp, Carrots and Zucchini

Makes 6 servings

As curries go, this one is low-calorie (about 275 calories per serving) because the base sauce is compounded of minced vegetables *à la cuisine minceur* instead of being thickened with flour or cream. The order in which the various vegetables are processor-chopped is important, because each succeeding vegetable can be added without washing out the work bowl, indeed each helps to clear the work bowl, simplifying final cleanup.

2 large garlic cloves, peeled
One ½-inch cube ginger root, peeled
3 tablespoons unsalted butter
3 medium-size yellow onions, peeled and cut into slim wedges

3 medium-size carrots, peeled and cut into 1-inch chunks

2 large celery ribs, washed, trimmed of tops and cut into 1-inch chunks

4 small zucchini, washed, trimmed and cut into 1-inch chunks

1 medium-size tart apple (such as a McIntosh), peeled, quartered and cored

3 large vine-ripe tomatoes, peeled, cored and cut into slim wedges

2 tablespoons curry powder

2 pounds shelled and deveined raw shrimp

1 cup yogurt, at room temperature

1 teaspoon salt (or to taste)

⅛ teaspoon freshly ground black pepper

1 teaspoon brown sugar (if needed to mellow the tartness of the tomatoes)

In a food processor fitted with the metal chopping blade, grind the garlic and ginger root to a paste (about 1 minute nonstop). Using the rubber spatula, scrape paste into a very large heavy skillet or a large, shallow kettle. Add butter, set over lowest heat and allow to mellow while you chop the vegetables.

Coarsely chop the onions in the processor, using the metal chopping blade and doing only about half of them at a time—use 2 or 3 pulses or on-offs for each batch. Scrape onions into skillet, and stir to blend with the garlic-ginger paste. Raise heat to moderate. Place all carrot chunks in work bowl, still fitted with the chopping blade, and chop moderately fine (about 10 seconds nonstop); transfer to skillet. Coarsely chop the celery with 2 or 3 pulses or fast bursts of speed; add to skillet. Then chop the zucchini the same way, doing about half of the full amount at a time; also add to skillet. Raise heat under skillet to moderately high and stir-fry mixture 10 to 15 minutes, until golden but not brown. Add apple and tomatoes to processor work bowl (again still fitted with the metal chopping blade) and reduce to liquid—10 to 15 seconds nonstop should do the job.

When skillet vegetables are limp and golden, sprinkle with curry powder and let mellow 5 minutes; add tomato mixture and simmer slowly over moderately low heat, uncovered, about 50 to 60 minutes, or until reduced to the consistency of a fairly thick sauce. Now add the shrimp, pushing them well down in the vegetable mixture, and simmer 5 minutes, just until they turn bright pink. Smooth in the yogurt, salt and pepper; taste and adjust seasonings if necessary, adding a little more salt and, if curry seems unduly tart, the teaspoon of brown sugar. Bring just to serving temperature—do not allow the sauce to boil or the yogurt will curdle. Serve over fluffy boiled rice with a hot and spicy chutney.

Shrimp de Jonghe

Makes 6 servings

Minced fresh tarragon, chives and parsley, buzzed into a paste with butter, shallots, garlic and soft bread crumbs, give this casserole its delicate color and balance of flavors. You may be interested to know that Shrimp de Jonghe is a relatively long-winded affair made the old-fashioned way, but with a food processor, total preparation time is about 30 minutes, *including* 20 to 25 minutes of unattended baking. Make the recipe several hours ahead of time, if you like, then cover and refrigerate. About 30 minutes before baking, bring the casserole from the refrigerator and let stand at room temperature. (This is to allow the ingredients to warm slightly so that you need not increase baking time and risk the shrimp's drying out.)

1½ pounds shelled and deveined raw shrimp
2 quarts boiling water
4 slices firm-textured white bread, broken into small pieces
1 large garlic clove, peeled
1 large shallot, peeled
¼ cup loosely packed parsley sprigs, washed and patted very dry on
*   paper toweling*
¼ cup snipped fresh chives
2 tablespoons fresh tarragon leaves, washed and patted dry on
*   paper toweling (do not substitute dried or crumbled leaf tarragon)*
1 teaspoon fresh marjoram leaves, washed and patted dry on paper
*   toweling, or ¼ teaspoon crumbled leaf marjoram*
1 teaspoon fresh chervil leaves, washed and patted dry on paper
*   toweling, or ¼ teaspoon crumbled leaf chervil*
½ cup (1 stick) butter, at room temperature
Juice of ½ lemon

3 tablespoons dry sherry or Port
¼ teaspoon salt
Several hefty grindings of black pepper

Parboil the shrimp in the boiling water for 2 minutes; drain and set aside. In a food processor fitted with the metal chopping blade, buzz the bread to crumbs, using two or three 5-second bursts of speed; empty onto a piece of wax paper and set aside. To the processor add the garlic, shallot, parsley, chives, tarragon, marjoram and chervil, and mince together by letting the motor run nonstop for 10 seconds. Add the crumbs and all remaining ingredients and buzz for another 60 seconds nonstop. Place the shrimp in a buttered shallow 1-quart casserole or *au gratin* dish and spread the herb mixture on top. Bake, uncovered, in a moderately hot oven (375° F.) for 20 to 25 minutes, or until the butter, which has melted and trickled down through the shrimp to the bottom of the casserole, is bubbly. Serve at once.

Shrimp Catupiry

Makes 6 servings

The Brazilian state of Minas Gerais, renowned for its topazes, tourmalines and aquamarines, is also famous for this delicate shrimp and cheese skillet dish. The best American cheese to use for *catupiry* is a white Cheddar such as a Vermont cheese or a Monterey Jack. If unavailable, use any pale, well-aged Cheddar.

2½ pounds raw shelled and deveined shrimp
3 tablespoons butter
⅓ cup brandy
6 shallots, peeled
½ cup dry white wine
2 cups light cream
⅓ pound sharp white or pale yellow Cheddar, cut into columns
    about the height and width of the food-processor feed tube
½ teaspoon salt
Pinch freshly ground black pepper

Stir-fry the shrimp in the butter in a very large, heavy skillet over moderate heat 8 to 10 minutes, or until they have turned pink and released their juices; drain off and reserve the juices. Remove skillet from heat, add brandy, return to heat and warm about 1 minute. Remove from heat and ignite with a match—the brandy will burst into blue flames. Let the flames die out, shaking the skillet all the while. Remove the shrimp from the skillet and reserve.

In a food processor fitted with the metal chopping blade, mince the shallots quite fine—5 or 6 pulses or quick bursts of speed should do the job. Add shallots to skillet, also the juices of the reserved shrimp, and cook over moderate heat, agitating the skillet, until almost all of the juices have evaporated—2 to 3 minutes. Pour in the wine and boil, uncovered, until the wine evaporates and only the shallots and a nice golden glaze remain in the skillet. Whisk in the cream and reduce heat to low. Equip the food processor with the shredding disc and shred the cheese. Add to skillet along with salt and pepper and cook, stirring constantly, until cheese has melted and sauce thickened—about 3 to 4 minutes. Do not allow the mixture to boil, or it may curdle. Return shrimp to skillet and bring just to serving temperature. Serve over boiled rice.

Eggs, Cheese, Pasta & Their Sauces

Basel Onion Tart

Makes 8 servings

This bacon-and-cheese tart is much like quiche Lorraine except that it is filled with thinly sliced onions. It should be served warm—not oven-hot or refrigerator-cold—and is perfect for a party luncheon. It also makes an appropriate first course for a not-too-rich dinner.

3 slices lean, smoky bacon, snipped crosswise in julienne strips
1 tablespoon unsalted butter
1 very large Spanish onion (about 4 inches in diameter), peeled and quartered lengthwise
1½ cups light cream
3 large eggs
¼ pound well-aged Gruyère cheese, cut into columns about the height and width of the food-processor feed tube
¼ teaspoon salt
⅛ teaspoon white pepper
⅛ teaspoon freshly ground nutmeg
One 9-inch unbaked pie shell (see Index for recipe page numbers for Pâte Brisée and Flaky Pastry)

In a large heavy skillet set over moderately high heat, sauté the bacon until crisp and brown; drain bacon on paper toweling and reserve. Pour drippings from skillet, measure out 2 tablespoons of them and return to the skillet along with the 1 tablespoon of butter.

In a food processor fitted with a slicing disc (the thin-slicing disc, if you have one), thin-slice the onion by pushing the quarters down the feed tube one at a time with gentle pressure. Dump onion slices into skillet and sauté over moderately low heat 8 to 10 minutes until limp and golden—do not allow to brown. Set off heat, but keep warm. Wash and dry the processor work bowl and equip with the shredding disc. In a mixing bowl, beat the cream and eggs until frothy. Set aside for the time being. Shred the cheese by pushing it through the feed tube with light pressure; add it to the cream mixture along with salt, pepper and nutmeg, and fold in.

Scatter the sautéed onion slices over the bottom of the pie shell, pour in the cream mixture, then sprinkle the bacon crumbles on top. Bake, uncovered, in a hot oven (400° F.) for 10 minutes, reduce heat to moderate (350° F.) and bake for 20 to 25 minutes longer, or until tart is puffy and lightly browned. Remove from oven and cool at least 30 minutes before serving.

Gruyère-and-Cheddar Strata

Makes 6 to 8 servings

This is that old-fashioned meat substitute—bread and cheese layered into a casserole, topped with a custard mixture, then baked just until set. It's far superior, I think, made with two kinds of cheese—and with plenty of both.

8 slices firm-textured white bread
½ cup melted butter
¼ pound well-aged Gruyère cheese, cut into columns about the
*   height and width of the food-processor feed tube*
¼ pound good sharp Cheddar cheese, cut into chunks the height and
*   width of the food-processor feed tube*
1 tablespoon finely grated yellow onion
4 large eggs, lightly beaten
2½ cups light cream
½ teaspoon salt
⅛ teaspoon freshly ground black pepper
⅛ teaspoon freshly ground nutmeg

Brush each side of each piece of bread generously with melted butter, spread the slices out one layer deep on a baking sheet and toast about 30 minutes in a moderately slow oven (325° F.) until crisp and golden—about like melba toast. Remove from oven and allow to cool while you proceed with the recipe.

Shred the Gruyère, then the Cheddar, by pushing the chunks of cheese firmly down the feed tube of a food processor fitted with the shredding disc. Dump the two cheeses into a mixing bowl and toss lightly to mix. Combine the onion, eggs, cream, salt, pepper and nutmeg in a separate bowl.

Arrange 4 pieces of toast in the bottom of a buttered 9x9x2-inch baking dish, and scatter half of the combined cheeses on top. Cover with the remaining toast slices, top with the rest of the shredded cheeses, then pour the egg mixture evenly over all. Set the baking dish in a large, shallow baking pan, pour water into the pan to a depth of about 1 inch, then set all in a moderate oven (350° F.) and bake, uncovered, for about 50 minutes, or until the casserole is lightly browned. Remove from the oven and from the water bath and cool 25 to 30 minutes. Cut into large squares to serve.

Pipérade
(Basque-Style Omelet)

Makes 4 to 6 servings

1 very large Spanish onion, peeled and quartered
2 tablespoons bacon or ham drippings
1 medium-size sweet red pepper, washed, halved and cored
1 medium-size sweet green pepper, washed, halved and cored
2 juicily ripe beefsteak tomatoes, peeled, cored and quartered
¼ teaspoon crumbled leaf chervil
¼ teaspoon crumbled leaf marjoram
A hefty pinch of crumbled leaf thyme
1 teaspoon salt
Several hefty grindings of black pepper
8 eggs, lightly beaten

In a food processor fitted with the slicing disc, slice the onion quarters very thin by pushing them through the feed tube with gentle pressure; dump into a large heavy skillet (not iron) in which you have already warmed the bacon or ham drippings. Stack the red and green pepper halves together (simply fit one against another spoon-fashion), stand them in the feed tube and push them through gently so that you have very thin slices. Empty the slices into the skillet. Remove the slicing disc from the processor and slip the metal chopping blade into place.

Set the skillet over moderately low heat and sauté the onion and peppers, stirring now and then, until very soft and golden—about 20 minutes. Add half of the tomato quarters to the food processor and with a couple of pulses or fast on-offs, chop fairly coarsely. Add to skillet; chop remaining tomato the same way and add to skillet also. Add the chervil, marjoram and thyme and simmer, uncovered, for about 30 minutes, or until about the consistency of pasta sauce. Combine the salt with the pepper and eggs, pour into the skillet on top of the sauce and cook slowly, tilting the skillet and pulling cooked eggs from edges in toward the center so that the uncooked portions run underneath. Serve as soon as the eggs are softly set.

Roquefort Eggs
Makes 4 servings

An unusual omelet akin to *Pipérade* that's a good choice for lunch or supper.

> *1 medium-size yellow onion, peeled and cut into slim wedges*
> *1 small garlic clove, peeled and minced (It's best to do this by hand so that the garlic flavor is not overpowering—machine-mincing does compound the impact of garlic.)*
> *2 tablespoons unsalted butter*
> *1 large very ripe tomato, peeled, cored and cut into slim wedges*
> *½ teaspoon crumbled leaf basil*
> *¼ teaspoon salt*
> *⅛ teaspoon freshly ground black pepper*
> *5 eggs, lightly beaten*
> *4 tablespoons crumbled Roquefort cheese*

In a food processor equipped with the metal chopping blade, chop the onion moderately fine, using 5 or 6 pulses or quick bursts of speed. Empty onion into a heavy 10-inch skillet in which you have already placed the garlic and butter. Set over moderate heat and sauté 8 to 10 minutes until onion is limp and golden. Meanwhile, chop the tomato moderately fine in the processor, using about 4 pulses or fast on-offs of the motor. Add tomato to skillet along with basil, salt and pepper, and simmer about 10 minutes until juices have cooked down and are no longer watery. Stir well, add remaining ingredients and cook *without stirring* just until set, but do lift the cooked portions occasionally so that the uncooked eggs can run underneath. Quarter and serve.

Leek Frittata
Makes 4 servings

4 large leeks, washed carefully, trimmed, cut into 4-inch lengths and
  patted dry on paper toweling
2 tablespoons olive oil (best quality)
6 eggs, lightly beaten
¼ teaspoon crumbled leaf rosemary
¾ teaspoon salt
Pinch of ground nutmeg or mace
Several hefty grindings of black pepper

In the feed tube of a food processor fitted with the slicing disc, stand as many pieces of leek as needed for a fairly tight fit; turn motor on or depress the Pulse button and thin-slice by pushing the leeks through the slicer with almost no pressure. Repeat until all leeks are sliced. Empty into a 10-inch heavy skillet to which you have already added the olive oil, set over moderate heat and stir-fry about 5 minutes, just until leeks are limp and golden but not brown. Mix the eggs with the rosemary, salt, nutmeg and pepper, pour into skillet, stir briskly just once, then cook without stirring for 3 to 4 minutes, or until browned underneath and set on top. Quarter and serve.

Zucchini Frittata
Makes 4 servings

2 tender young zucchini, washed, trimmed and cut into 4-inch
  lengths
1 medium-size yellow onion, peeled and halved lengthwise

3 tablespoons olive oil (top quality)
1 small garlic clove, peeled and minced (It's best to do this by hand.)
6 eggs, lightly beaten
1 teaspoon salt
¼ teaspoon crumbled leaf marjoram
Several hefty grindings of black pepper

In the feed tube of a food processor fitted with the slicing disc, stand as many pieces of zucchini as needed for a snug fit; turn motor on or depress the Pulse button and thin-slice by pushing the zucchini through the slicer, using almost no pressure. Slice the onion the same way. Place zucchini and onion in a 10-inch heavy skillet to which you have already added the olive oil and garlic, set over moderate heat and stir-fry 5 to 8 minutes, until limp and golden but not brown. Combine eggs with salt, marjoram and pepper, pour into skillet, stir once quickly, then cook without stirring for 3 to 4 minutes until browned underneath and set on top. Quarter and serve.

Curried Chopped Eggs

Makes 4 to 6 servings

You can serve this dish as an entrée, spooned over fluffy boiled rice, or as a cocktail spread accompanied by buttered melba-toast rounds. The food processor is a whiz at chopping hard-cooked eggs, and you can control the fineness of the chop simply by the number of on-off bursts of speed you use. This particular curry is relatively mild. For a truly torrid version (*vindaloo*, in the Indian venacular), increase the amount of chili peppers to 1½ teaspoons.

1 large Spanish onion, peeled and cut into 1-inch chunks
2 tablespoons ghee (melted unsalted butter poured off from its milk solids)
½ cinnamon stick
1 medium-size garlic clove, peeled
One 1-inch cube fresh ginger root, peeled
½ teaspoon ground turmeric
¼ to ½ teaspoon crushed dried red chili peppers (depending upon how "hot" you like things)
¼ teaspoon ground cardamom

⅛ teaspoon coriander seeds
⅛ teaspoon cumin seeds
⅛ teaspoon ground cloves
⅓ cup cider vinegar
1½ cups water
1 tablespoon light brown sugar (or to taste)
8 hard-cooked eggs, peeled and halved lengthwise
¾ teaspoon salt

Place half of the onion chunks in the food-processor work bowl fitted with the metal chopping blade and, with 3 or 4 pulses or fast bursts of speed, chop moderately coarsely. Empty into a large heavy skillet in which you have already placed the *ghee*. Machine-chop the remaining onion chunks the same way and add to skillet. Set skillet over moderate heat, add cinnamon stick and sauté, stirring now and then, 12 to 15 minutes, or until onions are soft and lightly browned.

Now add to the processor work bowl, still fitted with the metal chopping blade, the garlic, ginger root, turmeric, chili peppers, cardamom, coriander and cumin seeds, cloves and vinegar; buzz for 60 seconds nonstop, or until uniformly smooth. Add puréed spice mixture to the skillet along with the water and brown sugar. Cover, reduce heat to moderately low and simmer 40 minutes, or until onion is very tender. Taste for seasoning and add another teaspoon or two of brown sugar if mixture is too tart to suit you.

Wash and dry all parts of the food processor at this point, and reassemble. Place 6 hard-cooked egg halves in the food processor and, with 3 pulses or quick bursts of speed, chop moderately coarsely. Empty into skillet. Chop another 6 egg halves the same way and add to skillet, then the remaining 4 halves. Add these to the skillet, too, along with the salt. Stir gently to mix, cover and simmer slowly, stirring once or twice, 10 to 12 minutes longer—just until eggs are heated through. Remove the cinnamon stick, spoon over fluffy boiled rice and serve.

Lasagne with Veal, Chicken and Mushrooms
Makes 8 to 10 servings

A friend told me about this lasagne, which she had been served in Florence. "It was the best I've ever eaten," she said, "and I've never tasted anything else quite like it." From her detailed description, I've worked out the following recipe, which she says is very much like what she enjoyed so much in Italy.

Cream sauce:

3 tablespoons butter
3 tablespoons flour
¼ teaspoon ground mace or nutmeg
Pinch of white pepper
¾ teaspoon salt
1 cup milk
½ cup light cream
½ cup small mozzarella cheese cubes
1 tablespoon freshly grated Parmesan cheese
2 egg yolks, lightly beaten

Veal-and-chicken sauce:

1 medium-size yellow onion, peeled and halved lengthwise
1 small garlic clove, peeled and crushed
3 tablespoons butter
1 pound medium-size mushrooms, wiped clean and stemmed (reserve stems)
1 pound boneless veal shoulder, cut into 1-inch cubes, trimmed of sinew and chilled well
2 whole chicken breasts, split, skinned, boned, cut into 1-inch cubes, trimmed of sinew and chilled well
½ teaspoon crumbled leaf thyme
1½ cups of the cream sauce

Lasagne layers:

The veal and chicken sauce
1 pound lasagne noodles, cooked by package directions and drained
1½ pounds ricotta cheese blended with ¼ to ⅓ cup of the cream sauce
½ cup freshly grated Parmesan cheese
1 pound mozzarella cheese, sliced as thin as possible (Tip: You'll find the mozzarella much easier to slice if you use a very sharp slicing knife and dip it into boiling water each time you make a slice.)

Prepare the cream sauce first: Melt the butter in a heavy saucepan over moderate heat, blend in flour, mace, pepper and salt, then add milk and cream and heat, stirring constantly, until thickened and smooth. Add the mozzarella and Parmesan and cook, stirring, until cheese is melted and mixture smooth. Whisk a little of the hot sauce into the yolks, stir back into pan and remove from heat. Let cool while you prepare the veal and chicken sauce, but whisk occasionally to prevent a "skin" from forming on the surface of the sauce or the cheese from "stringing."

For the veal and chicken sauce: In a food processor fitted with the metal chopping blade, coarsely chop the onion with 2 or 3 pulses or fast bursts of speed. Empty into a large heavy skillet in which you have already placed the garlic and butter. Now machine-chop the mushroom caps the same way, doing about half of them at a time; add to skillet. Repeat until all mushroom caps and stems are coarsely chopped; add these to the skillet also. Set over moderate heat and sauté, stirring now and then, about 10 minutes until mushrooms are limp and their juices have cooked down. Meanwhile, chop the veal cubes fine—doing only half of them at a time—in the processor, still fitted with the metal chopping blade; two 5-seconds bursts of speed will be enough. Add to skillet. Now chop the chicken the same way, again doing only half of the full amount at a time. Add to skillet also. Mix well into onion and mushroom mixture and set off the heat immediately. Mix in the thyme and cream sauce. Now you are ready to begin assembling the lasagne.

Layer the lasagne into the pan: You will need, first of all, a lightly buttered 13x9x2-inch baking pan. Spread about one third of the veal and chicken sauce over the bottom of the pan. Add a single layer of cooked lasagne noodles, overlapping them slightly. Add a second layer of the meat sauce (use about one half of what's left); smooth a third of the ricotta mixture on top, sprinkle with ¼ cup of grated Parmesan, then arrange half of the mozzarella slices over all. Finish assembling the lasagne this way: another layer of pasta, the remaining meat sauce, pasta, ricotta, pasta, ricotta. Finally, top with the remaining mozzarella slices and grated Parmesan.

Set, uncovered, in a moderate oven (350° F.) and bake for 40 to 45 minutes, or until bubbly and lightly touched with brown. Remove from oven and let stand at room temperature for 15 minutes before cutting into squares and serving.

Pasta with Minced Broccoli and Garlic Sauce

Makes 4 servings

I first tasted this ambrosial pasta in a little restaurant tucked away on a back street in Florence and couldn't wait to try it out at home. With a food processor to mince the broccoli and garlic, you can prepare the recipe in about 20 minutes—start to finish.

> *1 large bunch of broccoli, trimmed, washed and cut into small flowerets (Include some of the tenderer stalks, cutting them into ½-inch cubes, and some of the younger leaves, too, because they will add pungency to the sauce.)*
> *2 large garlic cloves, peeled and halved*
> *1 cup boiling water mixed with 1 teaspoon salt*
> *2 tablespoons olive oil (best quality)*
> *4 tablespoons unsalted butter (at room temperature)*
> *1 cup light cream (at room temperature)*
> *⅛ teaspoon freshly ground black pepper*
> *1 pound thin spaghetti (No. 9), cooked by package directions and drained well*
> *Freshly grated Parmesan cheese (topping)*

Cook the broccoli and garlic in the salted water in a large, covered, heavy kettle over moderate heat 10 to 12 minutes, or until crisp-tender. Drain well, then chop moderately fine in a food processor fitted with the metal chopping blade—6 to 8 pulses or quick on-offs of the motor will be sufficient. While you are draining and chopping the broccoli and garlic, add the olive oil and butter to the kettle in which you cooked the broccoli and set over moderate heat to melt the butter. Smooth in the cream, salt and pepper, bring to a bubble, then add the chopped broccoli and garlic. Cover and let mellow 1 to 2 minutes. Pour over the drained pasta, toss well to mix, then serve with plenty of freshly grated Parmesan.

Spaghetti with Leek and Mushroom Sauce
Makes 4 servings

One of the most elegant pasta sauces I have ever tasted and, with an assist from the food processor, one of the quickest to prepare.

½ cup loosely packed parsley sprigs, washed and patted very dry on paper toweling
6 tablespoons unsalted butter
3 large leeks, trimmed, washed carefully to remove grit and sand, and cut into 1-inch chunks
2 pounds medium-size fresh mushrooms, wiped clean, stemmed and quartered (reserve stems)
2 cups light cream
1 teaspoon salt
Several hefty grindings of black pepper
Pinch of ground nutmeg
1 pound thin spaghetti (No. 9), cooked by package directions and drained well
Freshly grated Parmesan cheese (topping)

In a food processor fitted with the metal chopping blade, mince the parsley fine by using three 5-second churnings of the motor; empty onto a piece of wax paper and set aside. Melt 4 tablespoons of the butter in a very large heavy skillet over low heat. Meanwhile, coarsely chop the leeks in the processor by pulsing or snapping the motor on and off 3 times. Add to skillet and allow to sauté slowly while you chop the mushrooms.

Working with about one fifth of the quartered mushroom caps at a time, coarsely chop them in the food processor by pulsing or switching the motor on and off quickly 3 or 4 times. As each batch is chopped, dump into skillet. Finally, chop the mushroom stems the same way and add to skillet. Raise heat to moderately high and stir-fry leeks and mushrooms 12 to 15 minutes, or until they have cooked down to a fairly thick mixture (mushrooms will have released their juices and these will have cooked down). Pour in the cream, add salt, pepper and nutmeg, reduce heat to moderately low and cook, stirring now and then, until cream has cooked down slightly—about 5 minutes. Mix in the minced parsley.

Return the hot, drained spaghetti to the kettle in which you cooked it, add the remaining 2 tablespoons butter, return kettle to very low burner heat and toss briskly until butter is melted and strands of spaghetti are coated. Pour in the mushroom sauce, toss well to mix, then serve with plenty of Parmesan to accompany.

Processor Pasta Dough
Makes about ¾ pound, enough for 4 servings

It's simply amazing how quickly and easily the processor mixes and kneads fresh pasta dough—in less than 30 seconds if you were to clock the preparation. But try not to make this recipe on a humid day because the dough will take on moisture from the atmosphere and not roll or dry properly. This is an all-purpose pasta that can be used to make ravioli, *fettuccine*, or wide, medium or thin noodles.

2 large eggs
1 tablespoon olive oil
2 tablespoons cold water
2 cups sifted all-purpose flour

Break the eggs directly in the work bowl of a food processor fitted with the metal chopping blade; add olive oil and water and blend lightly by snapping the motor on and off twice. Add 1 cup of the flour, turn motor on and let run 5 seconds nonstop. Add the remaining cup of flour and buzz for 10 seconds nonstop. The dough will churn into a ball and ride up on the chopping blade's central spindle. Remove dough from processor, divide in half, shape each half into a round ball, set them on a lightly floured board and top with a bowl turned upside down. Let stand for 40 minutes.

Now roll 1 ball of the dough on a lightly floured pastry-cloth with a lightly floured, stockinette-covered rolling pin. Work with quick, short strokes, from the center outward, and roll the dough as thin as possible into a more or less rectangular shape. Now let the dough air-dry for 1 hour, or until surface is no longer sticky. Roll the dough up loosely, jelly-roll style, then, with a large, sharp knife, slice ½ inch thick for wide pasta, ¼ inch thick for medium, and ⅛ inch thick for thin. Roll and cut remaining dough the same way.

Unroll the pasta strands and cook in a large kettle of actively boiling, lightly salted water 3 to 4 minutes until *al dente*. Drain, then serve with any of your favorite pasta sauces.

Pasta Verde
(Green Noodles)

Makes about ¾ pound, enough for 4 servings

The processor does it all: mincing the spinach, mixing the pasta ingredients, kneading the dough—all except for a few final hand kneadings. This recipe, like the one for Processor Pasta Dough, should not be made in a damp weather because the dough will absorb moisture from the air and remain too soft to roll.

2 cups trimmed, washed and drained young spinach leaves (measure moderately firmly packed)
1 tablespoon olive oil
1 tablespoon cold water
2 large eggs
2 cups sifted all-purpose flour

Steam the spinach in a small, heavy, covered saucepan over moderate heat about 3 minutes until wilted (add no water; the rinse water clinging to the leaves will be sufficient to steam them). Drain spinach, then dump into a food-processor work bowl fitted with the metal chopping blade. Add the olive oil and water, turn the motor on and run 5 seconds nonstop; scrape the work bowl down, buzz 5 seconds longer, then scrape down work bowl once again. Break the eggs into the work bowl and blend, using 2 on-offs of the motor. Add 1 cup of flour, churn 5 seconds nonstop, add remaining cup of flour and churn 10 seconds nonstop. Dough will form a ball and ride up on the chopping-blade spindle. Remove dough to a lightly floured board, knead briskly about 10 to 12 times. Then divide dough in half, shape each into a ball and cover with a bowl turned upside down. Let stand 45 minutes.

Roll 1 ball of dough on a lightly floured pastry cloth with a lightly floured, stockinette-covered rolling pin into as thin a rectangle as possible. Let the dough air-dry for 1 hour or until surface is no longer sticky. Roll up loosely, jelly-roll style, then, with a large, sharp knife, slice ½ inch thick for wide noodles, ¼ inch thick for medium, and ⅛ inch thick for thin. Roll and cut the remaining pasta the same way.

Unroll the noodles, then cook in a huge kettle of lightly salted boiling water until *al dente*—3 to 4 minutes. Drain well, then dress with any of your favorite pasta sauces. Or, if you prefer, simply dress with salt, pepper, melted butter and freshly grated Parmesan.

Whole-Wheat Pasta Dough

Makes about 1½ pounds, enough for 6 hearty servings

This pasta dough and the two that follow (Fresh Basil Linguine and Tomato Pasta Dough) are geared to the new heavy-duty processors with larger work bowls and more powerful motors. All three are also geared to the pasta attachments, which many new models now feature as optional "extras," although there is nothing to prevent their being rolled and cut by hand. I favor this particular dough as *fettuccine* (flat strands about ¼ inch wide), but cut or shape it any way you fancy.

2¼ cups sifted all-purpose flour (about)
1 cup unsifted whole-wheat flour
¾ teaspoon salt
4 large eggs
1 tablespoon vegetable oil
1 to 3 tablespoons cold water (if needed)

Place 2 cups of the all-purpose flour, the whole-wheat flour and salt in the work bowl of a food processor fitted with the metal chopping blade and combine with three or four 1-second churnings of the motor.

In a 1-cup measuring cup, lightly beat the eggs and oil with a fork, then with the processor running, pour down the feed tube and buzz 10 seconds nonstop. The dough should roll into a ball and ride up on the central spindle. If it does not, *and if you intend to hand-roll and cut the dough*, add 1 tablespoon cold water and pulse or snap the motor on and off quickly about 10 times. If the dough still does not form a ball, repeat once or twice more—that is, adding 1 tablespoon cold water and pulsing it in each time with about 10 on-offs of the motor. As soon as the dough has become a single glutenous mass, divide it in half, then shape each half into a round ball, set on a lightly floured board and top each with a bowl turned upside down. Let stand for 40 minutes.

If, however, you intend to extrude the pasta with the processor pasta attachment, you must work in more flour. Indeed, the mixture should seem very dry and crumbly—about the texture of uncooked oatmeal, but it must also cling together when you gather a few lumps of it in your hand and squeeze gently.

To achieve the proper texture for the pasta attachment: After the dough has been buzzed 10 seconds nonstop, open the work bowl and with a wooden spoon or plastic scraper, break the dough into small clumps; sprinkle in 2 tablespoons of the remaining flour, scattering it evenly over the surface of the dough. Now pulse or snap the motor on and off quickly 10 times. Inspect the texture of the dough. If it is not thoroughly crumbly, again break up any large clumps, then sprinkle 1 tablespoon of the remaining flour evenly on top; pulse 10 more times, inspect the dough, and if still not uniformly fine and crumbly, add another tablespoon of flour, sprinkling it over the surface of the dough; pulse another 10 times. The dough should by now be the proper texture, but if not (this will vary with the quality of the flour you use, and indeed with where you live and the season of the year because not all flours are standardized), add another tablespoon or 2 of flour, pulsing each in with 10 quick on-offs of the motor.

To use the pasta attachment: Remove the work bowl and fit the pasta attachment, equipped with the *fettuccine* disc (or any disc you prefer), into place as the manufacturer directs; empty the pasta dough into the hopper and feed it through the chute according to the instruction manual. TIPS: *I find it helpful to extrude the pasta onto a clean dry dishtowel lightly dusted with stone-ground cornmeal, cornstarch or flour, to cut the strands of pasta into 12-inch lengths, then to transfer them to a second dishtowel, also lightly dusted with sifted stone-ground cornmeal, cornstarch or flour. The purpose of the cornmeal, cornstarch or flour is to help keep the strands of pasta separate. It also helps to sift a little cornmeal, cornstarch or flour on top of each fresh batch of strands as you transfer them to the second dishtowel. Don't worry if some of the strands stick together; they will separate as they cook.*

To hand-roll and cut the pasta: Roll the dough, one ball at a time, on a lightly floured pastry cloth with a lightly floured, stockinette-covered rolling pin. Work with quick, short strokes, from the center outward, and roll the dough as thin as possible into a more or less rectangular shape. Now let the dough air-dry for 1 hour, or until the surface is no longer sticky. Roll the dough up loosely, jelly-roll style, then with a large, sharp knife, slice ½ inch wide for large pasta, ¼ inch for medium (*fettuccine*) and ⅛ inch for thin (*linguine*). Roll and cut remaining dough the same way, then unroll the pasta strands.

You can, at this point, refrigerate or freeze the pasta if you don't plan to cook it straightaway. Divide in half, bundle in two large plastic bags, press out as much air as possible, twist the ends into goosenecks and secure with twist-bands, then store in the refrigerator (use within 2 to 3 days) or in the freezer (use within 4 to 6 weeks and be sure to label and date the packages before they go into the freezer).

To cook: Place 5 to 6 quarts of water in a 4-gallon kettle, add 1 tablespoon of salt and 1 tablespoon of olive or vegetable oil; set over moderately high heat and bring to a rolling boil. Now add the pasta, a handful at a time so that the water never ceases boiling. The instant all of the pasta is in the kettle, boil uncovered for about 2 minutes, or until *al dente* and no raw starch flavor lingers.

Drain well and serve with a favorite pasta sauce. I very much like this whole-wheat pasta with Creamed Onion Sauce (the recipe appears elsewhere in this section).

Fresh Basil Linguine
Makes about 1½ pounds, enough for 6 hearty servings

I've always been so fond of *pesto* (that thick green sauce compounded of fresh basil, garlic and *pignoli*) that I began to wonder if I could make a green pasta out of basil. This is the result, and I think it exceptionally good, particularly if tossed with Oil, Garlic and Pignoli Sauce (recipe appears later on in this section). NOTE: *If you have a pasta attachment for your processor, you will find this recipe tailor-made. But the pasta can also be rolled and cut the old-fashioned way.*

> 1 cup tender young basil leaves (measure very firmly packed),
>   washed in cool water, then wrung very dry in paper toweling
> ½ small garlic clove, peeled
> 1 teaspoon salt
> 4 cups sifted all-purpose flour (about)
> 4 large eggs
> 1 tablespoon olive oil

Place the basil leaves, garlic and salt in the work bowl of a food processor fitted with the metal chopping blade and buzz 15 seconds nonstop; scrape the work-bowl sides down, buzz 5 seconds; scrape down once again and buzz 5 seconds longer. Add 3¾ cups of the flour and combine with the minced basil and garlic by pulsing or snapping the motor on and off quickly 5 times; scrape the work-bowl sides down, pulse 5 seconds; scrape the work bowl down once again and pulse 5 to 10 times more, just until mixture is well combined.

In a 1-cup measuring cup, lightly beat the eggs with the oil using a fork, then with the processor running, pour down the feed tube. Buzz 10 seconds nonstop after all of the egg mixture has been added; the dough will roll into a ball and ride up on the central spindle. You can at this point take the dough out of the work bowl if you will roll and cut it by hand. Divide in half, shape each half into a round ball, set on a lightly floured board and top with a bowl turned upside down. Let stand for 40 minutes.

If, however, you intend to extrude the pasta with the processor pasta attachment, you must work in more flour. Indeed, the mixture should seem very dry and crumbly—about the texture of uncooked oatmeal, *but* it must cling together when you gather a few lumps of it in your hand and squeeze gently.

To achieve the proper texture for the pasta attachment: Open the work bowl after the dough has rolled into a ball and been buzzed 10 seconds nonstop; with a wooden spoon or plastic scraper, break the ball of dough into several small chunks and sprinkle 2 tablespoons of the remaining flour evenly over all. Now pulse or snap the motor on and off quickly 10 times. Inspect the texture of the dough. If it is not thoroughly crumbly, again break up any large clumps, then sprinkle 1 tablespoon of the remaining flour evenly on top; pulse 10 more times, inspect the dough, and if still not uniformly fine and crumbly, add another tablespoon of flour, sprinkling it over the surface of the dough; pulse another 10 times. The dough by now should be the proper texture, but if not, add another tablespoon or 2 of flour, pulsing each in with 10 quick on-offs of the motor.

To use the pasta attachment: Remove the work bowl and fit the pasta attachment, equipped with the *linguine* disc, into place as the manufacturer directs; empty the pasta dough into the hopper and feed it through the shute according to the instructions accompanying your particular machine. TIPS: *I find it helpful to extrude the pasta onto a* clean dry dishtowel lightly dusted with sifted stone-ground cornmeal, cornstarch or flour, to cut the strands when they've reached about 12 inches in length, then to transfer them to a second dishtowel, lightly dusted with sifted stone-ground cornmeal, cornstarch or flour. The purpose of the cornmeal, cornstarch or flour is to help keep the strands of pasta separate. It also helps to sift a little cornmeal, cornstarch or flour on top of each fresh batch of strands as you transfer them to the second dishtowel. Fret not if some of the strands are stuck together; they will separate as they cook.

To hand-roll and cut the pasta: Roll the dough, one ball at a time, on a lightly floured pastry cloth with a lightly floured, stockinette-covered rolling pin. Work with quick, short strokes, from the center outward, and roll the dough as thin as possible into a more or less rectangular shape. Now let the dough air-dry for 1 hour or until the surface is no longer sticky. Roll the dough up loosely, jelly-roll style, then, with a large, sharp knife, slice ⅛ inch thick. Roll and cut remaining dough the same way. Unroll the pasta strands.

You can, at this point, bundle the pasta into two large plastic bags, press out as much air as possible, twist the necks and secure with twist-bands, then store in the refrigerator (use within 2 to 3 days) or in the freezer (use within 4 to 6 weeks—and be sure to date and label the bags).

To cook: Place 5 to 6 quarts of water in a 4-gallon kettle, add 1 tablespoon of salt and 1 tablespoon of olive or vegetable oil; set over moderately high heat and bring to a full rolling boil. Now add the pasta, a handful at a time so that the water never ceases boiling. Once all of the pasta is in the kettle, boil uncovered for 1½ minutes, or until *al dente*. Drain very well, then serve with a favorite pasta sauce.

I personally like nothing better with this pasta than Oil, Garlic and Pignoli Sauce (which appears in this section) and the technique I use for dressing the pasta is this: Once I've drained the fresh basil *linguine* very dry, I dump it back into the kettle in which it cooked, pour the sauce evenly over all, then shake the kettle over moderate heat, tilting it first to one side and then to the other, until the pasta is evenly dressed. Serve with plenty of freshly grated Parmesan.

Tomato Pasta Dough

Makes about 1½ pounds, enough for 6 hearty servings

A lovely coral-colored pasta delicately flavored with tomato that is delicious with Creamed Onion Sauce, Marinara or White Clam Sauce (see Index for recipe page numbers). A heavy-duty processor buzzes it up without complaint. Roll and cut by hand or extrude with a processor pasta attachment.

> *3⅔ cups sifted all-purpose flour (about)*
> *¾ teaspoon salt*
> *4 large eggs*
> *¼ cup tomato paste*
> *1 tablespoon olive or vegetable oil*

Place the flour in the work bowl of a food processor fitted with the metal chopping blade, sprinkle in the salt and combine using three or four 1-second churnings of the motor.

In a 2-cup measuring cup, beat the eggs, tomato paste and oil until moderately well blended, then with the processor running, pour the mixture down the feed tube and buzz 10 seconds nonstop. The dough should roll into a ball and ride up on the central spindle. Remove the dough from the processor work bowl, shape into a ball, pressing any loose clumps together firmly, then halve and shape into two balls. Set on a lightly floured board and top each ball of dough with a bowl turned upside down. Let stand for 40 minutes.

If you intend to extrude the pasta with the processor pasta attachment, you must work in more flour—the mixture should be dry and crumbly—about like uncooked oatmeal, but it must also cling together when you gather a few lumps of it in your hand and squeeze gently.

To achieve the proper texture for the pasta attachment: After the dough has been buzzed 10 seconds nonstop, open the work bowl and with a wooden spoon or plastic scraper, break the dough into small clumps; sprinkle in 2 tablespoons additional flour, scattering it evenly over the surface of the dough. Now pulse or snap the motor on and off quickly 10 times. Inspect the texture of the dough. If it is not thoroughly crumbly, again break up any large clumps, then sprinkle 1 tablespoon of additional flour evenly on top; pulse 10 more times, inspect the dough, and if still not uniformly fine and crumbly, add another tablespoon of flour, sprinkling it over the surface of the dough;

pulse another 10 times. The dough should by now be the proper texture, but if not (and this will vary with the quality of the flour you use, indeed where you live and the season of the year because flours are not standardized), add another tablespoon or 2 of flour, pulsing each in with 10 quick on-offs of the motor.

To use the pasta attachment: Remove the work bowl and fit the pasta attachment equipped with the disc of your choice (I prefer the *linguine, fettuccine* or *vermicelli* disc) into place as the manufacturer directs; empty the pasta dough into the hopper and push it down the chute according to the instruction manual. TIPS: *I find it helpful to extrude the pasta onto a clean dry dishtowel lightly dusted with stone-ground cornmeal, cornstarch or flour, to cut the strands of pasta into 12-inch lengths, then to transfer them to a second dishtowel, also lightly dusted with sifted stone-ground cornmeal, cornstarch or flour. The purpose of the cornmeal, cornstarch or flour is to help keep the pasta strands separate. It also helps to sift a little cornmeal, cornstarch or flour on top of each fresh batch of pasta as you transfer it to the second dishtowel. But don't worry if some pasta strands should stick together; they will separate as they cook.*

To hand-roll and cut the pasta: Roll the dough, one ball at a time, on a lightly floured pastry cloth with a lightly floured, stockinette-covered rolling pin. Work with quick, short strokes, from the center outward, and roll the dough as thin as possible into a more or less rectangular shape. Now let the dough air-dry for 1 hour, or until the surface is no longer sticky. Roll the dough up loosely, jelly-roll style, then with a large, sharp knife, slice ½ inch thick for wide pasta, ¼ inch for medium (*fettuccine*) and ⅛ for thin (*linguine*). Roll and cut remaining dough the same way, then unroll the pasta strands.

You can, at this point, refrigerate or freeze the pasta if you don't plan to cook it straightaway. Divide in half, bundle in two large plastic bags, press out as much air as possible, twist the ends into goosenecks and secure with twist-bands, then store in the refrigerator (use within 2 to 3 days) or in the freezer (use within 4 to 6 weeks and be sure to label and date the bags before they go into the freezer).

To cook: Place 5 to 6 quarts of water in a 4-gallon kettle, add 1 tablespoon of salt and 1 tablespoon of olive or vegetable oil; set over moderately high heat and bring to a rolling boil. Now add the pasta, a handful at a time so that the water never stops boiling. The instant all of the pasta is in the kettle, boil, uncovered, for 1 to 2 minutes (depending upon how thick or thin the pasta was cut), or until *al dente* and no raw starch flavor remains. Drain well.

Serve with a favorite pasta sauce.

It goes without saying that you should read the instruction booklet that accompanies your machine carefully and proceed accordingly. The large attachment pieces, for the most part smoothly molded of plastic, cause little problem (most are even dishwasher-proof). But those little extruding discs full of slits and holes: It's best, I've found *not* to wash these—at least not right away. Instead, scrape off excess dough, then let the dough-clogged discs air-dry 24 to 36 hours. The pasta jamming all of the little holes and slits will dry, *shrink,* then pop right out with a couple of gentle raps on the counter. Once all of the disc openings are free and clear, wash the discs in warm sudsy water or if yours, like mine, are dishwasher-safe, slip them into the silver basket of your dishwasher and run them through anytime you have a full load. **CAUTION:** *Do not at any time try to pry bits of dough out of the disc's perforations because you may damage or deform them.*

Marinara Sauce

Makes 4 servings

1 large garlic clove, peeled and minced
3 tablespoons olive oil
1 large Spanish onion, peeled and cut into 1-inch chunks
½ teaspoon crumbled leaf marjoram
¼ teaspoon crumbled leaf thyme
¼ teaspoon crumbled leaf savory
Pinch of ground nutmeg
1 large bay leaf, crumbled
½ cup dry white wine
6 medium-size vine-ripe tomatoes, washed, cored and cut into slim
    wedges (no need to peel)
¾ cup tomato juice
1 can (6 ounces) tomato paste
1 teaspoon salt (or to taste)

Several hefty grindings of black pepper
1 tablespoon light brown sugar or honey (if needed to mellow the
tartness of the tomatoes)

Place the garlic and olive oil in a large, heavy skillet and set over low heat. Mince one half of the onion chunks in a food processor fitted with the metal chopping blade by pulsing or snapping the motor on and off 5 or 6 times; add onion to skillet. Processor-mince the remaining onion the same way and add to skillet. Sauté slowly, stirring now and then, about 20 minutes until onion and garlic are very soft and golden, but not brown. Blend in marjoram, thyme, savory, nutmeg, bay leaf and wine and allow to simmer while you chop the tomatoes.

Place one third of the tomatoes in the food processor (still equipped with the metal chopping blade—no need to wash) and chop moderately coarsely by pulsing or snapping the motor on and off 2 or 3 times. Add to skillet. Chop the remaining tomatoes the same way, in two batches, and add to skillet. Simmer, uncovered, stirring now and then, 20 to 25 minutes, or until tomatoes have cooked down somewhat and their tart flavor is beginning to mellow. Blend in the tomato juice, tomato paste, salt and pepper. Turn heat to lowest point and simmer the sauce, uncovered, for about 1½ hours, or until the flavors are well balanced and the consistency good and thick. If the sauce seems too tart, mix in the sugar. Also add more salt and pepper if needed.

Serve hot over freshly cooked pasta and pass plenty of freshly grated Parmesan.

Bolognese Sauce
(Meat Sauce for Pasta)

Makes 4 to 6 servings

½ cup loosely packed parsley sprigs, washed and patted very dry on
*   paper toweling*
1 cup loosely packed tender young basil leaves, washed and patted
*   very dry on paper toweling*
2 medium-size yellow onions, peeled and cut into slim wedges
2 tablespoons olive oil
2 tablespoons butter

2 medium-size garlic cloves, peeled and minced (by hand)

2 medium-size celery ribs, washed, trimmed and cut into 1-inch chunks

6 medium-size mushrooms, wiped clean, stemmed and quartered (reserve stems)

1 chicken breast, boned, skinned, cut into 1-inch chunks and chilled well

¼ pound boned lean beef chuck, cut into 1-inch chunks and chilled well

¼ pound boned pork shoulder, cut into 1-inch chunks and chilled well

6 medium-size vine-ripe tomatoes, washed, cored and cut into slim wedges (no need to peel)

3 tablespoons tomato paste

½ cup dry white wine

1 bay leaf, crumbled

1 teaspoon salt (or to taste)

Several hefty grindings of black pepper

In a food processor equipped with the metal chopping blade, mince the parsley and basil together until uniformly fine—two or three 5-second churnings of the motor will be about right. Empty onto a piece of wax paper and set aside. Now add onion wedges to work bowl and mince by pulsing or snapping the motor on and off 5 or 6 times. Let stand for the moment. Heat the olive oil and butter in a very large, heavy skillet over moderate heat just until butter melts, then add the garlic and onions and allow to sauté while you mince the celery and mushrooms. Add celery chunks, quartered mushroom caps and stems to the work bowl and mince, using 5 or 6 pulses or on-offs of the motor. Add to skillet along with the minced parsley and basil, reduce heat to low and sauté the mixture very slowly for about 20 minutes, or until vegetables are quite soft and golden. Do not allow to brown, as this will alter the flavor of the sauce.

Meanwhile, place the chicken in the processor (still fitted with the metal chopping blade—no need to wash either the work bowl or the blade) and mince quite fine with two 5-second churnings of the motor. Add to skillet. Mince the beef the same way (three or four 5-second churnings of the motor, because beef is a coarser meat than chicken); add to skillet. Now fine-mince the pork, using two or three 5-second churnings of the motor. Add to skillet also. Break up the clumps of meat and sauté slowly, stirring now and then, about 20 minutes until meat is no longer pink. Do not brown the meat.

Now coarsely chop the tomatoes, one third of the total amount at a time, in the processor (still fitted with the chopping blade—again no need to wash work bowl or blade) by pulsing or snapping the motor on and off quickly 2 or 3 times. Add tomatoes to skillet. Chop the remaining tomatoes the same way in two batches and add to skillet also. Blend in the tomato paste and wine and drop in the bay leaf. Cover the skillet and simmer very slowly for about 1½ hours. Uncover, stir in salt and pepper, reduce burner heat to lowest point, then allow the sauce barely to simmer for 1½ to 2 hours longer. If the burner heat is low enough (or if you place a flame tamer underneath the skillet), you can let the sauce laze along for as long as 3 hours. Its flavor and texture will improve with long slow simmering, but do check the skillet from time to time to see that the sauce is not cooking down too much. If so, thin with a little chicken stock or water. Also taste for salt and pepper and add more of each, if needed.

Serve over hot boiled pasta and pass plenty of freshly grated Parmesan cheese to accompany.

White Clam Sauce for Pasta

Makes 4 servings

½ cup loosely packed fresh parsley sprigs, washed and patted very
   dry on paper toweling
2 medium-size garlic cloves, peeled and minced (by hand)
4 tablespoons olive oil (best quality)
1 quart shucked cherrystone or littleneck clams, drained well
   (reserve juice)
2 tablespoons flour
2 cups clam juice (measure juice drained from clams, then add water
   or bottled clam juice to round out the measure at 2 cups)
Several hefty grindings of black pepper

In a food processor fitted with the metal chopping blade, mince the parsley quite fine, using two or three 5-second churnings of the motor. Empty onto a piece of wax paper and set aside for the time being.

Sauté the garlic in the olive oil in a large heavy skillet over low heat for about 2 minutes, or until soft and golden; do not allow the garlic to brown, as it will take on a bitter flavor. Dump the drained clams into the processor work bowl (still fitted with the metal chopping blade) and mince moderately coarsely by pulsing or snapping the motor on and off 5 times quickly. Let stand for the moment.

Blend the flour into the garlic and olive oil in the skillet and heat and stir 1 to 2 minutes. Pour in the clam juice and heat, stirring constantly, until thickened and smooth—3 to 5 minutes. Now cover the skillet, turn heat to lowest point, and simmer mixture slowly for 15 minutes; this is to mellow the flavors. Add the minced clams, half of the minced parsley, and the pepper and simmer, stirring now and then, about 3 minutes, just until clams are heated through. If you cook them any longer they will toughen.

Serve over cooked, drained *fettuccine* or thin spaghetti and top with the remaining minced parsley.

Anchovy-Tuna-Parsley Sauce for Pasta
Makes 4 servings

An unusual sauce, and a good one, which the processor buzzes up in no time at all.

*1 cup loosely packed parsley sprigs, washed and patted very dry on
    paper toweling
1 can (2 ounces) anchovy fillets, drained and rinsed well
1 large garlic clove, peeled and minced
⅓ cup olive oil (top quality)
¼ cup unsalted butter
1 can (7 ounces) chunk light tuna (do not drain)
Juice of 1 lemon
Several hefty grindings of black pepper*

In a food processor fitted with the metal chopping blade, mince the parsley and the anchovy fillets together until fairly fine, using two or three 5-second churnings of the motor; empty onto a piece of wax paper and set aside for the moment. Sauté the garlic in the oil and butter in a large heavy skillet over moderate heat 3 to 5 minutes until soft and golden, but not brown. Set skillet off the heat for the moment. Place the tuna in the processor work bowl (still fitted with the metal chopping blade) and distribute the chunks evenly around the blade. Flake moderately coarsely by pulsing or snapping the motor on and off 2 or 3 times. Add tuna to skillet with the minced parsley and the anchovies, lemon juice and pepper. Cover, turn burner heat to lowest point and simmer the mixture 5 minutes, or just until heated through.

Serve with hot cooked *linguine* or thin spaghetti that has been tossed with a fat lump of butter, and accompany, if you like, with freshly grated Parmesan cheese (Italians do not use cheese with seafood sauces for pasta).

Pesto

Makes about 1 cup, enough for 4 servings

The Italian way to make this green and garlicky pasta sauce is to pound fresh basil leaves, garlic and *pignoli* into submission by hand in a mortar and pestle. Few of us, of course, have the time, energy or inclination for such a task. Luckily, the food processor does a better job and in just one minute. This sauce, by the way, freezes well, so I like to make up a dozen or so batches of it—as long as the fresh basil season lasts—and freeze them in half-pint containers so that I can enjoy *pesto* the year round. NOTE: *The most aromatic basil of all and thus the best to use for* pesto *is that which is budding and ready to bloom.*

> 1 tightly packed quart tender young basil leaves, washed and patted
>   dry on paper toweling (The leaves must be very dry or the pesto
>   will be watery.)
> 2 medium-size garlic cloves, peeled and halved
> ⅓ cup pignoli (pine nuts)
> 6 tablespoons butter, at room temperature
> 2 tablespoons olive oil
> ½ teaspoon salt
> ⅛ teaspoon freshly ground black pepper

Place all ingredients in a food processor fitted with the metal chopping blade and buzz to a fine paste (about 1 minute nonstop). Serve the *pesto* over hot cooked spaghetti (this amount will dress about 1 pound), toss lightly to mix, then pass plenty of freshly grated Parmesan cheese.

Creamed Onion Sauce

Makes 4 to 6 servings

Because this sauce is so thick, it is better to spoon it generously over individual portions of pasta than to try to toss it with a huge kettleful. I like this sauce—nothing more than onions cooked down, down, down with butter and cream—over whole-wheat or tomato pasta, but it's perfectly delicious over *Pasta Verde*, and absolutely plain pasta, too.

> *12 large yellow onions, peeled and halved lengthwise (if you have a*
> *processor with an expanded feed tube, no need to halve the*
> *onions)*
> *¾ cup (1½ sticks) unsalted butter*
> *1½ cups heavy cream*
> *1 teaspoon salt (about)*
> *⅛ teaspoon freshly ground black pepper (about)*
> *⅛ teaspoon crumbled leaf rosemary*
> *⅛ teaspoon freshly grated nutmeg*

Equip a food processor with the thin- or medium-slicing disc, then slice all of the onions by pushing down the feed tube with the gentlest of pressure. Meanwhile, place the butter in a large, heavy saucepan and set over low heat. If your processor work bowl should fill up as you slice the onions, simply dump the sliced onions into the saucepan and continue slicing as before.

Raise burner heat to moderate, turn the onions in the butter 2 to 3 minutes until pale golden, then turn heat down low, cover the saucepan and cook very slowly for 1 hour, or until the onions are very soft. Check the pan now and then as the onions cook and if they threaten to cook dry (which should not happen if the heat is low enough), turn heat still lower or add a tablespoon or 2 of water.

When onions are very soft, add the cream, salt, pepper, rosemary and nutmeg, raise the heat to moderate and cook, stirring frequently, about 5 minutes until the cream thickens slightly. It should be about the consistency of a thin white sauce.

Taste for seasoning and add a bit more salt or pepper, if needed, then serve over individual portions of hot, well-drained pasta.

Oil, Garlic and Pignoli Sauce

Makes 4 to 6 servings

I include this recipe not so much because it is itself a good candidate for the processor but because it's sensational over Fresh Basil Linguine, which is a stellar candidate for the processor. You can, of course, use the processor to chop the sauce's garlic and nuts. It's best to begin the sauce just minutes before you cook the pasta (note that it calls for ½ cup hot pasta cooking water), then to toss it with the hot pasta as soon as it is drained.

2 large garlic cloves, peeled
1 cup olive oil (best quality)
1 small sprig fresh rosemary, sage or thyme
⅔ cup pignoli (pine nuts)
½ cup pasta cooking water or hot chicken broth

Equip the processor with the metal chopping blade, snap the motor on and drop the garlic cloves down the feed tube; the instant they are coarsely chopped—a matter of a second or two—snap the motor off.

Place the olive oil in a medium-size heavy skillet, dump in the chopped garlic, add the rosemary sprig and set over low heat. Meanwhile, chop the *pignoli* moderately coarse by pulsing or snapping the motor on and off 3 to 4 times. When the garlic has turned golden (but by no means let it brown or the oil will taste bitter), strain the oil and return it to the skillet (do not return the sprig of rosemary to the skillet). Dump the nuts into the hot oil and stir over moderately high heat 1 to 2 minutes until lightly browned. Pour in the pasta cooking water and boil a minute or two.

To dress the pasta, drain it well, return it to the kettle in which you cooked it, then pour in the hot sauce. Shake the kettle over moderate heat, tilting it first to one side and then to the other, until every strand of pasta glistens.

Serve at once with plenty of freshly grated Parmesan or Romano cheese.

Vegetables

Asparagus-Parmesan Soufflé
Makes 4 servings

The processor, as I've said many times by now, enables you to use tough asparagus stems and other vegetable parings that you would normally discard because the machine's powerful chopping blade reduces them to purées that can be used in soups and soufflés.

3 tablespoons unsalted butter
1 small yellow onion, peeled and cut into slim wedges
½ cup loosely packed dill fronds, washed and patted very dry on
  paper toweling
3 tablespoons flour
½ cup chicken broth
½ cup light cream
4 large eggs, separated
¾ teaspoon salt
⅛ teaspoon white pepper
¼ cup freshly grated Parmesan cheese
1 recipe Asparagus-Stem Purée, thawed (see Index for recipe page
  number)

Melt the butter in a medium-size saucepan set over moderate heat. At the same time, mince the onion and dill together in a food processor fitted with the metal chopping blade by pulsing or switching the motor on and off about 6 times. Dump the mince into the saucepan and sauté slowly 5 to 8 minutes, until onion is limp and golden, but not brown. Smooth in the flour, add chicken broth and cream and heat, stirring constantly, until thickened and smooth—about 3 minutes. Lightly whisk the egg yolks, spoon in a little of the hot sauce, then stir back into pan, set over lowest heat and cook, stirring constantly, for 1 minute. Do not allow to boil, or mixture will curdle. Remove from heat, blend in salt, pepper, grated Parmesan and Asparagus-Stem Purée. Cool to room temperature, whisking mixture from time to time to prevent a "skin" from forming on the surface.

Beat the egg whites to soft peaks, blend in a little of the asparagus sauce, them dump the beaten whites on top of the sauce and fold in gently but thoroughly until no streaks of green or white show. Bake in an ungreased 6-cup soufflé dish on the center rack of a moderate oven (350° F.) for 40 to 45 minutes, or until soufflé is puffed and touched with brown. Serve immediately.

Shredded Beets with Horseradish and Sour Cream
Makes 4 servings

It was in Vienna that I was first served beets prepared this way, and they've been a favorite of mine ever since. Before I had a food processor, I simply used canned julienne-style beets. But fresh beets, boiled just until firm-tender, then peeled and processor-shredded, have far more character and flavor. TIP: *To keep the beets from losing their rich red color, cook them unpeeled with both the root ends and about two inches of the tops left on.*

> 20 small beets, washed and trimmed of all but about 2 inches of the
>   tops (do not peel and do not cut off the root ends)
> Cold water (enough to cover the beets)
> 2 tablespoons butter
> 2 tablespoons prepared horseradish
> 1 teaspoon salt
> ⅛ teaspoon freshly ground black pepper
> ½ cup sour cream, at room temperature

Cook the beets in the water in a large, covered saucepan over moderate heat about 30 minutes, or until firm-tender. Drain, cool, then peel, removing tops and root ends. In the feed tube of a food processor fitted with the shredding disc (the medium-shredding disc, if you have one), stack as many beets as will fit snugly, then turn the motor on or depress the Pulse button and push beets through the feed tube with gentle pressure. Repeat until all beets are shredded. Place shredded beets in a medium-size saucepan with the butter, horseradish, salt and pepper, set over moderate heat and warm for 2 to 3 minutes—just until butter is melted. Blend in the sour cream, warm for 2 to 3 minutes longer (do not allow mixture to boil or cream will curdle) and serve.

Creamed Chopped Broccoli with Walnuts
Makes 4 servings

Here is an imaginative way to rejuvenate broccoli that has perhaps waited too long in the refrigerator and is beginning to wither and yellow around the edges. Needless to say, crisp, fresh young broccoli is equally delicious prepared this way.

1 large bunch broccoli, trimmed of coarse or discolored stems and
*   leaves, divided into flowerets and washed*
1½ cups boiling water
½ cup walnut meats
2 tablespoons butter
¾ cup light cream
1 teaspoon salt
Several hefty grindings of black pepper
Pinch of ground nutmeg

Boil the broccoli flowerets in the water in a covered saucepan about 10 to 12 minutes, or until crisp-tender. Meanwhile, chop the walnuts quite fine in a food processor fitted with the metal chopping blade by letting the motor run nonstop for 10 seconds. Empty the walnuts onto a piece of wax paper and set aside. As soon as the broccoli is crisp-tender, drain well. Place half of it in the food processor (still equipped with the chopping blade) and chop moderately coarsely, using 3 or 4 pulses or on-offs of the motor. Empty into a large heavy skillet (not iron, which will react with the broccoli and walnuts, creating an unpleasant metallic flavor) and drop in the butter. Chop the remaining broccoli the same way and add to skillet. Set over moderate heat, add cream, salt, pepper and nutmeg and heat and stir 1 to 2 minutes. Add the walnuts and cook and stir 1 to 2 minutes longer, just until steaming hot.

Baked Broccoli Pudding

Make 6 servings

This rich, custard-like pudding is best served with a simply prepared meat—broiled chicken, for example, or butter-browned veal scallops.

1 large bunch of broccoli, trimmed of coarse stems and leaves,
*   divided into flowerets and washed well*
1 cup water
1 medium-size yellow onion, peeled and cut into slim wedges
6 tablespoons butter
6 tablespoons flour
2 cups milk
1⅔ cups light cream
4 large eggs, lightly beaten
1½ teaspoons salt
¼ teaspoon freshly ground nutmeg
⅛ teaspoon freshly ground black pepper
½ cup freshly grated Parmesan cheese

Cook the broccoli in the water in a covered saucepan over moderate heat about 15 minutes until crisp-tender. Drain well, then purée in a food processor fitted with the metal chopping blade by using 5 or 6 pulses or fast bursts of speed; empty into a mixing bowl and set aside. Machine-mince the onion fine in the processor, still equipped with the metal chopping blade (no need to wash it or the bowl) by using 5 or 6 pulses or on-offs of the motor. Empty into a medium-size heavy saucepan in which you have already melted the butter. Sauté the onion over moderate heat 8 to 10 minutes until lightly browned; blend in the flour, add the milk and cream and cook, stirring constantly, about 5 minutes until thickened and smooth. Ladle a little of the hot sauce into the eggs, then stir back into pan. Turn heat under sauce to lowest point, mix in salt, nutmeg, pepper and parmesan and heat and stir for 1 minute—no longer or eggs may curdle. Pour sauce on top of broccoli and fold in using a gentle over-and-over motion until mixture is uniform.

Pour into a buttered 2-quart soufflé dish. Set a large shallow pan on the middle oven rack, pour in hot water to a depth of 1½ inches, then set the soufflé dish in the center of the water bath. Bake, uncovered, in a moderate oven (350° F.) for 1 hour and 15 minutes. Remove pudding from the water bath and cool for 30 minutes before serving. Don't worry, it will still be quite hot. The cooling period is to give the mixture a chance to firm up slightly; it will still be rather soft, the texture about halfway between that of a soufflé and a custard.

Shredded Cabbage Baked in Puréed Leeks and Cream
Makes 4 to 6 servings

The best way to shred cabbage in a food processor is not with the shredding disc but with the metal chopping blade because with it—and with the number of bursts of speed you use—you can control the coarseness of the shred. For this particular recipe (delicious, by the way, with roast pork or fowl), the shred should be moderately coarse—a few bursts of speed are all that's necessary.

*4 large leeks trimmed of green tops, washed well and cut into 4-inch
  pieces*
⅓ cup chicken broth
*1 small cabbage, quartered and cored (for this recipe you will need 4
  cups shredded cabbage)*
1 large egg
½ cup light cream
2 tablespoons melted butter
1 teaspoon sugar
1 teaspoon salt
⅛ teaspoon freshly ground nutmeg
⅛ teaspoon freshly ground black pepper

In a food processor fitted with the slicing disc, slice the leeks thin, using gentle pressure on the pusher. Cook leeks in chicken broth about 10 minutes, or until very tender; drain well and reserve. Remove slicing disc from processor and set metal chopping blade in place. Cut 2 of the cabbage quarters into 1½-inch chunks, dump about half of them into the processor work bowl and, with 5 or 6 pulses or quick bursts of speed, chop moderately coarsely. Empty into a 1-quart measure; continue chopping cabbage the same way until you have exactly 1 quart of it. Leave the chopping blade in place and add to the work bowl the drained leeks and all remaining ingredients. Purée zip-quick, using 2 or 3 pulses or on-offs of the motor. Pour over cabbage and toss well. Spoon into a well-buttered 6-cup baking dish, cover and bake about 45 minutes in a moderate oven (350° F.), or until bubbly and softly set.

Braised Chopped Carrots
with Ginger Root and Green Pepper
Makes 4 servings

Here's an unusual way of serving carrots, made easy by the food processor. Total preparation time is less than 5 minutes, cooking time less than half an hour. Especially good with pork or ham.

1 medium-size yellow onion, peeled and cut into slim wedges
One 2-inch slice of green pepper
2 tablespoons butter
One ½-inch cube ginger root, peeled
1 pound medium-size carrots, peeled and cut into 1-inch chunks
3 tablespoons water
½ teaspoon salt (or to taste)
⅛ teaspoon pepper (or to taste)

Chop the onion and green pepper together in the food processor, using the metal chopping blade—2 or 3 pulses or on-offs will be sufficient. Melt butter in a large heavy skillet, add onion mixture, set over moderate heat and allow to sauté while you chop the ginger root and carrots. Add them to the processor work bowl, still fitted with the chopping blade, and chop moderately fine—30 to 45 seconds nonstop should be about right. Add to skillet. Stir-fry the mixture about 5 minutes over moderate heat, just until lightly glazed and golden. Add water, cover, turn heat to low and simmer about 20 minutes, or until carrots are tender. Season with salt and pepper to taste and serve.

Carrots Vichy

Makes 6 servings

2 pounds tender young carrots, peeled and cut into 4-inch lengths
⅔ cup water
3 tablespoons unsalted butter
2 teaspoons sugar (I like to use raw sugar or light brown sugar)
½ teaspoon salt (or to taste)
Several grindings of black pepper
*¼ cup freshly minced parsley (for an amount this small, I prefer to
    do the mincing by hand)*

Thin-slice the carrots by pushing them with as little pressure as possible through the feed tube of a food processor fitted with the slicing disc. Dump into a medium-size heavy saucepan, add the water, butter, sugar, salt and pepper, cover, set over moderate heat and cook for about 20 minutes, or until carrots are tender. If all of the water has not evaporated, uncover and cook about 5 minutes longer, just until carrots are nicely glazed. But watch the pan carefully at this point and shake it often over the heat lest the carrots scorch. As soon as the water has cooked away, add the parsley, and toss lightly into the carrots. Taste for salt, add more if needed and serve.

Creamed Carrot and Parsnip Rounds
with Onion

Makes 4 servings

6 medium-size carrots, peeled and cut into 4-inch lengths
*2 medium-size tender young parsnips, peeled and cut into 4-inch
    lengths*
1 medium-size yellow onion, peeled and halved lengthwise
½ cup chicken broth
¼ teaspoon salt (or to taste)
⅛ teaspoon freshly ground black pepper
Pinch of crumbled leaf rosemary
Pinch of ground mace or nutmeg

1 tablespoon butter
¼ cup light cream

Thin-slice the carrots, then the parsnips and onion halves, in a food processor fitted with the slicing disc by exerting as little pressure as possible when you push the vegetables down the feed tube. Place all in a large heavy saucepan. Add broth, salt, pepper, rosemary and mace, cover and simmer slowly about 30 minutes, or until carrots and parsnips are tender. If at any time they seem to be cooking dry, add a bit more chicken broth. Add butter and cream and simmer, uncovered, over moderate heat until the liquids reduce to the consistency of a thin cream sauce—about 5 minutes. Taste for salt, add more if needed and serve.

Scalloped Carrots and Potatoes with Rosemary
Makes 6 servings

5 baking potatoes, peeled and halved lengthwise
6 medium-size carrots, peeled and cut into 4-inch lengths
3 tablespoons bacon drippings or butter
1½ teaspoons salt
⅛ teaspoon freshly ground black pepper
⅛ teaspoon crumbled leaf rosemary
¼ cup minced parsley (with an amount this small, it's quicker to hand-mince than to machine-mince)
2 cups hot milk (about)

Thin-slice the potatoes with the food processor. (Use the thin-slicing disc if your machine has one; if not, simply push the potatoes through the slicing disc with as little pressure as possible). Transfer potatoes to a large bowl. Thin-slice the carrots the same way. In the bottom of a well-greased 9x9x2-inch baking dish (use bacon drippings for greasing) make a layer of sliced potatoes, using one third of the total amount. Drizzle lightly with bacon drippings or dot with butter; sprinkle with salt, pepper, rosemary and parsley, using one third of the total amount of each seasoning. Layer one half of the carrot slices into the dish on top of the potatoes, add a second potato layer and season as before. Lay remaining carrot slices on top, then, for the final layer, the remaining potato slices; season once again. Pour in the hot milk—just enough so that it is visible but does not cover potatoes. Cover baking dish snugly with foil and bake 1 hour in a moderate oven (350° F.). Uncover baking dish, stir carrots and potatoes well, raise oven temperature to moderately hot (375° F.) and bake, uncovered, 1 hour longer, or until potatoes and carrots are tender and tipped with brown.

Shredded Carrots in Mustard Cream
Makes 4 to 6 servings

This is one of those recipes that must move very quickly once the cooking begins, so have all ingredients measured and at the ready.

3 tablespoons unsalted butter
1 medium-size yellow onion, peeled and cut into slim wedges
1 pound carrots, trimmed, pared and cut into 4-inch lengths
¼ teaspoon crumbled leaf thyme
Several grindings of the peppermill
¼ teaspoon salt
¼ cup water
½ cup dry white wine
1 tablespoon Dijon mustard
⅓ cup heavy cream, at room temperature
¼ cup half-and-half, at room temperature

Melt the butter in a large heavy skillet over low heat and set aside. In a food processor fitted with the metal chopping blade, chop the onion moderately fine by pulsing or snapping the motor on and off quickly 4 or 5 times. Dump the onion into the skillet with the butter and set over moderate heat.

Meanwhile, remove the chopping blade from the processor work bowl and slip the medium-shredding disc into place. Shred the carrots by pushing down the feed tube with moderate pressure. Dump the carrots into the skillet, add the thyme, pepper and salt and stir-fry 2 to 3 minutes until golden. Add the water, cover, reduce heat to moderately low and simmer 10 to 12 minutes until carrots are crisp-tender. Empty the carrot mixture into a large bowl and keep warm.

Return the skillet to moderate heat, pour in the wine and cook and stir 3 to 4 minutes until the wine has cooked down by about half. Smooth in the mustard, then continue cooking until the mixture is reduced to a glaze on the bottom of the skillet. Pour in the heavy cream and half-and-half and cook and stir 2 or 3 minutes until about the consistency of a light cream sauce. Return the carrots to the skillet and warm in the mustard cream, stirring all the while, 2 or 3 minutes. Serve at once.

Carottes Râpées
(Shredded Carrot Salad)

Makes 4 to 6 servings

A sunny dish of shredded carrots from the South of France that's delicious hot or cold. Make sure that the carrots you use are young and tender and full of flavor.

1 pound carrots, trimmed, pared and cut into 4-inch lengths
1 medium-size yellow onion, peeled and cut into slim wedges
1 medium-size garlic clove, peeled and minced
¼ cup olive oil (top quality)
¼ teaspoon crumbled leaf savory
¼ teaspoon crumbled leaf chervil
¼ teaspoon crumbled leaf thyme
3 to 4 tablespoons lemon juice
¼ teaspoon salt (about)
Several grindings of the peppermill

Equip the processor with the medium-shredding disc, then shred the carrots by pushing down the feed tube with moderate pressure; dump the carrots into a large heavy skillet and set aside. Remove the shredding disc from the processor and set the metal chopping blade into place. Chop the onion moderately fine by pulsing or snapping the processor on and off 4 or 5 times; dump into the skillet, add the garlic, olive oil, savory, chervil and thyme and toss all well. Set over moderately high heat and stir-fry about 5 minutes—just until carrots are crisp-tender. Add 3 tablespoons of the lemon juice, the salt and pepper and toss well. Taste for lemon juice, salt and pepper and adjust as needed. Toss well again, then serve hot, at room temperature or well chilled.

Cauliflower-Gruyère Soufflé
Makes 4 servings

1 medium-size cauliflower, trimmed and divided into flowerets
1 quart lightly salted water
4 tablespoons butter
4 tablespoons flour
1¼ cups milk
¼ pound Gruyère cheese, cut into columns about the size of the
*   processor feed tube*
1 teaspoon salt
¼ teaspoon white pepper
¼ teaspoon ground mace or nutmeg
4 eggs, separated, plus 1 egg white

Cook the cauliflowerets in the salted water in a covered saucepan over moderate heat about 25 minutes until very tender. Drain well, then return pan to heat and shake 1 to 2 minutes to drive off excess moisture. Purée half of the cauliflowerets in a food processor fitted with the metal chopping blade by running the motor for about 10 seconds nonstop; empty into a large bowl. Purée remaining cauliflowerets the same way and add to bowl. Quickly wash and dry the processor work bowl, reassemble and equip with the shredding disc. You will use it for shredding the Gruyère a bit later on.

Melt the butter in a medium-size saucepan, blend in the flour, then add the milk and cook and stir about 5 minutes until thickened and smooth. Set aside for the moment. Shred the cheese in the processor and stir into the sauce along with the salt, pepper and nutmeg. Now measure out exactly 2 cups of the cauliflower purée (any remaining— and there shouldn't be much—can be added to a soup or snacked on as is) and smooth into the sauce. Whisk about ½ cup of the sauce into the egg yolks, beating briskly to blend, then stir back into sauce.

Using a rotary beater, whip the egg whites to soft peaks. Blend about 1 cup of the whites into the sauce, then gently fold the sauce into the beaten whites so as not to break down the volume. Spoon the soufflé mixture into an ungreased 6-cup soufflé dish and bake, uncovered, on the center rack of a moderate oven (350° F.) for about 45 minutes to 1 hour, or until puffy and golden. Rush to the table and serve straightaway.

Cauliflower Purée with Fresh Dill and Browned Ginger Butter

Makes 4 servings

1 large cauliflower, trimmed and divided into flowerets
1½ cups water mixed with 1 teaspoon salt
6 tablespoons butter
One 1-inch cube fresh ginger root, peeled and scored deeply
  crisscross fashion
½ cup fresh dill fronds, loosely packed, washed and patted very dry
  on paper toweling
⅛ teaspoon white pepper

Boil the cauliflowerets in the salted water in a large saucepan over moderate heat 12 to 15 minutes until crisp-tender. Drain well, return pan to heat and shake 3 to 4 minutes to drive off all excess moisture. (It is important that the cauliflower be very dry, otherwise the purée will be watery.) While the cauliflower cooks, brown the butter slowly with the ginger root in a small heavy saucepan over low heat—it should be a rich topaz brown, not blackened or burned. Dump the dill fronds into a food-processor work bowl fitted with the metal chopping blade and, with 1 or 2 pulses or fast bursts of speed, mince coarsely; leave the dill in the work bowl. Add the cauliflower to the work bowl, and with 1 or 2 pulses or quick on-offs, partially purée. Remove ginger from butter, pour half the butter into the work bowl, add the white pepper and give 1 or 2 pulses or quick on-offs of the motor. Add remaining butter and purée until fluffy with 2 or 3 pulses or bursts of speed. Particularly good served with baked ham, roast pork, chicken or turkey.

Celery Soufflé

Makes 6 servings

2 *medium-size bunches of celery, trimmed of tops, washed,*
   separated into individual ribs, and each cut into 4-inch lengths
1 *small yellow onion, peeled and halved lengthwise*
1 *parsley stalk*
¼ *teaspoon crumbled leaf thyme*
¼ *teaspoon crumbled leaf chervil*
2 *cups chicken broth*
3 *tablespoons butter*
4 *tablespoons flour*
4 *eggs, separated, plus 1 egg white*
¾ *teaspoon salt*
⅛ *teaspoon white pepper*
½ *cup soft white bread crumbs*
Pinch of cream of tartar

In the feed tube of a food processor fitted with the slicing disc, stack enough celery ribs for a fairly tight fit, then turn the motor on or depress the Pulse button and thin-slice. Continue until all celery is sliced. You'll probably have to empty the work bowl a couple of times en route, so dump the celery slices into a large, heavy saucepan. Also thin-slice the onion halves and add to saucepan along with the parsley, thyme, chervil and chicken broth. Cover and simmer over moderate heat about 45 minutes to 1 hour, or until celery is very tender. Remove parsley, then drain the celery, reserving the cooking liquid.

Remove slicing disc from the food processor and slip the metal chopping blade into place. Purée the celery mixture, about one third of the total amount at a time, by letting the processor motor run nonstop for about 10 seconds. As you purée the batches of celery, scrape into a 1-quart measure. You will need exactly 1 quart (4 cups) of the purée for the soufflé. (Save any remaining to add to a soup or sauce later on, or even to whip into mashed potatoes.)

Melt the butter in a large saucepan over moderate heat, blend in flour to make a smooth paste, then whisk in reserved cooking liquid and heat, stirring constantly, until thickened and smooth—about 5 minutes. Mix in the celery purée. Beat the egg yolks lightly with a fork, blend in about ½ cup of the hot celery mixture, then stir back into saucepan and cook and stir for 1 to 2 minutes—no longer, or mixture may curdle. Transfer all to a large mixing bowl, stir in salt, pepper and bread crumbs and set aside for the moment.

Whip the egg whites to soft peaks with the cream of tartar, using a rotary beater or whisk. Blend about 1 cup of the whites into the celery mixture, then carefully fold in the remaining beaten whites until no streaks of white remain. Spoon into an ungreased 2-quart soufflé dish and bake, uncovered, on the middle rack of a moderate oven (350° F.) for about 1 hour, or until puffy and touched with brown. Serve at once as a vegetable or as a main course topped with cheese sauce.

Chestnut Purée

Makes 4 servings

The dried Italian chestnuts, now being sold in this country in many specialty groceries, are a godsend for those of us who like chestnuts. Unlike fresh chestnuts, they are available the year around, but best of all, they have been shelled and blanched, meaning that you can finesse the shelling—surely one of the peskiest of all kitchen details. Their flavor, moreover, is so like that of fresh chestnuts that it would take a discerning palate indeed to tell the difference. This particular chestnut purée, ever so slightly aromatic of onion, is especially good with roast turkey, chicken, goose or game.

1 cup dried, shelled and blanched chestnuts, washed and sorted
7 cups cold water
1 large onion, peeled
1 large celery rib, washed
2 tablespoons unsalted butter
½ cup heavy cream
½ teaspoon salt (or to taste)
Several hefty grindings of black pepper
Pinch of ground nutmeg or mace

Place the chestnuts and 2 cups of the water in a large, heavy saucepan, bring to a boil, remove from heat, cover and let stand 4 hours. Drain the chestnuts in a colander, then remove any recalcitrant bits of skin. (There will be a few, but these slip right off after the chestnuts have been soaked.) Return chestnuts to pan, add the remaining 5 cups of water, the onion and celery, cover and simmer over moderately low heat about 1 hour, or until chestnuts are very tender. Drain well. Remove celery and all but 1 or 2 pieces of onion. (The onion will have separated into layers, so simply hold back a layer or two to purée with the chestnuts.)

Dump half of the chestnuts into the work bowl of a food processor fitted with the metal chopping blade and add 1 tablespoon of the butter, ¼ cup of the cream and half of the salt, pepper and nutmeg. Turn motor on and purée for 10 seconds nonstop, uncover work bowl, scrape down the sides, re-cover and purée 5 seconds longer. Spoon into a dish and keep warm. Purée the rest of the chestnuts the same way with the remaining butter, cream and seasonings. Add to the first batch, whisk together lightly to blend, then taste for salt, add more if needed and serve.

Creamed Skillet Corn
Makes 4 to 6 servings

The food processor, it turns out, makes excellent fresh cream-style corn. All you have to do is cut the *whole* kernels from the cob (none of that messy scratching of the *cut* kernels off the cob) and dump them into the work bowl fitted with the metal chopping blade. Buzz, buzz, buzz—and presto!—cream-style corn.

8 large ears of sweet corn, husked
1 large yellow onion, peeled and cut into slim wedges
5 teaspoons butter
1⅓ cups light cream
¾ teaspoon salt (or to taste)
Several grindings of black pepper
Several grindings of nutmeg

With a sharp knife, cut the kernels from the cob, letting them fall into a large bowl. Place about half the corn in the food processor fitted with the metal chopping blade, and then cream, using three to four 1-second bursts. Examine the texture of the corn and, if it is not as fine as cream-style corn, give it one or two more short bursts of speed. Dump corn into a bowl and reserve. Chop the remaining corn the same way and add to bowl.

Quickly rinse and dry the processor work bowl and chopping blade, then reassemble. Chop the onion moderately fine, using 4 or 5 pulses or quick on-offs. Melt the butter in a large heavy skillet over moderate heat, add the onion and sauté 5 minutes until limp and pale golden. Add the corn and all remaining ingredients, cover, reduce heat to *very* low and simmer slowly, stirring now and then, about 45 minutes, or until corn is tender.

Fresh Corn Pudding

Makes 4 servings

6 medium-size ears sweet corn, husked
2 tablespoons sugar
1 tablespoon flour
½ teaspoon salt
Pinch of freshly ground black pepper
Pinch of ground mace
1 very small yellow onion, peeled and quartered
1 cup light cream
2 eggs
1 tablespoon melted butter

TOPPING:

12 saltines (the 2-inch-square ones)
1 tablespoon melted butter

With a sharp knife, cut the whole kernels from the cobs, place in the work bowl of a food processor fitted with the metal chopping blade, and with four 1-second bursts of speed, churn into a cream-style corn. Let stand for the moment. Combine sugar, flour, salt, pepper and mace in a mixing bowl; dump in cream-style corn. Mince the onion fine in the processor, using 5 or 6 pulses or on-offs of the chopping blade; add to corn. Lightly beat together cream, eggs and melted butter, add to corn and stir well. Spoon into a buttered 6-cup casserole.

Quickly rinse and dry the processor work bowl and metal chopping blade; reassemble. Add the saltines and reduce to moderately coarse crumbs by letting the motor run nonstop for 10 seconds. While the motor is running, drizzle the melted butter down the feed tube and buzz for about 5 seconds longer—just long enough to blend. Scatter buttered crumbs on top of casserole. Set casserole in a baking pan, pour in water to a depth of 1½ inches, then bake, uncovered, in a moderate oven (350° F.) for 45 to 50 minutes, or until corn mixture is set and lightly browned.

Eggplant Croquettes
Makes 6 to 8 servings

> *1 medium-size eggplant, peeled and cut into 1-inch cubes*
> *¾ cup boiling water*
> *2 teaspoons salt*
> *2 slices very dry firm-textured white bread, torn into about 1-inch pieces*
> *1 small white onion, peeled and halved*
> *1 egg, lightly beaten*
> *¼ cup freshly grated Parmesan cheese*
> *¼ teaspoon crumbled leaf marjoram*
> *¼ teaspoon crumbled leaf rosemary*
> *⅛ teaspoon freshly ground black pepper*

COATING:

> *40 soda crackers (the single ones that come packed in individually wrapped stacks)*
> *1 egg lightly beaten with 1 tablespoon cold water*

> *3 tablespoons unsalted butter (for browning the croquettes)*

Place eggplant, boiling water and 1 teaspoon of the salt in a heavy saucepan, cover, set over moderate heat and boil about 5 minutes, or until eggplant is tender. Drain well, pressing out as much water as possible. Set aside for the moment. In a food processor fitted with the metal chopping blade, buzz the bread to fine crumbs, using three 5-second churnings of the motor. Dump the crumbs onto a piece of wax paper and set aside. Now mince the eggplant in the processor, still fitted with the metal chopping blade, using 2 or 3 pulses or quick churnings of the motor. Empty eggplant into a mixing bowl. Place onion halves in the processor and mince fairly fine with 3 or 4 pulses or quick on-offs. Add to eggplant along with the bread crumbs, egg, cheese, the remaining teaspoon of salt, the marjoram, rosemary and pepper. Mix well, cover and chill 2 to 3 hours, or until firm enough to shape.

Wash and dry the processor work bowl and metal chopping blade and reassemble. Place about one fourth of the crackers in the work bowl and reduce to moderately fine crumbs by buzzing about 10 seconds nonstop. Empty into a pie plate and continue until all crackers have been buzzed to crumbs. In a second pie plate, place the egg-water mixture.

Using ¼-cup measure, shape the eggplant mixture into croquettes. Dip each in egg, then in crumbs, then arrange one layer deep on a baking sheet; cover and chill 1 hour. (This is to make the crumb coating stick.)

Heat the butter in a large, heavy skillet, then sauté the croquettes 4 to 5 minutes over moderate heat, flipping them over about halfway through so that they brown nicely on both sides. Drain on paper toweling and serve.

Baked Lamb-Stuffed Eggplant

Makes 4 to 6 servings

2 small eggplants, halved lengthwise but not peeled
¼ cup olive oil
¾ cup water

LAMB STUFFING:

The eggplant pulp scooped from the 2 eggplants
1 pound boneless lamb shoulder, cut into 1-inch cubes, trimmed of
  sinew and chilled well
1 medium-size yellow onion, peeled and cut into slim wedges
1 garlic clove, peeled and minced (by hand)
1 bay leaf, crumbled
½ teaspoon crumbled leaf basil

1 tablespoon minced parsley
¼ cup tomato paste
½ cup water
2 teaspoons salt
⅛ teaspoon freshly ground black pepper
1 cup cooked unseasoned rice

Sear the cut surface of each eggplant half in 1 tablespoon olive oil in a large heavy skillet over moderately high heat 3 to 4 minutes; cool slightly. Scoop the pulp from the eggplant halves, leaving shells ¼ inch thick. Set eggplant shells aside and coarsely chop the pulp in a food processor equipped with the metal chopping blade—5 or 6 pulses or on-offs of the motor should do it. Empty chopped eggplant into the same large skillet and set aside while you proceed with the stuffing.

Place half the lamb cubes in the processor work bowl, still fitted with the metal chopping blade, and with two or three 5-second bursts of speed, chop fairly fine. Add to skillet; repeat until all lamb is chopped. Now coarsely machine-chop the onion with 2 or 3 pulses or on-offs of the motor. Add to skillet along with the garlic, bay leaf, basil and parsley. Set over moderate heat and stir-fry about 10 minutes, or until lamb is no longer pink. Mix in the tomato paste, water, salt and pepper, cover and simmer 10 minutes. Off heat, stir in the rice.

Pile mixture into the eggplant shells. Place the eggplant on a rack in a moderately deep kettle, add the ¾ cup water, cover and bake in a moderate oven (350° F.) for about 1 hour, until eggplant shells are tender. To brown, run quickly under the broiler.

Curried Dhal (Lentils) with Vegetables

Makes 8 servings

An inexpensive vegetarian curry rich enough in protein to be served as a main dish.

½ pound lentils, washed and sorted
5 cups cold water
½ teaspoon ground turmeric
1½ teaspoons salt (about)

2 medium-size Irish potatoes, peeled and cut into 1½-inch chunks
3 medium-size sweet and ripe tomatoes, cored and cut into slim
    wedges (no need to peel)
One 1-inch cube fresh ginger root, peeled
1 large garlic clove, peeled
½ teaspoon cumin seeds
¼ to ½ teaspoon crushed dried red chili peppers (more if you like a
    "hot" curry)
¼ teaspoon coriander seeds
1 large yellow onion, peeled and cut into slim wedges
3 tablespoons ghee (melted unsalted butter poured off from its milk
    solids)
⅛ teaspoon ground cinnamon
⅛ teaspoon ground cardamom
Pinch of ground cloves
1 to 2 tablespoons light brown sugar (if needed to mellow the
    tartness of the tomatoes)

Place lentils, water, turmeric and salt in a large, heavy kettle, bring to a boil over moderate heat, reduce heat so that liquid simmers gently, cover and cook 30 to 40 minutes until lentils are tender but still firm.

Place potato chunks in food-processor work bowl fitted with the metal chopping blade and chop coarsely—4 or 5 pulses or quick bursts of speed should be about right; mix potatoes into kettle. Add tomatoes to work bowl, still fitted with metal chopping blade, and buzz for about 15 seconds, until nicely puréed; stir into kettle. Add ginger root, garlic, cumin seeds, chili peppers and coriander seeds to processor work bowl and buzz to a paste (about 30 seconds). Scrape from work bowl with a rubber spatula and set aside on a piece of wax paper. Now machine-chop the onion, using 2 or 3 pulses or quick bursts of speed. Heat the *ghee* in a heavy skillet over moderate heat just until a piece of minced onion will sizzle in it. Add onion and the ginger-garlic mixture, also the cinnamon, cardamom and cloves and stir-fry 8 to 10 minutes, until onion is limp and lightly browned.

Stir skillet mixture into the lentils. Continue simmering the lentils, covered, for about 1 hour, or until they are very tender and begin to fall apart. Taste and, if mixture seems too tart, mix in 1 or 2 tablespoons light brown sugar. Also add a little extra salt if needed. Uncover and simmer until lentils cook down to the consistency of a thick gravy—20 to 30 minutes. Ladle over fluffy boiled rice and serve.

Mushrooms in Cream Finlandia

Makes 4 to 6 servings

For this recipe, Finns would use wild mushrooms that they had gathered themselves in the fields and forests. But the commercially grown, snowy American mushrooms can be substituted. They are in fact unusually elegant prepared this way.

> 2 pounds medium-size mushrooms, wiped clean and trimmed of
>   stems (save stems to use later in soups or stews)
> 5 tablespoons unsalted butter
> 1 large yellow onion, peeled and halved lengthwise
> ¾ teaspoon salt (or to taste)
> ⅛ teaspoon freshly ground black pepper
> ⅛ teaspoon freshly ground nutmeg
> 1 cup light cream, at room temperature
> ½ cup loosely packed fresh dill fronds, washed and patted very dry
>   on paper toweling
> ½ cup loosely packed parsley sprigs, washed and patted very dry on
>   paper toweling
> 1 cup sour cream, at room temperature
> Paprika

In the feed tube of a food processor fitted with the slicing disc, stand as many mushrooms on their sides as will fit fairly snugly; turn machine on or depress the Pulse button and push the mushrooms through, using gentle pressure on the pusher. Repeat until all mushrooms are sliced. (If work bowl threatens to overflow before all of the mushrooms are sliced, dump contents into a very large heavy skillet in which you have already placed the butter.) Thin-slice the onion halves the same way and add to skillet. Set over moderate heat and stir-fry onions and mushrooms 8 to 10 minutes, just until onions are limp and mushroom juices have cooked down. Add the salt, pepper, nutmeg and light cream and simmer, stirring now and then, about 10 minutes, or until cream is reduced by about one half.

Meanwhile, remove the slicing disc from the food processor. Wash and dry the work bowl and its lid thoroughly, set work bowl on power base and slip the metal chopping blade into place. Pile the dill and parsley into the work bowl and, with about 2 pulses or fast bursts of speed, mince fairly coarsely. Stir into skillet and let simmer about 2 minutes. Smooth in the sour cream and heat and stir just until steam begins to rise from the skillet—do not allow mixture to boil, or the sour cream will curdle. Sprinkle lightly with paprika, taste for salt, add more if needed, then ladle over crisp triangles of lightly buttered toast.

Baked Walnut-Stuffed Mushrooms
Makes 6 servings

These elegant mushrooms may be served as a first course, or as a vegetable, or used to garnish a roast platter.

½ *cup walnut meats*
1 *slice firm-textured white bread, torn into small chunks*
⅓ *cup loosely packed parsley sprigs, washed and patted very dry on*
  paper toweling
2 *dozen medium-size very fresh mushrooms, wiped clean and*
  stemmed (reserve stems)
½ *cup unsalted butter, at room temperature*
1 *tablespoon shallots, very finely minced (by hand)*
1 *teaspoon salt*
¼ *teaspoon crumbled leaf thyme*
⅛ *teaspoon freshly ground nutmeg*
Several hefty grindings of black pepper
1 *tablespoon dry sherry*
1⅔ *cups light cream*

In a food processor fitted with the metal chopping blade, chop the walnuts quite fine, using 5 or 6 pulses or on-offs of the motor; empty into a mixing bowl. Add the bread and parsley to the processor and buzz for 5 seconds nonstop. Uncover the work bowl and examine the texture; the crumbs and parsley should both be moderately finely chopped. If not, buzz for several seconds longer; add to nuts. Now place the reserved mushroom stems in the processor and mince quite fine—4 or 5 pulses or on-offs of the motor should be about right. Add to bowl. Also add the butter, shallots, salt, thyme, nutmeg, pepper and sherry and beat hard with a wooden spoon to blend all ingredients.

Stuff each mushroom cap with the mixture, mounding it up on top. Arrange the stuffed mushrooms in a single layer in an ungreased

9x9x2-inch baking dish. Gently pour the cream around the mushrooms and bake, uncovered, in a moderately slow oven (325° F.) for 1 hour. Baste the mushrooms with the cream in the pan 2 to 3 times as they bake, but do so gently, lest the mounds of stuffing skitter off into the pan. Serve as an appetizer or as a vegetable with a little of the hot cream spooned over each portion, or use the mushrooms to garnish a meat platter. (The leftover cream may be saved and whisked into a sauce or soup later.)

Mushroom Soufflé

Makes 6 to 8 servings

1 pound medium-size fresh mushrooms, wiped clean and stemmed
(reserve stems)
6 tablespoons butter
1 small yellow onion, peeled and cut into slim wedges
4 tablespoons flour
2 cups milk
6 eggs, separated
1 teaspoon salt
⅛ teaspoon freshly ground black pepper
Pinch of ground nutmeg

Place half of the mushroom caps in a food processor fitted with the metal chopping blade and, with 4 or 5 pulses or quick bursts of the motor, chop fairly fine. Dump chopped mushrooms into a large heavy skillet in which you have already melted 2 tablespoons of the butter. Chop remaining mushroom caps the same way and add to skillet, then chop mushroom stems and onion quite fine; add to skillet. Set skillet over moderate heat and sauté, stirring occasionally, about 10 minutes, or until mushrooms are lightly browned and all of their juices have cooked away. Remove from heat and allow mixture to cool while you prepare the sauce.

In a medium-size saucepan, melt the remaining 4 tablespoons of butter over moderate heat, then blend in the flour to make a smooth paste. Whisk in the milk and heat, stirring constantly, until thickened and smooth—about 5 minutes. Remove from heat. Briskly mix a little of the hot sauce into the egg yolks, then stir back into saucepan. Season with salt, pepper and nutmeg. Place a piece of plastic food wrap flat on the surface of the sauce and cool to room temperature.

Combine cooled mushroom mixture and sauce. With a rotary beater, beat the egg whites to soft peaks (you cannot do this in the processor), then gently fold about 1 cup of them into the mushroom sauce to lighten it. Using a rubber spatula and a light touch, fold the mushroom sauce into the remaining beaten whites with a delicate over-and-over motion so that you don't break down the whites' volume. Spoon into an ungreased 8-cup soufflé dish and bake, uncovered, on the middle rack of a moderate oven (350° F.) for about 1¼ hours, or until puffed and golden. Serve at once as a vegetable, or as a main course topped with a mild cheese sauce.

Old New England Creamed Hashed Onions
Makes 6 servings

For this recipe you must use the sweetest onions you can find, preferably the giant fawn-skinned Spanish onions (erroneously called Bermuda onions). You must then simmer the onions in a milk bath to minimize their pungency. Finally, you must chop them coarsely—easy with a food processor—and bring them to serving temperature with butter and cream. An exquisite dish, and a simple one, too, delicious with roast turkey, chicken or pork.

4 large Spanish onions, peeled and halved crosswise
¾ cup milk
2 cups water
⅛ teaspoon freshly ground nutmeg
3 tablespoons unsalted butter
½ cup light cream
Salt and freshly ground pepper to taste
¼ cup minced parsley

Simmer the onions in a large heavy covered kettle in a combination of the milk and water over moderate heat for 15 minutes, or until crisp but tender; drain well. Quarter each onion half, then chop coarsely, doing only about one third of the onions at a time, in a food processor fitted with the metal chopping blade. One or two pulses or on-offs should be sufficient. Place chopped onions in a large, heavy skillet (not iron), sprinkle with nutmeg, add butter and cream and simmer, uncovered, over very low heat for about 10 minutes, or until flavors blend. Add salt and pepper to taste, stir in minced parsley and serve.

Egg-Stuffed Sweet Peppers
Makes 4 servings

4 large sweet green or red peppers
2 quarts boiling water mixed with 1 teaspoon salt
4 tablespoons butter
4 tablespoons flour
2 cups milk
½ pound sharp Cheddar cheese, cut into columns about the height
    of the processor feed tube
½ teaspoon salt
⅛ teaspoon freshly ground black pepper
8 hard-cooked eggs, peeled and halved lengthwise
¼ cup freshly grated Parmesan cheese
1 cup water

With a sharp knife, cut around the stem of each pepper and lift out, scoop out seeds and any pithy portions inside and discard. Lay peppers on their sides in a large kettle, pour in boiling salted water, cover and parboil for 6 to 8 minutes, or just until crisp-tender. With tongs, carefully lift peppers from water and stand upside down on several thicknesses of paper toweling to drain.

Melt the butter in a heavy saucepan over moderate heat, blend in the flour to make a smooth paste, then add the milk and cook, stirring constantly, until thickened and smooth—about 5 minutes. Set off heat for the time being. Equip a food processor with the shredding disc (the medium-shredding disc, if you have one). Stand as many pieces of cheese in the feed tube as will fit fairly snugly, turn motor on or depress the Pulse button and push cheese through to shred. Repeat until all cheese is shredded, add to sauce and heat and stir until melted. Season with salt and pepper and set aside while you chop the hard-cooked eggs.

Remove shredding disc from the food processor (no need to wash the work bowl) and slip the metal chopping blade into place. Add 4 hard-cooked egg halves and, with about 3 pulses or on-offs of the motor, chop moderately coarsely. Empty into a mixing bowl and repeat until all eggs are chopped. Combine cheese sauce with chopped eggs and stir well to mix. Stand the peppers close together in an ungreased shallow 1-quart casserole. Fill each with the egg mixture, mounding it up, then sprinkle each with 1 tablespoon of grated Parmesan. Pour water around peppers and bake, uncovered, for 45 minutes to 1 hour, or until tender.

VARIATION:

Egg-and-Rice-Stuffed Sweet Peppers: Prepare as directed, but reduce the number of hard-cooked eggs to 4 and substitute 1 cup of cooked and seasoned rice.

Jansson's Temptation
Makes 6 to 8 servings

This Swedish classic is nothing more than thinly sliced potatoes and onions scalloped in cream with minced anchovies. The food processor deftly slices both the potatoes and the onions, but it should not be used to mince the anchovies because it will grind them to a paste.

8 medium-size potatoes, peeled and halved lengthwise
2 large yellow onions, peeled and halved lengthwise
Several hefty grindings of black pepper
3 tablespoons unsalted butter
2 cans (2 ounces each) flat anchovy fillets, drained and minced
1 cup heavy cream
2 cups milk (about)

In a food processor fitted with the slicing disc (the thin-slicing disc, if you have one), slice the potatoes as thin as possible by pushing them through the feed tube with very little pressure. As the work bowl fills up, empty sliced potatoes onto a large square of wax paper. Repeat until all potatoes are sliced, then thin-slice the onions the same way and dump onto a second large square of wax paper.

Now layer the ingredients this way in a buttered shallow 2-quart casserole: a thin layer of potatoes, one of onions, a sprinkling of peppe., a dotting of butter and a scattering of minced anchovies; then more potatoes, onions, butter, anchovies and pepper. To top, a final layer of potatoes dotted with butter and sprinkled with pepper. Pour in the heavy cream and just enough milk so that it is visible in the casserole; it should not cover the potatoes. Bake, uncovered, in a hot oven (425° F.) for about 1 hour, or until bubbling and nicely browned. Let stand at room temperature 10 minutes before serving.

Gratin Dauphinois
(French Scalloped Potatoes)

Makes 6 servings

For a proper *gratin dauphinois,* the potatoes must be sliced tissue-thin, a job the food processor does to perfection. In choosing potatoes for this recipe, try to pick out baking potatoes that are slim enough to slip lengthwise into the feed tube (no more than 2¾ inches wide and 1¾ inches thick). Otherwise, you'll have to halve the potatoes the long way in order to fit them into the feed tube and the slices will not be as attractive as they should be.

8 long, slim baking potatoes, peeled (Halve lengthwise, if necessary, to fit the potatoes into the processor feed tube.)
⅓ cup butter
1½ teaspoons salt
¼ teaspoon freshly ground pepper
¼ teaspoon freshly ground nutmeg
2½ cups light cream (about)

In a food processor fitted with the slicing disc (the thin-slicing disc, if you have one), slice the potatoes as thin as possible by pushing them through the feed tube with minimal pressure. As the work bowl fills up, dump sliced potatoes into a large mixing bowl and reserve. Continue until all potatoes are sliced. Arrange a thin layer of sliced potatoes in a well-buttered 9x9x2-inch baking dish, dot with chips of butter, sprinkle with salt, pepper and nutmeg. Add two more layers of potatoes, using about half of the remaining amount for each layer and dotting with butter and sprinkling with salt, pepper and nutmeg as before. Now pour light cream until it is visible in the potatoes; it should not cover them. Bake, uncovered, in a slow oven (300° F.) for 1½ to 1¾ hours, or until potatoes are dappled with brown and most of the cream has been absorbed.

Potatoes and Onions Scalloped in Cream
Makes 6 servings

6 large baking potatoes, peeled and halved lengthwise
2 large yellow onions, peeled and halved lengthwise
1½ teaspoons salt
½ teaspoon crumbled leaf thyme
¼ teaspoon freshly ground black pepper
4 tablespoons flour
4 tablespoons buttter, cut into small chips
2½ cups light cream (about)
Sprinkling of ground mace

Equip the food processor with the slicing disc (the thin-slicing disc, if you have one), then push the potato halves through gently, two at a time. Empty into a bowl and set aside. Thin-slice the onions the same way and set aside in a separate bowl. Layer half of the potato slices in the bottom of a very well buttered 9x9x2-inch baking dish and top with half of the onion slices. Sprinkle with half of the salt, thyme, pepper and flour, then dot with half of the butter. Make a second layer of potatoes, then one of onions, and sprinkle with remaining salt, thyme, pepper and flour; dot with the rest of the butter. Pour in enough cream to come up to the top layer of potatoes; it should just be visible. Scatter mace on top, then bake, uncovered, in a slow oven (300° F.) for about 2 hours, or until the potatoes are tender and nicely browned on top.

Pommes de Terre Anna
(Potatoes Anna)

Makes 4 to 6 servings

This French classic has always been considered a tricky recipe—the thinnest-sliced potatoes, layered into a shallow, round-bottomed casserole, weighted down, and baked at high heat so that they emerge as a golden-crusted, thick "pancake" that can be inverted onto a serving plate with its precise design of overlapping slices intact. I haven't found *pommes de terre Anna* particularly difficult, but two things are essential if the recipe is to succeed: You must use waxy potatoes that will adhere to one another as they bake, and you must slice them tissue-thin. All-purpose Maine or Eastern potatoes work well, as do California Long Whites, which are akin to new potatoes in flavor and texture. Baking potatoes won't work because they are too mealy to stick together. As for the thin-slicing, the processor works best if you exert no pressure at all on the feed tube pusher; simply let the action of the slicing disc pull the potatoes down the feed tube. And, of course, use the thin-slicing disc, if you have one. When choosing potatoes for the recipe, try to select those slim enough to fit into the feed tube whole (no more than 1¾ inches in diameter). Only then will you get the perfect oval circlets of potato essential to the design of a proper *pommes de terre Anna*.

6 medium-size boiling potatoes, peeled (Halve lengthwise any that
are too chunky to fit into the feed tube.)
⅓ cup butter, melted and skimmed of all milk solids
1 teaspoon salt (about)
Several hefty grindings of black pepper

Stand one potato in the feed tube of a food processor fitted with the slicing disc (preferably the thin-slicing disc), turn the motor on and let the action of the machine pull the potato down the feed tube. Turn the machine off, add a second potato, then slice as before. Repeat until all potatoes are sliced.

Brush an 8-inch ovenproof glass pie plate well with melted butter. Now, beginning in the center of the plate, arrange potato slices, slightly overlapping, in concentric rings until they cover the bottom and sides of the pie plate. Brush with melted butter, then sprinkle with salt and pepper. Continue building up single layers of potatoes, always overlapping them, brushing each layer with butter and sprinkling with salt and pepper, until all potatoes are used up. Cut a circle of heavy-duty foil to fit the pie plate, lay on top of potatoes, then weight firmly, using an 8-inch cast-iron skillet or a heavy 8-inch flat-bottomed heatproof plate. Press down hard, set all on the middle rack of a very hot oven (450°F.) and bake 1 hour. Check the bottom layer of potatoes and, if they are not a rich amber brown, transfer to the bottom oven rack and bake about 10 minutes longer.

Remove from the oven and let the potatoes stand, still weighted down, for 15 minutes. Remove the weight and the foil, carefully loosen the potatoes around the edge of the dish with a thin-bladed spatula, then place a serving plate on top and invert. The potatoes should come out in one piece with their design intact, but if any stick to the bottom of the pie plate, simply lift them out and replace in the design. Cut into wedges to serve.

Rösti
(Shredded Swiss Potato Pancake)
Makes 4 to 6 servings

In making *rösti*, it is important to use waxy potatoes rather than mealy ones. The best, I have found, are either new potatoes or California Long Whites, because they form a crisp-crusted pancake that is less apt to break apart as you turn it in the skillet. Turning the *rösti* is tricky. To minimize the risk of breakage, loosen the pancake around the edges, slide onto a dinner plate, then invert in the skillet. Or, if you prefer, instead of making one large ten-inch *rösti*, opt for two five-inch ones—decidedly easier to manipulate.

12 medium-size new potatoes, peeled
4 tablespoons butter
½ teaspoon salt (or to taste)
Several grindings of black pepper

Using the food processor fitted with the shredding disc (the medium-shredding disc, if you have a choice), shred the potatoes. (The advantage of using new potatoes here is that they are small enough to pass through the feed tube without being halved.) Melt 3 tablespoons of the butter in a well-seasoned, heavy 10-inch iron skillet over moderately high heat and when it froths, tilt skillet with a circular motion so that the sides are also well coated with butter. Dump the shredded potatoes into the skillet and flatten into a single pancake; press down hard so that shreds adhere to one another. Brown for about 5 minutes, continuing to press and flatten the pancake. Lower heat to moderate, cover skillet, and cook 5 minutes. Uncover skillet and cook 5 to 8 minutes longer, again pressing and flattening the pancake, until surface looks fairly dry.

Carefully loosen edges of pancake all around, slide pancake turner underneath *rösti* and ease out onto a dinner plate. Scrape up any recalcitrant bits of potato from skillet and pat onto pancake. Melt remaining tablespoon of butter in the skillet and when it foams, flop pancake back into skillet, uncooked side down. Raise heat to moderately high and brown for about 5 minutes—the *rösti* should be crusty and dark brown on each side. Sprinkle liberally with salt and pepper and cut into 4 to 6 large wedges to serve. The traditional accompaniment—in Switzerland at least—is *Émincé de Veau* (see Index for recipe page number).

Hashed Brown Potatoes
Makes 2 to 4 servings

The usual way to make hashed browns is to slice or dice cold boiled potatoes, then to fry them in butter or bacon drippings with minced onion until crusty and brown. If you intend to use the food processor to cut the potatoes, however, you will have to cut them up raw, because the machine's power and speed make rubber of cooked potatoes.

1 large yellow onion, peeled and cut into 1-inch chunks
3 tablespoons butter or bacon drippings
4 large Maine or Eastern potatoes, peeled and cut into 1-inch chunks
¾ teaspoon salt
Several hefty grindings of black pepper

In a food processor fitted with the metal chopping blade, coarsely chop the onion, using 2 or 3 pulses or on-offs of the motor. Melt the butter in a large, heavy skillet over moderate heat, add the onion and allow to sauté while you chop the potatoes.

For best results, chop only one fourth of the total amount of potatoes at a time; if you overload the processor, you'll wind up with an uneven mince. Place the potato chunks in the processor, distributing them evenly around the chopping blade, cover the work bowl and pulse or snap the motor on and off quickly 4 times. Empty potatoes into the skillet and chop the remaining potatoes the same way, in three separate batches. Add to skillet and sauté slowly for 10 minutes. Turn the heat to its lowest point, clap the lid on the skillet and let the potatoes simmer 10 minutes (this is to cook them through). Now raise the heat and brown the potatoes, stirring them up from the bottom with a pancake turner. Sprinkle with salt and pepper and serve.

French Fried Potatoes
Makes 4 to 6 servings

If you have a French-fry-cutting disc, you may be interested in French-frying potatoes at home. Unlike the twice-fried French fries of most fast-food chains, these are remarkably crisp and light and *un*-greasy. To simplify cutting the potatoes, pick out baking potatoes that are slim enough to fit into the food processor feed tube without being halved.

8 medium-size baking potatoes, peeled
2 quarts vegetable or peanut oil (for frying the potatoes)
Salt and freshly ground pepper

Equip a food processor with the French-fry-cutting disc. Slice the round end off a potato so that it will stand in the feed tube without tilting or wobbling, turn the motor on and push through, exerting medium pressure on the pusher. Continue until work bowl fills up, dump the cut potatoes into a large bowl of ice water, then cut the remaining potatoes the same way; dump them into the ice water, too. Let the potatoes soak for 10 minutes in the ice water, then drain well and pat very dry on paper toweling.

Meanwhile, heat the oil in a deep-fat fryer to 375°F. Place about one third of the potatoes in a fryer basket, lower into the hot fat and fry 8 to 10 minutes until crisp and golden. Drain on paper toweling, then arrange one layer deep on a baking sheet lined with paper toweling and set, uncovered, in a very slow oven (250°F.) to keep crisp and hot while you fry the remaining potatoes. When all are done, sprinkle with salt and pepper and toss lightly. Serve oven-hot with hamburgers, steak or fish sticks.

Potato Chips

Makes 4 to 6 servings

I doubt that it ever would have occurred to me to make potato chips if I hadn't had a food processor to thin-slice the potatoes. And why, you may wonder, is it worth the bother when commercial potato chips are so available and cheap? The best reason I can offer is that homemade potato chips are so wonderfully fresh and pure—no additives or preservatives at all. The potatoes, of course, must be shaved into the thinnest possible slices. The thin-slicing disc works best, I find, so use it if you have one; if not, use no pressure at all as you feed the potatoes down to the slicing disc. When buying the potatoes, choose Idahos that have approximately the dimensions of the food-processor feed tube.

3 pounds of baking potatoes, peeled
2 quarts corn oil or peanut oil
Salt and pepper to taste

Slice the potatoes very thin in a food processor fitted with the slicing disc by pushing them down the feed tube gently one at a time. When work bowl fills up, dump the potato slices into a large bowl of ice water. Repeat until all potatoes have been sliced. Soak the potatoes in ice water for 2 hours. (Keep adding more ice cubes as needed; the potatoes must be kept icy cold as they soak.) Drain the potatoes very dry in a colander, pushing gently to force out as much water as possible. Then pat the slices bone-dry between several thicknesses of super-absorbent paper toweling.

Meanwhile, heat the oil in a deep-fat fryer over high heat until the oil reaches 380°F. on a deep-fat thermometer. Place about 1 cup of the dry potato slices in the fryer basket, lower into the hot oil, stirring to keep the slices from sticking to one another, and fry 3 minutes until crisp and golden. Drain on paper toweling. Keep frying the potatoes, about a cup at a time, adjusting burner heat as needed to keep the temperature of the oil at 380°F. Sprinkle with salt and pepper and serve.

Fluffy Mashed Potatoes
Makes 6 servings

After working with food processors for more than ten years, I have at last learned to produce good processor-mashed potatoes—something once thought impossible. First, you must choose a *mealy* variety of potato, *not a waxy one*, meaning that the best candidates for processor-mashing are Idaho or baking potatoes (Russet Burbanks, to give their proper name). Second, you must boil them until *very* soft—almost falling-apart soft. Finally, you must peel, then shred the potatoes *steaming-hot* because once cooled, even baking potatoes will turn to glue in the processor. Here, then, is the technique for processor-mashing potatoes, step by step. If you follow it to the letter, your mashed potatoes should be fluffy and light (with a few small lumps to give them character).

2 pounds (3 to 4 medium-size to large) baking potatoes, scrubbed
   well but not peeled
2½ quarts (10 cups) cold water
¾ cup half-and-half
3 tablespoons unsalted butter
1 teaspoon salt
¼ teaspoon freshly ground black pepper (or white pepper, if you
   prefer)
Pinch freshly ground nutmeg

Place the potatoes and water in a large heavy saucepan, set over moderately high heat and bring to a boil. Adjust burner so that the water bubbles moderately vigorously, set the pan lid on askew (to discourage "boil-over") and cook the potatoes until a fork will pierce them with no resistance whatsoever. This will take from 1 to 1½ hours depending upon the size and shape of the potatoes. Some of the potatoes may even break apart in the water, but no harm done. Merely scoop out the pieces, peel and shred. As soon as the potatoes are very tender, turn the heat off but leave the potatoes in the hot water.

Place the half-and-half, butter, salt, pepper and nutmeg in a small heavy saucepan and bring quickly to a simmer. Remove from the heat and pour half of the mixture into the processor. Keep the remainder hot over lowest heat.

Equip the processor with the medium-shredding disc. Now lift a potato from the hot water with a slotted spoon and place on several thicknesses of paper toweling. With a paring knife, quickly peel off all skin, rolling the potato over the paper toweling as you peel it. Halve the potato lengthwise, stand a potato half in the processor feed tube, turn the motor on or depress the Pulse button and allow the potato half to ease down the feed tube of its own accord. If you apply pressure with the pusher, you risk compacting the potato into a gluey mass. Your aim is for light, fluffy shreds. Repeat with the remaining potato half, then peel and shred the remaining potatoes the same way, *one by one*, keeping the balance in the hot water until you are ready for them.

As soon as you have shredded all of the potatoes, remove the shredding disc and fit the metal chopping blade into place. Drizzle the remaining hot cream mixture evenly over the shredded potatoes, then with 1 or 2 pulses or on-offs of the motor—**no more**—"mash" the potatoes. They will not be perfectly smooth, but they *will* be nice and fluffy. Be content. If you try to smooth the mashed potatoes out with longer churning, you will merely make them gluey. Serve the mashed potatoes straightaway before they have a chance to cool.

VARIATION:

Fluffy Parmesan Potatoes: Prepare precisely as directed, but just before adding the final half of the cream mixture, sprinkle 2 tablespoons of *freshly* grated Parmesan cheese over the hot shredded potatoes. Add the remaining cream mixture and "mash" as directed.

Spanakopita
(Greek Spinach-Cheese Pie)

Makes about 10 servings

A splendid buffet dish, this, because it can be made ahead of time. It's best served warm rather than oven-hot, which unharries the hostess at the last minute, too. To make the *spanakopita* properly, that is with plenty of "top and bottom crust," you will need a full pound of *filo* pastry. (These are the wispy, thin leaves used in making *baklava* and dozens of other honey-drenched Greek and Turkish pastries.) Fortunately, *filo* pastry is now marketed across the country, both fresh and frozen. The best place to find it is at a specialty grocery or at an ethnic one specializing in Middle Eastern delicacies. Rich enough to be served as a main dish, *spanakopita* needs nothing more to accompany it than a light salad—perhaps of beautifully diced, perfectly ripe tomatoes.

½ cup loosely packed fresh dill fronds, washed and patted very dry on paper toweling
½ cup loosely packed parsley sprigs, washed and patted very dry on paper toweling
3 tablespoons olive oil
2 medium-size yellow onions, peeled and cut into slim wedges
1 large garlic clove, peeled and minced (by hand)
2 pounds tender, young spinach, trimmed of coarse stems and washed in several changes of tepid water to remove grit and sand
1 pound feta *cheese, cut into 1-inch cubes*
⅔ cup light cream
4 eggs, lightly beaten
¼ teaspoon freshly ground nutmeg
⅛ teaspoon freshly ground black pepper
Salt to taste, if needed (it's not likely that you'll need any, because of the saltiness of the feta *cheese)*
½ cup freshly grated Parmesan cheese

1 pound filo *pastry (fresh, or frozen and thawed)*
1¾ cups melted butter

In a food processor fitted with the metal chopping blade, mince the dill and parsley together, using two or three 5-second bursts of speed; empty onto a piece of wax paper and set aside. Heat the olive oil in a large heavy saucepan set over moderate heat and, at the same time, processor-mince the onions, using 5 or 6 on-offs of the motor. Add the onion and garlic to the saucepan and sauté over moderate heat about 10 minutes until limp and golden; mix in the minced dill and parsley.

Drain the spinach well and pile into the pan—it may seem to overflow the pan, but simply push it down firmly and snap the lid on the pan. Steam the spinach about 5 minutes, or until wilted, then uncover the saucepan and let the spinach cook 15 to 20 minutes, or until very dry. Stir from time to time so that the spinach is well mixed with the onions, garlic and herbs. Empty the saucepan mixture into the processor (still fitted with the metal chopping blade) and purée by letting the motor run nonstop for 10 seconds. Turn motor off, scrape down the sides of the work bowl, re-cover and buzz once or twice quickly until uniformly smooth. Empty into a large mixing bowl.

Now add half of the *feta* and ⅓ cup of the cream to the processor work bowl and churn until smooth, using two 10-second buzzings of the motor. Empty into bowl with spinach; churn the remaining *feta* and cream the same way and add to spinach. Also add eggs, nutmeg, pepper, salt, if needed, and grated Parmesan cheese. Stir well to mix and set aside.

The next step is to layer the *filo* pastry into a well-buttered 13x9x2-inch pan—not as difficult a feat as it sounds, because the *filo* leaves are not nearly as fragile as they look. In a 1-pound package you will get about 22 leaves, each folded in half and measuring about 13x9 inches (13x18 inches when unfolded). The easiest way to arrange these in the pan is to lay a folded leaf in the pan lengthwise—a perfect fit since both are 13 inches long. Carefully unfold the top layer (just as you would turn the page of a book) and lop over the pan rim. Brush the bottom layer well with melted butter, refold the top layer so that it lies smoothly over the bottom one and brush with melted butter also. Continue building up layers in this fashion, brushing each generously with melted butter, until you have used

11 more of the folded leaves of *filo*. Spread the spinach-cheese filling smoothly on top, now layer the remaining leaves of *filo* on the filling, one folded leaf at a time and brushing each layer with melted butter as before. Brush the top layer well with butter, too.

Bake, uncovered, in a slow oven (300°F.) for 1 hour, then raise heat to moderately hot (375°F.) and bake 8 to 10 minutes longer, or until pastry is puffy and golden. Remove the *spanakopita* from the oven and cool about 20 minutes. To serve, cut into 2-.to 3-inch squares.

Finnish Fresh Spinach Pancakes
Makes 4 to 6 servings

In Finland these are served in place of potatoes and they are simply gorgeous—light, delicately flavored and flecked with green. They are equally good with roasts, seafood or fowl.

> *1 medium-size yellow onion, peeled and cut into slim wedges*
> *2 tablespoons butter*
> *1 bag (10 ounces) fresh spinach, washed and trimmed of coarse stems*

BATTER:

> *1 cup sifted all-purpose flour*
> *2 teaspoons sugar*
> *1 teaspoon salt*
> *¼ teaspoon ground mace*
> *⅛ teaspoon ground cardamom*
> *⅛ teaspoon freshly ground black pepper*
> *2 large eggs*
> *1 cup light cream*
> *1 tablespoon melted butter*

In a food processor equipped with the metal chopping blade, mince the onion fine, using 5 or 6 pulses or on-offs of the motor. Empty into a large saucepan in which you have already melted the butter, set over moderate heat and brown lightly; this will take 10 to 12 minutes. In this instance, you *do* want the onion to brown—it's important for flavor. Pile the spinach on top, cover and steam just long enough to wilt it—3 to 5 minutes. Dump all into a large sieve and drain well.

Now begin the batter: Place the flour, sugar, salt, mace, cardamom and black pepper in a mixing bowl and stir well to combine. Dump the spinach mixture into the processor work bowl, still fitted with the metal chopping blade, and purée by running 3 seconds nonstop. Scrape down the sides and lid of the bowl, re-cover and buzz 1 or 2 seconds longer. Break the eggs into the work bowl, add the cream and melted butter and with 2 or 3 pulses or fast bursts of speed, blend the mixture. Make a well in the center of the dry ingredients and pour the spinach mixture in all at once. Stir lightly—just enough to mix.

Drop the batter from a tablespoon onto a hot, lightly oiled griddle or skillet, smooth each pancake out until about 3 inches in diameter, and cook over moderately high heat 3 to 5 minutes, or until tops of pancakes seem lightly set. Turn with a pancake turner and brown the flip side lightly. Serve at once.

Note: *This batter can be made ahead of time and refrigerated until about 30 minutes before time to cook the pancakes.*

Spinach Purée
Makes 4 servings

1 large yellow onion, peeled and cut into slim wedges
2 tablespoons butter
2 bags (10 ounces each) fresh spinach, washed and trimmed of
  coarse stems
¾ teaspoon salt
Several hefty grindings of black pepper

In a food processor fitted with the metal chopping blade, mince the onion fine, using 6 to 8 pulses or on-offs of the motor. Empty into a large saucepan in which you have already melted the butter, set over moderate heat and brown the onion lightly—10 to 12 minutes. Dump the spinach leaves on top (do not add any water), cover and steam about 5 minutes, or until spinach is wilted. Drain well in a large, fine sieve, pressing out as much water as possible with a wooden spoon, then dump spinach and onions into the processor work bowl, still fitted with the metal chopping blade. Add the salt and pepper, then purée with a few pulses or bursts of speed. Serve at once.

VARIATIONS:

Creamed Puréed Spinach: Prepare the spinach as directed, but just before serving, mix in 3 or 4 tablespoons of room-temperature sour cream and a generous pinch of ground nutmeg or mace.

Puréed Spinach and Watercress: Prepare as directed, but steam along with the spinach 2 cups of tender young watercress leaves. Drain, season and purée as directed.

Esparregado (Portuguese Puréed Spinach and Garlic): Brown the minced onion with 1 large minced clove of garlic in 2 tablespoons of olive oil instead of butter. Add the spinach, then steam, drain, season and purée as directed.

Shaker Turnip Pudding
Makes 4 to 6 servings

I call this Shaker Turnip Pudding because it's very much like one I enjoyed at the magnificently restored Shakertown at Pleasant Hill, Kentucky. Women of the Shaker communities, which thrived throughout New England and the Middle West during the nineteenth century, were uncommonly creative cooks—but none more so, I'm told, than the Shakertown Sisters, whose reputation for culinary excellence was known all over the Bluegrass Country.

1 large yellow onion, peeled and halved lengthwise
4 tablespoons butter
4 large white turnips, peeled and halved lengthwise
1½ cups boiling water
1 tablespoon sugar
Turnip cooking water plus enough heavy cream to total 1½ cups
3 tablespoons flour

1 teaspoon salt
⅛ teaspoon ground mace
⅛ teaspoon white pepper
¼ cup freshly grated Parmesan cheese
3 large eggs, lightly beaten
½ cup soda cracker crumbs mixed with 1 tablespoon melted
   butter (optional topping)

In a food processor fitted with the slicing disc, thin-slice the onion halves by pushing them down the feed tube with light pressure. Melt 1 tablespoon of the butter in a large heavy skillet, add the onion slices, set over very low heat and allow to sauté while you slice the turnips. Timing is not important in cooking the onions, texture is; after about 20 minutes of sautéing, they should be golden and very limp. At this point, simply set the skillet off the heat and let stand until you are ready to use the onions.

Thin-slice the turnips in the processor the same way you did the onions, place in a large saucepan with the boiling water and sugar, cover, set over moderate heat and cook 1 hour, or until turnips are very tender. Drain the turnips, reserving their cooking water. Measure the cooking water, then pour in heavy cream until the combined liquids total 1½ cups. Set aside.

Remove the slicing disc from the food processor and slip the metal chopping blade into place. Scrape the sautéed onions into the work bowl, then dump in all of the turnips. Turn the motor on and let run nonstop for 30 seconds; snap the motor off, uncover the work bowl and scrape down the sides, re-cover the bowl and churn the mixture for 10 seconds longer, or until creamy and smooth. Empty into a large mixing bowl.

Melt the remaining 3 tablespoons of butter in a heavy saucepan over moderate heat, blend in the flour, salt, mace and pepper and cook and stir for about a minute, just until you have a smooth, golden roux. Pour in the cream-and-cooking-water mixture and heat, stirring constantly, until thickened and smooth—about 5 minutes. Mix in the grated Parmesan and heat and stir a minute or two longer, just until the cheese is melted and no raw floury taste is discernible in the sauce. Whisk a little of the hot sauce into the beaten eggs, then stir back into the pan. Now fold the sauce into the turnip purée, using a gentle over-and-over motion until the two mixtures are thoroughly combined.

Pour the pudding batter into a well-buttered 6-cup baking dish and, if you like, scatter the crumb mixture on top. Set the baking dish in a large shallow pan, pour water into the pan to a depth of 1½ inches, set all on the center rack of a moderate oven (350°F.) and bake, uncovered, for 1 hour and 20 minutes. Remove the turnip pudding from the oven and from the water bath and cool for 20 minutes before serving.

Ratatouille

Makes 6 to 8 servings

This Provençal ragout of eggplant, tomatoes, zucchini and onions is somewhat tricky to make with the food processor, because the machine cuts the vegetables more finely than you would do them by hand. I've learned, however, that the recipe works well if I alter the method of cooking to compensate. The best trick is to simmer the tomatoes, onions and sweet pepper down to a fairly thick sauce, then to lay the sautéed slices of zucchini and strips of eggplant on top so that they steam until tender without cooking down to mush. For cutting the eggplant, I use the French-fry disc. If you don't have one, slice the eggplant ½ inch thick, then cut into ½-inch cubes *after* the slices have been salted and weighted down between paper towels for an hour or so to draw out the bitter juices.

> 1 small eggplant, washed, stemmed and cut into columns about
>   the height and width of the food-processor feed tube (do not
>   peel the eggplant)
> 1 tablespoon salt
> 4 medium-size zucchini, washed and stemmed (but not peeled),
>   then cut into 4-inch lengths
> 5 tablespoons olive oil (top quality)
> 1 large Spanish onion (about 4 inches in diameter), peeled and
>   quartered lengthwise
> 1 medium-size sweet green or red pepper, washed, halved
>   lengthwise, cored and seeded
> 2 large garlic cloves, peeled
> 3 large vine-ripe tomatoes, peeled, quartered and cored

2 tablespoons minced fresh parsley (for an amount this small, I
  prefer to do the mincing by hand)
¼ teaspoon crumbled leaf basil
¼ teaspoon crumbled leaf marjoram
⅛ teaspoon freshly ground black pepper

Equip the food processor with the French-fry disc, stand a chunk of eggplant in the feed tube with the skin facing the cutting blade, turn the motor on or depress the Pulse button and cut into long, thin strips; repeat until all eggplant is cut. Empty onto several thicknesses of paper toweling, sprinkle with 2 teaspoons of salt, cover with more paper toweling and weight down with a heavy platter. Let stand at room temperature for 1 hour to draw out the eggplant's bitter juices.

Meanwhile, remove the French-fry disc from the processor and slip the slicing disc into place (the medium-slicing disc, if you have a choice). Stand 2 chunks of zucchini in the feed tube, arranging so that they fit snugly, turn motor on or depress the Pulse button and then push them through the feed tube, using firm pressure on the pusher. Repeat until all zucchini is sliced; empty onto several thicknesses of paper toweling, sprinkle with the remaining 1 teaspoon of salt, cover with more paper toweling and weight down as you did the eggplant. Let stand for 1 hour also.

Heat 2 tablespoons of the olive oil in a large heavy kettle over moderately high heat, dump in one half of the drained eggplant and stir-fry 3 to 4 minutes until golden. Lift with a slotted spoon to fresh paper toweling to drain. Add 1 more tablespoon of olive oil to the kettle and stir-fry the remaining eggplant the same way; lift to paper toweling to drain. Add another tablespoon of oil to the kettle, add all of the zucchini and stir-fry about 10 minutes until lightly touched with brown; drain on paper toweling. Add the remaining olive oil to the kettle and set off the heat for the time being.

Thin-slice the onion quarters by pushing them through the feed tube of the food processor (still fitted with the slicing disc) with minimal pressure. Stack the sweet pepper halves together, spoon-fashion, then thin-slice them in the processor as you did the onion. Dump the onion and pepper into the kettle, set over moderate heat and sauté, stirring now and then, until onion is limp and golden. Meanwhile, remove the slicing disc from the processor and slip the metal chopping blade into place. Turn the motor on, drop the garlic cloves down the feed tube into the spinning blade, then mince quite fine by letting the motor run nonstop for about 5 seconds. Without removing the garlic, add one of the tomatoes and, with a couple of pulses or fast whirs of the motor, chop coarsely. Add to kettle. Chop the remaining tomatoes the same way and add to kettle also. Mix in the parsley, basil, marjoram and pepper, cover and simmer 15 minutes; uncover and simmer 25 to 30 minutes longer, or until tomato mixture has cooked down into a fairly thick sauce. Layer the zucchini slices on top, then the strips of sautéed eggplant; do not stir. Simmer, uncovered, for 1 hour over low heat; again, do not stir.

Remove from the heat; now stir the *ratatouille* well, then let stand uncovered until it reaches room temperature. Delicious either as a vegetable or as an hors d'oeuvre.

Vegetable Kofta Curry
(Vegetable-Ball Curry)

Makes 4 servings

A not-too-spicy vegetarian curry from the south of India, surprisingly good and economical, too. The most important point to remember in preparing this curry is to drain the cooked vegetables "bone dry" before puréeing them in the food processor. Otherwise they will be too soft to shape into balls.

VEGETABLE KOFTA:

> 2 large Irish potatoes, peeled
> 1½ cups small cauliflowerets (about ¼ medium-size cauliflower)
> 1½ cups freshly shelled or frozen green peas
> ¼ cup parsley sprigs, washed and patted very dry on paper toweling
> 1 teaspoon salt
> ¾ teaspoon chili powder
> ⅛ teaspoon ground cinnamon
> ⅛ teaspoon ground coriander
> ⅛ teaspoon ground cardamom
> ⅛ teaspoon freshly ground black pepper
> Pinch of ground cloves

1 egg, beaten lightly with 1 tablespoon cold water
Peanut oil or vegetable oil for deep-fat frying (about 1 quart)

CURRY SAUCE:

One 1-inch cube fresh ginger root, peeled
2 medium-size yellow onions, peeled and cut into slim wedges
2 tablespoons ghee (melted unsalted butter poured off from its
* milk solids)*
1 teaspoon ground turmeric
1 teaspoon chili powder
1 teaspoon salt
½ teaspoon ground coriander
¼ teaspoon ground cinnamon
Pinch of ground cloves
Pinch of ground cardamom
Pinch of freshly ground black pepper
4 juicily ripe large tomatoes, cored and cut into slim wedges (no
* need to peel)*
1 to 2 tablespoons light brown sugar (if needed to mellow the
* tartness of the tomatoes)*

TOPPING:

2 hard-cooked eggs, peeled and sliced
1½ cups roasted salted cashew nuts

Prepare the vegetable kofta: Each in separate saucepans, boil the potatoes, cauliflowerets and green peas in lightly salted boiling water (use as little water as possible for the cauliflowerets and peas) just until tender. Drain each vegetable well in a fine sieve, then return vegetables to their respective saucepans and set over low heat for a minute or so, shaking pans, to drive off excess moisture. It is imperative that the vegetables be as dry as possible so that, when they are puréed, they are firm enough to shape into balls.

Mash the potatoes well by hand and set aside (the processor would turn them to glue). Equip the food processor with the metal chopping blade and in it place the drained cauliflowerets and peas, along with all of the remaining *kofta* ingredients except the beaten egg and the peanut oil. With 4 or 5 pulses or fast bursts of speed, purée the mixture. Examine and, if not smooth, give another couple of bursts of speed. Scrape into a bowl, mix in the mashed potatoes, cover and chill for about an hour, or until firm enough to shape. Roll into 1-inch balls, arrange on a baking sheet and chill for at least 1 hour.

Prepare curry sauce: Wash the processor work bowl and dry it, also the metal chopping blade, then reassemble. Turn the motor on, drop the ginger root down the feed tube into the spinning blade, then reduce to paste with about 1 minute of nonstop action. Add the onions and, with 2 or 3 pulses or short on-offs, chop coarsely. Place the *ghee* in a large heavy skillet, add onions and ginger-root paste, set over moderate heat and sauté 12 to 15 minutes, stirring now and then, until onions are lightly browned and very soft. Blend in turmeric, chili powder, salt, coriander, cinnamon, cloves, cardamom and black pepper and heat, stirring occasionally, 10 minutes—just enough to mellow the flavors.

Place half of the tomatoes in the food-processor work bowl, still fitted with the chopping blade, and reduce to juice with two to three 20-second churnings; add to skillet, then purée the remaining tomatoes the same way and add to skillet. Turn heat under skillet to low and simmer, uncovered, for about 1 hour, stirring now and then, until the consistency of a pasta sauce. Taste for seasoning and, if too tart, add 1 to 2 tablespoons light brown sugar.

Fry the kofta: Heat peanut or vegetable oil in a fairly large heavy skillet to 360°F. on a deep-fat thermometer. Dip each vegetable ball quickly in the beaten-egg mixture, then deep-fry 5 to 8 minutes until golden brown on all sides. With a slotted spoon, transfer *kofta* to curry sauce and simmer, uncovered, for about 10 minutes, spooning some of the gravy over the balls to coat them well.

To serve: Ladle *kofta* over fluffy boiled rice, including plenty of the gravy. Top with sliced hard-cooked eggs and the roasted cashew nuts, which have been coarsely chopped in the food processor fitted with the metal chopping blade. The processor work bowl should be clean and dry before the nuts go into it. For a coarse chop, you'll need 4 or 5 quick bursts of speed only.

Carolina Yellow Squash Casserole
Makes 4 to 6 servings

So that you don't have to keep rinsing and drying the processor work bowl, begin with the dry ingredients, i.e., the topping, then proceed to the wet.

TOPPING:

2 slices firm-textured white bread, broken into 1-inch chunks
1 tablespoon freshly grated Parmesan cheese
1 tablespoon melted unsalted butter

CASSEROLE:

2 ounces Swiss cheese, cut to fit the processor feed tube
2 ounces sharp Cheddar cheese, cut to fit the processor feed tube
1 pound tender young yellow squash, trimmed, washed and cut
　　into 4-inch lengths
1 medium-size yellow onion, peeled and cut into slim wedges
4 scallions, trimmed and cut into 1-inch chunks (include a few
　　green tops)
½ cup water
¼ teaspoon crumbled leaf rosemary
Pinch crumbled leaf thyme
Pinch ground mace
¼ teaspoon salt
⅛ teaspoon freshly ground black pepper
1 egg, beaten until frothy

For the topping: Equip the processor work bowl with the metal chopping blade, drop in the bread chunks, add the Parmesan and buzz the bread to moderately fine crumbs by pulsing or snapping the motor on and off 5 or 6 times. Dump into a small mixing bowl, sprinkle the melted butter over all and toss well to mix. Set aside.

For the casserole: Remove the metal chopping blade from the work bowl and slip the medium-shredding disc into place. Stand first the Swiss cheese, then the Cheddar, in the processor feed tube, snap the motor on or depress the Pulse button and shred by pushing down the feed tube with light pressure. Tap the cheeses out onto a piece of wax paper and set aside.

Remove the shredding disc from the processor and set the medium-slicing disc into place. Slice the yellow squash by pushing down the feed tube with moderate pressure. Dump into a large heavy saucepan.

Remove the slicing disc from the work bowl and set the metal chopping blade back into place. Dump the onion and scallions into the work bowl and chop moderately coarsely by pulsing or snapping the motor on and off about 3 times. Dump into the saucepan with the squash, add the water, rosemary, thyme, mace, salt and pepper. Set over moderate heat and bring to a boil, cover and cook 10 to 12 minutes until squash is quite tender; drain well and cool 20 minutes. Mix in the reserved cheeses, then fold in the beaten egg.

Spoon into a well-buttered 1-quart casserole and sprinkle the reserved topping evenly over the surface. Bake, uncovered, in a hot oven (400° F.) for 25 to 30 minutes, or until bubbly and nicely browned.

Sautéed Shredded Zucchini with Onion
Makes 6 servings

I can't think of a lovelier accompaniment to veal scallops or broiled chicken than these delicate shreds of zucchini glazed with butter and olive oil and flavored with onion, dill and marjoram. But if this dish is to have the proper subtlety of flavor and texture, you must use only tenderest young zucchini to make it. Large, aged, or coarse zucchini is too pithy to produce good results; moreover, it oozes an inordinate amount of water as it cooks and even as you serve it.

1 large Spanish onion, peeled and cut into 1½-inch chunks
2 tablespoons unsalted butter
1 tablespoon olive oil
3 pounds tender young zucchini, washed, trimmed and cut into 4-inch lengths
½ teaspoon crumbled leaf marjoram
½ teaspoon dill weed
1 teaspoon salt (or to taste)
¼ teaspoon freshly ground black pepper

Place about half of the onion chunks in a food processor fitted with the metal chopping blade and, with 4 or 5 pulses or short bursts of speed, chop moderately fine; repeat with remaining onion. Warm butter and olive oil in a large heavy skillet, add onion, set over moderate heat and let sauté while you shred the zucchini. Fit the food processor with the shredding disc (the medium-shredding disc, if you have a choice), stand about 2 lengths of zucchini in the feed tube and shred. Continue until the work bowl fills up, transfer zucchini to skillet, then continue until all zucchini has been shredded. (You will have to do the zucchini in 5 or 6 batches.) Add herbs, salt and pepper to skillet and sauté, stirring now and then, for 5 minutes. Cover and simmer 5 minutes. Then uncover and simmer 5 to 10 minutes longer, just until the excess juices evaporate.

Batter-Fried Zucchini Sticks

Makes 6 to 8 servings

For this recipe you will need the French-fry disc. You will also need a large shallow French-fryer at least 12 inches in diameter. Handy to have, too: two Oriental mesh skimmers, one for lifting the zucchini from the batter, a second for removing it from the hot fat.

2 pounds tender young zucchini, washed, trimmed and cut into
1¼ inch lengths, but not peeled
1½ cups unsifted cornstarch (for dredging the zucchini)
2 pounds vegetable shortening (for deep-fat drying)

BATTER:

1½ cups sifted cornstarch
2 teaspoons salt
1 teaspoon baking powder
3 eggs, beaten until frothy
1 cup flat beer

Equip the food processor with the French-fry disc and fit the cover in place. Lay 3 chunks of zucchini on their *sides* in the feed tube, turn motor on or depress the Pulse button and push them through, using gentle pressure on the pusher. When work bowl fills up—after about half of the zucchini is cut—empty the zucchini onto several thicknesses of paper toweling. Cut the remaining zucchini the same way and dump onto paper toweling. Cover with more layers of paper toweling and pat as dry as possible. Let stand while you mix the batter.

In a shallow mixing bowl, combine the cornstarch, salt and baking powder. Add the eggs alternately with the beer, making about three additions of each and beating well. Spread out fresh paper toweling, several thicknesses deep, on the counter. Dump about 1 cup of the zucchini into the batter, stir to coat lightly, then lift out with a mesh skimmer or slotted spoon and spread out on the fresh paper toweling. Continue until all the zucchini has been batter-dipped. Let air-dry on the paper toweling for about 10 minutes while the fat heats.

Heat the shortening in a large French-fryer until it registers 375°F. on a deep-fat thermometer. Place the 1½ cups unsifted cornstarch in a large, heavy plastic bag (I used a 4-gallon garbage bag). When squash no longer seems wet, dump about 1 cup of it into the plastic bag and shake to dredge. Remove squash from bag, shaking off any excess cornstarch, then, with the skimmer, plunge immediately into the hot fat. Let fry 3 to 4 minutes until golden brown, then remove with a skimmer to paper toweling to drain. Transfer at once to a paper-towel-lined baking sheet and set in a very slow oven (250°F.) to keep warm and crisp while you fry the remaining squash. (Keep the oven door ajar.) NOTE: *Do not attempt to batter-dip, dredge or fry more than 1 cup of squash at a time—it will clump together. Also, keep lowering and raising the burner heat as needed to keep the temperature of the fat as nearly at 375°F. as possible. If the fat cools too much (below 350°F.), the squash will be greasy. If its temperature exceeds 400°F., the squash will char before it cooks.*

Salads & Salad Dressings

Tuna Salad with Fresh Dill, Parsley and Capers
Makes about 8 servings

The food processor does a first-rate job of flaking tuna. You can easily control the size of the flakes by the number of pulses or on-offs you use (one or two for coarse flakes when the tuna salad is indeed to be served as a salad; three to five when you want a texture fine enough for a sandwich spread). The processor, of course, also chops the onions, slices the celery and minces the fresh parsley neatly together with the dill *and* emulsifies the mayonnaise. This particular tuna salad is loaded with onions (I happen to be fond of onions). If you prefer a milder flavor, use one onion only. The order of ingredients below may seem odd, but food-processor preparation often alters the conventional order. The parsley and dill, for example, should be minced first, when the processor work-bowl is pristine (only then will the fresh chopped herbs be fluffy and light). The tuna follows, and finally the onions and celery, which help clear the tuna residue from the work bowl. NOTE: *As I have said about herbs before, if the parsley and dill are to be minced properly, rather than to be reduced to mush, they must be completely dry. I sometimes wash them several hours before, then roll them up snugly in super-absorbent paper toweling and stow in the refrigerator.*

1 cup loosely packed, washed and thoroughly dried parsley sprigs
⅓ cup loosely packed, washed and thoroughly dried dill sprigs
4 cans (7 ounces each) white chunk tuna, well drained

3 medium-size yellow onions, peeled and cut into slim wedges

2 medium-size celery ribs, washed, trimmed of tops and cut into 4-inch lengths

1 cup mayonnaise (see Index for recipe page number)

¼ cup small capers, drained

3 to 4 tablespoons light cream, milk or water (just enough to give the tuna salad the consistency you prefer)

¼ teaspoon freshly ground pepper

Salt (if needed to taste; you probably will need none at all)

Pile the parsley and dill in the processor work bowl fitted with the metal chopping blade, fit cover in place and give a single pulse or fast burst of speed—on-off, no more. Check the fineness of the mince, and if parsley and dill are too coarse, give a second pulse or on-off burst, then a third, if needed. Empty into a large mixing bowl. Flake half the tuna at a time, again using the metal chopping blade—1 or 2 pulses or on-off bursts for a fairly coarse flake, 3 to 5 for fine. Empty into mixing bowl. Place about half the onion wedges into the work bowl, again using the metal chopping blade, and with about 3 fast pulses or bursts of speed, chop fairly coarsely. Transfer to mixing bowl, then repeat with remaining onion wedges. Remove chopping blade, scrape out bowl with rubber spatula and fit metal slicing disc in place. Stand enough celery lengths in feed tube for a snug fit, then slice. Repeat until all celery is sliced; add to mixing bowl along with all remaining ingredients. Toss lightly until well mixed. Cover and chill several hours before serving.

Herb-Garden Egg Salad

Makes 4 servings, or enough filling for 6 to 8 sandwiches

If you grow your own herbs, do try this delicate egg salad, because only fresh herbs will give it the proper flavor. The food processor, of course, whirs the herbs into a fine mince, then chops the hard-cooked eggs, scallions and celery.

½ cup loosely packed parsley sprigs, washed and patted very dry on paper toweling

⅓ cup loosely packed dill fronds, washed and patted very dry on
  paper toweling
1 teaspoon rosemary leaves, washed and patted very dry on paper
  toweling
12 hard-cooked eggs, chilled, peeled and halved lengthwise
2 small scallions, trimmed of green tops and root ends, washed and
  cut into 1-inch lengths
1 small celery rib, trimmed, washed and cut into 1-inch lengths
1 teaspoon salt
Several grindings of black pepper
⅓ cup mayonnaise (see Index for recipe page number)
3 tablespoons light cream (about)

Toss fresh herbs together lightly to mix, put into a processor fitted with
the metal chopping blade, then mince fairly fine with 2 or 3 fast pulses
or on-offs of the motor. Empty into a large bowl. Place 6 hard-cooked
egg halves in the processor, fitting them around the chopping blade
and, with a couple of pulses or fast bursts of speed, chop moderately
coarsely; empty into bowl. Repeat until all eggs are chopped. Machine-
chop the scallions and celery the same way and add to bowl along with
all remaining ingredients. Stir well to mix, and if salad seems drier than
you like, mix in an additional tablespoon or so of cream. Cover and
refrigerate several hours before serving.

Tabbouleh
(Bulgur, Tomato, Onion and Mint Salad)
Makes 4 servings

Every Arab country has its own version of this crunchy cracked-wheat
salad. This particular recipe comes from Lebanon, where the proportions of mint, parsley and lemon are somewhat higher than in the more
arid countries. In Beirut, *tabbouleh* is traditionally served with *mezza*,
that nonstop procession of hors d'oeuvre that amounts to a meal in
itself. *Tabbouleh* is equally good, however, with grilled fish, lamb or
chicken. Bed each portion on crisp romaine leaves.

⅔ cups bulgur wheat
2 cups boiling water

1 cup Italian flat-leafed parsley leaves, washed and patted very dry
    on paper toweling
½ cup fresh mint leaves, washed and patted very dry on paper
    toweling
1 medium-size yellow onion, peeled and cut into slim wedges
1 large, ripe tomato, washed, cored and cut into 1-inch chunks (do
    not peel)
Juice of 1 large lemon
¼ teaspoon salt
Several hefty grindings of black pepper
3 tablespoons olive oil (top quality)

Soak the bulgur wheat in the boiling water for 15 minutes; drain well, then bundle the bulgur up in a clean, dry towel and squeeze out as much water as possible. Place the bulgur in a deep mixing bowl. In a food processor fitted with the metal chopping blade, mince the parsley fairly fine by using two or three 5-second churnings of the motor; empty onto a piece of wax paper and set aside. Mince the mint the same way and empty onto a separate piece of wax paper. Now chop the onion fine, using 5 or 6 pulses or on-offs of the processor, and add to the bulgur. Squeeze each tomato chunk lightly to extract excess juice and seeds, then chop chunks moderately coarsely, using 2 or 3 pulses or on-offs of the motor. Add to onion and bulgur along with lemon juice, salt, pepper, parsley and mint. Toss lightly. Sprinkle the olive oil evenly over the surface and again toss well. Cover and refrigerate until about 30 minutes before serving.

Céleri Rémoulade

Makes 6 to 8 servings

A bonus in having one of the big, powerful new food processors is that you can make this once-tedious French classic altogether by machine, something not possible with early processors because they hadn't the strength and stamina to shred the tough celery root. NOTE: *Have all ingredients measured and ready to use before you begin the Rémoulade sauce because once you start, things should move like clockwork.* For the small amounts of parsley, tarragon and dill, I prefer to do the mincing ahead, by hand.

2 pounds celery root, trimmed, peeled and cut into columns the
    height and width of the processor feed tube
Juice of 1 medium-size lemon
½ teaspoon salt

RÉMOULADE SAUCE:

1 large shallot, peeled
¼ cup Dijon mustard
½ teaspoon dry mustard
⅛ teaspoon freshly ground black pepper
2 jumbo-size egg yolks
¼ cup boiling water
2 tablespoons boiling tarragon vinegar
¾ cup olive oil (top quality)
2 tablespoons minced parsley
1 tablespoon minced fresh tarragon or 1 teaspoon crumbled leaf
    tarragon
1 tablespoon snipped fresh dill or ½ teaspoon dill weed

In a processor fitted with the coarse-shredding disc (or failing that, the medium-shredding disc), shred the celery root, chunk by chunk, by pushing down the feed tube with moderate pressure. If at any time the machine seems to balk, pulse or snap the motor on and off 3 or 4 times. If the shredding disc still seems to reject the celery root, stop the motor, open the work bowl and rearrange the celery root in the feed tube. Then depress the Pulse button or snap the machine on and push the remaining celery root down the feed tube with moderate pressure.

When all of the celery root has been shredded, dump into a large nonmetallic mixing bowl. Drizzle the lemon juice over all, sprinkle with salt, toss well, then cover and marinate in the refrigerator about 2 hours. Drain the celery root very dry and set aside for the moment.

For the Rémoulade Sauce: Equip the processor with the metal chopping blade, snap the motor on, drop the shallot down the feed tube and buzz 5 seconds; scrape the sides of the work bowl down and buzz 5 seconds longer. To the work bowl add the Dijon mustard, dry mustard, pepper and egg yolks. Pulse or snap the machine on and off 3 or 4 times to mix. Now with the motor running, drizzle first the boiling water, then the boiling vinegar down the feed tube. Next, drizzle the oil down the feed tube in the finest of streams. Once all of the oil has been added, buzz the sauce 30 seconds nonstop.

Uncover the work bowl, sprinkle the parsley, tarragon and dill evenly over the surface of the sauce, then mix in using 2 or 3 pulses or on-offs of the motor.

Place the celery root in a large nonmetallic mixing bowl and drizzle the sauce evenly over all. Toss well to mix, cover and marinate 2 to 3 hours in the refrigerator. Toss well again and serve on leaves of Boston or Bibb lettuce.

Old-Fashioned Herbed Potato Salad
Makes 8 to 10 servings

You won't be able to cube the potatoes in the food processor for this particular potato salad, but you will be able to machine-mince the celery, green pepper, onions, herbs and hard-cooked eggs in a fraction of the time it would take you to prepare them by hand. I like to make this salad with baked potatoes, because they impart a unique nutty flavor. Moreover, cooled baked potatoes are so easy to peel.

12 large baking potatoes
1 cup loosely packed parsley sprigs, washed and patted very dry on
    paper toweling
½ cup loosely packed snipped chives (Snip into about ⅛-inch lengths
    directly into measuring cup.)
¼ cup loosely packed dill fronds, washed and patted very dry on
    paper toweling or ½ teaspoon dill weed
2 tablespoons fresh marjoram leaves, washed and patted dry on
    paper toweling. (If you don't have the fresh, use ½ teaspoon
    crumbled leaf marjoram.)
4 medium-size yellow onions, peeled and cut into slim wedges
4 large celery ribs, trimmed, washed and cut into 1-inch chunks
1 small sweet green pepper, washed, cored, seeded and cut into 1-
    inch squares
10 hard-cooked eggs, cooled, peeled and halved lengthwise
1½ cups mayonnaise (see Index for recipe page number)
1 cup sour cream (at room temperature)
½ cup India relish
2 tablespoons cider vinegar or tarragon vinegar

2 tablespoons Dijon mustard
2 teaspoons salt (or to taste)
¼ teaspoon freshly ground pepper
*3 to 4 tablespoons light cream or milk (if needed to soften the
    consistency of the salad)*

Bake the potatoes for 1 hour in a hot oven (400° F.), then let cool
thoroughly, peel and cut into 1-inch cubes; put in a very large mixing
bowl. Pile the parsley, chives, dill and marjoram in the work bowl of a
food processor fitted with the metal chopping blade, then mince quite
fine, using two or three 5-second bursts of speed. Scrape herbs into
bowl with potatoes. Now fine-mince the onions in the processor, half of
them at a time, using 5 or 6 pulses or quick on-offs of the motor; add to
bowl. Mince the celery, then the green pepper, the same way and add
to bowl. Chop the eggs in the processor (you'll only be able to do 6
halves at a time) using 2 or 3 pulses or on-offs of the motor; add each
batch of eggs to bowl as it is chopped.

Now place the mayonnaise, sour cream, India relish, vinegar, mustard, salt and pepper in the processor work bowl, still fitted with the
chopping blade, and pulse or buzz 2 or 3 times (on-off each time, no
more) just to blend. Leave the chopping blade in place and lift the
work bowl from the processor; the mixture is fairly liquid and if you
remove the chopping blade at this point, it will ooze down inside the
spindle. Pour this mixture over the salad, scrapping the processor bowl
out well with a rubber spatula, then toss the salad well to mix. If it
seems somewhat dry, work in several tablespoons of light cream or
enough to make the salad a consistency you like. Taste for salt and add
more if needed. Cover and chill several hours before serving, so that
the flavors have a chance to mellow and mingle.

Pennsylvania Dutch Sweet-Sour Potato Salad
Makes 8 servings

Only if you have a French-fry-cutting disc will you be able to machine-
cut the potatoes for this salad. (And you cannot successfully boil machine-sliced raw potatoes, because they are so thin and fragile they will
disintegrate as they cook.) You will, of course, be able to chop the
celery, onion, hard-cooked eggs, parsley and chives in any food pro-

cessor. If you do have a French-fry-cutting disc, you must cut the potatoes up *raw*. And you must alter your way of boiling potatoes. It's best, in fact, to treat them as you would pasta: Boil them gently in a huge pot of bubbling water just until firm-tender—no longer or the potatoes will break apart and turn to mush. I used Idaho or baking potatoes for testing this recipe and found that they work well if a dab of cream of tartar is added to the cooking water to help keep them firm and white.

8 medium-size baking potatoes, peeled and halved lengthwise, or 7
  cups cooked, peeled, diced potatoes
2 quarts cold water mixed with ¼ teaspoon cream of tartar
  (acidulated water for cooking raw potatoes)
4 medium-size celery ribs, trimmed, washed and cut into 1-inch
  lengths
1 medium-size yellow onion, peeled and cut into slim wedges
1 cup loosely packed parsley sprigs, washed and patted very dry on
  paper toweling
¼ cup loosely packed chives (Snip into about 1-inch lengths directly
  into the measuring cup.)
3 hard-cooked eggs, peeled and halved lengthwise
¾ teaspoon salt
Several hefty grindings of black pepper

SWEET-SOUR DRESSING:

⅓ cup sugar
1 tablespoon flour
1 teaspoon dry mustard
1 teaspoon salt
2 eggs
⅔ cup cider vinegar
2 tablespoons cold water

If you are going to machine-cut raw potatoes with a French-fry-cutting disc, stack 2 potato halves vertically in the feed tube and push them through firmly. Repeat until the work bowl is filled, then dump cut potatoes into a very large kettle (the kind in which you would cook spaghetti) and add the acidulated water at once. Continue until all potatoes are cut, adding each successive batch to the kettle. Set kettle over high heat (do not cover) and bring to a boil, then cook potatoes 6 to 8 minutes, just until firm-tender. Keep tasting the potatoes (just as you would pasta) and the minute they no longer taste of raw starch, turn out into a large colander and drain thoroughly. Submerge potatoes immediately in a large bowl of ice water and let stand 30 minutes. Then drain very dry, spread out on several thicknesses of super-absorbent paper toweling, top with more toweling and pat as dry as possible. Place potatoes in a very large mixing bowl. (If you are using diced cooked potatoes, you will begin the recipe at this point.)

Remove the French-fry-cutting disc from the processor, then slip the metal chopping blade into place. Add the celery and, with 3 or 4 pulses or fast on-offs of the motor, chop moderately coarsely. Add to bowl of potatoes. Chop the onion the same way, then the parsley and chives together, then the hard-cooked eggs, adding each successive ingredient to the potatoes as it is chopped. Sprinkle salt and pepper on top, toss lightly to mix and set aside while you prepare the dressing.

In the top of a double boiler, mix together sugar, flour, mustard and salt, smoothing out any lumps. Beat in eggs. Add vinegar and water. Set over simmering water and cook and stir just until thickened, about 3 to 4 minutes. Pour hot dressing over salad, toss well, cover and refrigerate several hours before serving.

Chopped Zucchini-and-Rice Salad with Fresh Basil and Pine Nuts

Makes 8 servings

1 cup loosely packed parsley sprigs, washed and patted dry on paper toweling
6 to 8 young and tender basil leaves, washed and patted dry on paper toweling
4 medium-size young and tender zucchini, trimmed and scrubbed, but not peeled
5 tablespoons olive oil (best quality)
1 medium-size yellow onion, peeled and cut into 1-inch chunks
2 medium-size garlic cloves, peeled and minced
1½ cups long-grain rice, cooked by package directions
½ cup pignoli (pine nuts)
¼ cup freshly grated Parmesan cheese

Juice of ½ lemon
1 teaspoon salt (or to taste)
Freshly ground black pepper to taste

In a food processor fitted with the metal chopping blade, mince the parsley and basil together, using about three 5-second bursts of speed; empty onto a piece of wax paper and set aside for the time being. Cut the zucchini into 1-inch chunks, then chop them moderately fine—one half of the total amount at a time—using 4 or 5 pulses or on-offs of the processor motor.

Place 2 tablespoons of the olive oil in a large heavy skillet, then add the chopped zucchini; set over moderately low heat and let sauté while you mince the onion. Place the onion chunks in the processor and, with 5 or 6 pulses or fast bursts of speed, mince moderately fine; add to skillet along with the garlic. Sauté the onion, zucchini and garlic slowly over low heat for about 15 minutes, or until tender and golden. Transfer to a large mixing bowl and add the rice, *pignoli* and the reserved chopped parsley and basil. Toss well and let mixture cool to room temperature. Add the remaining olive oil, scattering it over the surface of the salad, then the grated Parmesan, lemon juice, salt and pepper and toss well again. Taste for seasoning and add more salt and pepper if needed. Cover and refrigerate until about 30 minutes before serving and toss well again before serving.

Zucchini-and-Green-Bean Salad with Tarragon
Makes 6 to 8 servings

The processor French-fry disc cuts zucchini into slim, uniform sticks about the size of snapped green beans. I used to cut the squash by hand—a good hour's work. With the machine, a full pound of squash is cut in five seconds with far greater precision.

1 pound tender young zucchini, washed, trimmed and cut into 2¼-
   inch lengths, but not peeled
1 medium-size Italian (red) onion, peeled and halved lengthwise
1 pound tender young green beans, washed, tipped, snapped in half
   and boiled in lightly salted water just until tender (about 15 to 20
   minutes)

*2 tablespoons minced fresh tarragon, or ½ teaspoon crumbled leaf
    tarragon*
1 teaspoon salt
⅛ teaspoon freshly ground black pepper

DRESSING:

1 garlic clove, peeled and quartered
½ cup olive oil (top quality)
¼ cup tarragon vinegar (about)

Prepare the dressing first: Drop the garlic into the oil and let stand an hour or so at room temperature. Remove and discard the garlic. Pour oil into a shaker jar, add vinegar and shake well to blend.

Equip the food processor with the French-fry disc and fit the cover in place. Lay 3 chunks of zucchini on their sides in the feed tube, turn motor on or depress the Pulse button and push them through, using gentle pressure. Repeat until all zucchini is cut; empty into a large mixing bowl. Remove the French-fry disc from the processor and slip the slicing disc into place. Thin-slice the onion halves by pushing them through the feed tube with minimal pressure; add to bowl. Drain the beans well and, while they are still hot, dump them on top of the zucchini. Let stand 10 minutes, then toss well. Add the tarragon, salt and pepper and toss well again. Let stand another 10 minutes. Shake the dressing well, drizzle about two thirds of it over the salad and toss well. Taste. If salad needs more dressing, drizzle in a little more and toss lightly again. The objective is to glaze the zucchini and beans lightly with dressing, but not to drench them. Let salad marinate several hours in the refrigerator, then serve at room temperature.

Raw Mushroom-and-Zucchini Salad

Makes 4 to 6 servings

DRESSING:

3 tablespoons tarragon vinegar
¼ teaspoon salt
⅛ teaspoon white pepper
⅔ cup olive oil (finest quality)
1 large garlic clove, peeled and quartered

1 pound medium-size mushrooms, wiped very clean and trimmed of
stems (save stems to use in soups or stews later)
4 tender young zucchini, washed, trimmed and cut into 4-inch
lengths
1 small sweet red onion, peeled and halved lengthwise
¼ cup coarsely chopped fresh tarragon (for an amount this small, I
prefer to do the chopping by hand)
1 tablespoon snipped fresh dill

It's best if you make the dressing first and let it stand at room temperature 2 to 3 hours before dressing the salad. In a small bowl, combine
the vinegar, salt and pepper. Pour the oil in a thin stream, mixing
briskly with a fork. Drop in the pieces of garlic. Just before using,
remove the garlic and stir the dressing well.

For the salad: Fit the food processor with the slicing disc. Stack
mushroom caps in the feed tube on their sides—as many as needed for
a fairly snug fit—and slice thin by pushing them through the slicing
disc with minimal pressure. Repeat until all mushrooms are sliced,
then machine-slice the zucchini and onion the same way. Dump into a
mixing bowl, add tarragon and dill and toss lightly to mix. Drizzle a
little of the dressing over the salad, then toss well. Taste and, if more
dressing is needed, drizzle in an additional tablespoon or two and toss
well again. Cover and marinate in the refrigerator at least 1 hour. Toss
lightly again just before serving.

Cacik
(Turkish Cucumber-and-Mint Salad)

Makes 6 to 8 servings

4 medium-size cucumbers, peeled and cut in half lengthwise
1 teaspoon salt
1 cup tender young mint leaves, rinsed and patted very dry on paper
toweling
1 cup yogurt
1 tablespoon olive oil
¼ teaspoon freshly ground black pepper

Scoop out and discard the central seedy portion of each cucumber half with a teaspoon; cut each half into 4-inch lengths. Set the slicing disc in place in the food processor work bowl (a medium-slicing disc, if you have one). Wedge enough cucumbers into the feed tube for a tight fit. (This is to keep them from slithering around, so that the slices will be uniform.) Turn the machine on or depress the Pulse button and slice the cucumbers, using gentle pressure on the pusher; repeat until all cucumbers are sliced. Put them into a large mixing bowl and sprinkle with salt. Toss lightly, let stand at room temperature for 1 hour, then drain off as much liquid as possible.

Rinse and dry the work bowl, return to machine base and equip with the metal chopping blade. Pile mint into processor and, with a couple of fast pulses or on-offs, mince fairly coarsely. Add to cucumber along with yogurt, olive oil and pepper. Toss well, cover and refrigerate several hours before serving. Marvelous on a hot summer day with cold salmon or ham.

Great-Grandma's Sweet-Sour Coleslaw

Makes 6 to 8 servings

Our family always liked this old-fashioned coleslaw best. The cabbage is very finely shredded or chopped, and how I used to dread the job of pushing a whole head of cabbage through the hand grater, then the onion, then the carrots, then the green pepper. I never escaped without a nick or two on the knuckles. The best way to deal with cabbage in the food processor is to use the metal chopping blade. The shredding disc often reduces the cabbage to mush, and the slicing blade cuts it more coarsely than I like for this particular slaw.

1 medium-size cabbage, trimmed, quartered, cored, then cut into 1-inch chunks
1 medium-size yellow onion, peeled and cut into slim wedges
½ small sweet green pepper, cored, seeded and cut into 1½-inch pieces
2 medium-size carrots, peeled and cut into 1-inch lengths
⅔ cup mayonnaise (see Index for recipe page number)
½ cup sour cream (about)
¼ cup India relish

⅓ cup capers
1 tablespoon Dijon mustard
¾ teaspoon dill weed
1 teaspoon sugar
½ teaspoon salt (or to taste)
¼ teaspoon freshly ground black pepper

Pile about 2 cups of cabbage chunks in a food processor fitted with the metal chopping blade, then, with 7 or 8 pulses or quick bursts of speed, chop moderately fine. Empty into a large bowl; repeat until all cabbage is chopped. Machine-chop the onion and the green pepper together with 2 or 3 pulses or on-offs of the motor and add to the bowl, then the carrots with 6 or 7 pulses or on-offs. Add carrots to bowl along with all remaining ingredients. Stir well to mix, taste for salt and add more if needed. If coleslaw seems too dry, mix in a bit of additional sour cream. Cover and chill several hours before serving.

Purple Caraway Coleslaw

Makes 8 servings

1 medium-size yellow onion, peeled and cut into slim wedges
1 tablespoon butter
1 pint sauerkraut (do not drain)
1 tablespoon Dijon mustard
1 tablespoon prepared horseradish
1 cup mayonnaise (see Index for recipe page number)
¼ cup sugar
2 teaspoons caraway seeds
1 teaspoon celery seeds
Several hefty grindings of black pepper
½ red cabbage, cored and cut into columns about the height and
    width of the food-processor feed tube
1 cup sour cream, at room temperature

In a processor fitted with the metal chopping blade, mince the onion fine, using 6 to 8 pulses or on-offs of the motor. Transfer to a medium-size heavy saucepan in which you have already melted the butter. Set over moderate heat and sauté about 5 minutes, until limp and golden.

Add the sauerkraut, mustard, horseradish, mayonnaise, sugar, caraway, celery seeds and pepper, and heat and stir 8 to 10 minutes until steam rises from surface of mixture. (Do not allow to boil, or the mayonnaise may curdle.) Set off the heat, but keep warm.

Remove the metal chopping blade from the processor and slip the slicing disc into place. Thin-slice the cabbage by pushing a column of it at a time down the feed tube with gentle pressure. As work bowl fills up, empty sliced cabbage into a large mixing bowl. Continue until all cabbage is sliced; add to bowl. Dump the sauerkraut mixture on top of the cabbage and toss well to mix. Now add the sour cream and toss well again. Serve straightaway.

Sweet-Sour Coleslaw
Makes 8 servings

For this slaw, you'll again need cabbage finely sliced rather than shredded. Cut the cabbage into columns approximately the size of the processor feed tube, then push the cabbage through the slicing disc with gentlest pressure.

1 medium-size cabbage, trimmed, quartered, cored, then cut into columns about the height and width of the processor feed tube
1 medium-size yellow onion, peeled and cut into slim wedges
1 small sweet red pepper, washed, cored, seeded and cut into 1-inch squares

DRESSING:

¼ cup sugar
¼ cup cider vinegar
¼ cup boiling water
¾ teaspoon salt
¾ teaspoon celery seeds
⅛ teaspoon freshly ground black pepper
⅓ cup corn oil or peanut oil

Prepare the dressing first: Place all ingredients in a shaker jar, screw the lid down tight and shake vigorously to blend. Let stand at room temperature for several hours, then shake well again before using.

For the slaw: Thin-slice the cabbage by standing columns of it, one by one, in the feed tube of a food processor fitted with the slicing disc (the thin-slicing disc, if you have one) and pushing them through with minimal pressure. When the work bowl fills up, empty cabbage into a large bowl. Continue until all cabbage is sliced. Remove the slicing disc from the processor, then slip the metal chopping blade into place. Mince the onion fairly finely using 6 to 8 pulses or on-offs of the motor; add to cabbage. Mince the red pepper the same way and add to cabbage. Toss well to mix, then drizzle in about half of the dressing and toss well again. Taste and, if cabbage does not seem tart enough, drizzle in a little more dressing and toss again. Keep adding dressing and tossing until the flavors suit you. (Any remaining dressing will keep awhile and may be used to dress other salads.) Cover the slaw with plastic food wrap and marinate in the refrigerator for several hours. Toss well once again and serve.

Roquefort Dressing

Makes about 2 cups

With a food processor you can make this dressing faster than it takes to assemble the ingredients. Use to dress any green salad.

⅓ pound Roquefort cheese, crumbled
1 small garlic clove, peeled
1 small scallion, trimmed, washed and cut into 1-inch lengths
2 tablespoons tarragon vinegar
¾ cup mayonnaise (see Index for recipe page number)
½ cup sour cream
1 tablespoon Dijon mustard
2 teaspoons sugar
Several hefty grindings of black pepper

In a food processor fitted with the metal chopping blade, cream the Roquefort with the garlic, scallion and vinegar until creamy-smooth—about 10 seconds of nonstop buzzing. Add remaining ingredients and buzz 2 or 3 times until well blended. That's all there is to it.

Green Goddess Dressing

Makes about 2 cups

Few dressing recipes show the food processor off to better advantage. You can plop all the ingredients into the processor at once and buzz them up into a creamy mixture in about one minute. The recipe is an American classic.

> ½ cup loosely packed parsley sprigs, washed and patted very dry on paper toweling
> ½ cup loosely packed tarragon leaves, washed and patted very dry on paper toweling
> ¼ cup loosely packed chives (The easiest way to measure is to snip them into 1-inch lengths directly into the measuring cup.)
> 1 scallion, washed, trimmed and cut into 1-inch lengths
> 1 small garlic clove, peeled
> 4 anchovy fillets, rinsed and well drained
> 1 cup mayonnaise (see Index for recipe page number)
> ½ cup sour cream
> 3 tablespoons tarragon vinegar
> 3 to 4 grindings of black pepper

Put all ingredients into a food processor fitted with the metal chopping blade. Turn the motor on and let run steadily for about 1 minute, or until dressing is uniformly creamy and smooth. Pour into a jar, cover and refrigerate until ready to serve. Use to dress crisp green salads.

Avocado-Watercress Dressing

Makes about 2 cups

This zingy salad dressing is magnificent ladled over grapefruit and orange sections and also when it is used to dress the Belgian salad made of about equal parts sliced endive and slim wedges of tart, unpeeled red apple.

> 1 small very ripe avocado, halved, pitted, peeled and cut into 1-inch cubes

1½ cups loosely packed young watercress leaves, washed and patted
very dry on paper toweling
1¼ cups mayonnaise (see Index for recipe page number)
1 tablespoon Dijon mustard
1 tablespoon lemon juice (or to taste)
½ teaspoon salt (or to taste)
⅛ teaspoon cayenne pepper

Place all ingredients in a food processor fitted with the metal chopping blade, turn the motor on and let run continuously for 45 to 60 seconds, or until mixture is uniformly creamy. Pour into a bowl. Taste for lemon juice and salt and add a bit more of each, if needed; cover and chill several hours. Whisk briskly before using.

Scallion-and-Watercress Dressing
Makes about 2 cups

This piquant dressing is particularly good with cold fish and shellfish.

2 medium-size scallions, trimmed, washed and cut into 1-inch
lengths (include some green tops)
1½ cups loosely packed young watercress leaves, washed and patted
very dry on paper toweling
1 cup mayonnaise (see Index for recipe page number)
½ cup sour cream
1 tablespoon tarragon vinegar
1 tablespoon lemon juice
½ teaspoon salt
⅛ teaspoon cayenne pepper

Chop the scallions and watercress together in a food processor fitted with the metal chopping blade, using about 8 pulses or on-offs of the motor. Add all remaining ingredients and, with a couple of whirs of the motor, blend until smooth. Empty into a small bowl, cover and refrigerate for several hours before using, to allow the flavors to mellow

Black Caviar Dressing
Makes about 2 cups

Absolutely delicious with cold boiled lobster, shrimp or scallops. Use this dressing also for crisp green salads.

1 cup loosely packed parsley sprigs, washed and patted very dry on
   paper toweling
½ cup snipped fresh chives (Snip into 1-inch lengths directly into the
   measuring cup.)
1 hard-cooked egg, peeled and halved lengthwise
1½ cups mayonnaise (see Index for recipe page number)
½ cup sour cream
2 tablespoons lemon juice
1 tablespoon olive oil
2 teaspoons Dijon mustard
2 tablespoons fresh black caviar

Chop the parsley and chives moderately fine in a food processor fitted with the metal chopping blade, using 6 to 8 pulses or quick bursts of the motor. Add hard-cooked egg and mince—3 or 4 on-offs should do it. Add all remaining ingredients except the caviar and buzz a couple of times just to blend. Empty into a small bowl and stir in the caviar.

Breads

Processor Brioche
Makes 12 to 15

Brioche dough has always been one of the trickiest to knead because it is impossibly sticky. You dare not add too much flour to the board, because you'll never obtain a fine and feathery *brioche* if you do. Yet knead the dough you must, again, and again, and again, until it no longer sticks to everything in sight. Since *brioche* is my favorite breakfast bread, I decided to put the processor to the test. Could it successfully knead the gluey, sticky *brioche* dough? I'm delighted to say that the most powerful processors can. If you think your machine will balk, simply knead one half of the dough at a time.

> *1 package active dry yeast*
> *¼ cup warm water (105° to 115° F.)*
> *1 cup unsalted butter, at room temperature*
> *3 tablespoons sugar*
> *½ teaspoon salt*
> *4 large eggs*
> *3¾ cups sifted all-purpose flour*
> *Melted butter*

GLAZE:

> *1 egg yolk whisked with 1 tablespoon cold water*

Sprinkle the yeast over the warm water and let stand about 5 minutes until dissolved. In a food processor fitted with the metal chopping blade, cream the butter with the sugar and salt by letting the motor run nonstop for 1 minute. Scrape down the sides of the work bowl, then cream for 1 minute longer. Add the yeast mixture and churn 10 seconds. Add the eggs, one at a time, and incorporate each by snap-

403

ping the motor on and off twice. Then add 1 cup of the flour, distributing it evenly over the surface of the work-bowl mixture, and run the machine nonstop for 10 seconds. Add a second cup of flour and churn 10 seconds, then a third cup and let the machine run nonstop for 60 seconds. Now add the remaining ¾ cup of flour and run the machine nonstop for 10 seconds. Let the machine and the dough rest 5 minutes, then snap the machine on and let run nonstop again for 15 seconds. Give the machine and the dough a 5-minute break, then run the motor nonstop for 15 seconds.

The dough at this point will be very soft, very sticky, very elastic. With the help of a rubber spatula, scrape it into a well-buttered mixing bowl. Brush the surface of the dough with melted butter, then cover with a clean dry cloth and set in a warm place, away from drafts, until doubled in bulk. The first rising will take about 1½ hours. With a wooden spoon, stir the dough down, beat hard a few times until dough more or less comes together in a ball, re-cover with cloth and let rise again until doubled in bulk—about 1 hour this time. Stir the dough down, then cover with plastic food wrap and refrigerate until firm enough to shape—at least 4 hours. NOTE: *You can, if you like, refrigerate the dough overnight and shape it the next morning. The dough will have risen considerably in the refrigerator, so again punch it down well.*

To shape the *brioches*, first butter your hands well. Pinch off hunks of dough and roll into balls slightly larger than golf balls. Place these in well-greased muffin-pan cups or *brioche* molds. Save about ½ cup of the dough to use for making the topknots for the *brioches*. Pinch off bits of this reserved dough and roll into marble-size balls. Push your thumb deep into the center of each *brioche,* then cradle the smaller ball in the depression. Cover the pans of *brioches* with dry cloth and set in a warm, dry spot to rise until doubled in bulk—about 1 to 1½ hours.

Brush the top of each *brioche* lightly with the egg-yolk glaze, taking care that it does not run down into the pan. (Once cooked, the glaze will act like a glue and the *brioches* will be very difficult to remove from the pan.)

Bake the *brioches,* uncovered, in a very hot oven (425° F.) for 12 to 15 minutes, or until puffed and richly browned, then lower the oven heat to moderate (350° F.) and bake 10 minutes longer. Remove from the oven and let the *brioches* cool in their pans about 5 minutes before removing.

Pain Ordinaire

(Plain French Bread)

Makes 1 loaf measuring about 14x4x3 inches

It *is* possible to approximate, though not duplicate, the crusty country bread of France using American flours and home ovens. The classic recipe calls for four ingredients only—yeast, flour, salt and water (as does this recipe). To thicken and crispen the crust as the bread bakes, set a large shallow baking pan of water directly on the floor of the oven—the steam generated is critical to the bread's texture.

1½ packages active dry yeast
¾ cup warm water (105° to 115° F.)
½ teaspoon salt
2¼ cups sifted all-purpose flour (about)

GLAZE:

1 egg white beaten with 1 tablespoon cold water

Sprinkle the yeast over the water and let stand about 5 minutes, or until completely dissolved. Stir in the salt, then pour mixture into a food-processor work bowl fitted with the metal chopping blade. Add 1 cup of the flour, snap motor on and let run 4 seconds. Add another cup of the flour, snap motor on and let run 5 seconds. Now add the remaining ¼ cup of flour, snap motor on and let run 10 seconds. Uncover work bowl and examine the texture of the dough. If it seems soft and sticky (as it may if you attempt to make the bread in rainy or humid weather), add another ¼ cup or so of sifted flour. Whether or not you add additional flour, switch the motor on and let run nonstop for 60 seconds, or until the dough forms a ball and rides up on the chopping blade's central spindle. Transfer dough to a greased mixing bowl, turn dough in bowl so that it is lightly greased all over, cover with a clean, dry cloth, set in a warm place away from drafts and allow to rise until double in bulk—1½ to 2 hours.

Punch the dough down, turn onto a lightly floured board and knead briskly for 2 to 3 minutes until dough feels soft and springy. Now, using the palms of your hands, roll the dough back and forth on the board to form a chunky rope about 14 inches long, 3 inches wide and 2 inches high. Ease onto an ungreased baking sheet, cover with a clean, dry towel and allow to rise until doubled in bulk—about 1 hour.

Set a shallow baking pan (I use the 13x9x2-inch size) on the oven floor and pour in water to a depth of 1 inch. Preheat oven to very hot (450° F.); this will take about 10 minutes. Meanwhile, brush the bread well with the egg-white glaze. Set it on the middle rack of the oven and bake, uncovered, for 30 minutes, or until loaf is richly browned and sounds hollow when thumped with your fingers. Remove the bread from the oven and cool to room temperature on a wire rack before cutting. Actually, this bread, like so many rustic breads, tears better than it cuts. Simply tear into chunks and enjoy with a ripe Camembert or Brie and dry red wine.

Pain de Mie
(White French Canapé Bread)

Makes 2 loaves of pain de mie

Each loaf will be 12 inches long and 1½ inches in diameter, or you can make one such long loaf and 1 round loaf about 5 inches in diameter.

Pain de mie is not a phrase that translates neatly into English. What it means, essentially, is white bread composed mostly of soft insides and very little crust. The French bake *pain de mie* expressly for making canapés or melba toast (more efficient and frugal than our practice of using the centers of conventional white bread and tossing away the crusts). Cuisinart® offers as an extra accessory a hinged metal *pain de mie* pan that bakes a loaf of bread exactly the right size for slicing in the processor. NOTE: *Wash and dry the pan well after each use by hand rather than in the dishwasher, which will rust it.*

1 package active dry yeast
1 cup warm water (105° to 115° F.)
1 tablespoon sugar
1 tablespoon unsalted butter
½ teaspoon salt
3 cups sifted all-purpose flour

Sprinkle the yeast over ¼ cup of the warm water and let stand 5 minutes. Meanwhile, heat together the remaining ¾ cup of water, the sugar, butter and salt over low heat just until the butter melts. Remove from heat and cool to between 105° and 115° F. (Water any hotter will kill the yeast; water any cooler will retard the leavening process.) Combine the yeast mixture with the water-butter-sugar mixture and pour into the work bowl of a food processor fitted with the metal chopping blade. Add 1 cup of the flour, sprinkling it over the surface of the liquid mixture. Cover work bowl, snap motor on and allow to run nonstop for 4 seconds. Add a second cup of flour, again distributing it over the surface of the mixture, and mix by running the processor nonstop for 5 seconds. Now add the third and final cup of flour, again distributing it evenly. Turn the processor motor on and allow to run for 1 minute nonstop—this both mixes and kneads the dough in one operation. After 1 minute of churning, the dough will come away from the sides of the work bowl, roll into a ball and ride up on the chopping blade's central spindle; this means the dough is ready to proof.

Remove dough from processor, pat into a round ball, place in a greased mixing bowl, then turn the dough in the bowl so that it is greased all over. Cover bowl with a clean, dry cloth and set in a warm, draft-free place until dough has doubled in bulk—this will take about 1 hour. Punch the dough down, knead briskly 60 times on a lightly floured board, again shape into a ball and place in a greased bowl (once more turning dough in the bowl so that it is greased all over). Cover with the cloth and allow to rise until doubled in bulk—40 to 45 minutes. Remove dough from bowl, punch down, knead lightly 5 to 10 times on a lightly floured board, shape into a ball and divide exactly in half.

If you intend to make two loaves and have only one *pain de mie* pan, wrap half the dough in plastic food wrap and refrigerate. (This is to keep it from overrising and developing an unpleasantly strong yeast flavor.) Shape the remaining dough into a rope the length of the *pain de mie* pan—I simply roll it back and forth on the lightly floured board, using light pressure with my palms (the same motion we used with modeling clay as children to make a "snake"). Oil the *pain de mie* pan, paying special attention to the hinged parts where the dough is apt to stick. Lay the shaped dough in one half of the pan (it is hinged to open like a book and the two halves are identical). Cover the open pan with clean, dry cloth and let stand in a warm, draft-free place until the dough has about doubled in bulk—this will take about 30 minutes. Then close the pan, pushing the dough snugly inside. Fasten with the brass hinge pin as the *pain de mie* pan's printed instructions direct. Baking the bread in this closed pan minimizes the crust.

Set in a moderately hot oven (375° F.) and bake for 35 minutes. Remove from oven, open the pan and set the loaf on a wire rack to cool. When the bread is at room temperature, trim off the ridged seam on each side of the loaf. The easiest way is to snip them off with kitchen shears; if you use a knife, you risk tearing the bread.

Shape the remaining dough into a second loaf of *pain de mie,* following the preceding directions step by step. Or, if you prefer, use the dough to make a small round loaf. If you opt for the round loaf, you need not refrigerate the balance of the dough when you shape the first *pain de mie,* because it will take the round loaf about twice as long to rise as the long one. Shape into a ball about 3 inches in diameter and place on an ungreased baking sheet. Cover with a clean, dry towel and set in a warm, draft-free spot to rise. It will take about 1 to 1¼ hours for the loaf to double in bulk. As soon as you remove the first *pain de mie* from the oven, raise the temperature to hot (400° F.). When the round loaf has doubled in bulk, bake, uncovered, at 400° for 35 to 40 minutes, or until loaf is richly browned and sounds hollow when thumped with your fingers. When you remove the round loaf from the oven, cool on a wire rack to room temperature before cutting into wedges and serving.

To processor-slice pain de mie: First of all, with a sharp bread knife, cut one end off the *pain de mie,* then divide loaf into 2-inch chunks, making each cut as square as possible; otherwise the bread will not stand vertically in the feed tube and the slices will not be round. Equip the processor with the *serrated* medium-slicing disc, then snuggle a chunk of bread into the curve of the feed tube on the right-hand side. (In this position, the action of the machine will push the bread into the curve as it is sliced, helping to support it and keep it vertical.) Anchor the bread in the feed tube with the pusher (use moderate pressure), turn the machine on and push the bread through the slicer. Slice the remaining bread the same way, taking great care to keep it vertical in the feed tube.

To make melba toast: Arrange the slices of *pain de mie* on an ungreased baking sheet, set, uncovered, in a slow oven (300° F.) and toast until crisp and dry and a light caramel color—about 30 minutes. Remove from oven and let cool. The melba toast can be frozen successfully; simply bundle into a plastic bag, twist the top into a tight gooseneck, secure with a twist-tie and pop into the freezer. Thaw before using.

To make canapé bases: Brown the slices of *pain de mie* lightly on each side in a little olive oil, vegetable oil or clarified butter (melted butter poured off from its milk solids) and drain on several thicknesses of paper toweling.

Old-Fashioned White Bread
Makes two 9x5x3-inch loaves

This recipe and the one for Honey Whole-Wheat Bread, which follows, prove what powerhouses the new heavy-duty processors are, also what miracle workers the stubby plastic dough blades are. The processor, in each instance, mixes and kneads—all at one time—enough dough for two large loaves of bread. You'll note that the method of mixing is altogether new, closer to the pastry method than to conventional bread-making because the fat is cut into the dry ingredients, then the liquids are added. There's a reason for this: The stubby dough blade is a whiz at cutting fats into dry ingredients, but once the liquids are added, it begins to knead rather than to mix. It's important that you do not overknead the dough—45 to 60 seconds of continuous kneading after the liquids are added is usually sufficient. Further kneading can not only overheat the processor but it can also overheat the dough, possibly to the point that the yeast is killed and the batch of bread ruined because it will not rise properly. **NOTE:** *Do not attempt either this recipe or the whole-wheat bread that follows unless your processor is one of the big, extra-powerful ones.*

> *2 packages active dry yeast*
> *½ cup warm water (105° to 115° F.)*
> *7½ cups sifted all-purpose flour*
> *¼ cup sugar*
> *2 teaspoons salt*
> *¼ cup (½ stick) cold unsalted butter, cut into slim pats*
> *1¾ cups cold milk*

Sprinkle the yeast over the water and let stand about 5 minutes, or until completely dissolved. Combine the flour, sugar and salt and place half of the combined dry ingredients in the work bowl of a processor fitted with the plastic dough blade. Scatter the pats of butter over the surface of the dry ingredients, then add the balance of the dry ingredients. Snap the processor on and buzz nonstop for 20 seconds; scrape the sides of the work bowl down, buzz 20 seconds longer, then scrape the work bowl down again. Repeat 2 to 3 more times until the butter has been completely cut into the dry ingredients and the mixture is the texture of coarse meal. Now with the motor running, drizzle first the yeast mixture, then the cold milk down the feed tube. Let the motor run 60 seconds nonstop after all of the liquids have been incorporated.

Empty the dough into a large, warm, well-buttered bowl, shape into a ball, turn the dough in the bowl so that it is buttered all over, then cover with clean dry cloth and set in a warm place away from drafts to rise until double in bulk—about 1 hour.

Punch the dough down, divide in half, then knead each half hard 15 to 20 times on a floured pastry cloth. Shape into 2 loaves, place in buttered 9x5x3-inch loaf pans, then cover with dry cloth and set in a warm place to rise until double in bulk—again about 1 hour.

Bake the loaves in a moderately hot oven (375° F.) for 35 to 40 minutes, or until nicely browned and the loaves sound hollow when thumped with your fingers. Remove the loaves from the oven and from their pans and cool upright on wire racks to room temperature before cutting.

Honey Whole-Wheat Bread
Makes two 9x5x3-inch loaves

2 packages active dry yeast
1 tablespoon sugar
1 cup warm water (105° to 115° F.)
3 cups unsifted whole-wheat flour
½ teaspoon freshly ground cardamom (the inner black seeds only, which can be buzzed to powder in one of the compact little electric coffee grinders)
½ teaspoon ground ginger
¼ teaspoon ground nutmeg
2 teaspoons salt
½ cup (1 stick) cold unsalted butter, cut into slim pats
3½ cups sifted all-purpose flour
½ cup cold milk

¼ cup molasses
¼ cup honey

Sprinkle the yeast and sugar over the water and let stand about 5 minutes, or until completely dissolved. In the work bowl of a food processor fitted with the plastic dough blade, combine the whole-wheat flour, cardamom, ginger, nutmeg and salt by pulsing or snapping the motor on and off 2 or 3 times. Scatter the butter pats over the surface of the dry ingredients, add the all-purpose flour, then with four or five 20-second churnings of the motor, cut the butter into the dry ingredients until the mixture is the texture of coarse meal. It's a good idea to scrape the work-bowl sides down between churnings.

Combine the milk, molasses and honey in a 2-cup measuring cup. Now with the processor motor running, pour first the yeast mixture, then the honey mixture down the feed tube. Buzz nonstop for 60 seconds after all liquids have been added. The dough will roll into a ball, ride up on top of the central spindle and the plastic blade's churning will move it up and down, round and round, kneading it all the way.

Scoop the dough into a large, warm, well-buttered bowl, shape into a ball, turn the dough in the bowl so that it is buttered all over, then cover with clean dry cloth and set in a warm place away from drafts to rise until double in bulk. This will take between 2 and 2½ hours because the whole-wheat dough is a very heavy one.

Punch the dough down, divide in half, then knead each half lightly 2 or 3 times on a floured pastry cloth. Shape into 2 loaves, place in buttered 9x5x3-inch loaf pans, then again cover with cloth and set in a warm place to rise until double in bulk—about 2 hours.

Bake the loaves in a moderately hot oven (375° F.) for 40 to 45 minutes, or until richly browned and the loaves sound hollow when thumped with your fingers. Remove the loaves from the oven and from their pans and cool upright on wire racks to room temperature before slicing.

Crêpes
Makes about ten 7-inch crêpes

The normal order of mixing *crêpe* batter is to sift the flour and salt into a bowl, to combine the eggs, cream and melted butter, then to add these slowly to the dry ingredients. With the processor, the order is exactly the reverse, but it works just as well and in a fraction of the time.

> *2 large eggs*
> *½ cup light cream*
> *1 tablespoon melted butter*
> *¼ teaspoon salt*
> *½ cup sifted all-purpose flour*

Beat eggs, cream, melted butter and salt together for 3 seconds non-stop in a food processor fitted with the metal chopping blade. Add the flour, churn for 5 seconds; uncover work bowl, scrape down sides, re-cover and whir 5 seconds longer. Let mixture stand 15 minutes.

Rub a well-seasoned 7-inch *crêpe* pan lightly with oil, then wipe out with paper toweling. Set the pan over moderate heat and warm about 1 minute. Spoon 2 tablespoons of *crêpe* batter into pan, then tilt quickly with a circular motion so that the batter covers the bottom of the pan in a tissue-thin layer. Set over moderately high heat and cook about 1½ minutes, or until top of *crêpe* seems dry. Loosen edges with a thin-bladed spatula, if necessary (*crêpe* really should slip right up of its own accord), then brown the flip side lightly. Ease the *crêpe* onto several thicknesses of paper toweling while you cook the remaining *crêpes*.

Fill *crêpes* with any creamed meat, poultry, seafood or vegetable: Spoon about 3 tablespoons of the creamed mixture onto the center of each *crêpe*, roll up jelly-roll style and place seam-side down in a shallow baking dish. (You'll need about 2 cups of creamed mixture for the 10 *crêpes*.) Top with Béchamel or Mornay sauce, sprinkle with freshly grated Parmesan and brown quickly under the boiler.

Variations:

Dessert Crêpes: Prepare as directed, but add 1 tablespoon of sugar to the blended liquid ingredients along with the flour. Fill with any tart fruit jelly or preserves or, if you prefer, with a thick applesauce, and roll up. Drizzle with melted butter and sprinkle with sugar or drift with whipped cream. *To flame:* Warm about ½ cup fine brandy or cognac 1 to 2 minutes over moderate heat and pour over filled *crêpes* that have been drizzled with melted butter and sprinkled with sugar. Blaze with a match and serve when the flames subside.

Chocolate Crêpes: Prepare as directed, but add 1 tablespoon of sugar and 1 tablespoon of Dutch cocoa to the blended liquid ingredients along with the flour. Fill with sweetened whipped cream, or with ice cream, or with cream cheese whipped up with enough light cream to give it about the consistency of hard sauce (flavor with vanilla, rum, brandy, or with a coffee liqueur). Serve topped with whipped cream and chocolate sauce.

Processor Popovers
Makes 10 to 12

Mixing time, less than 20 seconds. I've learned, after preparing this recipe a number of times, that the popovers will puff higher if you let the batter stand at room temperature for 30 minutes before baking and if you preheat the greased muffin tins for 5 minutes in a very hot oven (450° F.)—this is the same temperature at which the popovers will then be baked. **NOTE:** *Do not double this recipe; it will overflow the processor work bowl.*

2 large eggs
1 cup milk
½ teaspoon salt
1 cup sifted all-purpose flour

Place eggs, milk and salt in a processor work bowl fitted with the metal chopping blade and buzz for 3 seconds nonstop. Add the flour, sprinkling it over the surface of the beaten egg mixture, re-cover work bowl, then buzz 10 seconds nonstop. Uncover work bowl, scrape down sides, re-cover and buzz 5 seconds longer. Let batter stand for 30 minutes before baking.

Meanwhile, grease a standard muffin pan well (one that will hold 12 muffins). Five minutes before you're ready to bake the popovers, set the pan in a very hot oven (450° F.) to preheat. Remove pan from oven, ladle batter into each muffin cup, filling about two thirds full—no more. Return pan to oven and bake popovers, uncovered, for 25 to 30 minutes, or until nicely puffed and brown. Serve straightaway with plenty of butter.

Processor Biscuits

Makes about 1 dozen

The secret of tender, flaky baking-powder biscuits is *not* to overmix—which may well lead you to wonder if biscuits can be made successfully in a machine as fast and furious as a processor. The answer is yes if you pay meticulous attention to the timing; one second too long with the processor blades spinning, and your biscuits may indeed be unchewably tough. To help safeguard against rubbery biscuits, I have slightly increased the amount of shortening. If you follow this recipe to the letter, you should have no difficulty making very good biscuits in your processor, although their volume may not be quite as much as for those mixed by hand.

> 2 cups sifted all-purpose flour
> 1 tablespoon baking powder
> ¾ teaspoon salt
> ½ cup very cold vegetable shortening, cut into small chunks
> (I set the measured-out shortening in the freezer for about 1 hour.)
> ¾ cup cold milk

Combine the flour, baking powder and salt in a food processor fitted with the metal chopping blade by snapping the motor on and off quickly 5 times. Add the shortening to the work bowl, distributing it evenly over the surface of the dry ingredients, then cut in, using three or four 3-second churnings of the motor. When it is of the proper consistency, the flour-fat mixture will resemble raw oatmeal. With the work bowl uncovered, pour in the milk, again distributing uniformly over the work-bowl contents. Re-cover work bowl, snap motor on and run exactly 3 seconds—no longer.

Turn the biscuit dough onto a lightly floured pastry cloth and, with your hands, shape quickly into a flat round. Now, using a lightly floured, stockinette-covered rolling pin, roll the dough ½ inch thick. Cut with a floured 2½-inch biscuit cutter. Space the biscuits 2 inches apart on an ungreased baking sheet and bake, uncovered, for about 15 minutes in a very hot oven (450° F.), or until lightly browned. Split and butter while hot, then enjoy.

Sour Cream Banana-Walnut Bread

Makes one 9x5x3-inch loaf

If you intend to make fruit-nut breads in your processor, you will have to alter the sequence and method of mixing somewhat to compensate for the machine's powerful action and the work bowl's small capacity. In this recipe, for example, the nuts are chopped at the outset, the butter, sugar and banana are creamed with the flavorings, the eggs are mixed in, and then, finally, the flour and sour cream. (Normally the bananas and seasonings would go in toward the end.) Quick breads such as this one are apt to be critical—meaning that a slight alteration here or there can produce a failure. The danger with processor-mixing these breads is *overmixing*, particularly after the eggs and flour have been added, which will produce a tough, tunnel-riddled loaf. I don't recommend *carte blanche* use of the processor for making quick breads; as a matter of fact, for most of them, I find the electric mixer a better choice. With this particular bread, however, there are adequate reasons to use the processor—nuts must be chopped, a banana mashed and creamed with the butter, sugar and flavorings.

> 1½ cups walnut meats
> ½ cup butter, at room temperature
> 1 cup firmly packed light brown sugar
> 1 large ripe banana, peeled and cut into 1-inch chunks
> ½ teaspoon vanilla
> Pinch of ground cinnamon
> Pinch of ground nutmeg
> Pinch of ground cardamom
> 2 large eggs
> 2 cups sifted all-purpose flour
> 1 teaspoon baking powder
> 1 teaspoon baking soda
> ½ cup sour cream

In a food processor fitted with the metal chopping blade, chop the walnuts moderately fine using 5 or 6 pulses or on-offs of the motor; empty onto a piece of wax paper and set aside. Cream the butter and sugar in the processor by letting the motor run nonstop for 30 seconds; scrape down the sides of the work bowl and churn 30 seconds longer. Add the banana, vanilla, cinnamon, nutmeg and cardamom, and cream into the mixture, using two 30-second churnings of the motor (scrape down the bowl between the two). Now add the eggs and incorporate by snapping the motor on and off twice—quickly.

Sift the flour with the baking powder and soda, then spoon about one third of the flour mixture into the work bowl, distributing it evenly; snap the motor on and off 3 times. (The flour will not be fully incorporated—no matter, it *will* be by the time you've added the remaining ingredients. What's critical at this point is not to overbeat the batter.) Add half of the sour cream and mix in with 2 on-offs of the motor, add another one third of the flour and mix in with 3 on-offs of the motor, then blend in the remaining sour cream with 2 on-offs of the motor. Sprinkle the remaining flour into the work bowl and snap the motor on and off quickly. Scrape down the sides of the work bowl, then switch the motor on and off twice again.

Finally, sprinkle the chopped walnuts over the batter and, with the plastic spatula, push them down into it with a gentle folding motion (work carefully because the razor-sharp chopping blade is down there in the batter). Re-cover work bowl, and snap the motor on and off 2 times, just enough to mix the walnuts in.

Pour the batter into a well-greased and -floured 9x5x3-inch loaf pan and bake, uncovered, in a moderate oven (350° F.) for about 45 minutes, or until loaf has pulled from sides of the pan and the top is springy to the touch. Remove loaf from the oven and cool upright in its pan on a wire rack for 10 minutes. Loosen loaf from pan with a thin-bladed spatula, then turn out onto a wire rack and cool to room temperature before slicing.

Fresh Hazelnut Bread
Makes one 9x5x3-inch loaf

For this nut bread (and the Butternut Squash Bread that follows), I have adopted the muffin method of mixing (combined liquids briskly tossed with the combined dry ingredients), a technique that works well when processor-mixing quick breads because there is little danger of overmixing. This particular bread is feathery of crumb, not very sweet—a perfect tea bread. Spread it with softened *chèvre*, cream cheese or unsweetened butter. Or, if you prefer, serve absolutely plain.

1 cup fresh unblanched hazelnuts or filberts
2 cups sifted all-purpose flour
½ cup unsifted whole-wheat flour
½ cup firmly packed light brown sugar
1½ teaspoons baking powder
1 teaspoon baking soda
¾ teaspoon salt
½ teaspoon ground mace
⅓ cup melted butter
1 cup cold buttermilk
1 large egg, lightly beaten

Spread the hazelnuts out on a pie plate, set uncovered in a slow oven (300° F.) and toast 40 to 45 minutes until the skins crackle and nuts smell irresistible. Remove from the oven, then "skin" the nuts by bundling a few of them at a time in a small terry towel and rubbing vigorously. Repeat until all nuts have been "skinned." Inevitably, some bits of skin will cling to the nuts—but no harm done. The processor will pulverize the skin in short order. Dump the nuts into the work bowl of a processor fitted with the metal chopping blade and buzz 15 seconds nonstop; tap the nuts out onto a piece of wax paper and reserve.

To the processor work bowl (still fitted with the metal chopping blade), add the all-purpose and whole-wheat flours, the brown sugar (crumble it into the work bowl), the baking powder, soda, salt and mace. In a 2-cup measuring cup, whisk the butter briskly with the buttermilk and egg until reasonably smooth; set aside for the moment. Combine the dry ingredients in the processor with three or four 3-second churnings of the motor, scraping the work bowl sides down between each. Dump in the reserved hazelnuts and "dredge" well by pulsing or snapping the processor motor on and off 5 or 6 times.

Now open the processor work bowl and pour the combined liquids evenly over the surface of the dry ingredients. Close the work bowl and mix by pulsing or snapping the motor on and off 4 or 5 times—just until dry ingredients are moistened, no longer. The dough will be quite lumpy and a few dabs of the dry ingredients may even be visible, but that is as it should be. Further mixing at this point will toughen the bread.

Spoon the dough into a well-buttered 9x5x3-inch loaf pan, smooth the surface, then bake in a moderately hot oven (375° F.) for 40 to 45 minutes, or until nicely browned and the loaf sounds hollow when thumped with your fingers.

Remove the bread from the oven and cool upright in the pan on a wire rack 10 minutes. Loosen the bread around the edges with a thin-bladed knife or spatula and turn out on the rack to cool. Do not attempt to slice the bread until after it has reached room temperature—it's so tender and short it may crumble if sliced hot.

Butternut Squash Bread with Pecans
Makes one 9x5x3-inch loaf

1 cup pecan halves
½ pound butternut squash, seeded, peeled and cut into columns the height and width of the processor feed tube
1 cup granulated sugar
1 strip orange rind (orange part only and about ½ inch wide and 2 inches long)
½ cup firmly packed light brown sugar
3 cups sifted all-purpose flour
2 teaspoons baking powder
1 teaspoon baking soda
½ teaspoon ground cinnamon
½ teaspoon ground ginger
¼ teaspoon ground nutmeg
¾ cup peanut or vegetable oil
¼ cup cold milk
3 large eggs
1 teaspoon vanilla

Dump the pecans into a food processor work bowl fitted with the metal chopping blade and chop moderately coarse by snapping the motor on and off or pulsing 3 or 4 times; tap the nuts out onto a piece of wax paper and reserve.

Remove the metal chopping blade and slip the medium-shredding disc into place. Now shred the squash by pushing the columns down the feed tube with moderate pressure. When all of the squash has been shredded, measure out and reserve 2 cups of it (measure lightly packed) for the bread. Save any remaining shredded squash to add to a soup or stew or stir-fried skillet dish. Quickly rinse and dry the processor work bowl and lid; re-equip with the metal chopping blade.

Add the granulated sugar and orange rind to the work bowl and "grate" the rind by letting the motor run nonstop for 10 seconds. Inspect the texture of the rind and if it is not as finely grated as you would like, snap the motor on for 5 seconds, then off, then on for another 5 seconds, then off.

Crumble the brown sugar into the work bowl, add the flour, baking powder, soda, cinnamon, ginger and nutmeg. In a 2-cup measuring cup, whisk the oil, milk, eggs and vanilla until reasonably smooth; set aside for the moment. Now combine the dry ingredients in the work bowl using four or five 5-second churnings of the motor, and scraping the work-bowl sides down and the mixture up from the bottom of the work bowl between each churning. You are dealing here with a lot of combined dry ingredients and it's critical that they be thoroughly combined before any liquids are added. Dump in the reserved pecans and "dredge" well by pulsing or snapping the motor on and off 5 or 6 times.

Now open the processor work bowl and spoon the reserved shredded squash evenly over the top of the combined dry ingredients; pour the combined liquids evenly over all, then with a rubber spatula, push the liquids down the sides of the work bowl at regular intervals—every 2 or 3 inches.

Close the work bowl and mix by pulsing or snapping the motor on and off 4 or 5 times. The mixture will be very thick (about like cookie dough), lumpy, and a few clumps of dry ingredients may be clearly visible. That's just as it should be and additional mixing at this stage will mean a tough bread.

Spoon the dough into a well-greased and -floured 9x5x3-inch loaf pan, smooth the surface, then bake in a moderate oven (350° F.) for about 1 hour, or until the loaf is nicely browned and feels springy to the touch.

Remove the bread from the oven and cool upright in the pan on a wire rack 10 minutes. Loosen the bread around the edges with a thin-bladed knife or spatula and turn out on the rack to cool. Do not slice the bread until after it has reached room temperature, otherwise it may crumble as you cut it.

Dill and Chestnut Bread
Makes one 9x5x3-inch loaf

Here's another quick bread that can be successfully mixed by processor. Be sure that the dill you select is young and tender but full of flavor. Be sure, too, that you dry it thoroughly before you processor-mince it, otherwise it will churn to paste and dye the bread an unappetizing green.

30 fragrant young stalks of dill (6 to 8 inches in length)
3 cups sifted all-purpose flour
½ cup unsifted chestnut flour (available in specialty food shops)
⅓ cup firmly packed light brown sugar
3 teaspoons baking powder
½ teaspoon salt
¼ teaspoon freshly ground black pepper
¼ teaspoon freshly grated nutmeg
1½ cups milk
½ cup melted unsalted butter
2 large eggs

Remove the feathery fronds of dill from the stalks, rinse well in cool water, then rub very dry between several sheets of paper toweling. Dump the dill fronds into a food processor work bowl fitted with the metal chopping blade and mince very fine by letting the motor run nonstop 10 seconds; tap the dill out onto a piece of wax paper and reserve.

With paper toweling, wipe the processor work bowl, lid and blade very dry. Place the all-purpose and chestnut flours in the work bowl, again fitted with the metal chopping blade, crumble in the brown sugar, then add the baking powder, salt, pepper and nutmeg. In a 1-quart measuring cup, briskly whisk the milk, melted butter and eggs until reasonably smooth; set aside. Now combine the dry ingredients in the work bowl using four or five 5-second churnings of the motor, and scraping the work-bowl sides down and the mixture up from the bottom of the work bowl between each churning. You are dealing here with a hefty amount of dry ingredients and it is essential that they be mixed thoroughly before any liquid is added. Dump in the reserved minced dill and mix in well using five or six 3-second buzzings of the motor.

Open the processor work bowl and pour the combined liquids evenly over the surface of the combined dry ingredients, then with a rubber spatula, push the liquids down the sides of the work bowl at regular intervals—every 2 or 3 inches.

Close the work bowl and mix by pulsing or snapping the motor on and off 4 or 5 times. The mixture will be quite thick and lumpy, but that's normal. Do not mix the bread further at this point even though a few small clumps of dry ingredients may be visible because you will toughen the bread.

Spoon the dough into a well-buttered 9x5x3-inch loaf pan, smooth the surface, then bake in a moderately hot oven (375° F.) for 40 to 45 minutes, or until nicely browned and the loaf feels firm to the touch.

Remove the bread from the oven and cool upright in the pan on a wire rack 10 minutes. Loosen the bread around the edges with a thin-bladed knife or spatula and turn out on the wire rack to cool. Do not slice the bread until after it has reached room temperature or it may crumble as you cut it.

Pastries, Desserts
& Confections

Pâte à Chou

Makes enough for 1 dozen éclairs or cream puffs or about 4½ dozen profiteroles

This is the egg-rich French pastry of cream puffs, *profiteroles* and *éclairs*, and it can, I am delighted to say, be whirled up in the food processor in about two minutes. The processor pastry is slightly thinner than that beaten by hand, but it puffs majestically in the oven. Do not make this recipe on a rainy or humid day, because the baked puffs will quickly go limp and soggy.

1 cup water
½ cup (1 stick) unsalted butter
¼ teaspoon salt
1 cup sifted all-purpose flour
4 eggs

In a small, heavy saucepan bring the water, butter and salt to a boil over high heat. Meanwhile, place the flour in the work bowl of a food processor fitted with the metal chopping blade. With the motor running, carefully pour the boiling mixture down the feed tube of the processor in a moderately slow stream. Let the motor run nonstop for 40 seconds after all of the mixture has been incorporated. The pastry at this point will be glistening, thick and translucent. Now add the eggs, one at a time: Snap the motor on, crack an egg, then let the white yolk slide down the feed tube into the spinning pastry. Run the motor nonstop for 10 seconds after each egg has been added, then uncover work bowl and scrape down the sides with the plastic spatula before proceeding.

For cream puffs: Drop the pastry by rounded tablespoonsful onto ungreased baking sheets, spacing the cream puffs about 3 inches apart. Bake in a hot oven (400° F.) for 40 to 45 minutes, or until cream puffs are richly browned and sound hollow when tapped with your fingers. Transfer to wire racks, cool to room temperature, then slice about ¾ inch off the tops of the cream puffs and scoop out and discard any doughy bits inside. Fill with your favorite cream or custard filling (or use Cream Puff Filling included elsewhere in this book; see Index for recipe page number). Dust with confectioners' sugar and serve.

To make éclairs: Spoon the pastry into a large pastry bag fitted with a large plain tip, then press the pastry onto ungreased baking sheets into mounds about 4 inches long, 1½ inches wide and 1 inch high, spacing the *éclairs* at least 2 inches apart. Bake in a hot oven (400° F.) for 35 to 40 minutes, or until *éclairs* are a rich nut brown and sound hollow when tapped. Remove from oven and transfer at once to wire racks to cool. Split each *éclair* lengthwise, scoop out any doughy portions inside, then fill with your favorite cream or custard filling and glaze with chocolate. (Use the recipes for Cream Puff Filling and Chocolate Glaze included elsewhere in this book; see Index for recipe page numbers.)

To make profiteroles: Spoon the *chou* pastry into a large pastry bag fitted with a medium-size plain tip, then press the pastry onto ungreased baking sheets into little mounds about 1 inch in diameter and 1 inch high (space the mounds about 2 inches apart). Bake in a hot oven (400° F.) for 20 to 25 minutes, or until puffs are nicely browned and sound hollow when tapped. Remove from oven and transfer at once to wire racks to cool. To fill, make a tiny slit in the side of each *profiterole*. Fill a large pastry bag fitted with a medium-size plain tip with your favorite filling, then squirt into each *profiterole;* dust with confectioners' sugar. Or, for *Profiteroles au Chocolat*, fill with Chocolate Filling (see Index for recipe page number) and sauce with your favorite chocolate syrup.

Sonhos
(Portuguese Dreams)

Makes about 2½ dozen

Once you taste these deep-fried puffs, you'll understand why the Portuguese call them "dreams." *Sonhos* are popular two ways—drizzled with a thin sugar syrup (often flavored with raspberry, strawberry, apricot or orange) or dusted lavishly with cinnamon sugar.

½ cup unsalted butter
1 tablespoon sugar
¼ teaspoon salt
1 cup water
1 cup sifted all-purpose flour
4 eggs
Vegetable oil or shortening for deep-fat frying (about 2 quarts oil or 2 pounds shortening)
½ cup sugar blended with 1 teaspoon ground cinnamon (cinnamon sugar)

In a small, heavy saucepan, bring the butter, sugar, salt and water to a boil over high heat. Meanwhile, scatter flour over the bottom of a processor work bowl fitted with the metal chopping blade. With the motor running, carefully pour the boiling mixture down the processor feed tube in a moderate stream, then run the motor for 40 seconds nonstop. Now add the eggs, one at a time—snap the motor on, crack an egg, then let the white and yolk slide down the feed tube into the whirling mixture. Run the motor for 10 seconds after each egg has been added, then uncover the work bowl and scrape down the sides with the plastic spatula before proceeding.

Pour enough vegetable oil or melt enough vegetable shortening in a deep-fat fryer to measure about 2 inches deep. Insert a deep-fat thermometer and heat to 370° F. Drop the *sonhos* into the hot fat by the rounded tablespoonful and fry, 3 to 4 at a time, just until puffed and golden-brown on all sides—2 to 3 minutes. Keep the temperature of the fat as nearly as possible at 370° F. by raising and lowering burner heat as needed. Drain the fried *sonhos* on several thicknesses of paper toweling and sprinkle with cinnamon sugar while hot.

Baklava
Makes 12 to 15 servings

This sinfully rich Greek and Middle Eastern pastry is astonishingly easy to make if you have a processor to grind up the walnut filling and can rely on the fresh or frozen *filo* pastry now available in many better groceries across the country. The most tedious part of it is layering the *filo* in the baking pan and brushing each wispy layer with melted butter.

> *4 cups shelled walnuts*
> *1 cup sugar*
> *½ teaspoon ground cinnamon*
> *1 pound* filo *pastry (fresh, or frozen and thawed)*
> *2 cups (1 pound) melted butter*

SYRUP:

> *¾ cup water*
> *1½ cups sugar*
> *1 cinnamon stick*
> *2 strips lemon peel (each measuring about 2 inches long and ½ inch wide)*

Place 2 cups of the walnuts in a food processor fitted with the metal chopping blade and grind very fine by letting the motor run nonstop for 15 seconds; empty into a mixing bowl. Grind the remaining nuts the same way and add to bowl along with sugar and ground cinnamon. Stir well to mix.

Now begin layering the *filo* pastry in a well-buttered 13x9x2-inch baking pan. Don't be intimidated by the fragile look of the *filo* leaves; they have the sheerness of a fine silk scarf, but they are sturdier than you think. In a 1-pound package you will get about 22 leaves, each folded in half and measuring 18x13 inches when unfolded. The easiest way to arrange these in the pan is to lay a folded leaf in the pan lengthwise—both the pastry and the pan are 13 inches long, so it's a perfect fit. Carefully unfold the top layer (just as you would turn the page of a book) and lop over the pan rim. Brush the bottom layer well with melted butter, refold the top layer so that it lies smoothly over the bottom one and brush with melted butter also. Continue building up layers in this fashion, brushing each generously with melted butter, until you have used 6 folded leaves of *filo.* Now spread one third of the walnut mixture on top, packing it down gently but firmly with the back of a spoon. Layer 6 more folded leaves of *filo* on top, again brushing each with melted butter. Spread with one half of the remaining walnut mixture, packing it down firmly, then top with 6 more folded leaves of *filo*, brushing them with the melted butter as you go. Spread with the last of the walnut mixture, then layer the remaining *filo* leaves on top, again brushing each generously with melted butter—and that includes the final layer, too.

Bake, uncovered, in a moderately slow oven (325° F.) for 45 to 50 minutes, or until a rich golden brown. Meanwhile, prepare the syrup: Simmer all ingredients slowly in an uncovered saucepan for about 40 to 45 minutes. Remove from the heat and discard the cinnamon stick and lemon peel.

After the *baklava* comes from the oven, cool for 10 minutes, then pour the syrup evenly over all. Let cool 30 minutes, then cut into squares or diamonds—not too large because this *baklava* is far richer than that served in most Middle Eastern restaurants; there's been no stinting on walnuts or butter or pastry. Let the *baklava* stand 4 to 6 hours before serving, so that all of the syrup is absorbed by the pastry and filling.

Swedish Almond Tarts
Makes about 1 dozen

Every step of this recipe can be done in the food processor—the grinding of the almonds, the creaming of the butter and sugar, the addition of the egg white, and finally, the kneading in of the flour and ground almonds. What could be easier?

1 cup whole blanched almonds
½ cup (1 stick) refrigerator-cold unsalted butter
½ cup sugar
1 egg white
½ teaspoon vanilla
½ teaspoon almond extract
1½ cups sifted all-purpose flour

In a food processor fitted with the metal chopping blade, grind the almonds until very fine and almost paste-like by letting the motor run nonstop for 1 minute. Scrape nuts onto a piece of wax paper and set aside. Add butter and sugar to processor work bowl (no need to wash it or the metal chopping blade) and beat until smooth and creamy, using three 20-second bursts of speed. You'll notice that the action of the blade whirls the mixture up on the sides of the work bowl, so scrape down with the plastic spatula after each 20-second churning. Add the egg white, vanilla and almond extract and mix in by snapping the motor on and off 4 times. Now add the flour, one third of the total amount at a time, and incorporate each batch by using 3 quick bursts of speed. Uncover work bowl after all flour has been beaten, scrape down the sides, add the almonds, re-cover and let the motor run nonstop for 10 seconds. Uncover work bowl, once again scrape down the sides, then let the motor run 2 or 3 seconds longer, or until the dough forms a ball that rides up on the blade. The mixture is now ready to shape.

Pinch off bits of dough (about equal to a rounded tablespoonful) and press into ungreased fluted tart tins measuring about 2½ inches in diameter and 1 inch deep. Fill the tart tins to within about ¼ inch of the tops, pressing the dough firmly into the contours of the tins. The dough is sticky, but if you moisten your hands with cool water, you'll find it easy to work with. NOTE: *If you do not have tart tins and do not want to invest in them, simply use small muffin tins, packing about 1 inch of the dough into the bottom of each cup.*

Place the filled tart tins on a baking sheet and set on the middle rack of a slow oven (300° F.). Bake, uncovered, for 40 minutes, or until tarts are firm and faintly tan. Remove from oven and cool to room temperature. To loosen the tarts from the tins, use a toothpick or a poultry pin—insert it down around the fluted edge of the tin and the almond tart will ease right out.

Tarte aux Pommes à la Normande
(Norman Apple Tart)

Makes 8 servings

You may wonder if a food processor is much help with this recipe since you must peel, quarter and core the apples by hand. Isn't it simpler just to slice them by hand, too? Not if you slice the apples the Norman way, which is to say in perfect, tissue-thin crescents. This is an open-face pie with apple slices spiraling across the surface; looks are important, and the food processor can thin-slice the apples far faster and more uniformly than you can. How you stack the apple quarters in the feed tube is the secret. I lay them in sideways, cut-sides down, with the curves of the apple quarters facing the front of the tube. You will only be able to fit four quarters into the feed tube at one time. Don't try to force more in—you will bruise the apples and push them out of alignment. And don't try to feed the apples into the tube with the motor turned on. That would be quicker, but the apple slices would be far from perfect. NOTE: *You will need apples that hold their shape as they bake. The best varieties, I've found, are Golden Delicious, Rome Beauty, York Imperial or the tarter, crisper McIntosh.*

7 medium-size apples, quartered, cored and peeled
⅓ cup sugar
Finely grated rind of 1 lemon
¼ teaspoon salt
¼ teaspoon ground cinnamon
Pinch of ground mace or nutmeg

CRUST:

One 9-inch partially baked pie shell made with Pâte Sablée *(see Index for recipe page number)*

CUSTARD GLAZE:

2 large eggs
2 tablespoons flour
¼ cup sugar
⅓ cup light cream
2 tablespoons Calvados or fine brandy

In the feed tube of a food processor fitted with the slicing disc, lay 4 apple quarters on their sides with the cut surfaces down. Turn motor on or depress the Pulse button and push apple quarters through, using gentle pressure on the pusher. Repeat until work bowl fills up—after about half of the apples have been sliced. Empty into a large mixing bowl. Thin-slice the remaining apples the same way and add to bowl.

In a second mixing bowl, combine the sugar, lemon rind, salt, cinnamon and mace, rubbing mixture with your fingers so that ingredients are perfectly blended. Now begin filling the crust by starting at the center and laying apple slices slightly overlapping in a spiral pattern. When you have covered the bottom of the crust, sprinkle liberally with the sugar mixture. Continue building up spiral layers of apples, sprinkling with the sugar mixture as you go. Inevitably, there will be a few less-than-perfect apple slices; use these in the lower layers where they will not show. Arrange the top layer as artfully as possible and sprinkle well with the sugar mixture.

Bake, uncovered, in a moderate oven (350° F.) for 20 minutes. Meanwhile, remove slicing disc from the food processor and slip the metal chopping blade into place (no need to wash out the work bowl). Add all custard glaze ingredients and buzz quickly once or twice to blend. When pie has baked 20 minutes, remove from oven and drizzle the glaze slowly over the surface, letting it seep down between the apples. Return pie to the oven (still set at 350° F.) and bake, uncovered, for 30 to 35 minutes longer, or until apples have taken on a nice amber color. Remove the pie from the oven and cool to room temperature before cutting.

Fresh Chopped-Apple Pie with Butter-Crumb Topping
Makes one 9-inch pie

The beauty of this pie is that you don't have to peel the apples. Simply wash and dry them well, then quarter, core, cut into chunks and drop into the processor. It chops them up beautifully, skin and all. The skins, of course, give the pie a slight crunch as well as a fresh orchard flavor.

FILLING:

*6 large McIntosh or other fairly tart apples, washed, dried,
    quartered, cored and cut into 1-inch chunks*
Juice of 1 lemon
⅔ cup firmly packed light brown sugar
¼ cup unsifted all-purpose flour
¼ teaspoon ground cinnamon
Pinch of ground nutmeg or mace
Pinch of salt
2 tablespoons melted butter

TOPPING:

⅔ cup firmly packed light brown sugar
⅔ cup unsifted all-purpose flour
¼ cup refrigerator-cold butter, cut into small cubes
Pinch of ground cardamom
Pinch of salt

PIE CRUST:

One 9-inch unbaked pie shell

Place one third of the apple chunks in a food processor equipped with the metal chopping blade and chop moderately coarsely, using 3 pulses or on-offs of the motor. Uncover the work bowl, scrape down the sides with a rubber spatula, then re-cover and snap the motor on and off 3 or 4 more times. Empty chopped apples into a large bowl. Chop the remaining apples the same way in two batches and add to bowl. Mix in all remaining filling ingredients and let stand for the time being.

Quickly wash and dry the processor work bowl and chopping blade; reassemble. Place all topping ingredients in the work bowl in the order listed, then reduce to crumbs, using 5 or 6 pulses or on-offs of the motor.

Pour the chopped apple filling into the unbaked pie shell, then spread the crumb mixture evenly on top so that no apples show. Bake, uncovered, in a hot oven (400° F.) for 10 minutes, lower heat to moderately hot (375° F.), and bake the pie for 30 to 35 minutes longer, or until bubbling and lightly browned. Cool to room temperature before cutting.

Open-Face Sliced-Lemon Pie
Makes one 9-inch pie

This is an extraordinary pie made with thinly sliced whole lemons, and it is not unlike the ones the Shaker women used to bake. In fact, I tasted a pie much like this one at Shakertown at Pleasant Hill in Kentucky and determined then to try a similar one, using the processor to slice the lemons. It works beautifully, but do not push the lemons through the feed tube; let the action of the machine pull them through instead. That way you'll get the thinnest possible slices. If the slices are too thick, the bitter rind flavor will predominate. Properly prepared, the pie filling is rather like lemon marmalade—very sweet, but plenty tart, too.

3 medium-size seedless lemons, washed and halved lengthwise
3 cups sugar
5 eggs, lightly beaten
2 tablespoons melted butter
One 9-inch unbaked pie shell

Thin-slice the lemon halves, one at a time, in a food processor fitted with the slicing disc (the thin-slicing disc, if you have one). Do not push the lemons down the feed tube; let the action of the slicing disc pull them through so that the slices are tissue-thin. Dump all lemon slices into a large bowl. Add all the sugar, stir lightly, then let stand at room temperature for 3 hours, stirring the mixture occasionally so that all sugar dissolves. Combine the eggs and the butter, pour over the lemons, then fold in thoroughly, using an over-and-over motion. Pour into the pie shell and bake, uncovered, in a moderately slow oven (325° F.) for 1 hour, or until puffy and golden brown. Cool to room temperature before cutting with a very sharp knife.

Apricot-Lemon Mousse Pie
Makes one 10-inch open-face pie

2 cups dried apricots
1¼ cups sugar
2½ cups cold water
Juice of 2 lemons
1 cinnamon stick
1 envelope plain gelatin
2 eggs, separated
1 cup refrigerator-cold heavy cream
One 10-inch baked pie shell

1½ cups heavy cream beaten to soft peaks with 2 tablespoons sugar

Place the apricots, sugar, 1 cup of the water, the lemon juice and the cinnamon stick in a large, heavy saucepan, bring to a simmer, adjust heat so that liquid barely ripples, cover and cook for 1 hour. Set off the heat and cool 20 minutes. Meanwhile, pour the remaining 1½ cups water into a small saucepan and sprinkle in the gelatin. Set over moderate heat and cook, stirring, until gelatin dissolves—3 to 5 minutes. Remove from heat and cool also.

Remove the cinnamon stick from the apricots, then pour them and their cooking liquid into a food processor fitted with the metal chopping blade; turn the motor on and run 15 seconds nonstop until apricots are reduced to purée. Empty into a large mixing bowl and blend in the cooled gelatin and egg yolks. Quickly wash and dry both the processor work bowl and chopping blade.

In a separate bowl, hand-beat the egg whites to soft peaks and fold into the apricot mixture. Now pour the cream into the processor and whip, using about three 10-second churnings of the motor. Inspect the cream closely after each churning, and the minute it mounds softly, dump it into the apricot mixture; fold in gently but thoroughly until no streaks of white or orange remain. Pour into the baked pie shell, swirling the mixture up on top, then chill 4 to 5 hours until firm.

Just before serving, top, if you like, with whipped cream, swirling it into peaks and valleys and covering the apricot filling completely. NOTE: *For greater volume, whip the cream by hand. The processor will softly whip cream, but its swift action releases much of the beaten-in air needed for volume.*

Almond-Cheese Tart
Makes about 8 servings

In Sintra, Portugal, they make a splendid cheese tart that has a ground almond crust. The filling contains ground almonds, too, so that crust and filling seem to merge, one into the other. Though this recipe isn't the original, it comes very close to it. Both the crust and the filling can be wholly prepared in the processor.

ALMOND CRUST:

> 1 cup whole blanched almonds
> ½ cup butter
> ⅔ cup sugar
> 1 teaspoon vanilla
> ½ teaspoon almond extract
> 1 egg white
> 1½ cups sifted all-purpose flour

CHEESE FILLING:

> 1 package (8 ounces) cream cheese, at room temperature
> 1 cup cream-style cottage cheese
> ½ cup sugar
> 1 teaspoon vanilla
> ¼ teaspoon almond extract
> ½ cup of the raw almond-crust mixture
> ¼ cup heavy cream
> 2 eggs
> 1 egg yolk

In a food processor fitted with the metal chopping blade, grind the almonds until quite fine and almost paste-like by letting the motor run nonstop for 1 minute. Scrape nuts onto a piece of wax paper and set aside. Add butter, sugar, vanilla and almond extract to processor work bowl and beat until smooth and light, using three 20-second bursts of speed. The action of the blade throws the mixture against the sides of the work bowl, so scrape it down with the plastic spatula after each 20-second churning. Add the egg white and beat in by pulsing or snapping the motor on and off 4 times quickly. Now add the flour, ½ cup at a time, and incorporate each batch with a couple of pulses or fast on-offs of the motor. Uncover work bowl after all flour has been mixed in, scrape down the sides, add ground almonds and "knead in" by letting the motor run nonstop for 10 seconds.

Measure out and reserve ½ cup of this mixture to use in the filling. Pat the rest firmly into the bottom and up the sides of an ungreased 9-inch springform pan, moistening hands as needed to facilitate shaping the crust (the mixture is quite sticky). Bake the crust, uncovered, in a slow oven (300° F.) for 25 minutes. Remove from oven and cool to room temperature.

For the filling: In the processor work bowl, still fitted with the metal chopping blade (no need to wash it or the bowl), blend together the cream cheese, cottage cheese, sugar, vanilla and almond extract by running the motor nonstop for 10 seconds; scrape down the work bowl and blend 5 seconds longer. Add the almond-crust mixture and heavy cream and blend for 5 seconds. Add the eggs and egg yolk and incorporate, using 4 pulses or quick on-offs of the motor. Scrape down the work bowl (also run spatula along the bottom and around the blade), re-cover and buzz 1 second longer.

Pour the filling into the cooled crust and bake, uncovered, in a moderately hot oven (375° F.) for 30 minutes. Remove the tart from the oven and cool to room temperature before cutting.

Ginger Root Mousse
Makes 6 servings

The fragrance and bite of fresh ginger root captured in a cool mousse that can be totally prepared by processor—right down to the beating of the egg whites! What makes it possible to beat the egg whites to surprising volume and stability is the drizzling of a boiling lemon syrup down the feed tube into the whirling meringue, which effectively "cooks" or "sets" it. This is a soft, moist meringue, not stiff enough or dry enough to bake, but perfect to lighten cold mousses and soufflés.

2 (1½-inch) cubes of fresh ginger root, peeled
⅔ cup plus 2 tablespoons sugar
1 tablespoon unsalted butter
Juice of 2 large lemons
Juice of 1 medium-size orange
1 envelope plain gelatin
5 large eggs, separated
⅛ teaspoon salt
⅓ cup water
1 cup heavy cream

Equip the food processor with the metal chopping blade, snap the motor on and drop the ginger root down the feed tube into the spinning blade; buzz 5 seconds nonstop. Scrape the work bowl down, sprinkle the 2 tablespoons sugar over the ginger root, then snap the motor on and buzz 5 seconds nonstop (the sugar's abrasiveness will help reduce the ginger root to fine particles). Scrape the work-bowl sides down once again, then buzz nonstop another 5 seconds. Inspect the texture of the ginger—it should be quite fine; if not, scrape the work bowl down again, then pulse or snap the motor on and off quickly 4 or 5 times.

Melt the butter in a small heavy skillet over low heat; scrape in the ginger-sugar mixture; raise heat to moderate and stir-fry 1 to 2 minutes; turn heat to its lowest point and allow ginger mixture to mellow 1 to 2 minutes; set off the heat and reserve. Quickly wash and dry the processor work bowl and blade and reassemble.

Measure out and reserve 2 tablespoons of the lemon juice; place the remaining lemon juice and the orange juice in a small heavy saucepan (preferably not aluminum, which might make the mousse taste metallic). Sprinkle the gelatin over the combined juices and let stand 5 minutes. Now add ⅓ cup of the remaining sugar, set over moderately low heat and cook and stir about 3 minutes until both the gelatin and sugar are dissolved.

Meanwhile, place the egg whites in the processor work bowl and sprinkle the salt evenly over the surface. Lightly whisk the yolks, beat a little of the hot gelatin mixture into them, then stir back into the remaining gelatin mixture, and cook and stir over low heat 3 to 4 minutes until the mixture has the consistency of custard and no raw egg flavor remains. Mix in the reserved ginger mixture, transfer to a medium-size mixing bowl and set in an ice bath. Whisk or stir frequently until mixture begins to thicken.

At the same time, place the remaining ⅓ cup sugar, the reserved 2 tablespoons of lemon juice and the water in a small heavy saucepan (again not aluminum) and set over moderately low heat; boil gently 5 minutes, turn heat to its lowest point and keep the syrup hot.

When the gelatin mixture is thick and syrupy enough to mound on a spoon (it should take about 15 minutes for the mixture to cool sufficiently to mound), begin processor-beating the egg whites. First pulse or snap the machine on and off 4 or 5 times to incorporate the salt (this also helps to stabilize the egg whites as you beat them). With the motor running, drizzle about one fourth of the boiling syrup down the feed tube; beat the whites 5 seconds nonstop. Scrape the work-bowl sides down; snap the motor on and drizzle one third of the remaining syrup down the feed tube; buzz 5 seconds nonstop. Now drizzle the remaining syrup down the feed tube very slowly with the blade spinning; buzz 10 seconds nonstop. You should have a soft and billowing meringue.

Whisk about one fourth of the meringue into the gelatin mixture—this is to lighten it and facilitate folding in the remaining meringue. Dump the balance of the meringue on top, scraping the work bowl and blade very dry. Using a light touch, fold the meringue into the gelatin mixture until no streaks of white or yellow remain.

Reassemble the work bowl and metal chopping blade (no need to wash either). Pour the cream into the work bowl and whip to soft peaks using two 10-second churnings of the motor (scrape the work-bowl sides down between churnings).

Fold the whipped cream into the gelatin mixture, then continue to chill, stirring frequently, in the ice bath until the mixture is about the consistency of angel-cake batter.

Cover with plastic food wrap and chill several hours until softly set. To serve, spoon into stemmed goblets and top each portion with a dollop of whipped cream and a scattering of finely minced candied ginger, if you like.

Fresh Pear Mousse
Makes about 8 servings

So many of the world's great recipes are the result of happy accidents or of making do with what food there is on hand. I count this pear mousse in that category, for it evolved from a last-ditch attempt to salvage fresh pears that were on the verge of going bad. I'd bought them for an open-face pear pie, but as so often happens, time got away from me and before I knew it, they had ripened almost beyond the point of no return. Certainly, they were too soft to slice for pie. So, with the help of the food processor, I whirred them into this fresh-pear mousse, which, I must say, is as lovely and delicate as any mousse I've eaten.

1 cup sugar
2 envelopes plain gelatin
¼ teaspoon salt
3 large eggs, separated

2 egg whites
1½ cups milk
6 large very ripe pears (I used Bartletts), peeled, cored and
   quartered
Juice of ½ lemon
1 tablespoon Poire William (pear eau de vie) or Cointreau
1 cup refrigerator-cold heavy cream

In the top of a double boiler, blend ¾ cup of the sugar with the gelatin and salt, smoothing out any lumps with a wooden spoon. Blend in the 3 egg yolks. Place the 5 egg whites in a large mixing bowl and set aside for the time being. Mix the milk into the gelatin mixture, set over simmering water and cook and stir for 5 to 8 minutes, or until gelatin and sugar are both dissolved and mixture lightly coats a metal spoon with a custard-like film. Remove from heat and cool. Stir from time to time to prevent a "skin" from forming on the surface of the sauce.

Halve the pear quarters crosswise and place half of them in a food processor fitted with the metal chopping blade. Drizzle half of the lemon juice over all. Purée the pears by using three or four 5-second churnings of the motor. Transfer to a large bowl and set aside. Now purée the remaining pears the same way, drizzling first with lemon juice, and add to bowl. Stir in the cooled custard sauce and the Poire William or Cointreau, cover with plastic food wrap and chill for about 40 minutes, or until tacky. Then whisk lightly until smooth.

With a rotary beater, beat the egg whites with 1 tablespoon of the remaining sugar to soft peaks, then continue beating, adding the remaining 3 tablespoons of sugar gradually, until the consistency of meringue. Ladle about 1 cup of the pear mixture into the whites and fold in to lighten the meringue. Then dump the meringue on top of the pear purée and let stand for the moment.

In a clean, dry work bowl fitted with the metal chopping blade (also clean and dry), whip the cream to soft peaks, using three or four 5-second churnings of the motor. Examine the consistency of the cream closely after each 5-second churning and, the minute it mounds softly, scoop on top of the meringue in the bowl. The reason you must watch the cream so carefully as it whips is that the processor action is so powerful it may create butter flakes while you look away for only an instant.

Gently but thoroughly fold the meringue and whipped cream into the pear mixture with an over-and-over motion until no streaks of pink or white remain. Cover with plastic food wrap and chill for 8 hours, or overnight. This is a soft and billowing mousse, wonderfully fresh of flavor and fragile of texture. Spoon into stemmed crystal goblets and serve.

Fresh Strawberry Mousse Ring
Makes 6 to 8 servings

2 envelopes plain gelatin
1 cup sugar
3 eggs, separated
1½ cups light cream
2 pints ripe strawberries, washed and hulled (halve any that are
  large)
Juice of ½ lemon
2 tablespoons Cointreau or Grand Marnier
1 cup refrigerator-cold heavy cream

In the top of a double boiler, blend the gelatin with ¾ cup of the sugar. Beat the egg yolks lightly with the light cream, just enough to blend. (Reserve the egg whites in a separate large bowl.) Pour the yolk mixture into the sugar and gelatin and stir well. Set over simmering water and heat and stir 5 to 8 minutes, or until mixture will coat a metal spoon with a thin custard-like film. Remove from the heat and from the double-boiler bottom; let cool while you prepare the strawberries, but do stir the mixture from time to time to prevent a "skin" from forming on the surface.

Place half of the strawberries and the lemon juice in a food processor fitted with the metal chopping blade, turn the motor on and let run nonstop for 20 seconds. Turn motor off, uncover bowl and scrape down the sides. Re-cover and buzz 20 seconds longer. Uncover and scrape down the bowl once again, then whir 20 seconds longer, or until purée is uniformly smooth. Empty into a large bowl. Purée the remaining strawberries the same way with the Cointreau; add to bowl. Blend about 1 cup of the purée into the custard mixture, then pour back into the purée and fold in thoroughly so that no streaks of red or yellow remain. Chill for about 40 minutes, or until tacky.

With a rotary beater, beat the egg whites until frothy, add 1 tablespoon of the remaining sugar and beat until billowing and soft. Continue beating, adding the remaining 3 tablespoons of sugar gradually, until the egg whites peak stiffly. Quickly whisk the gelatin mixture until light, then dump the beaten egg whites on top.

Equip the processor with a clean work bowl and metal chopping blade; pour in the heavy cream and whip to soft peaks, using three or four 5-second churnings of the motor. Watch the cream closely as it whips, and the instant it mounds softly, turn the motor off—it's very easy to overbeat the cream in the processor. Empty the cream into the bowl with the beaten whites and strawberry mixture, then fold all three together, using a gentle over-and-over motion until no streaks of red or white remain.

Pour into an oiled 6-cup ring mold, cover with plastic food wrap and chill 8 hours, or overnight, until set. To unmold, dip quickly in warm water, place a flat serving plate on top of mold, then invert quickly, giving the mold a couple of shakes to loosen the mousse. Lift the mold off.

Fill the center of the mousse with sliced fresh strawberries, sweetened to taste, and sprig with mint, lemon verbena or rose geranium.

Alsatian Apple Ice
Makes 4 to 6 servings

It was at l'Arsenal, a Strasbourg restaurant pledged to serving old Alsatian specialties, that I first sampled this ambrosial ice. What makes it special, owner Tony Schneider pointed out, is that it contains the chopped apple peel and a local apple *eau de vie*. I have taken the liberty of substituting the more readily available apple brandy of Normandy—Calvados, but plain old-fashioned applejack would work well, too. NOTE: *The ice trays you use for freezing the cubes of puréed apple should be metal, with pry-out levers. Once the apple purée is frozen, pop the cubes into a plastic bag and store in the freezer.*

> 2 pounds tart green-skinned apples (Granny Smiths are perfect), washed well
> Juice of 1 medium-size lemon
> ¼ to ⅓ cup superfine sugar (depending upon the tartness of the apples)

2 tablespoons apple cider or juice
3 tablespoons Calvados or applejack

Halve one of the apples, core, cut into slim wedges but do not peel. Drop into a processor work bowl fitted with the metal chopping bowl; add the lemon juice, sprinkling it evenly over the apple (this is to prevent the apple from turning brown), dump in the sugar, then sprinkle in the apple cider and Calvados. Snap the motor on and buzz 30 seconds nonstop; scrape the work-bowl sides down, buzz 30 seconds longer—just until the apple peel is finely chopped.

Now working with the remaining apples *one by one* (so they don't have a chance to darken), peel, core, cut in slim wedges and drop down the feed tube of the processor; pulse the machine 3 or 4 times or snap the motor on and off quickly 3 or 4 times to coat the apple with the tart processor mixture (this also prevents the apple from turning dark). Once all apples are in the work bowl, buzz 30 seconds nonstop; scrape down the work-bowl sides, buzz 30 seconds longer, or until velvety smooth.

Divide the apple mixture between two metal ice cube trays (those with pry-out levers). **TIP:** *It's easiest to fill the trays with the ice cube inserts removed, then to set these carefully into place after the trays have been filled.* Freeze the apple mixture 8 hours, or overnight, until firm. Remove the frozen apple cubes from the trays, drop into a sturdy plastic bag, press out as much air as possible, twist the ends of the bag into a gooseneck, secure with a twist band, label, date and store in the freezer.

When you are ready to buzz up the apple ice, equip the processor with the metal chopping blade and snap the motor on. Drop the apple cubes down the feed tube, one by one, then when all of the cubes are in the work bowl, buzz 30 seconds nonstop. Open the work bowl and with a wooden spoon, break up any large clumps of ice. Buzz 30 seconds longer. If at this point the apple ice is not nice and feathery, pulse the machine or snap the motor on and off quickly 10 to 15 times.

Spoon into stemmed goblets and serve immediately or, if you prefer, spoon lightly into a 1-quart freezer container and store in the freezer. **NOTE:** *Once the apple ice has been buzzed up, do not attempt to store it for more than a day or two in the freezer because it will begin to lose its lovely spring green color, its fresh apple taste and its velvety texture.*

Pink Apple Snow
Makes 6 servings

Here's a simple, old-fashioned New England dessert that is nothing more than puréed raw apples mixed with whipped cream. It keeps well in the refrigerator for 24 hours, so make it ahead of time, if you like.

6 medium-size tart apples (McIntoshes are a good choice), peeled,
   cored and quartered
Juice of 1 lemon
6 tablespoons sugar
⅛ teaspoon ground nutmeg
⅛ teaspoon ground cardamom
1 cup refrigerator-cold heavy cream

In a food processor fitted with the metal chopping blade, place 8 apple quarters (halve any that are large), drizzle with lemon juice and sprinkle with 2 tablespoons of the sugar. With two or three 5-second churnings of the motor, reduce to sauce. Empty into a bowl and continue until all apples are puréed. Mix in the spices. Pour the heavy cream into the processor, still fitted with the metal chopping blade, and beat to soft peaks, using three or four 5-second bursts of speed. Inspect the texture of the cream closely after each 5-second churning and the minute it mounds softly, fold into the applesauce lightly but thoroughly until no streaks of apples or cream are visible. Cover and chill until ready to serve.

VARIATION:

Whipped Apples with Cheese: Prepare the apples as directed and add to a large mixing bowl. Pour the heavy cream into the processor, fitted with the metal chopping blade; add 1 cup of ricotta cheese and 3 tablespoons Calvados or cognac. Beat until creamy-smooth, using three or four 5-second bursts of the motor. Fold into the applesauce and chill until ready to serve.

Raw Applesauce

Makes 4 to 6 servings

The traditional way to make applesauce is to cook apples to mush with a little water and sugar. With a processor, however, you can purée raw apples into a sauce that will have a deliciously tart, fresh flavor. Raw applesauce will darken somewhat on standing, even though you mix in the juice of a lemon, so my advice is to make it just before serving— easy enough in the processor.

> *8 medium-size tart apples (McIntoshes are particularly good),*
>   *peeled, cored and quartered*
> *Juice of 1 lemon*
> *½ cup sugar*
> *½ teaspoon ground cinnamon*
> *Pinch of ground nutmeg*

In a food processor fitted with the metal chopping blade, place 8 apple quarters (halve any that are large), drizzle with lemon juice and sprinkle with 2 tablespoons of the sugar. With two or three 5-second churnings of the motor, reduce to sauce. Empty into a bowl and continue until all apples are puréed, doing no more than 2 apples at a time and adding lemon juice and sugar as before. Add each batch to the bowl as it is puréed. Mix in the spices and serve.

Lemon-Lime Granité

Makes 4 to 6 servings

One of the easiest desserts imaginable, thanks to the food processor, which fluffs frozen cubes of lemon-lime syrup into snowy drifts. This is a good dessert to end a festive summer meal because it's tart, light and marvelously refreshing.

> *2 lemons*
> *2 limes*
> *1¾ cups sugar*
> *1 envelope plain gelatin*
> *3½ cups cold water (about)*

Using a swivel-bladed vegetable peeler, strip off all the thin, colored part of the rind (zest) of each lemon and lime. I simply run the peeler the length of the lemon or lime, end to end, and the zest comes off in long, thin strips. Now juice the lemons and limes, strain the juice, pour into a 1-quart measure and set aside.

Place the lemon and lime rinds and ½ cup of the sugar in a food processor fitted with the metal chopping blade and mince the rind quite fine, using three or four 10-second churnings of the motor. Scrape down the work bowl after each successive churning. Empty the sugar-rind mixture into a heavy saucepan, add the remaining sugar and the gelatin and stir to combine. Now add enough cold water to the lemon and lime juices to total 4 cups liquid; pour into the saucepan. Set over moderate heat, and heat and stir about 3 minutes until sugar and gelatin are both thoroughly dissolved. Cool the syrup to room temperature, then divide between two metal ice-cube trays and freeze several hours, or until mushy-firm.

Meanwhile, wash and dry the processor work bowl and chopping blade and reassemble. When the cubes of syrup are semi-frozen, buzz them to fluff in the processor, doing only 10 to 12 cubes at a time, and allowing 3 or 4 pulses or on-offs of the motor for each batch. Spoon at once into freezer containers and store in the freezer.

Frozen Nectarine Velva

Makes 4 to 6 servings

Be sure that the nectarines you select for this recipe are sun-ripened and full of fragrance because it is an intense, tree-sweet flavor that you want. Nectarines picked green, then shipped cross country, will never develop or ripen properly. And any frozen velva made from them will have a bitter aftertaste.

Juice of 1 medium-size lemon
1½ pounds dead-ripe nectarines
¼ to ⅓ cup superfine sugar, depending upon the tartness of the
  nectarines
2 tablespoons Cointreau

Place the lemon juice in the work bowl of a food processor fitted with the metal chopping blade. Now, working with one nectarine at a time, blanch 30 seconds in boiling water, slip off the skin, then remove pit and cut into slim wedges; drop wedges into the work bowl and pulse or snap the machine on and off 3 or 4 times to coat the wedges with lemon juice (this helps keep the nectarines from darkening). NOTE: *A quick way to pit the nectarine and cut into wedges all at the same time is to hold a whole, peeled nectarine in one hand, then with a paring knife, cut straight through the flesh to the pit; now make a second cut about ¾ inch from the first cut and at about a 40-degree angle to it; when the knife reaches the pit (and the end of the first cut), twist the knife slightly and a wedge of nectarine will pop out. Repeat until only the pit remains in your hand. You can do this directly over the feed tube, letting the wedges of fruit drop straight into the work bowl as they are cut.*

When all of the nectarines are in the work bowl, add the sugar and Cointreau; buzz 30 seconds nonstop, scrape down the sides of the work bowl, then buzz 30 seconds longer or until absolutely smooth.

Spoon the nectarine mixture into a metal ice cube tray (one with a pry-out lever). TIP: *It's easiest to fill the tray with the ice cube insert removed, then to set it carefully in place in the filled tray.* Freeze the nectarine mixture 8 hours, or overnight, until very firm. Remove the frozen nectarine cubes from the tray, drop into a sturdy plastic bag, press out as much air as possible, twist the ends of the bag into a gooseneck, secure with a twist band, label, date and store in the freezer.

When you are ready to buzz up the nectarine velva, equip the processor with the metal chopping blade and snap the motor on. Drop the nectarine cubes down the feed tube, one by one, then when all of the cubes are in the work bowl, buzz 30 seconds nonstop. Open the work bowl and with a wooden spoon, break up any large clumps of velva. Buzz 30 seconds longer. If at this point the velva is not nice and smooth, pulse the machine or snap the motor on and off quickly 10 to 15 times.

Spoon into stemmed goblets and serve immediately or, if you prefer, spoon lightly into a 1-quart freezer container and store in the freezer. NOTE: *Once the nectarine velva has been buzzed up, don't try to keep it for more than a day or two because it will quickly discolor and lose flavor.*

Frozen Peach Velva: Prepare precisely as directed, but substitute tree-ripened peaches for nectarines, add ½ teaspoon almond extract, and substitute Grand Marnier for Cointreau.

Fresh Pear Ice

Makes 4 to 6 servings

Despite all precautions (peeling the pears one by one and coating them well with lemon) juice), this ice will quite quickly turn from pale ivory to rosy beige. So if you object to the darker color, serve the pear ice without delay.

> *⅓ cup lemon juice*
> *2 pounds tree-ripened pears (I favor Comice because of their rich flavor)*
> *⅓ cup superfine sugar*
> *¼ cup Poire William (pear eau de vie)*

Place the lemon juice in the work bowl of a processor fitted with the metal chopping blade. Now working with the pears, *one by one*, peel, core, cut into slim wedges and drop down the feed tube of the processor; pulse the machine 3 or 4 times or snap the motor on and off quickly 3 or 4 times to coat the pear with the lemon juice and retard discoloration. Repeat until all pears are in the work bowl, then buzz 30 seconds nonstop. Add the sugar and Poire William, scrape down the work-bowl sides, then buzz 30 seconds longer. Again scrape down the work bowl and buzz 30 seconds.

Divide the pear mixture between two metal ice cube trays (those with pry-out levers). **Tip:** *It's easiest to fill the trays with the ice cube inserts removed, then to set these carefully back into place after the trays have been filled.* Freeze the pear mixture 8 hours, or overnight, until firm. Remove the frozen pear cubes from the trays, drop into a sturdy plastic bag, press out as much air as possible, twist the ends of the bag into a gooseneck, secure with a twist band, and store in the freezer.

When you are ready to buzz up the pear ice (and it's best to do this within 24 hours so that the ice does not become unappetizingly brown), equip the processor with the metal chopping blade and snap the motor on. Drop the frozen pear cubes down the feed tube, one by one, then when all of the cubes are in the work bowl, buzz 30 seconds nonstop. Open the work bowl and with a wooden spoon, break up any large clumps of ice. Buzz 30 seconds longer. If at this point the pear ice is not nice and feathery, pulse the machine or snap the motor on and off quickly 10 to 15 times.

Spoon into stemmed goblets and serve.

Fresh Pineapple-Yogurt Sherbet
Makes 6 servings

A fresh pineapple somehow seems formidable, especially when the canned is so readily available. However, the flavor of fresh pineapple is vastly superior, as this recipe readily proves. Moreover, if you have a food processor, you can slice or crush fresh pineapple in seconds, preserving all of its tart tropical flavor. Try this recipe, also the one that follows for Pineapple Fans with Mint. Neither takes more than five minutes to prepare, start to finish.

1 medium-size ripe pineapple, trimmed, peeled and cut into 1-inch chunks (do not core)
⅔ cup sugar
2 cups plain yogurt
2 tablespoons rum or Cointreau

Place about one third of the pineapple chunks in a food processor fitted with the metal chopping blade, add one third of the sugar and chop fairly coarsely, using about two 3-second bursts of speed. Empty into a large bowl. Chop the remaining pineapple with the remaining sugar the same way in two batches and add to the bowl. Blend in the yogurt and rum and pour into a 13x9x2-inch pan and freeze until mushy. Remove from freezer, beat mixture hard with a wooden spoon (you can do this right in the pan), return to freezer and freeze until almost firm. Serve at once.

Pineapple Fans with Mint

Makes 6 servings

*1 medium-size ripe pineapple, trimmed, peeled and cut lengthwise
into sixths or eighths (whichever will fit most easily into the feed
tube of a food processor)*
¼ cup sugar (or more if pineapple is unduly tart)
*¼ cup freshly chopped mint (for an amount this small I prefer to do
the chopping by hand)*
2 tablespoons white crème de menthe or *Cointreau*

Test the core of the pineapple for tenderness (it will be at the point of
each wedge) and if woody or fibrous, trim off. Stand a wedge of pineapple in the feed tube of a processor equipped with the slicing disc (the
medium-slicing disc, if you have one) and slice thin by pushing it
through with gentle pressure. Repeat with three or four more wedges
and then empty into a large, shallow mixing bowl. Thin-slice the remaining wedges the same way and add to bowl. Sprinkle with sugar
and mint and drizzle with *crème de menthe.* Toss lightly and allow to
marinate at room temperature for 1 hour. Toss lightly again and serve.

Mother's Fresh Banana Ice Cream

Makes 6 servings

This is a recipe my mother worked out during World War II when sugar
was rationed. The recipe, you'll note, calls for only half a cup of it.

3 very ripe bananas, peeled and cut into 1-inch chunks
Juice of 2 lemons
1½ cups fresh orange juice
½ cup light corn syrup
½ cup sugar
½ teaspoon vanilla
1 cup refrigerator-cold heavy cream

Place the bananas and lemon juice in a food processor fitted with the
metal chopping blade and purée, using 3 or 4 pulses or on-offs of the
motor. Empty into a large bowl, scraping the processor work bowl out

as well as possible (you'll use it in a minute to whip the cream, but there's no need to wash it). Blend in the orange juice, corn syrup, sugar and vanilla. Now pour the cream into the processor, still fitted with the chopping blade, and with three or four 5-second churnings of the motor, whip to soft peaks. Inspect the consistency of the cream closely after each 5-second churning, and the minute it mounds softly, fold into the banana mixture. Pour into a 13x9x2-inch pan and freeze until mushy. Empty about one third of the "mush" into the processor fitted with the metal chopping blade and buzz 3 to 5 seconds until fluffy-smooth; pack into a half-gallon freezer container. Beat the remaining banana mixture the same way in two separate batches, add to freezer container, cover and freeze until firm.

Silky Strawberry Ice
Makes 4 to 6 servings

Nothing more than fresh strawberries picked at their peak of flavor, puréed with a little orange rind, Grand Marnier, freshly squeezed lemon juice and sugar to sweeten, then frozen in ice cube trays. Once the strawberry cubes are frozen, you can bundle them up in plastic bags and store in the freezer—welcome insurance against drop-in guests because with a processor at the ready, you can buzz them into the featheriest of ices in seconds. NOTE: *For making the strawberry cubes, I use two metal ice cube trays with pry-out levers, which simplify the task of removal (the strawberry cubes never freeze as hard and dry as ice, thus won't pop out of the plastic ice trays).*

1 strip (2 inches by ½ inch) orange rind (orange part only)
¼ to ⅓ cup superfine sugar (depending upon how tart the berries are)
3 pints dead-ripe strawberries, hulled, washed and halved
2 tablespoons lemon juice
2 tablespoons Grand Marnier

In a processor equipped with the metal chopping blade, grate the orange rind by letting it churn nonstop with the sugar for 10 seconds. Inspect the texture of the rind and if it is not as finely grated as you would like, snap the motor on for 5 seconds, then off, then on for another 5 seconds, then off. Add strawberries, lemon juice and Grand Marnier, buzz 30 seconds nonstop, scrape the sides of the work bowl down, buzz 30 seconds longer, and if the mixture is not velvety smooth, scrape the work bowl down once again and buzz 30 seconds longer. Dump the strawberry mixture into a fine sieve set over a large nonmetallic mixing bowl; press all the strawberry purée through the sieve (the purpose of the sieve is to remove the seeds).

Divide the sieved strawberry mixture between two metal ice cube trays (with pry-out levers) and freeze overnight, or at least 8 hours, until firm. Remove the frozen strawberry cubes from the tray, drop into a sturdy plastic bag, press out as much air as possible, twist the ends of the bag into a gooseneck, secure with a twist band, label and date and store in the freezer.

When you are ready to buzz the strawberry cubes into a feathery ice, equip the processor with the metal chopping blade and snap the motor on. Drop the strawberry cubes down the feed tube, one by one, then when all of the cubes are in the work bowl, buzz 30 seconds nonstop. Open the work bowl and with a wooden spoon, break up any large clumps of ice. Buzz 30 seconds nonstop, rearrange the chunks of ice as before, buzz 30 seconds longer. If at this point the strawberry ice is not nice and fluffy, pulse the machine or snap the motor on and off quickly 10 to 15 times.

Spoon into stemmed goblets and serve or, if you prefer, spoon lightly into a 1-quart freezer container and store in the freezer. **NOTE:** *Once the strawberry ice has been buzzed up, do not attempt to store it for more than a day or two because it will begin to lose flavor and become gritty.*

VARIATION:

Silky Fresh Raspberry Ice: Prepare exactly as directed for the strawberry ice, but substitute lemon rind for the orange rind and *Framboise* for the Grand Marnier.

Fresh Strawberry Ice Cream
Makes 6 to 8 servings

1 quart fresh ripe strawberries, washed and hulled
Juice of 2 lemons

2 cups sugar
3 eggs
1 cup milk
2 cups refrigerator-cold heavy cream

Crush the strawberries, half of them at a time, in a food processor fitted with the metal chopping blade, using 3 or 4 pulses or fast bursts of speed. Empty into a large mixing bowl. Now add to the processor the lemon juice, sugar and eggs and let motor run nonstop for 15 seconds. Stir into the strawberries along with the milk. Pour into a 13x9x2-inch baking pan and freeze until mushy.

Pour 1 cup of the heavy cream into the processor work bowl, which you have washed and dried and fitted with the metal chopping blade (also clean and dry) and whip to soft peaks, using three or four 5-second bursts of speed. Check consistency of the cream often, and the minute it mounds softly, pour into a large mixing bowl. Whip the remaining cream the same way and add to bowl. Now empty one fourth of the semi-frozen strawberry mixture into the processor work bowl (no need to wash it or the blade) and beat about 5 seconds until fluffy. Add to cream in bowl. Beat the remaining strawberry mixture the same way in three separate batches and add to bowl. Fold the two together, using a gentle over-and-over motion, until no streaks of white or red remain. Pour back into pan and freeze until firm.

Orange-Walnut Torte
Makes one 10-inch tube cake

I frankly see no reason to make standard butter cakes in the food processor—sponge or angel cakes either, for that matter. The electric mixer does a superior job and its work-bowl capacity far exceeds that of the processor. There is, in fact, a danger of overmixing cake batter in a food processor, particularly after the eggs and sifted dry ingredients have been added, which can result in a rubbery cake shot through with tunnels. The temptation, of course, with a machine as new and revolutionary as the processor, is to try all of the old favorites in it. And, indeed, a number of the first-published processor cookbooks do recommend mixing yellow and silver cakes in the processor. I don't. I do, however, urge you to make this exquisitely moist and tender torte in the processor. It contains no flour at all, and uses finely ground walnuts and bread crumbs instead for body. You can, if you like, substitute an equal quantity of pecans, blanched filberts or almonds for the walnuts, and the rind of one lemon for the orange rind. This torte is uncommonly rich, so I prefer to serve it unfrosted. You may, however, want to ice it with Walnut Butter-Cream Frosting for a festive occasion (see Index for recipe page number) or simply top each portion with softly whipped cream.

2 slices firm-textured white bread, torn into small pieces
2 cups walnut meats
Rind of ½ orange (remove the thin, colored part only, using a
    swivel-bladed vegetable peeler)
1½ cups sugar
½ teaspoon almond extract
8 eggs, separated
Pinch of cream of tartar

It's wise to prepare the cake pan first, so that it will be ready for the batter as soon as it is mixed. Line the bottom of a 10-inch tube pan (I prefer to use one with a removable bottom) with wax paper. Do not grease the wax paper and do not grease the pan.

In a food processor fitted with the metal chopping blade, buzz the bread to fine and feathery crumbs by using three 5-second churnings of the motor; empty the crumbs into a large bowl. Now chop the walnuts very fine, again using three 5-second churnings of the motor; empty into bowl with the crumbs. Place the strips of orange rind and ¼ cup of the sugar in the processor work bowl and mince the rind very fine, using three 10-second churnings of the motor. Uncover the work bowl after each churning, lift out the chopping blade, then scrape the bottom and sides of the work bowl well; the sugar and rind tend to cake on the bottom of the bowl below the level of the blade. Replace the chopping blade, re-cover the work bowl and proceed until the rind is reduced to fine particles. Leave this mixture in the work bowl.

Now add the almond extract and the egg yolks and beat lightly by switching the motor on and off twice. If you have a feed-tube funnel, insert it. If not, shape a heavy piece of paper into a wide-mouthed cone and insert it in the top of the feed tube. Turn the processor on and gradually add 1 cup of the remaining sugar, letting it trickle down the feed tube into the whirling egg mixture. When all of the sugar has been incorporated, beat the mixture for 25 seconds longer, nonstop. Pour this mixture on top of the nuts and crumbs and stir lightly but thoroughly to mix.

Place the egg whites in a large bowl and sprinkle the cream of tartar on top (the reason for using cream of tartar is that it helps to whiten and stabilize the beaten whites, insuring a cake of good volume). Using a rotary beater or hand electric mixer, beat the egg whites until frothy, then add the remaining ¼ cup of sugar, 1 tablespoon at a time, beating well after each addition. Continue whipping the egg whites until they peak softly. Stir about 1 cup of the beaten whites into the walnut mixture, then add the remaining beaten whites and fold in gently but thoroughly, using a rubber spatula.

Pour the batter into the prepared pan, then bake, uncovered, in a moderate oven (350° F.) for 1 hour, or until torte is lightly browned and feels springy to the touch. The surface of the baked torte will seem soft and moist; that is as it should be. Remove the torte from the oven, turn the pan upside down at once and allow the torte to stand in the pan for 1 hour, or until it has cooled to room temperature.

Then turn the pan right-side up, loosen the torte around the edges of the pan and around the central tube. Then, grasping the central tube, lift the pan bottom out, bringing the torte with it. Now slide a thin-bladed knife or spatula between the wax paper and the pan bottom to loosen the torte. Place a cake plate on top of the central spindle, then invert the torte. Peel off the wax paper. NOTE: *If you intend to frost the torte, do not do so until after it has stood at room temperature for at least 3 hours. This torte is a particularly fragile one, and the waiting period is to give it a chance to firm up somewhat before you apply the frosting.*

Old-Fashioned Macaroons
Makes about 3 dozen

To make this recipe, you needn't track down a can of almond paste (not so easily found these days) or a hunk of marzipan; all you require is 1¼ cups of whole, shelled, unblanched almonds (either fresh or canned). With the processor, you can make your own almond paste, and from it, these deliciously chewy cookies. NOTE: *Do try the variation—Orange Macaroons. They are even better.*

1 recipe Almond Paste (see Index for recipe page number)
1¼ cups sugar
¼ teaspoon salt
1 teaspoon vanilla
1 teaspoon almond extract
2 egg whites

Place the almond paste, sugar, salt, vanilla and almond extract in a food processor fitted with the metal chopping blade, snap the motor on and churn for 30 seconds nonstop. Add the egg whites and blend 10 seconds nonstop; uncover the work bowl, scrape the sides down, recover and churn 5 seconds longer, or until uniformly smooth.

Drop the cookies from a teaspoon onto baking sheets that have been lined with ungreased brown paper, spacing the cookies about 2 inches apart. Bake, uncovered, in a moderately slow oven (325° F.) for 30 minutes, or until faintly tan. Remove macaroons from the oven and cool to room temperature. Then, to remove them from the brown paper, set the paper on wet towels. Let stand several minutes, then peel the cookies off.

VARIATION·

Orange Macaroons: Prepare as directed, but reduce the amount of vanilla to ½ teaspoon and add 1 teaspoon of very finely grated orange rind to the work-bowl mixture at the outset.

Filbert or Almond Meringue Cookies
Makes about 3 dozen

One of my childhood memories is of watching my mother painstakingly grind the filberts for this recipe into featheriness, and the bitter chocolate, too. The recipe is an old Czechoslovakian one, given to my mother by a friend who had been brought up in Prague. *One note of caution: If you are to grate the chocolate to the proper degree of fineness in the food processor, the chocolate must be well chilled—also the metal chopping blade and the work bowl. Otherwise, the heat of the machine may melt the chocolate.*

1 square (1 ounce) unsweetened chocolate, refrigerator-cold
¾ cup whole unblanched filberts or almonds
2 egg whites
1 cup sifted confectioners' sugar
½ teaspoon ground cinnamon
½ teaspoon vanilla

Place the chocolate in the chilled work bowl of a food processor; insert the chilled metal chopping blade, turn the motor on and, with about four 10-second bursts of speed, grate very fine; the consistency should be about that of finely ground coffee. Empty onto a square of wax paper and set aside. Now add the nuts to the processor and let the machine run nonstop for 15 to 20 seconds, or until nuts are very fine and powdery. Empty onto a second square of wax paper and set aside.

With a rotary beater, beat the egg whites with 2 tablespoons of the confectioners' sugar to very stiff peaks. Combine the cinnamon with the remaining confectioners' sugar and fold into the egg whites, about one third of the total amount at a time. Fold in the chocolate and nuts, then stir in the vanilla.

Line a baking sheet with foil, the shiny side up. Drop the batter onto the foil by the half-teaspoonful, spacing 2 inches apart. Bake in a slow oven (300° F.) for 20 minutes. Remove from oven, let cool 10 minutes, then peel cookies from the foil.

Cream-Puff Filling

Makes enough to fill 12 cream puffs or éclairs

Blending the ingredients for this recipe in the food processor almost guarantees you a butter-smooth consistency. The only critical step is heating the mixture at the end after the eggs have been added. To safeguard against curdling, use a double boiler. However, if you keep a watchful eye on the pot, turn the burner heat to its lowest point and stir the filling constantly, it won't curdle over direct heat.

⅔ cup sugar
6 tablespoons flour
1 cup heavy cream

1 cup light cream
5 eggs
1 teaspoon vanilla

Place ⅓ cup of the sugar and all of the flour in a food processor fitted with the metal chopping blade; whir nonstop for 5 seconds to combine sugar and flour. Now, with the motor running, drizzle the heavy cream down the feed tube. The instant all of the cream has been incorporated, stop the motor; scrape the mixture into a medium-size heavy saucepan and blend in the light cream. To the work bowl add the remaining ⅓ cup sugar, the eggs and the vanilla; pulse or snap the motor on and off about twice to beat lightly. Let mixture stand for the moment.

Set saucepan over moderate heat and cook, stirring constantly, until sauce mixture is quite thick—about 3 minutes—and no raw starch taste remains. Quickly spoon half of the hot sauce into the processor mixture and pulse or snap the motor on and off about 3 times to combine; scrape down the bowl with a plastic spatula, add the remaining hot sauce and combine as before.

Spoon all of this mixture back into the saucepan and whisk lightly. (Or if you are afraid of the mixture's curdling over direct heat, spoon into the top of a double boiler and set over simmering water.) Set the saucepan over lowest heat (moderate heat if you're using the double boiler) and cook, stirring constantly, until quite thick and no raw egg taste remains—about 2 to 3 minutes over direct heat, 8 or more in the double boiler. (The water, by the way, should never actually *boil*, only simmer gently.) Remove thickened filling from the heat and cool to room temperature, whisking often to prevent a "skin" from forming on the surface. (Another trick is to brush the surface of the filling lightly with melted butter, which keeps it from drying.) Cover the cooled filling with plastic food wrap and chill until quite firm—about the consistency of a cornstarch pudding. Use to fill cream puffs or *éclairs*.

VARIATION:

Chocolate Filling: Prepare the cream-puff filling exactly as directed, but before combining the sugar and flour in the processor at the outset, also add 3 tablespoons of Dutch cocoa to the work bowl. From here on the recipe remains precisely the same.

Chocolate Glaze

Makes about 2 cups, enough to glaze 12 éclairs
or one 9-inch layer cake

The advantages of using the processor to make this glaze are (1) that you don't have to melt the chocolate (you can simply grind it up) and (2) that the glaze will be incomparably silky. Do not attempt to make the glaze in rainy or humid weather, because it will not harden properly.

4 squares (1 ounch each) unsweetened chocolate, broken in half
3 cups sifted confectioners' sugar
½ cup water
1 tablespoon butter
1 teaspoon vanilla

Place the chocolate in a food processor fitted with the metal chopping blade, turn the motor on and let run nonstop for about 35 seconds, or until the chocolate is the texture of coffee grounds. Add half the confectioners' sugar and buzz for 10 seconds nonstop to blend; add the remaining confectioners' sugar and buzz 10 seconds longer. Meanwhile, bring the water and butter to a boil in a small saucepan. With the processor motor running, pour the boiling mixture down the feed tube in a fine stream, then beat for 10 seconds longer. Uncover work bowl and scrape down sides. Also lift off the chopping blade and scrape the glaze mixture up from the bottom of the work bowl; replace blade. Add vanilla and buzz for 10 seconds nonstop. The glaze is now ready to use.

Old-Fashioned Butter-Cream Frosting

Makes enough to frost one 2-layer, 9-inch cake
or one 10-inch tube cake

One of the advantages of making butter-cream frosting in the processor is that you don't have to sift the confectioners' sugar—any lumps will be reduced to powder at first touch of the powerful chopping blade. Another advantage is that the sugar, contained as it is in the enclosed work bowl, can't spew out, dusting everything in sight, as so often happens with the electric mixer. This particular recipe is eminently adaptable, as the accompanying variations prove.

⅓ cup unsalted butter, at room temperature
1 teaspoon vanilla
Pinch of salt
4 cups unsifted confectioners' sugar
5 tablespoons light cream

In the work bowl of a food processor equipped with the metal chopping blade, cream the butter, vanilla, salt and 2 cups of the confectioners' sugar by running the motor nonstop for 20 seconds. The mixture will be quite thick and crumbly. With the plastic spatula, carefully scrape down the work-bowl sides and bottom; for safety's sake, lift out the metal chopping blade, then replace as soon as you've scraped the bowl down. Now add 3 tablespoons of the cream and beat the mixture 10 seconds nonstop. Add the remaining 2 cups of sugar and 2 tablespoons of cream and beat another 10 seconds. Quickly scrape the work bowl down and buzz 5 seconds longer. The frosting is now ready to spread.

VARIATIONS:

Walnut Butter-Cream Frosting: Prepare the recipe above as directed, add ½ cup finely chopped walnuts and blend into the frosting by running the processor 5 seconds. You can, of course, substitute chopped pecans, hazelnuts or toasted almonds for the walnuts.

Lemon or Orange Butter-Cream Frosting: Prepare Old-Fashioned Butter-Cream Frosting as directed, but substitute ¼ cup lemon or orange juice for the light cream and beat in 1 tablespoon very finely grated lemon or orange rind. Omit the vanilla, but add ¼ teaspoon almond extract.

Chocolate Butter-Cream Frosting: Prepare the basic recipe as directed, but cream, along with the butter, vanilla, salt and confectioners' sugar, 4 tablespoons of Dutch cocoa. Otherwise, the recipe remains the same.

Mocha Butter-Cream Frosting: Prepare Chocolate Butter-Cream Frosting as directed, but add to the work bowl at the outset 1 level tablespoon of freeze-dried instant-coffee crystals; then add the butter, vanilla, salt, confectioners' sugar and cocoa and proceed as recipe directs.

Mock Crème Fraîche for Fresh Fruit
Makes about 2 cups, enough for 4 to 6 servings

1 cup light cream
½ cup heavy cream
⅓ cup sugar
½ teaspoon unflavored gelatin
1 cup sour cream, at room temperature
¼ teaspoon vanilla

Cook and stir together light and heavy creams, sugar and gelatin in a small, heavy saucepan over moderate heat about 20 minutes until gelatin and sugar are thoroughly dissolved. Cool 10 minutes, stirring now and then to prevent a "skin" from forming on the surface.

Place sour cream and vanilla in a food processor fitted with either the plastic mixing blade or the metal chopping blade. Snap cover in place, turn machine on and add gelatin mixture in a slow but steady stream through the feed tube. When all is incorporated, switch machine off and lift the work bowl from the power base with the blade still in place (this is to prevent the mixture from draining through the spindle tube in the center of the work bowl). Pour mixture into a bowl, cover and chill at least overnight until thickened; mixture should be slightly thinner than a stirred custard. Whisk lightly, then serve over fresh strawberries, raspberries or blackberries, or over fresh sliced peaches or apricots.

Melba Sauce
Makes about 2¼ cups

3 cups fresh raspberries, rinsed
½ cup sugar

½ cup red currant jelly
4 teaspoons cornstarch blended with 2 tablespoons cold water

In a food processor fitted with the metal chopping blade, buzz the raspberries to purée with the sugar by running the motor nonstop for about 10 seconds. Set a fine sieve over a medium-size stainless steel or enameled saucepan and push the purée through, extracting as much of it as possible. Stir in the jelly and cornstarch paste, set over moderate heat and cook, stirring constantly, about 3 minutes, or until thickened and clear. Remove from heat, cool and serve over ice cream, fresh fruit, angel or sponge cake. Or use to make Peach Melba, which is nothing more than scoops of vanilla ice cream topped with poached peach halves and Melba Sauce.

Hot Fudge Sauce
Makes about 1 cup

I can't believe how easy this is, or how delicious.

2 packages (4 ounces each) German-style sweet chocolate
⅔ cup heavy cream, heated just to the simmering point
¼ teaspoon salt

Break the chocolate into smallish chunks directly into the work bowl of a food processor fitted with the metal chopping blade. Turn the motor on and let run nonstop for 10 seconds, or until chocolate is about the texture of coarsely ground coffee. With the motor running, trickle the heavy cream down the feed tube, add the salt, and beat about 5 seconds longer until creamy-smooth. Serve at once. NOTE: *Any leftover sauce may harden on standing. To smooth out, scrape all of the hardened sauce back into the processor work bowl fitted with the metal chopping blade, then, with the motor on, drizzle in 1 to 2 tablespoons of hot cream. Beat a few seconds longer until silky-smooth.*

VARIATIONS:

Mocha Fudge Sauce: Add chocolate to processor work bowl as above, spoon in 1 level teaspoon of instant-coffee powder, then proceed as directed.

Brazilian Fudge Sauce: Add chocolate to processor work bowl as above, spoon in 1 level teaspoon of instant-coffee powder and ¼ teaspoon of ground cinnamon, then proceed as directed.

Minty Fudge Sauce: Prepare Hot Fudge Sauce as directed, then, with the motor still running, drizzle 1 tablespoon *crème de menthe* down the feed tube. Beat 1 to 2 seconds longer, then serve.

Candied Grapefruit Rind
Makes about 1 pound

If you have a serrated slicing disc for your processor that cuts between 4 and 8 slices to the inch (you can test it by slicing a 1-inch chunk of carrot), you will be able to machine-cut the grapefruit rind for this confection. Do not attempt to make this recipe in rainy or humid weather, because the candied rind will hydrolyze (absorb water from the atmosphere and become impossibly sticky) rather than crystallize. Also, in order for the machine to cut *uniform* slices of rind, stack as many pieces in the feed tube on end as needed for a tight fit (otherwise the rind will slither around and the slices will be irregular). Needless to add, the grapefruit rind you choose to candy should be good and thick. Don't waste time with thin-skinned varieties of grapefruit.

2 thick-skinned grapefruits, halved
5 quarts cold water
3 cups sugar
½ cup boiling water
½ teaspoon plain gelatin softened in 1 tablespoon cold water

Remove sections from each half of grapefruit (save for dessert, salad, or breakfast), then scrape all membrane from each half so that you have only the thick rind. Quarter each half of the grapefruit rind as evenly as possible, giving you 4 triangles of rind. In the feed tube of a food processor equipped with the *serrated* thick-slicing disc, fit 3 quarters (or triangles) of grapefruit rind, which have been stacked together, then folded together in half; arrange so that the fold is on the right side of the feed tube. Before turning the processor motor on, even up the edges of rind at the bottom of the feed tube; if the first slices are cut straight, the successive ones are much more likely to be also. Turn the motor on or depress the Pulse button, then push the folded slices of rind through the feed tube, using gentle pressure on the pusher. Turn the motor off, refill the feed tube with rind, being as meticulous about the arrangement as you were the first time around, then slice as before. Continue until all rind is sliced.

Dump the sliced rind into a large heavy saucepan, pour in 1 quart of cold water, set, uncovered, over moderate heat and bring to the boil. As soon as the water boils, pour rind into a colander. Again place the rind in the saucepan, add 1 quart of cold water and again bring to the boil and drain. Repeat three more times; this is to extract as much of the bitterness from the rind as possible. While rind drains the last time, place 2 cups of the sugar and the ½ cup boiling water in the saucepan and heat without stirring about 3 minutes—just until all sugar dissolves. Add the drained grapefruit rind, again without stirring, and simmer slowly 20 to 25 minutes, or until grapefruit rind becomes translucent and glistening. Then stir in the gelatin mixture and cook and stir 5 minutes. Remove candied rind from heat and let stand 5 minutes.

Scatter the remaining 1 cup of sugar on a baking pan lined with wax paper, pour the candied rind on top and toss lightly so that each strip of rind is coated with sugar. Let air-dry several hours before eating.

Index

chicken
Country Captain, 263–65
with ground coconut balls, 261–63
chutney dip, 164
dhal (lentils) with vegetables, 351–52
eggs
chopped, 310–11
spread, 157–58
ham mousse with sour cream-caper sauce, cold, 251–53
mayonnaise, 109–10
meatballs, 234–36
shrimp, carrots and zucchini, 299–301
turkey hash, 276
vegetable-ball, 376–78

Danish-style liver *pâté*, 152–53
Desserts, 423-62
apple snow, pink, 442
crêpes, 412–13
orange-walnut torte, 451-53
pineapple fans with mint, 448
pineapple-yogurt sherbet, 447
whipped apples with cheese, 442
See also under Breads; Cookies; Ice cream; Ices; Mousse; Pastry; Pies; Tarts
Dessert sauces and toppings
chocolate glaze, 457
crème fraîche, mock, 459
frostings, butter-cream, 457–58
hot fudge, 460
variations, 460–61
Melba sauce, 459–60
Deviled
clams, 142
crab meat and mushroom casserole, Eastern Shore-style, 291–93
ham spread, 163
Dhal, curried lentil with vegetable, 351–52
Dictionary of Foods and How to Process Them, 41–87
Dictionary of Processes and Techniques, 31–38
Dill
cauliflower purée with browned ginger butter and, 344
and chestnut bread, 420–21

cold fresh salmon mousse with, 287–89
salmon-broccoli loaf with capers and, 286–87
tuna salad with parsley, capers and, 383–84
Dressings, *see* Salad dressings; Stuffing
Duxelles, 134–35

Eastern Shore-style
deviled crab meat and mushroom casserole, 291–93
stuffed ham, 247–48
Éclairs, 423–24
filling for, 455–56
Egg(s)
Basque-style omelet, 307–8
curried chipped, 310–11
curried spread, 157–58
frittatas
leek, 309
zucchini, 309–10
hard-cooked, 65
Roquefort, 308–9
salad, herb-garden, 384–85
-stuffed sweet peppers, 357–58
rice-and-, 358
Eggplant, 65
baked lamb-stuffed, 350–51
croquettes, 349–50
and lamb loaf, 237–39
ratatouille, 374–76
Sicilian-style appetizer, 144–45
Turkish-style caviar, 145–46
Emincé de veau à la Zürichoise, 219–21
Endive *velouté*, Belgian, 168
Escalopes de veau chasseur, 222–23
Escarole, lentil soup with leek and, 189–90
Esparregado, 372

Feijão preto, sopa de, 186–87
Fennel, **65–66**
Feta cheese-spinach pie, Greek-style, 368–70
Figaro sauce, 104
Filbert(s), **66**, **93**
bread, 416–18
meringue cookies, 454–55

Poultry, **58–59**, 255–70
  sage and onion stuffing for, 113–14
  See also Chicken; Turkey
Processor, the, *see* Food processing;
  Food processor
Profiteroles, 423–24
  au chocolat, 424
Provençal-style
  mayonnaise (*aïoli*), **17**, 107
  ratatouille, 374–76
  vegetable soup with garlic-tomato-
    basil sauce, 190–93
Pudding
  broccoli, baked, 336–37
  corn, 348–49
  fish, Norwegian-style, 277–78
  turnip, Shaker-style, 372–74
Purées, **80–81, 95**
  asparagus-stem, 135–36
  chestnut, 346–47
  spinach, 371–72
Purple caraway coleslaw, 375

Quenelles, gratinéed haddock, 279–81

Radishes, **82**
Râpées, carottes, 342
Raspberry ice, 449–50
Ratatouille, 374–76
Red peppers, **77, 95**
  egg-stuffed, 357–58
  rice-and-, 358
Relish, pickle, *see* Pickle relish
Rémoulade sauce, 387–88
Rhubarb, **82**
Rice
  and chopped zucchini salad with
    basil and pine nuts, 391–92
  sweet peppers stuffed with eggs and,
    358
Romano cheese, **55–56, 91**
Root soup, 201–3
Roquefort cheese
  eggs, 308–9
  salad dressing, 398
  veal sandwich roast with pecans and,
    228–29
Rosemary, scalloped carrots and pota-
  toes with, 340–41
Rösti, 362–63
Rôti de porc à la boulangère, 242–43

Russian-style
  beef Stroganoff, 210–11
  borsch with beef and pork, Ukrai-
    nian, 211–13
  pork and mushroom *piroshki*, 155–
    56
Rutabaga, **82**

Sage
  and Cheddar spread, 160–61
  and onion stuffing for poultry, 113–
    14
Salad, 383–96
  bulgur, tomato, onion and mint,
    385–86
  carrot, shredded, 342
  celery root *rémoulade*, 386–88
  coleslaw
    great-grandma's sweet-sour, 395–
      96
    purple caraway, 396–97
    sweet-sour, 397–98
  cucumber-and-mint, Turkish-style,
    394–95
  egg, herb-garden, 384–85
  parslied ham sandwich spread, 154–
    55
  potato
    old-fashioned herbed, 388–89
    Pennsylvania Dutch-style sweet-
      sour, 389–91
  tabbouleh, 385–86
  tuna, with dill, parsley, and capers,
    383–84
  zucchini
    and green beans, with tarragon,
      392–93
    and mushrooms, raw, 393–94
    and rice, with basil and pine nuts,
      391–92
Salad dressings, 398–401
  avocado-watercress, 399–400
  black caviar, 401
  Green Goddess, 399
  Roquefort, 398
  scallion-and-watercress, 400–401
Salmon
  -broccoli loaf with dill and capers,
    286–87
  mousse with dill, cold fresh, 287–89
Salt cod
  brandade de morue, 143–44